www.wadsworth.com

wadsworth.com is the World Wide Web site for Wadsworth and is your direct source to dozens of online resources.

At *wadsworth.com* you can find out about supplements, demonstration software, and student resources. You can also send email to many of our authors and preview new publications and exciting new technologies.

wadsworth.com
Changing the way the world learns®

Foundations of Computer Science
From Data Manipulation to Theory of Computation

Behrouz A. Forouzan

De Anza College

with

Sophia Chung Fegan

THOMSON

™

BROOKS/COLE

Australia • Canada • Mexico • Singapore • Spain
United Kingdom • United States

THOMSON

BROOKS/COLE

Computer Science Editor: *Kallie Swanson*
Senior Editorial Assistant: *Carla Vera*
Technology Project Manager: *Burke Taft*
Marketing Director: *Tom Ziolkowski*
Marketing Assistant: *Darcy Poole*
Advertising Project Manager: *Laura Hubrich*
Project Manager, Editorial Production: *Kelsey McGee*
Print/Media Buyer: *Vena M. Dyer*
Permissions Editor: *Sue Ewing*

Production Service: *Matrix Productions*
Text Designer: *Adriane Bosworth*
Copy Editor: *Frank Hubert*
Cover Designer: *Roy R. Neuhaus*
Cover Image: *Jude Maceren/SIS*
Cover Printing, Printing, and Binding: *Transcontinental/ Louiseville*
Compositor: *ATLIS Graphics & Design*

For more information about our products, contact us at:
Thomson Learning Academic Resource Center
1-800-423-0563
For permission to use material from this text, contact us by:
Phone: 1-800-730-2214
Fax: 1-800-730-2215
Web: http://www.thomsonrights.com

Library of Congress Cataloging-in-Publication Data
Forouzan, Behrouz A.
  Foundations of computer science : from data manipula-
    tion to theory of computation/Behrouz A. Forouzan
    with Sophia Chung Fegan
        p.   cm.
  Includes index.
  ISBN 0 534-37968-0
  1. Computer science. I. Fegan, Sophia Chung. II. Title

QA76.F623 2002   2002019780
004-dc21

Brooks/Cole—Thomson Learning
511 Forest Lodge Road
Pacific Grove, CA 93950
USA

Asia Thomson Learning
5 Shenton Way #01-01
UIC Building
Singapore 068808

Australia Nelson Thomson Learning
102 Dodds Street
South Melbourne, Victoria 3205
Australia

Canada Nelson Thomson Learning
1120 Birchmount Road
Toronto, Ontario M1K 5G4
Canada

Europe/ Thomson Learning
Middle East/ High Holborn House
Africa 50/51 Bedford Row
London WC1R 4LR
United Kingdom

Latin America Thomson Learning
Seneca, 53
Colonia Polanco
11560 Mexico D.F.
Mexico

Spain Paraninfo Thomson Learning
Calle/Magallanes, 25
28015 Madrid, Spain

To my wife Faezeh

— Behrouz Forouzan

Contents

Preface

Welcome to computer science! You are about to start the exploration of a wonderful and exciting world that offers many challenging and exciting careers. Computers play a large part in our everyday lives and will continue to do so in the future.

Computer science is a young discipline that is evolving and progressing. Computer networks have connected people from far-flung points of the globe. Virtual reality is creating three-dimensional images that amaze the eyes. Space exploration owes part of its success to computers. Computer-created special effects have changed the movie industry. And computers have played important roles in genetics.

ORGANIZATION OF THE BOOK

This book is designed for a CS0 course. It covers in breadth all areas in computer science. We divided the text into five parts: Computers and Data, Computer Hardware, Computer Software, Data Organization, and Advanced Topics (Figure P.1).

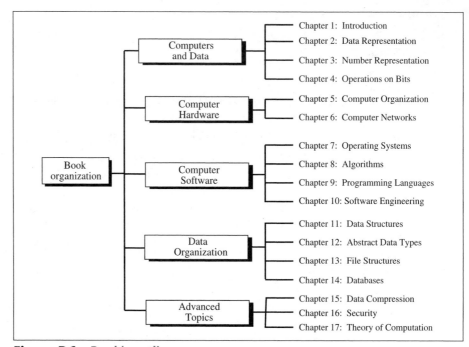

Figure P.1   Book's outline

Part I: Computers and Data

In Part I, we look at a computer and the data that it processes. This part contains four chapters.

Chapter 1: Introduction   In this chapter, we look at the computer as a data processing entity. We introduce the von Neumann concept and discuss the general components of a computer. We postpone the detailed discussion of computer components until Chapter 5.

Chapter 2: Data Representation   In this chapter, we discuss the representation of text, images, audio, and video as bit patterns. Numeric representation is postponed until Chapter 3.

Chapter 3: Number Representation   In this chapter, we present the representation of numbers. We show how integers and floating-point numbers are stored in a computer.

Chapter 4: Operations on Bits   In this chapter, we discuss the manipulation of bit patterns, both arithmetic and logical.

Part II: Computer Hardware

In Part II, we look at computer hardware. This part is divided into two chapters.

Chapter 5: Computer Organization   In this chapter, we discuss the computer as a stand-alone machine. We describe the parts of computer hardware and how they work.

Chapter 6: Computer Networks   In this chapter, we discuss how computers are connected to create computer networks and internetworks.

Part III: Computer Software

In Part III, we look at various aspects of computer software.

Chapter 7: Operating Systems   In this chapter, we discuss the operating system as the most important part of system software. We present the duties of an operating system and how they evolved. We also discuss the parts of a modern operating system.

Chapter 8: Algorithms   In this chapter, we discuss algorithms. Algorithms play such an important role in computer science that some people believe computer science means the study of algorithms. We define the concept of algorithms and use some tools to represent algorithms. A full discussion of these tools is presented in Appendixes C, D, and E.

Chapter 9: Programming Languages   In this chapter, we first present computer languages in general. Then we discuss the elements of C, a popular language.

Chapter 10: Software Engineering   In this chapter, we discuss software engineering, a very important discipline for the computer major.

Part IV: Data Organization

In Part IV, we look again at data, but from the user's point of view.

Chapter 11: Data Structures   In this chapter, we discuss data structures. Data, at the higher level, are organized into structures. We present common data structures in use today such as arrays, records, and linked lists.

Chapter 12: Abstract Data Types   In this chapter, we discuss abstract data types (ADTs). In data processing, you need to define data as a package including the operations defined for the package. We describe lists, stacks, queues, trees, and graphs so that students think about data in the abstract.

Chapter 13: File Structures   In this chapter, we discuss file structures. We show how files are logically organized. We discuss sequential access and random access files. A student needs to know these concepts before taking a first course in programming.

Chapter 14: Databases   In this chapter, we discuss databases. Files in an organization are very rarely stored separately and in isolation. Often, they are organized into one entity called a database. We present the relational database and touch on a language (SQL) that can retrieve information from this type of database.

Part V: Advanced Topics

In this part, we discuss three advanced topics that are gaining importance in computer science: data compression, security, and the theory of computation. These topics can be skipped if time is a factor or if the background of students is lacking.

Chapter 15: Data Compression   In this chapter, we present two categories of data compression: lossless and lossy. We discuss run-length encoding, Huffman coding, and the Lempel Ziv algorithm as examples of lossless compression. We discuss JPEG and MPEG as examples of lossy compression.

Chapter 16: Security   In this chapter, we discuss four aspects of security: privacy, authentication, integrity, and nonrepudiation. We show how to use encryption/decryption and the digital signature to create a secure system.

Chapter 17: Theory of Computation   In this chapter, we briefly explore the theory of computation. We show how no language is superior to another in solving a problem. We show that there are some problems that cannot be solved by any computer program written in any language.

BIRD'S-EYE VIEW

The reader should keep in mind that this book does not discuss any topic in computer science in depth; to do so would require multiple volumes. The book tries to cover in breadth topics related to computer science. Our experience shows that knowing data representation and manipulation, for example, helps students better understand programming in low- and high-level languages. Knowing general information about computer science will help students be more successful when taking courses in networking and internetworking. The book is a bird's-eye view of computer science.

FEATURES OF THE BOOK

There are several features of this book that not only make it unique but make it easier for beginning students to understand.

Concepts

Throughout the book, we have tried to emphasize the concept rather than the mathematical model. We believe an understanding of the concept leads to an understanding of the model.

Visual Approach

A brief examination of the book will show that our approach is very visual. There are nearly 300 figures. While this tends to increase the length of a book, figures aid in understanding the text.

Examples

Whenever appropriate, we have used examples to demonstrate the concept and the mathematical model.

End-of-Chapter Material

The end material of each chapter contains three parts: key terms, summary, and practice set.

Key Terms   The key terms provide a list of the important terms introduced in the chapter. Every key term is defined in the glossary.

Summary   The summaries contain a concise overview of all the key points of the chapter. They are bulleted for readability.

Practice Sets   Each practice set contains three parts: review questions, multiple-choice questions, and exercises.

- **Review questions** test the overall key points and concepts of the chapter.
- **Multiple-choice questions** are designed to test the understanding of the materials.
- **Exercises** are designed to see if students can apply the concepts and formulas.

Appendixes

Seven appendixes are included for quick reference to tables or materials that are discussed in various chapters. These appendixes are

- ASCII table
- Unicode
- Flowcharts
- Pseudocode
- Structure Charts
- Discrete Cosine Transform
- Acronyms

Glossary

A glossary of all key terms is included at the end of the book.

Solutions to Practice Sets

The solutions to the odd-numbered review questions, multiple-choice questions, and exercises are available online at www.brookscole.com/compsci.

INSTRUCTIONAL MATERIALS

The Powerpoint presentation of all figures and highlighted points in addition to the solution of all review questions, multiple-choice questions, and exercises is available online at www.brookscole.com/compsci.

ACKNOWLEDGMENTS

No text of this scope can be developed without the support of many people. This is especially true for this text.

We would like to acknowledge the support of the De Anza staff for their continuing encouragement and their comments. We particularly acknowledge the contribution of Scott DeMouthe for reading the manuscript and solving the problems.

To anyone who has not been through the process, the value of peer reviews cannot be appreciated enough. Writing a text rapidly becomes a myopic process. The important guidance of reviewers who can stand back and review the text as a whole cannot be measured. To twist an old cliché, "They are not valuable; they are priceless." We would especially like to acknowledge the contributions of the reviewers: Essam El-Kwae, University of North Carolina at Charlotte; Norman J. Landis, Fairleigh Dickinson University; John A. Rohr, University of California at Los Angeles; Robert Signorile, Boston College; and Robert Statica, New Jersey Institute of Technology

Our thanks also go to our publisher, Bill Stenquist; acquisition editor, Kallie Swanson; editorial assistant, Carla Vera; and production editor, Kelsey McGee. We also wish to thank Merrill Peterson of Matrix Productions, copy editor Frank Hubert, and proofreader Amy Dorr.

Last, and most obviously not least, is the support of our families and friends. Many years ago, an author described writing a text as "a locking yourself in a room" process. While the authors suffer through the writing process, families and friends suffer through their absence. We can only hope that as they view the final product, they feel that their sacrifices were worth it.

Foundations of Computer Science
From Data Manipulation to Theory of Computation

I

Computers and Data

1 Introduction

The phrase "**computer science**" has a very broad meaning today. However, in this book, we define the phrase as "issues related to the computer". This introductory chapter first tries to find out what a computer is and then discovers other issues directly related to computers. We look at the computer as a **black box** and try to guess its behavior. We then try to penetrate this box to uncover what is common to every computer. This leads to the **von Neumann model,** which is universally accepted as the basis of the computer. We then briefly discuss the ramifications and issues of accepting the von Neumann model. At this time, we refer to the chapter or chapters in the text that pertain to these issues. The chapter ends with a brief history of this culture-changing device: the computer.

1.1 THE COMPUTER AS A BLACK BOX

If you are not concerned with the internal mechanisms of a computer, you can simply define it as a black box. However, you still need to define the job performed by a computer to distinguish it from other types of black boxes. We provide two common computer models.

DATA PROCESSOR

You can think of a computer as a **data processor.** Using this definition, a computer acts as a black box that accepts input data, processes the data, and creates output data (Figure 1.1). Although this model can define the functionality of a computer today, it is too general. Under this model, a pocket calculator is also a computer (which it is, literally).

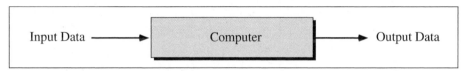

Figure 1.1   Data processor model

Another problem with this model is that it does not specify the type of processing or whether more than one type of processing is possible. In other words, it is not clear how many types or sets of operations a machine based on this model can perform. Is it a specific-purpose machine or a general-purpose machine?

This model could represent a specific-purpose computer (or processor) that is designed to do some specific job such as controlling the temperature of a building or controlling the fuel usage in a car. However, computers, as the term is used today, are *general-purpose* machines. They can do many different types of tasks. This implies that we need to change our model to reflect the actual computers of today.

PROGRAMMABLE DATA PROCESSOR

A better model for a general-purpose computer is shown in Figure 1.2. This figure adds one extra element to the computer: the program. A **program** is a set of instructions that tells the computer what to do with data. In the early days of computers, the instructions were implemented by changing the wiring or turning a set of switches on and off. Today, a program is a set of instructions written in a **computer language.**

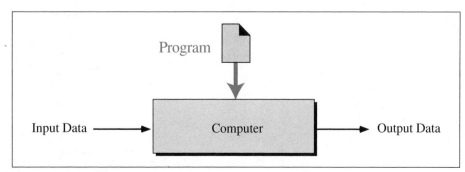

Figure 1.2   Programmable data processor model

In the new model, the **output data** depend on the combination of two factors: the **input data** and the program. With the same input data, you can generate different output if you change the program. Similarly, with the same program, you can generate different outputs if you change the input. Finally, if the input data and the program remain the same, the output should be the same. Let us look at three cases.

Same Program, Different Input Data

Figure 1.3 shows the same sorting program with different data. Although the program is the same, the output is different because different input data are processed.

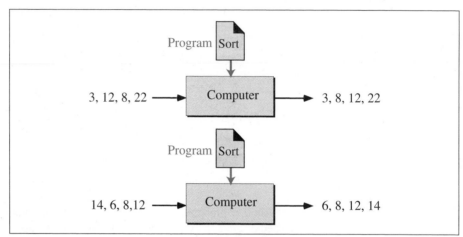

Figure 1.3   Same program, different data

Same Input Data, Different Programs

Figure 1.4 shows the same input data with different programs. Each program makes the computer perform different operations on the same input data. The first program sorts the data, the second adds the data, and the third finds the smallest number.

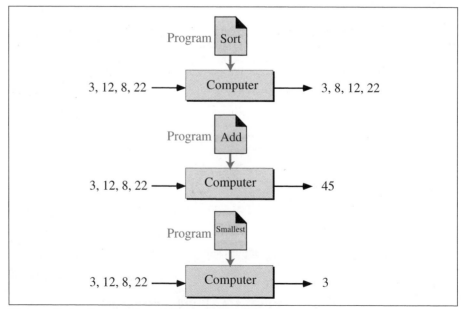

Figure 1.4   Same data, different programs

**Same Input Data,
Same Program**

You, of course, expect the same result each time both input data and the program are the same. In other words, when the same program is run with the same input, you expect the same output.

1.2   VON NEUMANN MODEL

Every computer today is based on the von Neumann model (named after John von Neumann). The model looks at the inside of the computer (black box) and defines how processing is done. It is based on three ideas.

FOUR SUBSYSTEMS

The model defines a computer as four subsystems: memory, arithmetic logic unit, control unit, and input/output (Figure 1.5).

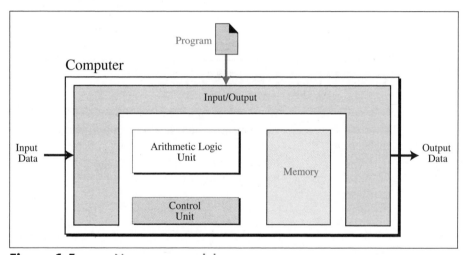

Figure 1.5   von Neumann model

Memory

Memory is the storage area. It is where programs and data are stored during processing. We discuss the reason for storing programs and data later in the chapter.

**Arithmetic
Logic Unit**

The **arithmetic logic unit (ALU)** is where calculation and logical operations take place. If a computer is a data processor, you should be able to do arithmetic operations on data (e.g., adding a list of numbers). You should also be able to do logical operations on data (e.g., finding the smaller of two elements of data, as in the previous sorting example).

Control Unit

The **control unit** controls the operations of the memory, ALU, and the input/output subsystem.

Input/Output

The input subsystem accepts input data and the program from outside the computer; the output subsystem sends the result of processing to the outside. The definition of the input/output subsystem is very broad; it also includes the secondary storage devices such as disk or tape that stores data and programs for processing. When a disk stores data that results from processing, it is considered an output device; when you read data from the disk, it is considered an input device.

STORED PROGRAM CONCEPT

The von Neumann model states that the program must be stored in memory. This is totally different from the architecture of early computers in which only the data were stored in memory. The program for a task was implemented by manipulating a set of switches or changing the wiring system.

The memory of modern computers hosts both a program and its corresponding data. This implies that both the data and programs should have the same format because they are stored in memory. They are, in fact, stored as binary patterns (a sequence of 0s and 1s) in memory.

SEQUENTIAL EXECUTION OF INSTRUCTIONS

A program in the von Neumann model is made of a finite number of **instructions.** In this model, the control unit fetches one instruction from memory, interprets it, and then executes it. In other words, the instructions are executed one after another. Of course, one instruction may request the control unit to jump to some previous or following instruction, but this does not mean that the instructions are not executed sequentially.

1.3   COMPUTER HARDWARE

Without question, the von Neumann model set the standard for essential computer components. A physical computer must include all four components, referred to as computer hardware, defined by von Neumann. But you can have different types of memory, different types of input/output subsystems, and so on. We discuss computer hardware in more detail in Chapter 5.

1.4   DATA

This model clearly defines a computer as a data processing machine that accepts the input data, processes it, and outputs the result.

STORING DATA

The von Neumann model does not define how data must be stored in a computer. If a computer is an electronic device, the best way to store data is in the form of an electrical signal, specifically its presence or absence. This implies that a computer can store data in one of two states.

Obviously, the data you use in daily life are not just in one of two states. For example, our numbering system uses digits that can take one of ten states (0 to 9). You cannot (as yet) store this type of information in a computer. It needs to be changed to another system that uses only two states (0 and 1).

You also need to process other types of data (text, image, audio, video). They also cannot be stored in a computer directly, but need to be changed to the appropriate form (0s and 1s).

In Chapters 2 and 3, you will learn how to store different types of data as a binary pattern, a sequence of 0s and 1s. In Chapter 4, we show how data are manipulated, as a binary pattern, inside a computer.

ORGANIZING DATA

Although data should be stored only in one form (a binary pattern) inside a computer, data outside a computer can take many forms. In addition, computers (and the notion of data processing) have created a new field of study known as **data organization**. Can you organize your data into different entities and formats before storing them inside a computer? Today, data are not treated as a rough sequence of information. Data are organized into small units, small units are organized into larger units, and so on. You will look at data from this point of view in Chapters 2 to 4.

1.5 COMPUTER SOFTWARE

The main feature of the von Neumann model is the concept of the stored program. Although early computers did not use this model, they did use the concept of programs. *Programming* these early computers meant changing the wiring systems or turning on and off a set of switches. Programming was a task done by an operator or engineer before the actual data processing began.

The von Neumann model changed the meaning of the term "**programming**." In this model, there are two aspects of programming that must be understood.

PROGRAMS MUST BE STORED

In the von Neumann model, the programs are stored in computer memory. Not only do you need memory to hold data, but you also need memory to hold the program (Figure 1.6).

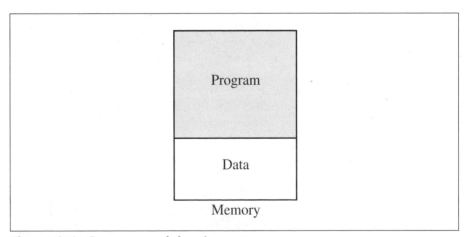

Figure 1.6   Program and data in memory

A SEQUENCE OF INSTRUCTIONS

Another requirement of the model is that the program must be a sequence of instructions. Each instruction operates on one or more data items. Thus, one instruction can change the effect of a previous instruction. For example, Figure 1.7 shows a program that inputs two numbers, adds them, and prints the result. This program consists of four individual instructions.

A person might ask why a program must be made of instructions. The answer is reusability. Today, computers do millions of tasks. If the program for each task was an independent entity without a common section with other programs, programming would be difficult. The von Neumann model makes programming easier by carefully defining the different instructions that can be used by computers. A programmer

```
1. Input first data item into memory.
2. Input second data item into memory.
3. Add the two together and store the result in memory.
4. Output the result.
```
Program

Figure 1.7   Program made of instructions

combines these instructions to make any number of programs. Each program can be a different combination of different instructions.

ALGORITHMS

The previous requirement made programming possible, but it brought another dimension to using a computer. A programmer must not only learn the task done by each instruction but also learn how to combine these instructions to do a particular task. Looking at this issue differently, a programmer should first solve the problem in a step-by-step manner and then try to find the appropriate instruction (or series of instructions) that solves the problem. The step-by-step solution is called an **algorithm.** Algorithms play a very important role in computer science and are discussed in Chapter 8.

LANGUAGES

At the beginning of the computer age, there was no computer language. Programmers wrote instructions (using binary patterns) to solve a problem. However, as programs became larger, writing long programs using these patterns became tedious. Computer scientists came up with the idea of using symbols to represent binary patterns, just as people use symbols (words) for commands in daily life. But of course, the symbols used in daily life are different from those used in computers. So the concept of computer languages was born. A natural language (e.g., English) is a rich language and has many rules to combine words correctly; a computer language, on the other hand, has a more limited number of symbols and also a limited number of words. You will study computer languages in Chapter 9.

SOFTWARE ENGINEERING

Something that was not defined in the von Neumann model is **software engineering,** which is the design and writing of structured programs. Today, it is not acceptable just to write a program that does a task; the program must follow strict principles and rules. We discuss these principles, collectively known as software engineering, in Chapter 10.

OPERATING SYSTEMS

During the evolution of computers, scientists became aware that there was a series of instructions common to all programs. For example, instructions to tell a computer where to receive data and where to send data are needed by almost all programs. It is more efficient to write these instructions only once for the use of all programs. Thus, the concept of the **operating system** emerged. An operating system originally worked as a manager to facilitate access of the computer components for a program. Today, operating systems do much more. You will learn about them in Chapter 7.

1.6 HISTORY

Before closing this chapter, we briefly review the history of computing and computers. We divide this history into three periods.

MECHANICAL MACHINES (BEFORE 1930)

During this period, several computing machines were invented that bear little resemblance to the modern concept of a computer.

- In the 17th century, Blaise Pascal, a French mathematician and philosopher, invented Pascaline, a mechanical calculator for addition and subtraction operations. In the 20th century, when Niklaus Wirth invented a structured programming language, he called it Pascal to honor the inventor of the first mechanical calculator.

- In the late 17th century, German mathematician Gottfried Leibnitz invented a more sophisticated mechanical calculator that could do multiplication and division as well as addition and subtraction. It was called Leibnitz's Wheel.

- The first machine that used the idea of storage and programming was the Jacquard loom, invented by Joseph-Marie Jacquard at the beginning of the 19th century. The loom used punched cards (like a stored program) to control the raising of the warp threads in the manufacture of textiles.

- In 1823, Charles Babbage invented the Difference Engine, which could do more than simple arithmetic operations; it could solve polynomial equations, too. Later, he invented a machine called the Analytical Engine that, to some extent, parallels the idea of modern computers. It had four components: a mill (modern ALU), a store (memory), an operator (control unit), and output (input/output).

- In 1890, Herman Hollerith, working at the U.S. Census Bureau, designed and built a programmer machine that could automatically read, tally, and sort data stored on punched cards.

BIRTH OF ELECTRONIC COMPUTERS (1930–1950)

Between 1930 and 1950, several computers were invented by scientists who could be considered the pioneers of the electronic computer industry.

Early Electronic Computers

The early computers of this period did not store the program in memory; all were programmed externally. Five computers were prominent during these years:

- The first special-purpose computer that encoded information electrically was invented by John V. Atanasoff and his assistant Clifford Berry in 1939. It was called the ABC (Atanasoff Berry Computer) and was specifically designed to solve a system of linear equations.

- At the same time, a German mathematician named Konrad Zuse designed a general-purpose machine named Z1.

- In the 1930s, the U.S. Navy and IBM sponsored a project at Harvard University under the direction of Howard Aiken to build a huge computer named Mark I. This computer used both electrical and mechanical components.

- In England, Alan Turing invented a computer called Colossus that was designed to break the German Enigma code.

■ The first general-purpose, totally electronic computer was made by John Mauchly and J. Presper Eckert and was called ENIAC (Electronic Numerical Integrator and Calculator). It was completed in 1946. It used 18,000 vacuum tubes, was 100 feet long by 10 feet high, and weighed 30 tons.

Computers Based on the von Neumann Model

The preceding five computers used memory only for storing data. They were programmed externally using wires or switches. John von Neumann proposed that the program and the data should be stored in memory. That way, every time you use a computer to do a new task, you need only change the program instead of rewiring the machine or turning on and off hundreds of switches.

The first computer based on von Neumann's idea was made in 1950 at the University of Pennsylvania and was called EDVAC. At the same time, a similar computer called EDSAC was made at Cambridge University in England by Maurice Wilkes.

COMPUTER GENERATIONS (1950–PRESENT)

Computers built after 1950 are following, more or less, the von Neumann model. The computers have become faster, smaller, and cheaper, but the principle is almost the same. Historians divide this period into generations, with each generation witnessing some major change in hardware or software (but not the model).

First Generation

The first generation (roughly 1950–1959) is characterized by the emergence of commercial computers. During this time, computers were used only by professionals. They were locked in rooms with access limited only to the operator or computer specialist. Computers were bulky and used vacuum tubes as electronic switches. At this time, computers were affordable only by big organizations.

Second Generation

Second-generation (roughly 1959–1965) computers used transistors instead of vacuum tubes. This reduced the size of computers as well as their cost and made them affordable to small and medium-size corporations. Two high-level programming languages, FORTRAN and COBOL (see Chapter 9), were invented and made programming easier. These two languages separated the programming task from the computer operation task. A civil engineer could write a FORTRAN program to solve a problem without being involved in the electronic details of computer architecture.

Third Generation

The invention of the **integrated circuit** (transistors, wiring, and other components on a single chip) reduced the cost and size of computers even further. Minicomputers appeared on the market. Canned programs, popularly known as **software** packages, became available. A small corporation could buy a needed package (e.g., for accounting) instead of writing its own program. A new industry, the software industry, was born. This generation lasted roughly between 1965 and 1975.

Fourth Generation

The fourth generation (approximately 1975–1985) saw the appearance of **microcomputers.** The first desktop calculator (Altair 8800) became available in 1975. Advances in the electronics industry allowed whole computer subsystems to fit on a single circuit board. This generation also saw the emergence of computer networks (see Chapter 6).

Fifth Generation

This open-ended generation started in 1985. It witnessed the appearance of laptop and palmtop computers, improvements in secondary storage media (CD-ROM, DVD, etc.), the use of multimedia, and the phenomenon of virtual reality.

1.7 KEY TERMS

algorithm	input data	program
arithmetic logic unit (ALU)	instruction	programmable data processor
black box	integrated circuit	software
computer language	memory	software engineering
computer science	microcomputer	von Neumann model
control unit	operating system	
data processor	output data	

1.8 SUMMARY

- Computer science, in this text, means issues related to a computer.

- A computer is a programmable data processor that accepts input data and programs and outputs data.

- A program is a set of instructions executed sequentially that tells the computer what to do with data.

- Every computer today is based on the von Neumann model.

- The von Neumann model specifies a memory subsystem, an arithmetic logic unit subsystem, a control unit subsystem, and an input/output subsystem.

- Data and programs are stored in computer memory.

- A step-by-step solution to a problem is called an algorithm.

- A program is written in a computer language.

- Software engineering is the design and writing of programs in a structured form.

1.9 PRACTICE SET

REVIEW QUESTIONS

1. How is computer science defined in this book?

2. What model is the basis for today's computers?

3. Why shouldn't you call a computer a data processor?

4. What does a programmable data processor require to produce output data?

5. What are the subsystems of the von Neumann computer model?

6. What is the function of the memory subsystem in von Neumann's model?

7. What is the function of the ALU subsystem in von Neumann's model?

8. What is the function of the control unit subsystem in von Neumann's model?

9. What is the function of the input/output subsystem in von Neumann's model?

10. Compare and contrast the memory contents of early computers with the memory contents of a computer based on the von Neumann model.

11. How did the von Neumann model change the concept of programming?

MULTIPLE-CHOICE QUESTIONS

12. The _____ model is the basis for today's computers.
    a. Ron Newman
    b. von Neumann
    c. Pascal
    d. Charles Babbage

13. In the von Neumann model, the _____ subsystem stores data and programs.
    a. ALU
    b. input/output
    c. memory
    d. control unit

14. In the von Neumann model, the _____ subsystem performs calculations and logical operations.
    a. ALU
    b. input/output
    c. memory
    d. control unit

15. In the von Neumann model, the _____ subsystem accepts data and programs and sends processing results to output devices.
    a. ALU
    b. input/output
    c. memory
    d. control unit

16. In the von Neumann model, the _____ subsystem serves as a manager of the other subsystems.
    a. ALU
    b. input/output
    c. memory
    d. control unit

17. According to the von Neumann model, _____ stored in memory.
    a. only data are
    b. only programs are
    c. data and programs are
    d. none of the above

18. A step-by-step solution to a problem is called _____.
    a. hardware
    b. an operating system
    c. a computer language
    d. an algorithm

19. FORTRAN and COBOL are examples of _____.
    a. hardware
    b. operating systems
    c. computer languages
    d. algorithms

20. A 17th-century computing machine that could perform addition and subtraction was the _____.
    a. Pascaline
    b. Jacquard loom
    c. Analytical Engine
    d. Babbage machine

21. _____ is a set of instructions in a computer language that tells the computer what to do with data.
    a. An operating system
    b. An algorithm
    c. A data processor
    d. A program

22. _____ is the design and writing of a program in structured form.
    a. Software engineering
    b. Hardware engineering
    c. Algorithm development
    d. Instructional architecture

23. The first electronic special-purpose computer was called _____.
    a. Pascal
    b. Pascaline
    c. ABC
    d. EDVAC

24. One of the first computers based on the von Neumann model was called _____.
    a. Pascal
    b. Pascaline
    c. ABC
    d. EDVAC

25. The first computing machine to use the idea of storage and programming was called _____.
    a. the Madeline
    b. EDVAC
    c. the Babbage machine
    d. the Jacquard loom

26. _____ separated the programming task from the computer operation tasks.
    a. Algorithms
    b. Data processors
    c. High-level programming languages
    d. Operating systems

EXERCISES

27. Use the Internet or the library to find when keyboards were invented.

28. Use the Internet or the library to find when printers were invented.

29. Use the Internet or the library to find when magnetic disks were invented.

30. According to the von Neumann model, can the hard disk of today be used as input or output? Explain.

31. A programming language has 10 different instructions. How many 5-instruction programs can be made in this language if no instruction is repeated? How many 7-instruction programs?

32. Which is more expensive today, hardware or software?

33. Which is more valuable today for an organization, hardware, software, or data?

34. How does what a word processor program sees impose organization on data?

35. Use the Internet or the library to find more information about Pascaline.

36. Use the Internet or the library to find more information about Leibnitz's Wheel.

37. Use the Internet or the library to find more information about the Jacquard loom and its social impact.

38. Use the Internet or the library to find more information about the Analytical Engine.

39. Use the Internet or the library to find more information about Hollerith and his tabulator.

Data
Representation

As discussed in Chapter 1, a computer is a data processing machine. But before we can talk about processing data, you need to understand the nature of data. In this chapter and the next, we discuss the different data and how they are represented inside a computer. In Chapter 4, we show how data are manipulated inside a computer.

2.1 DATA TYPES

Data today come in different forms such as numbers, text, images, audio, and video (Figure 2.1). People need to process all these data types.

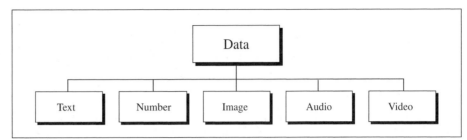

Figure 2.1   Different types of data

■ An engineering program uses a computer mostly to process numbers: to do arithmetic, to solve algebraic or trigonometric equations, to find the roots of a differential equation, and so on.

■ A word processing program, on the other hand, uses a computer mostly to process text: justify, move, delete, and so on.

■ An image processing program uses a computer to manipulate images: create, shrink, expand, rotate, and so on.

■ A computer also handles audio data. You can play music on a computer and can enter your voice as data.

■ Finally, a computer can be used not only to show movies, but also to create the special effects seen in movies.

> The computer industry uses the term *"multimedia"* to define information that contains numbers, text, images, audio, and video.

2.2 DATA INSIDE THE COMPUTER

The question now is: How do you handle all these data types? Do you have different computers process different types of data? That is, do you have a category of computers that processes only numbers? Do you have a category of computers that processes only text?

This solution of different computers to process different types of data is neither economical nor practical because data is usually a mixture of types. For example, although a bank primarily processes numbers, it also needs to store, in text, customers' names. As another example, an image is often a mixture of graphics and text.

The most efficient solution is to use a uniform representation of data. All data types from outside a computer are transformed into this uniform representation when stored in a computer and then transformed back when leaving the computer. This universal format is called a *bit pattern*.

BIT

Before further discussion of bit patterns, we must define a bit. A **bit (binary digit)** is the smallest unit of data that can be stored in a computer; it is either 0 or 1. A bit represents the state of a device that can take one of two states. For example, a **switch** can be either on or off. The convention is to represent the on state as 1 and the off state as 0. An electronic switch can represent a bit. In other words, a switch can store one bit of information. Today, computers use various two-state devices to store data.

BIT PATTERN

A single bit cannot possibly solve the data representation problem. If every piece of data could be represented by either one 0 or one 1, you would only need one single bit. However, you need to store larger numbers, you need to store text, you need to store graphics, and so on.

To represent different types of data, you use a **bit pattern,** a sequence, or as it is sometimes called, a string of bits. Figure 2.2 shows a bit pattern made of 16 bits. It is a combination of 0s and 1s. This means that if you need to store a bit pattern made of 16 bits, you need 16 electronic switches. If you need to store 1000 bit patterns, each 16 bits, you need 16,000 switches and so on.

---

1 0 0 0 1 0 1 0 1 0 1 1 1 1 1 1

Figure 2.2 Bit pattern

Now the question is: How does computer memory know what type of data a stored bit pattern represents? It does not. Computer memory just stores the data as bit patterns. It is the responsibility of input/output devices or programs to interpret a bit pattern as a number, text, or some other type of data. In other words, data are coded when they enter a computer and decoded when they are presented to the user (Figure 2.3).

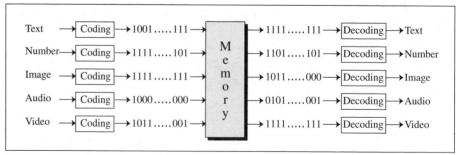

Figure 2.3 Examples of bit patterns

BYTE

By tradition, a bit pattern of length 8 is called a **byte**. This term has also been used to measure the size of memory or other storage devices. For example, a computer memory that can store 8 million bits of information is said to have a memory of 1 million bytes.

2.3 REPRESENTING DATA

Now we can explain how different data types can be represented using bit patterns.

TEXT

A piece of **text** in any language is a sequence of symbols used to represent an idea in that language. For example, the English language uses 26 symbols (A, B, C, . . . , Z) to represent uppercase letters, 26 symbols (a, b, c, . . . , z) to represent lowercase letters, 9 symbols (0, 1, 2, . . . , 9) to represent numeric characters (not numbers; you will see the difference later), and symbols (., ?, :, ; . . . , !) to represent punctuation. Other symbols such as the blank, the newline, and the tab are used for text alignment and readability.

You can represent each symbol with a bit pattern. In other words, text such as "BYTE", which is made of four symbols, can be represented as 4 bit patterns, each pattern defining a single symbol (Figure 2.4).

Figure 2.4   Representing symbols using bit patterns

Now the question is: How many bits are needed in a bit pattern to represent a symbol in a language? It depends on how many symbols are in the set. For example, if you create an imaginary language that uses only the English uppercase letters, you need only 26 symbols. A bit pattern in this language needs to represent at least 26 symbols. For another language, such as Chinese, you may need many more symbols. The length of the bit pattern that represents a symbol in a language depends on the number of symbols used in that language. More symbols mean a longer bit pattern.

Although the length of the bit pattern depends on the number of symbols, the relationship is not linear; it is logarithmic. If you need two symbols, the length is 1 bit ($\log_2 2$ is 1). If you need four symbols, the length is 2 bits ($\log_2 4$ is 2). Table 2.1 shows the relationship, which you can easily see. A bit pattern of 2 bits can take four different forms: 00, 01, 10, and 11. Each of these forms can represent a symbol. In the same way, a bit pattern of 3 bits can take eight different forms: 000, 001, 010, 011, 100, 101, 110, and 111.

Number of Symbols	Bit Pattern Length
2	1
4	2
8	3
16	4
. . .	. . .
128	7
256	8
. . .	. . .
65,536	16

Table 2.1   Number of symbols and bit pattern length

Codes

Different sets of bit patterns have been designed to represent text symbols. Each set is called a **code,** and the process of representing symbols is called coding. In this section, we explain the common codes.

ASCII   The **American National Standards Institute (ANSI)** developed a code called **American Standard Code for Information Interchange (ASCII).** This code uses 7 bits for each symbol. This means 128 (2^7) different symbols can be defined by this code. The full bit patterns for ASCII code are in Appendix A. Figure 2.5 shows how "BYTE" is represented in ASCII code.

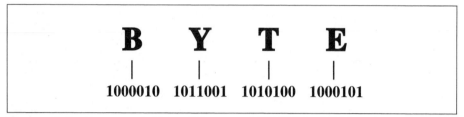

Figure 2.5   Representation of the word "BYTE" in ASCII code

The following highlights some features of this code:

■ ASCII uses a 7-bit pattern ranging from 0000000 to 1111111.

■ The first pattern (0000000) represents the null character (lack of character).

■ The last pattern (1111111) represents the delete character.

■ There are 31 control (nonprintable) characters.

■ The numeric characters (0 to 9) are coded before letters.

■ There are several special printable characters.

■ The uppercase letters (A . . . Z) come before the lowercase letters (a . . . z).

■ The upper- and lowercase characters are distinguished by only 1 bit. For example, the pattern for A is 1000001; the pattern for a is 1100001. The only difference is in the sixth bit from the right.

■ There are six special characters between the upper- and lowercase letters.

Extended ASCII   To make the size of each pattern 1 byte (8 bits), the ASCII bit patterns are augmented with an extra 0 at the left. Now each pattern can easily fit into 1 byte of memory. In other words, in **extended ASCII,** the first pattern is 00000000 and the last one is 01111111.

Some manufacturers have decided to use the extra bit to create an extra 128 symbols. However, this attempt has not been very successful due to the nonstandard set created by each manufacturer.

EBCDIC   In the early age of computers, IBM developed a code called **Extended Binary Coded Decimal Interchange Code (EBCDIC).** This code uses 8-bit patterns, so it can represent up to 256 symbols. However, this code is not used in any computers other than IBM mainframes.

Unicode   Neither of the foregoing codes represent symbols belonging to languages other than English. For that, a code with much more capacity is needed. A coalition of hardware and software manufacturers have designed a code named **Unicode** that uses 16 bits and can represent up to 65,536 (2^{16}) symbols. Different sections of the code are allocated to symbols from different languages in the world. Some parts of the code are used for graphical and special symbols. The Java™ language uses this code to represent characters. Microsoft Windows uses a variation of the first 256 characters. A brief set of Unicode symbols is in Appendix B.

ISO   The **International Organization for Standardization,** known as ISO, has designed a code using 32-bit patterns. This code can represent up to 4,294,967,296 (2^{32}) symbols, definitely enough to represent any symbol in the world today.

NUMBERS

In a computer, numbers are represented using the **binary system.** In this system, a pattern of bits (a sequence of 0s and 1s) represents a number. However, a code such as ASCII is not used to represent data. The reason for this and a discussion of number representation are presented in Chapter 3.

IMAGES

Images today are represented in a computer by one of two methods: **bitmap graphic** or **vector graphic** (Figure 2.6).

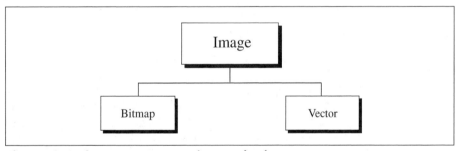

Figure 2.6   Image representation methods

Bitmap Graphic

In this method, an image is divided into a matrix of **pixels (picture elements),** where each pixel is a small dot. The size of the pixel depends on what is called the *resolution.* For example, an image can be divided into 1000 pixels or 10,000 pixels. In the second case, although there is a better representation of the image (better resolution), more memory is needed to store the image.

After dividing an image into pixels, each pixel is assigned a bit pattern. The size and the value of the pattern depend on the image. For an image made of only black-and-white dots (e.g., a chessboard), a 1-bit pattern is enough to represent a pixel. A pattern of 0 represents a black pixel and a pattern of 1 represents a white pixel. The patterns are then recorded one after another and stored in the computer. Figure 2.7 shows an image of this kind and its representation.

If an image is not made of pure white and pure black pixels, you can increase the size of the bit pattern to represent gray scales. For example, to show four levels of gray scale, you can use 2-bit patterns. A black pixel can be represented by 00, a dark gray pixel by 01, a light gray pixel by 10, and a white pixel by 11.

To represent color images, each colored pixel is decomposed into three primary colors: red, green, and blue (RGB). Then the intensity of each color is measured, and a

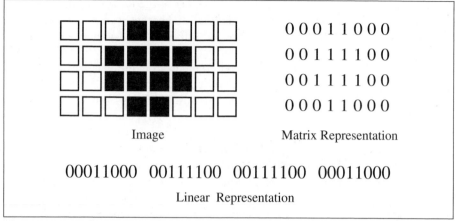

Figure 2.7   Bitmap graphic method of a black-and-white image

bit pattern (usually 8 bits) is assigned to it. In other words, each pixel has three bit patterns: one to represent the intensity of the red color, one to represent the intensity of the green color, and one to represent the intensity of the blue color. For example, Figure 2.8 shows four bit patterns for some pixels in a color image.

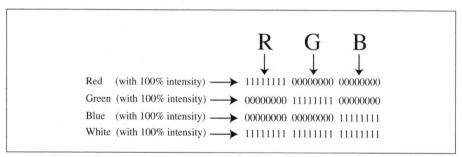

Figure 2.8   Representation of color pixels

Vector Graphic

The problem with the bitmap graphic method is that the exact bit patterns representing a particular image must be stored in a computer. Later, if you want to rescale the image, you must change the size of the pixels, which creates a ragged or grainy look. The vector graphic method, however, does not store the bit patterns. An image is decomposed into a combination of curves and lines. Each curve or line is represented by a mathematical formula. For example, a line may be described by the coordinates of its endpoints, and a circle may be described by the coordinates of its center and the length of its radius. The combination of these formulas is stored in a computer. When the image is to be displayed or printed, the size of the image is given to the system as an input. The system redesigns the image with the new size and uses the same formula to draw the image. In this case, each time an image is drawn, the formula is reevaluated.

AUDIO

Audio is a representation of sound or music. Although there is no standard to store sound or music, the idea is to convert audio to **digital** data and use bit patterns to store them. Audio is by nature **analog** data. It is continuous (analog), not discrete (digital). Figure 2.9 shows the steps to change audio data to bit patterns. They are as follows:

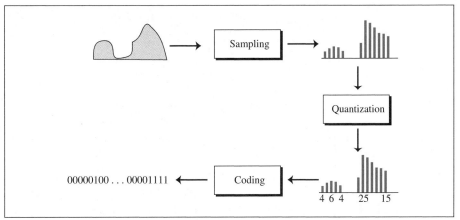

Figure 2.9 Audio representation

1. The analog signal is sampled. **Sampling** means measuring the value of the signal at equal intervals.
2. The samples are quantized. **Quantization** means assigning a value (from a set) to a sample. For example, if the value of a sample is 29.2 and the set is the set of integers between 0 and 63, the sample is assigned a value of 29.
3. The quantized values are changed to binary patterns. For example, the number 25 is changed to the binary pattern 00011001 (see Chapter 3 for number to pattern transformations).
4. The binary patterns are stored.

VIDEO

Video is a representation of images (called frames) in time. A movie is a series of frames shown one after another to create the illusion of motion. So, if you know how to store an image inside a computer, you also know how to store a video; each image or frame is changed to a set of bit patterns and stored. The combination of the images represents the video. Note that today video is normally compressed. In Chapter 15, we discuss MPEG, a common video compression technique.

2.4 HEXADECIMAL NOTATION

The bit pattern is designed to represent data when they are stored inside a computer. However, people find it difficult to manipulate bit patterns. Writing a long stream of 0s and 1s is tedious and prone to error. Hexadecimal notation helps.

Hexadecimal notation is based on 16 (*hexadec* is Greek for 16). This means there are 16 symbols (hexadecimal digits): 0, 1, 2, 3, 4, 5, 6, 7, 8, 9, A, B, C, D, E, and F. The importance of hexadecimal notation becomes clear when converting a bit pattern into hexadecimal notation.

Each hexadecimal digit can represent 4 bits, and 4 bits can be represented by a hexadecimal digit. Table 2.2 shows the relationship between a bit pattern and a hexadecimal digit.

A 4-bit pattern can be represented by a hexadecimal digit, and vice versa.

Bit Pattern	Hexadecimal digit	Bit Pattern	Hexadecimal digit
0000	0	1000	8
0001	1	1001	9
0010	2	1010	A
0011	3	1011	B
0100	4	1100	C
0101	5	1101	D
0110	6	1110	E
0111	7	1111	F

Table 2.2   Hexadecimal digits

CONVERSION

Converting from a bit pattern to hexadecimal is done by organizing the pattern into groups of four and finding the hexadecimal value for each group of 4 bits. For hexadecimal to bit pattern conversion, convert each hexadecimal digit to its 4-bit equivalent (Figure 2.10).

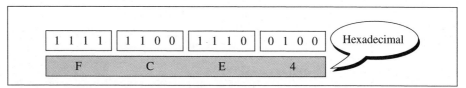

Figure 2.10   Binary to hexadecimal and hexadecimal to binary transformation

Note that hexadecimal notation is written in two formats. In the first format, you add a lowercase (or uppercase) x before the digits to show that the representation is in hexadecimal. For example, xA34 represents a hexadecimal value in this convention. In another format, you indicate the base of the number (16) as the subscript after the notation. For example, $A34_{16}$ shows the same value in the second convention. We use both conventions in this book.

EXAMPLE 1

Show the hexadecimal equivalent of the bit pattern 110011100010.

SOLUTION

Each group of 4 bits is translated to one hexadecimal digit. The equivalent is xCE2.   ■

EXAMPLE 2

Show the hexadecimal equivalent of the bit pattern 0011100010.

SOLUTION

Divide the bit pattern into 4-bit groups (from the right). In this case, add two extra 0s at the left to make the total number of bits divisible by 4. So you have 000011100010, which is translated to x0E2.   ■

EXAMPLE 3

What is the bit pattern for x24C?

SOLUTION

Write each hexadecimal digit as its equivalent bit pattern and get 001001001100.   ■

2.5 OCTAL NOTATION

Another notation used to group bit patterns together is octal notation. **Octal notation** is based on 8 (*oct* is Greek for 8). This means there are eight symbols (octal digits): 0, 1, 2, 3, 4, 5, 6, 7. The importance of octal notation becomes clear as you learn to convert a bit pattern into octal notation.

Each octal digit can represent 3 bits, and 3 bits can be represented by an octal digit. Table 2.3 shows the relationship between a bit pattern and an octal digit.

> A 3-bit pattern can be represented by an octal digit, and vice versa.

Bit Pattern	Octal Digit	Bit Pattern	Octal Digit
000	0	100	4
001	1	101	5
010	2	110	6
011	3	111	7

Table 2.3   Octal digits

CONVERSION

Converting from a bit pattern to octal is done by organizing the pattern into groups of three and finding the octal value for each group of 3 bits. For octal to bit pattern conversion, convert each octal digit to its 3-bit equivalent (Figure 2.11).

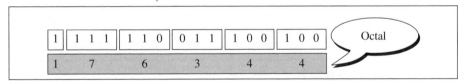

Figure 2.11   Binary to octal and octal to binary transformation

Note that octal notation is also written in two formats. In the first format, you add 0 (zero) before the digits to show that the representation is in octal (sometimes a lowercase o is used). For example, 0634 represents an octal value in this convention. In the other format, you indicate the base of the number (8) as the subscript after the notation. For example, 634_8 shows the same value in the second convention. We use both conventions in this book.

EXAMPLE 4

Show the octal equivalent of the bit pattern 101110010.

SOLUTION

Each group of 3 bits is translated to one octal digit. The equivalent is 0562, o562, or 562_8.

EXAMPLE 5

Show the octal equivalent of the bit pattern 1100010.

SOLUTION

Divide the bit pattern into 3-bit groups (from the right). In this case, add two extra 0s at the left to make the total number of bits divisible by 3. So you have 001100010, which is translated to 0142, o142, or 142_8. ■

EXAMPLE 6

What is the bit pattern for 24_8?

SOLUTION

Write each octal digit as its equivalent bit pattern to get 010100. ■

2.6 KEY TERMS

American National Standards Institute (ANSI)	byte	octal notation
American Standard Code for Information Interchange (ASCII)	code	picture element
	digital	pixel
analog	extended ASCII	quantization
binary digit	Extended Binary Coded Decimal Interchange Code (EBCDIC)	sampling
binary system		switch
bit	hexadecimal notation	text
bitmap graphic	image	Unicode
bit pattern	International Organization for Standardization (ISO)	vector graphic
		video

2.7 SUMMARY

- Numbers, text, images, audio, and video are all forms of data. Computers need to process all types of data.

- All data types are transformed into a uniform representation called a bit pattern for processing by computers.

- A bit is the smallest unit of data that can be stored in a computer.

- A switch, with its two states of on and off, can represent a bit.

- A bit pattern is a sequence of bits that can represent a symbol.

- A byte is 8 bits.

- Coding is the process of transforming data into a bit pattern.

- ASCII is a popular code for symbols.

- EBCDIC is a code used in IBM mainframes.

- Unicode is a 16-bit code, and the ISO has developed a 32-bit code. Both these codes allow a greater number of symbols.

- Images use the bitmap graphic or vector graphic method for data representation. The image is broken up into pixels which can then be assigned bit patterns.

- Audio data are transformed to bit patterns through sampling, quantization, and coding.

- Video data are a set of sequential images.

2.8 PRACTICE SET

REVIEW QUESTIONS

1. Name five types of data that a computer can process.

2. How does a computer deal with all the data types it must process?

3. What is a bit pattern?

4. What is the difference between ASCII and extended ASCII?

5. What is EBCDIC?

6. How is bit pattern length related to the number of symbols the bit pattern can represent?

7. How does the bitmap graphic method represent an image as a bit pattern?

8. What is the advantage of the vector graphic method over the bitmap graphic method?

9. What steps are needed to convert audio data to bit patterns?

10. What is the relationship between image data and video data?

MULTIPLE-CHOICE QUESTIONS

11. Which of the following can be classified as data?
    a. numbers
    b. video
    c. audio
    d. all of the above

12. To store a byte, you need _____ electronic switches.
    a. 1
    b. 2
    c. 4
    d. 8

13. A byte consists of _____ bits.
    a. 2
    b. 4
    c. 8
    d. 16

14. In a set with 64 symbols, each symbol requires a bit pattern length of _____ bits.
    a. 4
    b. 5
    c. 6
    d. 7

15. How many symbols can be represented by a bit pattern with 10 bits?
    a. 128
    b. 256
    c. 512
    d. 1024

16. In extended ASCII, each symbol is _____ bits.
    a. 7
    b. 8
    c. 9
    d. 10

17. If the ASCII code for E is 1000101, then the ASCII code for e is _____.
    a. 1000110
    b. 1000111
    c. 0000110
    d. 1100101

18. In extended ASCII, a _____ of the bit pattern for regular ASCII code.
    a. 0 bit is added to the left
    b. 0 bit is added to the right
    c. 1 bit is added to the left
    d. 1 bit is added to the right

19. _____ is a code used in IBM mainframes.
    a. ASCII
    b. Extended ASCII
    c. EBCDIC
    d. Unicode

20. _____ is a 16-bit code that can represent symbols in languages other than English.
    a. ASCII
    b. Extended ASCII
    c. EBCDIC
    d. Unicode

21. _____ is a code used by the Java language to represent characters.
    a. ASCII
    b. Extended ASCII
    c. EBCDIC
    d. Unicode

22. A 32-bit code was developed by _____ to represent symbols in all languages.
    a. ANSI
    b. ISO
    c. EBCDIC
    d. Hamming

23. An image can be represented in a computer using the _____ method.
    a. bitmap graphic
    b. vector graphic
    c. matrix graphic
    d. a or b

24. The bitmap graphic method and the vector graphic method are used to represent _____ in a computer.
    a. audio
    b. video
    c. images
    d. numbers

25. In the _____ graphic method of representing an image in a computer, each pixel is assigned one or more bit patterns.
    a. bitmap
    b. vector
    c. quantized
    d. binary

26. In the _____ graphic method of representing an image in a computer, the image is decomposed into a combination of curves and lines.
    a. bitmap
    b. vector
    c. quantized
    d. binary

27. In the _____ graphic method of representing an image in a computer, rescaling of the image creates a ragged or grainy image.
    a. bitmap
    b. vector
    c. quantized
    d. binary

28. When you want to download music to a computer, the audio signal must be _____.
    a. sampled
    b. quantized
    c. coded
    d. all of the above

EXERCISES

29. Given 5 bits, how many distinct 5-bit patterns can you have?

30. In some country, the vehicle license plates have two decimal digits (0 to 9). How many distinct plates can you have? If the digit 0 is not allowed on the license plate, how many distinct plates can you have?

31. Redo Exercise 30 for a license plate that has two digits followed by three uppercase letters (A to Z).

32. A machine has eight different cycles. How many bits are needed to represent each cycle?

33. A student's grade in a course can be A, B, C, D, F, W (withdraw), or I (incomplete). How many bits are needed to represent the grade?

34. A company has decided to assign a unique bit pattern to each employee. If the company has 900 employees, what is the minimum number of bits needed to create this system of representation? How many patterns are unassigned? If the company hires another 300 employees, should it increase the number of bits? Explain your answer.

35. If you use a 4-bit pattern to represent the digits 0 to 9, how many bit patterns are wasted?

36. A gray scale picture is digitized using four different gray levels. If the picture is composed of 100×100 pixels, how many bits are needed to represent the picture?

37. An audio signal is sampled 8000 times per second. Each sample is represented by 256 different levels. How many bits per second are needed to represent this signal?

38. Change the following bit patterns to hexadecimal notation:
    a. 100011110000
    b. 1000001101
    c. 10001
    d. 11111111

39. Change the following to bit patterns:
    a. x120
    b. x2A34
    c. x00
    d. xFF

40. Change the following bit patterns to octal notation:
    a. 100011110000
    b. 1000001101
    c. 10001
    d. 11111111

41. Change the following to bit patterns:
    a. o12
    b. o27
    c. o45
    d. o20

42. How many hexadecimal digits are needed to convert a 19-bit pattern?

43. How many octal digits are needed to convert a 19-bit pattern?

44. How many hexadecimal digits are needed to convert a 6-byte pattern?

Number Representation 3

In Chapter 2, we showed how text, image, audio, and video can be represented in a computer by bit patterns. We postponed discussing the representation of numbers because their representation is so different from nonnumeric data. Some reasons for this difference are as follows:

■ A character code such as ASCII is not efficient for representing numbers. ASCII can represent 128 symbols, but the decimal system needs only 10. (Note that if you consider other symbols such as +, −, and the decimal point, more symbols are needed, but still much fewer than 128.) For example, if you want to store 65,535 using ASCII, you need 5 bytes (1 byte for each digit). But if the number is represented as an unsigned integer (you will see this representation later in this chapter), you need only 2 bytes.

■ Operations on numbers (e.g., addition and subtraction) are very complicated if the digits of a number are represented in a character code.

■ Representation of the precision of a number (i.e., the number of places after the decimal point) is byte intensive. For example, storing 23454.00001 requires 11 bytes, but if the same number is represented in floating point (you will see this representation later in this chapter), you need far fewer bytes.

3.1 DECIMAL AND BINARY

Two numbering systems are dominant today in the world of computers: decimal and binary. We first discuss these two different systems before presenting how numbers are represented by a computer.

DECIMAL SYSTEM

Today, the world uses the **decimal system** for numbers developed by Arabian mathematicians in the eighth century. The first people to use a decimal numbering system were the ancient Egyptians. The Babylonians improved on the Egyptian system by making the positions in the numbering system meaningful.

We all readily understand the decimal numbering system. In fact, we have used it so much that it is basically intuitive. But is it really understood why the second position in the decimal system is tens and the third position is hundreds? The answer lies in the powers of the base of the system, which in decimal is 10. Thus, the first position is 10 raised to the power 0, the second position is 10 raised to the power 1, and the third position is 10 raised to the power 2. Figure 3.1 shows the relationship between the powers and the number 243.

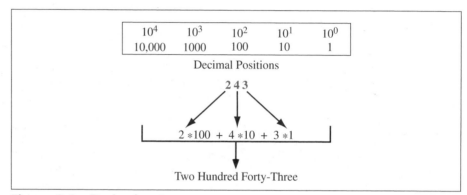

Figure 3.1 Decimal system

BINARY SYSTEM

Whereas the decimal system is based on 10, the **binary system** is based on 2. There are only two digits in the binary system, 0 and 1. Figure 3.2 shows the positional weights for a binary system and the value 243 in binary. In the position table, each position is double the previous position. Again, this is because the base of the system is 2. You should memorize the binary powers to at least 2^{10}.

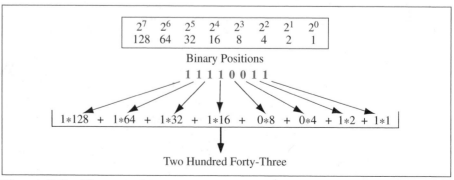

Figure 3.2 Binary system

3.2 CONVERSION

Before discussing how numbers in the form of bit patterns are stored inside a computer, you should understand how to manually convert a number from the decimal system to the binary system, and vice versa.

BINARY TO DECIMAL CONVERSION

We start by converting a number from the binary system to the decimal system. Start with the binary number and multiply each binary digit by its weight. Since each binary bit can be only 0 or 1, the result will be either 0 or the value of the weight. After multiplying all the digits, add the results. **Binary to decimal conversion** is shown in Figure 3.3.

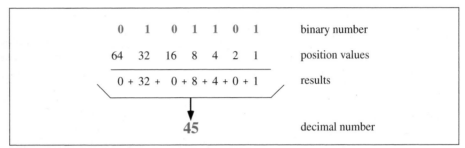

Figure 3.3   Binary to decimal conversion

EXAMPLE 1

Convert the binary number 10011 to decimal.

SOLUTION

Write the bits and their weights. Multiply the bit by its corresponding weight and record the result. At the end, add the results to get the decimal number.

Binary	1	0	0	1	1
Weights	16	8	4	2	1
	16 +	0 +	0 +	2 +	1
Decimal				19	

DECIMAL TO BINARY CONVERSION

To convert from decimal to binary, use repetitive division. The original number, 45 in the example, is divided by 2. The remainder (1) becomes the first binary digit, and the second digit is determined by dividing the quotient (22) by 2. Again, the remainder (0) becomes the binary digit, and the quotient is divided by 2 to determine the next position. This process continues until the quotient is 0. **Decimal to binary conversion** is shown in Figure 3.4.

EXAMPLE 2

Convert the decimal number 35 to binary.

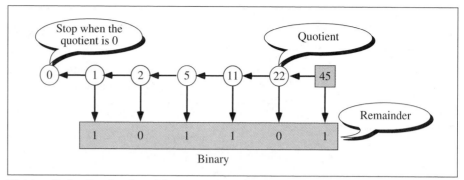

Figure 3.4   Decimal to binary conversion

SOLUTION

Write the number at the right corner. Divide the number continuously by 2 and write the quotient and the remainder. The quotients move to the left, and the remainder is recorded under each operation. Stop when the quotient is 0.

$$0 \leftarrow 1 \leftarrow 2 \leftarrow 4 \leftarrow 8 \leftarrow 17 \leftarrow 35 \qquad \textbf{(Decimal)}$$
$$\downarrow \quad \downarrow \quad \downarrow \quad \downarrow \quad \downarrow \quad \downarrow$$

Binary   1   0   0   0   1   1   ■

3.3   INTEGER REPRESENTATION

Now that you know how to transform from the decimal system to the binary system, let us see how to store integers inside a computer. **Integers** are **whole numbers** (i.e., numbers without a fraction). For example, 134 is an integer, but 134.23 is not. As another example, −134 is an integer, but −134.567 is not.

An integer can be positive or negative. A **negative integer** ranges from negative infinity to 0; a **positive integer** ranges from 0 to positive infinity (Figure 3.5). However, no computer can store all the integers in this range. To do so would require an infinite number of bits, which means a computer with infinite storage capability.

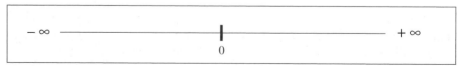

Figure 3.5   Range of integers

To use computer memory more efficiently, two broad categories of integer representation have been developed: unsigned integers and signed integers. Signed integers may also be represented in three distinct ways (Figure 3.6).

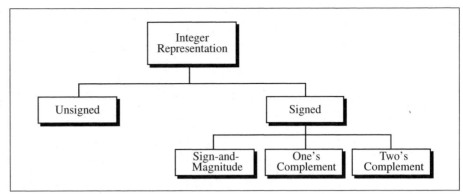

Figure 3.6 Taxonomy of integers

Note that today, the most commonly used representation is two's complement. However, we first discuss the other representations because they are simpler and serve as a good foundation for two's complement.

UNSIGNED INTEGERS FORMAT

An **unsigned integer** is an integer without a sign. Its range is between 0 and positive infinity. However, since no computer can possibly represent all the integers in this range, most computers define a constant called the maximum unsigned integer. An unsigned integer ranges between 0 and this constant. The maximum unsigned integer depends on the number of bits the computer allocates to store an unsigned integer. The following defines the range of unsigned integers in a computer, where N is the number of bits allocated to represent one unsigned integer:

$$\textbf{Range:} \quad 0 \ \ldots \ (2^N - 1)$$

Table 3.1 shows two common ranges for computers today.

Number of Bits	Range
8	0 . . . 255
16	0 . . . 65,535

Table 3.1 Range of unsigned integers

Representation

Storing unsigned integers is a straightforward process as outlined in the following steps:

1. The number is changed to binary.
2. If the number of bits is less than N, 0s are added to the left of the binary number so that there is a total of N bits.

EXAMPLE 3

Store 7 in an 8-bit memory location.

SOLUTION

First change the number to binary 111. Add five 0s to make a total of N (8) bits, 00000111. The number is stored in the memory location. ∎

EXAMPLE 4

Store 258 in a 16-bit memory location.

SOLUTION

First change the number to binary 100000010. Add seven 0s to make a total of N (16) bits, 0000000100000010. The number is stored in the memory location. ∎

Table 3.2 shows how unsigned integers are stored in two different computers: one using 8-bit allocation and one using 16-bit allocation. Note that decimal 258 and decimal 24,760 cannot be stored in a computer using 8-bit allocation for an unsigned integer. Decimal 1,245,678 cannot be stored in either of these computers. A condition called overflow occurs (discussed in Chapter 4).

Decimal	8-Bit Allocation	16-Bit Allocation
7	00000111	0000000000000111
234	11101010	0000000011101010
258	Overflow	0000000100000010
24,760	Overflow	0110000010111000
1,245,678	Overflow	Overflow

Table 3.2 Storing unsigned integers in two different computers

Interpretation

How do you interpret an unsigned binary representation in decimal? The process is simple. Change the N bits from the binary system to the decimal system as shown at the beginning of the chapter.

EXAMPLE 5

Interpret 00101011 in decimal if the number was stored as an unsigned integer.

SOLUTION

Using the procedure shown in Figure 3.3, the number in decimal is 43. ∎

Overflow

If you try to store an unsigned integer such as 256 in an 8-bit memory location, you get a condition called overflow.

Applications

Unsigned integers representation can improve the efficiency of storage because you do not need to store the sign of the integer. This means that the entire bit allocation can be used for storing the number. Unsigned integers representation can be used whenever you do not need negative integers. The following lists some cases:

■ Counting. When you count, you do not need negative numbers. You start counting from 1 (sometimes 0) and go up.

■ Addressing. Some computer languages store the address of a memory location inside another memory location. Addresses are positive numbers starting from 0 (the first byte of memory) and going up to a number representing the total memory capacity in bytes. Here again, you do not need negative numbers. Unsigned integers can easily do the job.

SIGN-AND-MAGNITUDE FORMAT

Storing an integer in the sign-and-magnitude format requires 1 bit to represent the sign (0 for positive, 1 for negative). This means that in an 8-bit allocation, you can only use 7 bits to represent the absolute value of the number (number without the sign). Therefore, the maximum positive value is one half the unsigned value. The following defines the range of sign-and-magnitude integers in a computer, where N is the number of bits allocated to represent one sign-and-magnitude integer:

$$\text{Range:} \quad -(2^{N-1}-1) \quad \ldots \quad +(2^{N-1}-1)$$

Table 3.3 shows common ranges for computers today. Note that in this system there are two 0s: +0 and −0.

There are two 0s in sign-and-magnitude representation: positive and negative. In an 8-bit allocation:

$$+0 \quad \longrightarrow \quad 00000000$$
$$-0 \quad \longrightarrow \quad 10000000$$

Number of Bits	Range				
8	−127	...	−0 +0	...	+127
16	−32,767	...	−0 +0	...	+32,767
32	−2,147,483,647	...	−0 +0	...	+2,147,483,647

Table 3.3 Range of sign-and-magnitude integers

Representation

Storing sign-and-magnitude integers is a straightforward process:

1. The number is changed to binary; the sign is ignored.
2. If the number of bits is less than $N-1$, 0s are added to the left of the number so that there is a total of $N-1$ bits.
3. If the number is positive, 0 is added to the left (to make it N bits). If the number is negative, 1 is added to the left (to make it N bits).

In sign-and-magnitude representation, the leftmost bit defines the sign of the number. If it is 0, the number is positive. If it is 1, the number is negative.

EXAMPLE 6

Store +7 in an 8-bit memory location using sign-and-magnitude representation.

SOLUTION

First change the number to binary 111. Add four 0s to make a total of $N-1$ (7) bits, 0000111. Add an extra zero, shown in bold, because the number is positive. The result is **0**0000111. ∎

EXAMPLE 7

Store -258 in a 16-bit memory location using sign-and-magnitude representation.

SOLUTION

First change the number to binary 100000010. Add six 0s to make a total of $N-1$ (15) bits 000000100000010. Add an extra 1, shown in bold, because the number is negative. The result is **1**000000100000010. ∎

Table 3.4 shows how sign-and-magnitude numbers are stored in two different computers: one using 8-bit allocation and one using 16-bit allocation.

Decimal	8-Bit Allocation	16-Bit Allocation
+7	00000111	0000000000000111
−124	11111100	1000000001111100
+258	Overflow	0000000100000010
−24,760	Overflow	1110000010111000

Table 3.4   Storing sign-and-magnitude integers in two different computers

Interpretation

How do you interpret a sign-and-magnitude binary representation in decimal? The process is simple:

1. Ignore the first (leftmost) bit.
2. Change the $N-1$ bits from binary to decimal as shown at the beginning of the chapter.
3. Attach a + or a − sign to the number based on the leftmost bit.

EXAMPLE 8

Interpret 10111011 in decimal if the number was stored as a sign-and-magnitude integer.

SOLUTION

Ignoring the leftmost bit, the remaining bits are 0111011. This number in decimal is 59. The leftmost bit is 1, so the number is −59. ∎

Applications

The sign-and-magnitude representation is not used to store signed numbers by computers today. There are at least two reasons. First, operations such as adding and subtracting are not straightforward for this representation. Second, there are two 0s in this representation, which makes programmers uncomfortable. However, sign-and-magnitude representation does have an advantage: Transformation from decimal to binary, and vice versa, is very easy. That makes this representation convenient for applications that do not need operations on numbers. One example is changing analog signals to digital signals. You sample the analog signal, you assign a positive or negative number to the sample, and you change it to binary to be sent over data communication channels.

ONE'S COMPLEMENT FORMAT

You may have noticed that the representation of a number in the binary system is a matter of convention. In sign-and-magnitude representation, we adopted the convention that the leftmost bit represents the sign; this bit is not part of the value.

The designers of **one's complement representation** adopted a different convention: To represent a positive number, use the convention adopted for an unsigned integer. To represent a negative number, complement the positive number. In other words, +7 is represented just like an unsigned number; −7 is represented as the complement of +7. In one's complement, the complement of a number is obtained by changing all 0s to 1s and all 1s to 0s.

The following defines the range of one's complement integers in a computer, where N is the number of bits allocated to represent a one's complement integer:

$$\text{Range:} \quad -(2^{N-1}-1) \quad \ldots \quad +(2^{N-1}-1)$$

There are two 0s in one's complement representation: positive and negative. In an 8-bit allocation:

$$+0 \quad \longrightarrow \quad 00000000$$
$$-0 \quad \longrightarrow \quad 11111111$$

Table 3.5 shows common ranges for computers today. Note that in this system there are also two 0s: a +0 and a −0.

Number of Bits	Range				
8	−127	... −0	+0	...	+127
16	−32,767	... −0	+0	...	+32,767
32	−2,147,483,647	... −0	+0	...	+2,147,483,647

Table 3.5 Range of one's complement integers

Representation

Storing one's complement integers requires the following steps:

1. The number is changed to binary; the sign is ignored.
2. 0s are added to the left of the number to make a total of N bits.
3. If the sign is positive, no more action is needed. If the sign is negative, every bit is complemented (changed from 0 to 1 or from 1 to 0).

In one's complement representation, the leftmost bit defines the sign of the number. If it is 0, the number is positive. If it is 1, the number is negative.

EXAMPLE 9

Store +7 in an 8-bit memory location using one's complement representation.

SOLUTION

First change the number to binary 111. Add five 0s so that there is a total of N (8) bits, 00000111. The sign is positive, so no more action is needed.   ■

EXAMPLE 10

Store –258 in a 16-bit memory location using one's complement representation.

SOLUTION

First change the number to binary 100000010. Add seven 0s so that there is a total of N (16) bits, 0000000100000010. The sign is negative, so each bit is complemented. The result is 1111111011111101.   ■

Table 3.6 shows how one's complement numbers are stored in two different computers: one using 8-bit allocation and one using 16-bit allocation.

Decimal	8-Bit Allocation	16-Bit Allocation
+7	00000111	0000000000000111
–7	11111000	1111111111111000
+124	01111100	0000000001111100
–124	10000011	1111111110000011
+24,760	Overflow	0110000010111000
–24,760	Overflow	1001111101000111

Table 3.6   Storing one's complement integers in two different computers

Interpretation

How do you interpret a one's complement binary representation in decimal? The process involves these steps:

1. If the leftmost bit is 0 (positive number),
   a. Change the entire number from binary to decimal.
   b. Put a plus sign (+) in front of the number.
2. If the leftmost bit is 1 (negative number),
   a. Complement the entire number (changing all 0s to 1s, and vice versa).
   b. Change the entire number from binary to decimal.
   c. Put a negative sign (–) in front of the number.

EXAMPLE 11

Interpret 11110110 in decimal if the number was stored as a one's complement integer.

SOLUTION

The leftmost bit is 1, so the number is negative. First complement it. The result is 00001001. The complement in decimal is 9. So the original number was –9. Note that the complement of a complement is the original number.   ■

One's complementing means reversing all bits. If you one's complement a positive number, you get the corresponding negative number. If you one's complement a negative number, you get the corresponding positive number. If you one's complement a number twice, you get the original number.

Overflow

If you try to store a one's complement integer such as +256 in an 8-bit memory location, you get a condition called overflow.

Applications

One's complement representation is not used to store numbers in computers today. There are at least two reasons. First, operations such as adding and subtracting are not straightforward for this representation. Second, there are two 0s in this representation, which makes programmers uncomfortable. However, this representation does have some significance. First, it is the foundation of the next representation (two's complement). Second, it has properties that make it interesting for data communication applications such as error detection and correction.

TWO'S COMPLEMENT FORMAT

As previously mentioned, one's complement representation has two 0s (+0 and –0). This can create some confusion in calculations. In addition, you will see in the next chapter that if you add a number and its complement (+4 and –4) in this representation, you get negative –0 instead of +0. **Two's complement representation** solves all these problems.

> Two's complement is the most common, the most important, and the most widely used representation of integers today.

The following defines the range of two's complement integers in a computer, where N is the number of bits allocated for a two's complement integer:

$$\text{Range:} \quad -(2^{N-1}) \quad \ldots \quad +(2^{N-1}-1)$$

Table 3.7 shows common ranges for computers today. Note that in this system there is only one 0 and that the beginning of the range is 1 less than that of one's complement.

Number of Bits	Range				
8	−128	...	−0	+0 ...	+127
16	−32,768	...	−0	+0 ...	+32,767
32	−2,147,483,648	...	−0	+0 ...	+2,147,483,647

Table 3.7   Range of two's complement numbers

Representation

Storing two's complement requires the following steps:

1. The number is changed to binary; the sign is ignored.
2. If the number of bits is less than N, 0s are added to the left of the number so that there is a total of N bits.
3. If the sign is positive, no further action is needed. If the sign is negative, leave all the rightmost 0s and the first 1 unchanged. Complement the rest of the bits.

> In two's complement representation, the leftmost bit defines the sign of the number. If it is 0, the number is positive. If it is 1, the number is negative.

EXAMPLE 12

Store +7 in an 8-bit memory location using two's complement representation.

SOLUTION

First change the number to binary 111. Add five 0s so that there is a total of N (8) bits, 00000111. The sign is positive, so no more action is needed.   ■

EXAMPLE 13

Store −40 in a 16-bit memory location using two's complement representation.

SOLUTION

First change the number to binary 101000. Add ten 0s so that there is a total of N (16) bits 0000000000101000. The sign is negative, so leave the rightmost 0s up to the first 1 (including the 1) unchanged and complement the rest. The result is 1111111111011**000.**   ■

Table 3.8 shows how two's complement numbers are stored in two different computers: one using 8-bit allocation and one using 16-bit allocation.

Decimal	8-Bit Allocation	16-Bit Allocation
+7	00000111	0000000000000111
−7	11111001	1111111111111001
+124	01111100	0000000001111100
−124	10000100	1111111110000100
+24,760	Overflow	0110000010111000
−24,760	Overflow	1001111101001000

Table 3.8   Example of two's complement representations in two computers

There is only one 0 in two's complement: In an 8-bit allocation:

0    $\longrightarrow$ 00000000

Interpretation

How do you interpret a two's complement binary representation in decimal? The process involves these steps:

1. If the leftmost bit is 0 (positive number),
   a. Change the whole number from binary to decimal.
   b. Put a plus sign (+) in front of the number.
2. If the leftmost bit is 1 (negative number),
   a. Leave the rightmost bits up to the first 1 (inclusive) unchanged. Complement the rest of the bits.
   b. Change the whole number from binary to decimal.
   c. Put a negative sign (−) in front of the number.

EXAMPLE 14

Interpret 11110110 in decimal if the number was stored as a two's complement integer.

SOLUTION

The leftmost bit is 1. The number is negative. Leave 10 at the right alone and complement the rest. The result is 0000l0**10**. The two's complement number is 10. So the original number was −10. ∎

> Two's complementing can be achieved by reversing all bits except the rightmost bits up to the first 1 (inclusive). If you two's complement a positive number, you get the corresponding negative number. If you two's complement a negative number, you get the corresponding positive number. If you two's complement a number twice, you get the original number.

Applications

The two's complement representation is the standard representation for storing integers in computers today. In the next chapter, you will see why this is the case when you see the simplicity of operations using two's complement.

**SUMMARY
OF INTEGER
REPRESENTATION**

To get you the big picture of number representation methods, examine Table 3.9. In this table, assume that N is 4. The memory location can store only 4 bits. If you look at the contents of the memory location, you can interpret the number in one of the four representations. Although the interpretation is the same for positive integers, it is different for negative integers.

Contents of Memory	Unsigned	Sign-and-Magnitude	One's Complement	Two's Complement
0000	0	+0	+0	+0
0001	1	+1	+1	+1
0010	2	+2	+2	+2
0011	3	+3	+3	+3
0100	4	+4	+4	+4
0101	5	+5	+5	+5
0110	6	+6	+6	+6
0111	7	+7	+7	+7
1000	8	−0	−7	−8
1001	9	−1	−6	−7
1010	10	−2	−5	−6
1011	11	−3	−4	−5
1100	12	−4	−3	−4
1101	13	−5	−2	−3
1110	14	−6	−1	−2
1111	15	−7	−0	−1

Table 3.9   Summary of integer representation

3.4   EXCESS SYSTEM

Another representation that allows you to store both positive and negative numbers in a computer is called the **Excess system.** In this system, it is easy to transform a number from decimal to binary, and vice versa. However, operations on the numbers are very complicated. The only application in use today is in storing the exponential value of a fraction. This is discussed in the next section.

In an Excess conversion, a positive number, called the magic number, is used in the conversion process. The magic number is normally (2^{N-1}) or ($2^{N-1}-1$), where N is the bit allocation. For example, if N is 8, the magic number is either 128 or 127. In the first case, we call the representation Excess_128, and in the second case, it is Excess_127.

Representation

To represent a number in Excess, use the following procedure:

1. Add the magic number to the integer.
2. Change the result to binary and add 0s so that there is a total of N bits.

EXAMPLE 15

Represent −25 in Excess_127 using an 8-bit allocation.

SOLUTION

First add 127 to −25 and get 102. This number in binary is 1100110. Add 1 bit to make it 8 bits in length. The representation is 01100110. ■

Interpretation

To interpret a number in Excess, use the following procedure:

1. Change the number to decimal.
2. Subtract the magic number from the integer.

EXAMPLE 16

Interpret 11111110 if the representation is Excess_127.

SOLUTION

First change the number to decimal. It is 254. Then subtract 127 from the number. The result is decimal 127. ■

3.5   FLOATING-POINT REPRESENTATION

To represent a **floating-point number** (a number containing an integer and a **fraction**), the number is divided into two parts: the integer and the fraction. For example, the floating-point number 14.234 has an integer of 14 and a fraction of 0.234.

CONVERTING TO BINARY

To convert a floating-point number to binary, use the following procedure:

1. Convert the integer part to binary.

2. Convert the fraction to binary.

3. Put a decimal point between the two parts.

Converting the Integer Part

This procedure is the same as that presented in Chapter 2.

Converting the Fraction Part

To convert a fraction to binary, use repetitive multiplication. For example, to convert 0.125 to binary, multiply the fraction by 2; the result is 0.250. The integer part of the result (0) is extracted and becomes the leftmost binary digit. Now multiply by 2 the fraction part (0.250) of the result to get 0.50. Again, the integer part of the result (0) is extracted and becomes the next binary digit. This process continues until the fraction part becomes 0 or you reach the limit of the number of bits you can use (Figure 3.7).

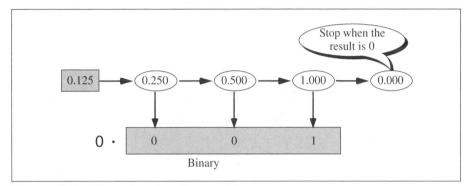

Figure 3.7   Changing fractions to binary

EXAMPLE 17

Transform the fraction 0.875 to binary.

SOLUTION

Write the fraction at the left corner. Multiply the number continuously by 2 and extract the integer part as the binary digit. Stop when the number is 0.0.

$$\text{Fraction} \quad 0.875 \;\rightarrow\; 1.750 \;\rightarrow\; 1.50 \;\rightarrow\; 1.0 \;\rightarrow\; 0.0$$
$$\qquad\qquad\qquad\quad\;\; \downarrow \qquad\; \downarrow \qquad \downarrow$$

Binary: 0 .   1   1   1

EXAMPLE 18

Transform the fraction 0.4 to a binary of 6 bits.

SOLUTION

Write the fraction at the left corner. Multiply the number continuously by 2 and extract the integer part as the binary digit. In this case, you can never get the exact binary representation because the original fraction reappears. However, you can continue until you get 6 bits.

$$\text{Fraction} \quad 0.4 \;\rightarrow\; 0.8 \rightarrow 1.6 \rightarrow 1.2 \rightarrow 0.4 \rightarrow 0.8 \rightarrow 1.6$$
$$\qquad\qquad\qquad\;\; \downarrow \quad\; \downarrow \quad\; \downarrow \quad\; \downarrow \quad\; \downarrow \quad\; \downarrow$$

Binary: 0 .   0   1   1   0   0   1

NORMALIZATION

To represent the number 71.3125 (+1000111.0101), store the sign, all of the bits, and the position of the decimal point in memory. Although this is possible, it makes operations on numbers difficult. You need a standard representation for floating-point numbers. The solution is **normalization,** the moving of the decimal point so that there is only one 1 to the left of the decimal point.

$$1 . xxxxxxxxxxxxxxxxx$$

To indicate the original value of the number, multiply the number by 2^e, where e is the number of bits that the decimal points moved: positive for left movement, negative for right movement. A positive or negative sign is then added depending on the sign of the original number. Table 3.10 shows examples of normalization.

Original Number	Move	Normalized
+1010001.11001	← 6	$+2^6$ × **1.01000111001**
−111.000011	← 2	$−2^2$ × **1.11000011**
+0.00000111001	6 →	$+2^{-6}$ × **1.11001**
−0.001110011	3 →	$−2^{-3}$ × **1.110011**

Table 3.10   Examples of normalization

SIGN, EXPONENT, AND MANTISSA

After a number is normalized, you store only three pieces of information about the number: sign, exponent, and mantissa (the bits to the right of the decimal point). For example, +1000111.0101 becomes

$$+ \quad 2^6 \qquad \times \quad 1.0001110101$$

Sign: +   Exponent: 6   Mantissa: 0001110101

Note that the 1 to the left of the decimal point is not stored; it is understood.

Sign

The sign of the number can be stored using 1 bit (0 or 1).

Exponent

The exponent (power of 2) defines the movement of the decimal point. Note that the power can be negative or positive. Excess representation is the method used to store the exponent. The number of bits allocated (N) defines the range of numbers that a computer can store.

Mantissa

The **mantissa** is the binary number to the right of the decimal point. It defines the precision of the number. The mantissa is stored as an unsigned integer.

IEEE STANDARDS

The Institute of Electrical and Electronics Engineers (IEEE) has defined three standards for storing floating-point numbers; two are used to store numbers in memory (single precision and double precision). These formats are shown in Figure 3.8. Note that the number inside the boxes is the number of bits for each field. We discuss the single-precision format and leave the **double-precision format** as an exercise.

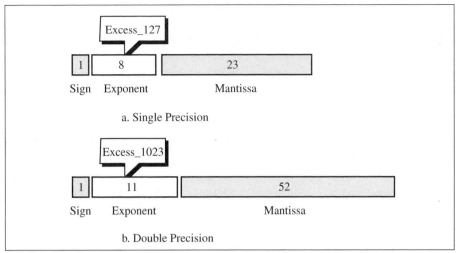

Figure 3.8 IEEE standards for floating-point representation

Single-Precision Representation

The procedure for storing a normalized floating-point number in memory using **single-precision format** is as follows:

1. Store the sign as 0 (positive) or 1 (negative).
2. Store the exponent (power of 2) as Excess_127.
3. Store the mantissa as an unsigned integer.

EXAMPLE 19

Show the representation of the normalized number

$$+ \quad 2^6 \quad \times \quad \mathbf{1.01000111001}$$

SOLUTION

The sign is positive, and it is represented as 0. The exponent is 6. In Excess_127 representation, add 127 to it and get 133. In binary, this is 10000101. The mantissa is 01000111001. When you increase the bit length to 23, you get 01000111001000000000000. Note that you cannot ignore the 0 on the left because this is a fraction. Ignoring that 0 is the same as multiplying the number by 2. Note that you add extra 0s on the right side (not the left) because it is a fraction. Adding 0s to the right side of a fraction does not change the fraction, but adding 0s to the left means dividing the number by a power of 2. The number in memory is a 32-bit number as shown next:

sign	exponent	mantissa
0	**10000101**	01000111001000000000000

■

Table 3.11 shows more examples of floating-point representation.

Number	Sign	Exponent	Mantissa
$-2^2 \times 1.11000011$	1	10000001	11000011000000000000000
$+2^{-6} \times 1.11001$	0	01111001	11001000000000000000000
$-2^{-3} \times 1.110011$	1	01111100	11001100000000000000000

Table 3.11 Examples of floating-point representation

Floating-Point Interpretation for Single Precision

The following procedure interprets a 32-bit floating-point number stored in memory.

1. Use the leftmost bit as the sign.

2. Change the next 8 bits to decimal and subtract 127 from it. This is the exponent.

3. Add 1 and a decimal point to the next 23 bits. You can ignore any extra 0s at the right.

4. Move the decimal point to the correct position using the value of the exponent.

5. Change the whole part to decimal.

6. Change the fraction part to decimal.

7. Combine the whole and the fraction parts.

EXAMPLE 20

Interpret the following 32-bit floating-point number

$$1\ 01111100\ 11001100000000000000000$$

SOLUTION

The leftmost bit is the sign (−). The next 8 bits are 01111100. This is 124 in decimal. If you subtract 127 from it, you get the exponent −3. The next 23 bits are the mantissa. If you ignore the extra 0s, you get 110011. After you add 1 to the left of the decimal point, the normalized number in binary is:

$$-2^{-3} \times 1.110011$$

3.6   HEXADECIMAL NOTATION

Numbers, as discussed in Chapter 2, can be represented in hexadecimal notation. For example, the number 48 can be represented in 8-bit unsigned format as 00110000 or as hexadecimal x30. Similarly, a number such as 81.5625 can be represented in IEEE standard as **01000010**10100011001000000000000 or in hexadecimal notation as x42A39000.

3.7   KEY TERMS

binary system	fraction	sign-and-magnitude representation
binary to decimal conversion	integer	single-precision format
decimal system	mantissa	two's complement representation
decimal to binary conversion	negative integer	unsigned integer
double precision format	normalization	whole number
Excess system	one's complement representation	
floating-point number	positive integer	

3.8   SUMMARY

■ The decimal system has 10 digits and is based on powers of 10.

■ The binary system, used by computers to store numbers, has 2 digits, 0 and 1, and is based on powers of 2.

■ The bit allocation is the number of bits used to represent an integer.

■ Integers can be represented as unsigned or signed numbers.

■ There are three major methods of signed number representation: sign-and-magnitude, one's complement, and two's complement.

■ Unsigned numbers are commonly used for counting and addressing.

■ In the sign-and-magnitude method of integer representation, 1 bit represents the sign of the number; the remaining bits represent the magnitude.

■ In the one's complement method of integer representation, a negative number is represented by complementing the corresponding positive number.

■ Complementing a number means to convert each 1 to 0 and each 0 to 1.

■ In the two's complement method of integer representation, a negative number is represented by leaving all the rightmost 0s and the first 1 unchanged and then complementing the remaining bits.

■ Most computers today use the two's complement method of integer representation.

■ Both sign-and-magnitude and one's complement methods have two representations for the 0 value; two's complement has just one representation for the 0 value.

■ A floating-point number is a whole number and a fraction. Conversion of the fraction to binary requires the denominator of the fraction to be expressed as a power of 2. The Excess_X system is used to store this power of 2.

■ A fraction is normalized so that operations are simpler.

■ To store a fraction in memory, you need its sign, exponent, and mantissa.

3.9   PRACTICE SET

REVIEW QUESTIONS

1. How do you convert a decimal number to binary?

2. How do you convert a binary number to decimal?

3. In a binary system, each column position is a power of what number?

4. In a decimal system, each column position is a power of what number?

5. What are three methods to represent signed integers?

6. What is the meaning of the term *maximum unsigned integer?*

7. What is the meaning of the term *bit allocation?*

8. Why can't you store decimal 256 in an 8-bit memory location?

9. Name two uses of unsigned integers.

10. What happens when you try to store decimal 130 using sign-and-magnitude representation with an 8-bit allocation?

11. Compare and contrast the representation of positive integers in sign-and-magnitude, one's complement, and two's complement.

12. Compare and contrast the representation of negative integers in sign-and-magnitude, one's complement, and two's complement.

13. Compare and contrast the representation of 0 in sign-and-magnitude, one's complement, and two's complement.

14. Compare and contrast the range of numbers that can be represented in sign-and-magnitude, one's complement, and two's complement.

15. Discuss the leftmost bit in sign-and-magnitude, one's complement, and two's complement.

16. What is the primary use of the Excess_X system? What does X represent?

17. Why is normalization necessary?

18. What is the mantissa?

19. After a number is normalized, what kind of information does a computer store in memory?

MULTIPLE-CHOICE QUESTIONS

20. The only digits used in the _____ number system are 0 and 1.
  a. decimal
  b. octal
  c. binary
  d. hexadecimal

21. When converting a decimal number to binary, you repeatedly divide by _____.
  a. 2
  b. 8
  c. 10
  d. 16

22. Which of the following is an integer representation method that handles both positive and negative numbers?
  a. sign-and-magnitude
  b. one's complement
  c. two's complement
  d. all of the above

23. In unsigned integers, a 4-bit allocation allows _____ nonnegative numbers.
  a. 7
  b. 8
  c. 15
  d. 16

24. In all signed integer representations, a 4-bit allocation allows _____ nonnegative numbers.
  a. 7
  b. 8
  c. 15
  d. 16

25. In _____ number representation, 1111 in memory represents −0.
  a. unsigned integers
  b. sign-and-magnitude
  c. one's complement
  d. two's complement

26. In _____ number representation, 1111 in memory represents −1.
  a. unsigned integers
  b. sign-and-magnitude
  c. one's complement
  d. two's complement

27. In _____ number representation, there are two representations for 0.
  a. sign-and-magnitude
  b. one's complement
  c. two's complement
  d. a and b

28. In _____ number representation, there is one representation for 0.
  a. unsigned integers
  b. one's complement
  c. two's complement
  d. a and c

29. If the leftmost bit is 0 in _____ number representation, then the decimal number is positive.
  a. sign-and-magnitude
  b. one's complement
  c. two's complement
  d. all of the above

30. If the leftmost bit is 1 in _____ number representation, then the decimal number is positive.
  a. sign-and-magnitude
  b. one's complement
  c. two's complement
  d. none of the above

31. Which number representation method is most widely used today for storing numbers in a computer?
  a. sign-and-magnitude
  b. one's complement
  c. two's complement
  d. unsigned integers

32. Which number representation method is often used to convert analog signals to digital signals?
  a. unsigned integers
  b. sign-and-magnitude
  c. one's complement
  d. b and c

33. Unsigned integers can be used for _____.
  a. counting
  b. addressing
  c. signal processing
  d. a and b

34. Which number representation method is often used to store the exponential value of a fraction?
  a. unsigned integers
  b. one's complement
  c. two's complement
  d. Excess_X

35. In an Excess_X conversion, you _____ the magic number X to the number to be converted.
  a. add
  b. subtract
  c. multiply
  d. divide

36. In Excess_X number representation, what is usually the relationship between X and *N*, the bit allocation?
    a. $X = 2^N - 1$
    b. $X = 2^N + 1$
    c. $X = 2^{N-1} - 1$
    d. a or c

37. When a computer stores a fraction, the _____ is usually expressed as a power of 2.
    a. numerator
    b. denominator
    c. whole number
    d. a or b

38. If the denominator of a fraction is 1024, then the numerator is _____ bits in length.
    a. 2
    b. 8
    c. 10
    d. 16

39. If the numerator of a fraction is 3 bits in length, then the denominator is _____
    a. 2
    b. 8
    c. 10
    d. 16

40. What is the Excess_128 representation of 5?
    a. 00000101
    b. 10000100
    c. 10000101
    d. 10000001

41. When a fraction is normalized, there is a _____ to the left of the decimal point.
    a. 0 bit
    b. 1 bit
    c. random bit sequence
    d. a or b

42. You multiply a normalized number by _____ where *e* is the number of bits that the decimal point moved.
    a. $2e$
    b. $e/2$
    c. e^2
    d. 2^e

43. When a fraction is normalized, the computer stores the _____.
    a. sign
    b. exponent
    c. mantissa
    d. all of the above

44. The precision of the fractional number stored in a computer is defined by the
    a. sign
    b. exponent
    c. mantissa
    d. any of the above

45. How is the mantissa stored in a computer?
    a. in one's complement
    b. in two's complement
    c. as an unsigned integer
    d. in sign-and-magnitude

46. An octal digit converted to binary is composed of _____ bits.
    a. 2
    b. 3
    c. 4
    d. 8

EXERCISES

47. Change the following decimal numbers to 8-bit unsigned integers if possible.
    a. 23
    b. 121
    c. 34
    d. 342

48. Change the following decimal numbers to 16-bit unsigned integers.
    a. 41
    b. 411
    c. 1234
    d. 342

49. Change the following decimal numbers to 8-bit sign-and-magnitude integers.
    a. 32
    b. −101
    c. 56
    d. 129

50. Change the following decimal numbers to 16-bit sign-and-magnitude integers.
    a. 142
    b. −180
    c. 560
    d. 2456

52. Change the following decimal numbers to 16-bit one's complement integers.
    a. 162
    b. −110
    c. 2560
    d. 12,123

53. Change the following decimal numbers to 8-bit two's complement integers.
    a. −12
    b. −101
    c. 56
    d. 142

54. Change the following decimal numbers to 16-bit two's complement integers.
    a. 102
    b. −179
    c. 534
    d. 62,056

55. Change the following 8-bit unsigned numbers to decimal.
    a. 01101011
    b. 10010100
    c. 00000110
    d. 01010000

56. Change the following 8-bit sign-and-magnitude numbers to decimal.
    a. 01111011
    b. 10110100
    c. 01100011
    d. 11010000

57. Change the following 8-bit one's complement numbers to decimal.
    a. 01100011
    b. 10000100
    c. 01110011
    d. 11000000

58. Change the following 8-bit two's complement numbers to decimal.
    a. 01110111
    b. 11111100
    c. 01110100
    d. 11001110

59. The following are sign-and-magnitude binary numbers. Show how to change the sign of the number.
    a. 01110111
    b. 11111100
    c. 01110111
    d. 11001110

60. The following are one's complement binary numbers. Show how to change the sign of the number.
    a. 01110111
    b. 11111100
    c. 01110111
    d. 11001110

61. The following are two's complement binary numbers. Show how to change the sign of the number.
    a. 01110111
    b. 11111100
    c. 01110111
    d. 11001110

62. In this chapter, we show how to make a two's complement of a number by skipping some bits and complementing the rest (changing 0 to 1 and 1 to 0). Another method is to first make a one's complement and then add 1 to the result. Try both methods using the following numbers. Compare and contrast the results.
    a. 01110111
    b. 11111100
    c. 01110100
    d. 11001110

63. If you apply the one's complement operation to a number twice, you get the original number. Apply the one's complement operation twice to each of the following numbers and see if you can get the original number.
    a. 01110111
    b. 11111100
    c. 01110100
    d. 11001110

64. If you apply the two's complement operation to a number twice, you should get the original number. Apply the two's complement operation to each of the following numbers and see if you can get the original number.
    a. 01110111
    b. 11111100
    c. 01110100
    d. 11001110

65. The equivalent of one's complement in decimal number is called nine's complement (10−1 is 9). In this way, the nine's complement of a number is obtained by subtracting each digit from 9. Find the nine's complement of the following decimal numbers. Assume you are using only three digits.
    a. +234
    b. +112
    c. −125
    d. −111

66. If you use three digits, what is the range of the numbers you can represent using nine's complement? In this system, how can you determine the sign of a number? Do you have two 0s in this system? What is the representation for +0? What is the representation for −0?

67. Normalize the following binary floats. Explicitly show the value of the exponent after normalization.
    a. 1.10001
    b. $2^3 \times 111.1111$
    c. $2^{-2} \times 101.110011$
    d. $2^{-5} \times 101101.00000110011000$

68. Show the following numbers in 32-bit IEEE format.
    a. $-2^0 \times 1.10001$
    b. $+2^3 \times 1.111111$
    c. $+2^{-4} \times 1.01110011$
    d. $-2^{-5} \times 1.01101000$

69. Show the following numbers in 64-bit IEEE format.
    a. $-2^0 \times 1.10001$
    b. $+2^3 \times 1.111111$
    c. $+2^{-4} \times 1.01110011$
    d. $-2^{-5} \times 1.01101000$

70. Change the following decimal fractions into binary fractions.
    a. $3\,{}^5\!/_8$
    b. $12\,{}^3\!/_{32}$
    c. $4\,{}^{13}\!/_{64}$
    d. $12\,{}^5\!/_{128}$

71. Table 3.12 shows how to rewrite a fraction so the denominator is a power of two (1, 4, 8, 16, etc.). However, sometimes you need a combination of entries to find the appropriate fraction. For example, 0.625 is not in the table, but you know that 0.625 is 0.5 + 0.125. This means that 0.625 can be written as $\frac{1}{2} + \frac{1}{8}$, or $\frac{5}{8}$,

Original	New	Original	New
0.5	$\frac{1}{2}$	0.25	$\frac{1}{4}$
0.125	$\frac{1}{8}$	0.0625	$\frac{1}{16}$
0.03125	$\frac{1}{32}$	0.015625	$\frac{1}{64}$

Table 3.12 Exercise 71

which is the appropriate form. Change the following decimal fractions to a fraction with a power of 2.
    a. 0.1875
    b. 0.640625
    c. 0.40625
    d. 0.375

72. Using the results of the previous problem, change the following decimal numbers to binary numbers.
    a. 7.1875
    b. 12.640625
    c. 11.40625
    d. 0.375

73. Using the result of the previous problem, show the following numbers in 32-bit IEEE format.
    a. +7.1875
    b. +12.640625
    c. −11.40625
    d. −0.375

74. Show the result of the following operations using IEEE format.
    a. x012A00 + x12AAFF
    b. x0000011 + x820000
    c. x9111111 + x211111
    d. xE111111 + x777777

4 Operations on Bits

In Chapters 2 and 3, we showed how to store different types of data in a computer. In this chapter, we show how to operate on bits. Operations on bits can be divided into two broad categories: arithmetic operations and logical operations (Figure 4.1).

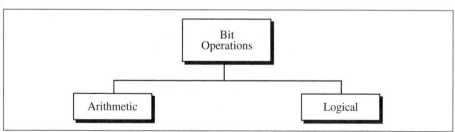

Figure 4.1   Operations on bits

4.1   ARITHMETIC OPERATIONS

Arithmetic operations involve adding, subtracting, multiplying, dividing, and so on. You can apply these operations to integers and floating-point numbers. Let us first concentrate on integers.

ARITHMETIC OPERATIONS ON INTEGERS

All arithmetic operations such as addition, subtraction, multiplication, and division can be applied to integers. However, we focus only on addition and subtraction. The multiplication operation can be implemented in software using repeated addition or in hardware using other techniques. The division operation can also be implemented in software using repeated subtraction or in hardware using other techniques.   However, an extended discussion of multiplication and division is beyond the scope of this book, and we leave it as the topic for books on computer architecture.

You can apply addition and subtraction to all representations of integers. However, we present the **two's complement** representation because this is the only method used to store integers in computers today.

Addition In Two's Complement

Adding numbers in two's complement is like adding the numbers in decimal; you add column by column, and if there is a carry, it is added to the next column. However, you should remember that you are dealing with binary digits, not decimal digits. When you add 2 bits, the result is 0 or 1. In addition, you have to **carry** a 1 that is propagated to the next column. Therefore, you need to be careful when adding 2 or 3 bits. Table 4.1 is a guide to adding bits.

Number of 1s	Result	Carry
None	0	
One	1	
Two	0	1
Three	1	1

Table 4.1   Adding bits

Now we can define the rule for adding two integers in two's complement:

Rule of Adding Integers in Two's Complement

Add 2 bits and propagate the carry to the next column. If there is a final carry after the leftmost column addition, discard it.

EXAMPLE 1

Add two numbers in two's complement representation:

$$(+17) \ + \ (+22) \ \longrightarrow \ (+39)$$

SOLUTION

These numbers in two's complement are represented as 00010001 and 00010110 for an 8-bit memory location. The result is similar for any allocation size.

```
Carry            1
          0  0  0  1  0  0  0  1  +
          0  0  0  1  0  1  1  0
         _____
Result    0  0  1  0  0  1  1  1
```

The result is 39 in decimal.

EXAMPLE 2

Add 24 and −17. Both numbers are in two's complement format.

$$(+24) \ + \ (-17) \longrightarrow (+7)$$

SOLUTION

The numbers in two's complement can be represented as follows:

```
Carry    1  1  1  1  1
          0  0  0  1  1  0  0  0  +
          1  1  1  0  1  1  1  1
         _____
Result    0  0  0  0  0  1  1  1
```

Note that the result is +7 and that the last carry (from the leftmost column) is discarded.

EXAMPLE 3

Add −35 and 20. Both numbers are in two's complement format.

$$(-35) \ + \ (+20) \longrightarrow (-15)$$

SOLUTION

The numbers in two's complement can be represented as follows:

```
Carry          1  1  1
          1  1  0  1  1  1  0  1  +
          0  0  0  1  0  1  0  0
         _____
Result    1  1  1  1  0  0  0  1
```

Note that the result is −15 (if you two's complement the result, you get 15).

EXAMPLE 4

Add 127 and 3. Both numbers are in two's complement format.

$$(+127) \ + \ (+3) \longrightarrow (+130)$$

SOLUTION

The numbers in two's complement can be represented as follows:

```
Carry    1  1  1  1  1  1  1
          0  1  1  1  1  1  1  1  +
          0  0  0  0  0  0  1  1
         _____
Result    1  0  0  0  0  0  1  0
```

We immediately see an error here. The leftmost bit of the result is 1, which means the number is negative (we expected a positive number). What is this number? The two's complement is 126. This means the number is −126 instead of 130. We discuss this issue in the next section on overflow. ■

Overflow

Overflow is an error that occurs when you try to store a number that is not within the range defined by the allocation. When you add numbers in two's complement using N bits, make sure that each number and the result are in the range defined for two's complement representation. In Chapter 3, we mentioned that the range of numbers that can be represented in two's complement is between -2^{N-1} and $2^{N-1}-1$.

Range of numbers in two's complement representation:
$$-(2^{N-1}) \qquad\qquad 0 \qquad\qquad +(2^{N-1}-1)$$

For Example 4, the range is -2^{8-1} to $+2^{8-1}-1$, which is −128 to 127. The result of the addition (130) is not in this range. But another question remains unanswered: Why is −126 the answer? The answer can be found if you visualize the numbers in two's complement as points on a circle (Figure 4.2).

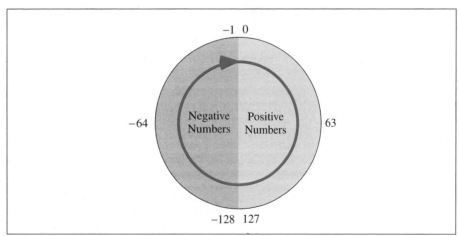

Figure 4.2   Two's complement numbers visualization

Start from 0 and continuously add 1 until you get to 127. If you add one more, you do not get 128; you get −128. Add one more and you get −127. Add one more and you get −126. This is what happened in Example 4.

When you do arithmetic operations on numbers in a computer, remember that each number and the result should be in the range defined by the bit allocation.

Subtraction in Two's Complement

One of the advantages of two's complement representation is that there is no difference between addition and subtraction. To subtract, negate (two's complement) the second number and add. In other words, the following two statements are the same:

$$\text{Number 1} \quad - \quad \text{Number 2} \quad \longleftrightarrow \quad \text{Number 1} \quad + \quad (-\text{Number 2})$$

EXAMPLE 5

Subtract 62 from 101 in two's complement format.

$$(+101) \quad - \quad (+62) \quad \longleftrightarrow \quad (+101) \quad + \quad (-62) \quad \longrightarrow \quad (+39)$$

SOLUTION

The numbers in two's complement can be represented as follows:

```
Carry    1 1
         0 1 1 0 0 1 0 1 +
         1 1 0 0 0 0 1 0
        _____
Result   0 0 1 0 0 1 1 1
```

The result is +39. Note that the leftmost carry is discarded.

ARITHMETIC OPERATIONS ON FLOATING-POINT NUMBERS

All arithmetic operations such as addition, subtraction, multiplication, and division can be applied on **floating-point numbers** (floats). However, we focus only on addition and subtraction because multiplication is just repeated addition and division is just repeated subtraction.

Addition and subtraction on floats, when stored in IEEE format, are very involved and detailed. We cannot cover all of the details and special cases here and only give the overall concept.

Addition and Subtraction

Addition and subtraction for floating-point numbers are one process. The steps are as follows:

- Check the signs.
    a. If the signs are the same, add the numbers and assign the sign to the result.
    b. If the signs are different, compare the absolute values, subtract the smaller from the larger, and use the sign of the larger for the result.
- Move the decimal points to make the exponents the same. This means if the exponents are not equal, the decimal point of the number with the smaller exponent is shifted to the left to make the exponents the same.
- Add or subtract the **mantissas** (including the whole part and fraction part).
- Normalize the result before storing in memory.
- Check for any overflow.

EXAMPLE 6

Add two floats:

```
0   10000100   10110000000000000000000
0   10000010   01100000000000000000000
```

SOLUTION

The exponent of the first number is 132–127, or 5. The exponent of the second number is 130–127, or 3. The numbers are therefore

$+2^5$ $\times$ 1.1011
$+2^3$ $\times$ 1.011

Make the exponents the same:

$+2^5$ $\times$ 1.1011
$+2^5$ $\times$ 0.01011
———————————————
$+2^5$ $\times$ 10.00001

Now normalize the result:

$+2^6$ $\times$ 1.000001

The float stored in the computer is:

0   10000101   00000100000000000000000

4.2 LOGICAL OPERATIONS

A single bit can be either 0 or 1. You can interpret 0 as the logical value *false* and 1 as the logical value *true*. In this way, a bit stored in the memory of a computer can represent a logical value that is either false or true.

If you interpret a bit as a logical value, then you can apply logical operations on this bit. A **logical operation** can accept 1 or 2 bits to create only 1 bit. If the operation is applied to only one input, it is a **unary operation.** If it is applied to 2 bits, it is a **binary operation.** (Figure 4.3).

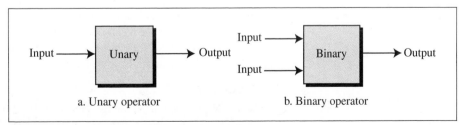

a. Unary operator   b. Binary operator

Figure 4.3   **Unary and binary operations**

We will discuss one unary operator and three binary operators in this section. They are shown in Figure 4.4.

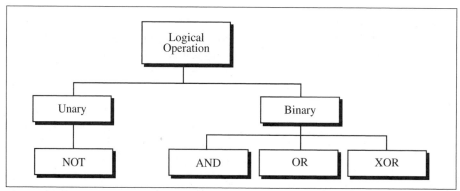

Figure 4.4   Logical operations

TRUTH TABLES

One way to show the result of a logical operation is with a truth table. A **truth table** lists all the possible input combinations with the corresponding output. In the case of a unary operator such as NOT, there are two output possibilities. In the case of a binary operator, there are four output possibilities. Figure 4.5 shows the truth tables for NOT, AND, OR, and XOR.

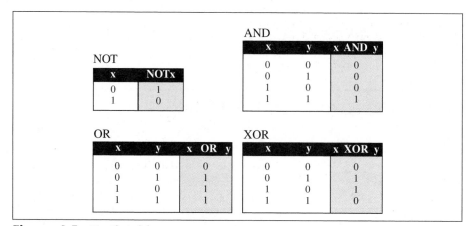

Figure 4.5   Truth tables

UNARY OPERATOR

The only **unary operator** we discuss is the NOT operator.

NOT Operator

The NOT operator has one input (a bit pattern). It inverts bits; that is, it changes 0 to 1 and 1 to 0. Figure 4.6 shows the result of applying the NOT operator to a bit pattern. We have used the conventional NOT icon that converts each bit and a NOT box that is an operation applied to the whole pattern. Note that a truth table is applied to each individual bit.

EXAMPLE 7

Use the NOT operator on the bit pattern 10011000.

SOLUTION

The solution is:

```
Target   10011000   NOT
Result   01100111
```

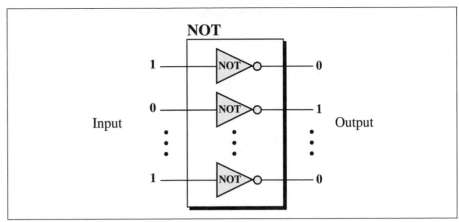

Figure 4.6   NOT operator

BINARY OPERATORS

We discuss three **binary operators** in this section: AND, OR, and XOR.

AND Operator

The **AND operator** is a binary operator. It takes two inputs (two bit patterns) and creates one output (bit pattern). It applies the truth table to a pair of bits, one from each input, and creates the corresponding output (Figure 4.7). We have used the conventional AND icon that ANDs each pair of bits and an AND box that is an operation applied to the pair of patterns. For each pair of input bits, the result is 1 if and only if both bits are 1; otherwise, it is 0.

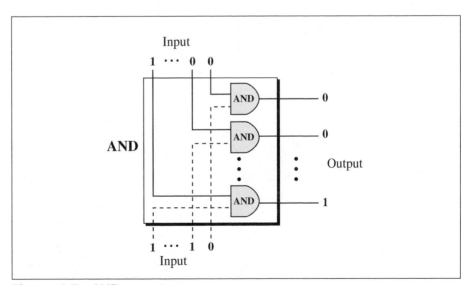

Figure 4.7   AND operator

EXAMPLE 8

Use the AND operator on bit patterns 10011000 and 00110101.

SOLUTION

The solution is:

```
Pattern 1   10011000   AND
Pattern 2   00110101
Result      00010000
```

Inherent Rule of the AND Operator   One interesting point about the AND operator is that if a bit in one input is 0, you do not have to check the corresponding bit in the other input; you can quickly conclude that the result is 0. We define this fact as the inherent rule of the AND operator (Figure 4.8).

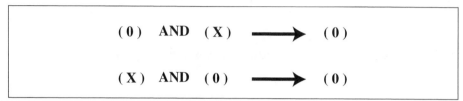

(0)   AND   (X)   ⟶   (0)

(X)   AND   (0)   ⟶   (0)

Figure 4.8   Inherent rule of the AND operator

OR Operator

The **OR operator** is a binary operator. It takes two inputs (two bit patterns) and creates one output (bit pattern). It applies the truth table to a pair of bits, one from each input, and creates the corresponding output (Figure 4.9). We have used the conventional OR icon that ORs each pair of bits and an OR box that is an operation applied to the pair of patterns. For each pair of input bits, the result is 0 if and only if both bits are 0; otherwise, it is 1.

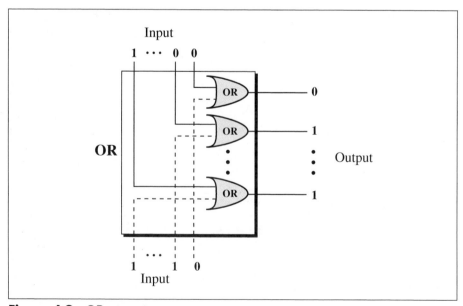

Figure 4.9   OR operator

EXAMPLE 9

Use the OR operator on bit patterns 10011000 and 00110101.

SOLUTION

The solution is:

```
Pattern 1   10011000   OR
Pattern 2   00110101
Result      10111101
```

Inherent Rule of the OR Operator   One interesting point about the OR operator is that if a bit in one input is 1, you do not have to check the corresponding bit in the other input; you can quickly conclude that the result is 1. We define this fact as the inherent rule of the OR operator (Figure 4.10).

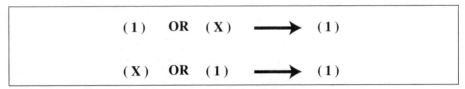

Figure 4.10   Inherent rule of the OR operator

XOR Operator

The **XOR operator** is a binary operator. It takes two inputs (two bit patterns) and creates one output (bit pattern). It applies the truth table to a pair of bits, one from each input, and creates the corresponding output (Figure 4.11). We have used the conventional XOR icon that XORs each pair of bits and an XOR box that is an operation applied to the pair of patterns. For each pair of input bits, the result is 0 if and only if both bits are equal; otherwise, it is 1.

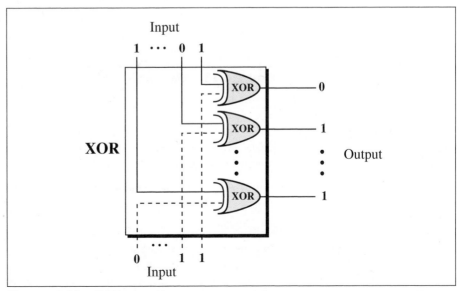

Figure 4.11   XOR operator

EXAMPLE 10

Use the XOR operator on bit patterns 10011000 and 00110101.

SOLUTION

The solution follows:

```
Pattern 1   10011000   XOR
Pattern 2   00110101
Result      10101101
```

Inherent Rule of the XOR Operator   One interesting point about the XOR operator is that if a bit in one input is 1, the result is the inverse of the corresponding bit in the other input. We define this fact as the inherent rule of the XOR operator (Figure 4.12).

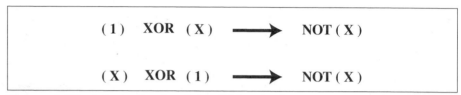

Figure 4.12   Inherent rule of the XOR operator

APPLICATIONS

The three logical binary operations can be used to modify a bit pattern. They can unset, set, or reverse specific bits. The bit pattern to be modified is ANDed, ORed, or XORed with a second bit pattern, which is called the **mask**. The mask is used to modify another bit pattern (Figure 4.13).

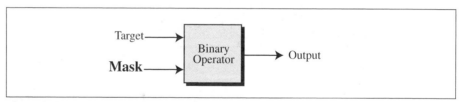

Figure 4.13   Mask

Unsetting Specific Bits

One of the applications of the AND operator is to **unset (force to 0)** specific bits in a bit pattern. To do so, use an unsetting mask with the same bit length. The rules for constructing an unsetting mask can be summarized as follows:

1. To unset a bit in the target bit pattern, use 0 for the corresponding bit in the mask.
2. To leave a bit in the target bit pattern unchanged, use 1 for the corresponding bit in the mask.

To understand why these rules work, refer back to the inherent rule of the AND operator in Figure 4.8.

For example, assume that you want to turn off the 5 leftmost bits of an 8-bit pattern. The mask should have five 0s at the left, followed by three 1s (Figure 4.14).

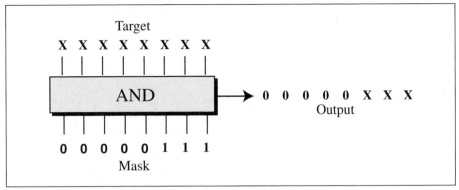

Figure 4.14   Example of unsetting specific bits

EXAMPLE 11

Use a mask to unset (**clear**) the 5 leftmost bits of a pattern. Test the mask with the pattern 10100110.

SOLUTION

The mask is 00000111. The result of applying the mask is:

```
Target      10100110   AND
Mask         00000111
Result      00000110
```

EXAMPLE 12

Imagine a power plant that pumps water to a city using eight pumps. The states of the pumps (on or off) can be represented by an 8-bit pattern. For example, the pattern 11000111 shows that pumps 1 to 3 (from the right), 7, and 8 are on while pumps 4, 5, and 6 are off. Now assume pump 7 shuts down. How can a mask show this situation?

SOLUTION

Use the mask 10111111 to AND with the target pattern. The only 0 bit (bit 7) in the mask turns off the seventh bit in the target.

```
Previous Situation  11000111   AND
Mask                 10111111
New Situation        10000111
```

Setting Specific Bits   One of the applications of the OR operator is to **set (force to 1)** specific bits in a bit pattern. To do so, use a setting mask with the same bit length. The rules for constructing a setting mask can be summarized as follows:

1. To set a bit in the target bit pattern, use 1 for the corresponding bit in the mask.

2. To leave a bit in the target bit pattern unchanged, use 0 for the corresponding bit in the mask.

To understand why these rules work, refer back to the inherent rule of the OR operator in Figure 4.10.

For example, assume that you want to turn on the 5 leftmost bits of an 8-bit pattern. The mask should have five 1s at the left followed by three 0s (Figure 4.15).

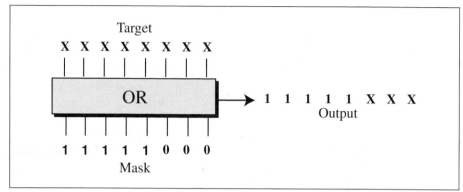

Figure 4.15   Example of setting specific bits

EXAMPLE 13

Use a mask to set the 5 leftmost bits of a pattern. Test the mask with the pattern 10100110.

SOLUTION

The mask is 11111000. The result of applying the mask is:

```
Target        10100110   OR
Mask          11111000
Result        11111110
```

EXAMPLE 14

Using the power plant example, how can you use a mask to show that pump 6 is now turned on?

SOLUTION

Use the mask 00100000 to OR with the target pattern. The only 1 bit (bit 6) in the mask turns on the sixth bit in the target.

```
Previous Situation  10000111   OR
Mask                00100000
New situation       10100111
```

Flipping Specific Bits

One of the applications of XOR is to **flip** bits, which means to change the value of specific bits from 0s to 1s, and vice versa. The rules for constructing an XOR mask can be summarized as follows:

1. To flip a bit in the target bit pattern, use 1 for the corresponding bit in the mask.

2. To leave a bit in the target bit pattern unchanged, use 0 for the corresponding bit in the mask.

To understand why these rules work, refer back to the inherent rule of the XOR operator in Figure 4.12.

For example, to flip the 5 leftmost bits of an 8-bit pattern, make a mask starting with five 1s at the left followed by three 0s (Figure 4.16).

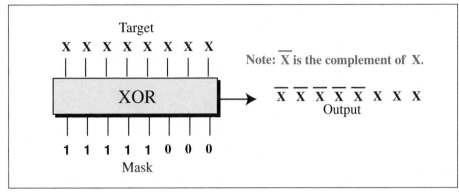

Figure 4.16   Example of flipping specific bits

EXAMPLE 15

Use a mask to flip the 5 leftmost bits of a pattern. Test the mask with the pattern 10100110.

SOLUTION

The mask is 11111000. The result of applying the mask is:

```
Target      10100110   XOR
Mask        11111000
Result      01011110
```

4.3   SHIFT OPERATIONS

Another common operation on bit patterns is the shift operation. A bit pattern can be shifted to the right or to the left. The right-shift operation discards the rightmost bit, shifts every bit to the right, and inserts 0 as the leftmost bit. The left-shift operation discards the leftmost bit, shifts every bit to the left, and inserts 0 as the rightmost bit. Figure 4.17 shows these two operations on 8-bit patterns, where a, b, . . . , h stand for individual bits.

You must be careful about shift operations if the pattern represents a signed number. A shift operation may change the leftmost bit of the pattern, which in a signed number represents the sign of the number. Shift operations can only be used when a pattern represents an unsigned number.

EXAMPLE 16

Show how you can divide or multiply a number by 2 using shift operations.

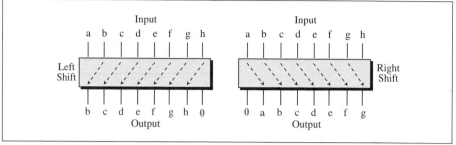

Figure 4.17   Shift operations

SOLUTION

If a bit pattern represents an unsigned number, a right-shift operation divides the number by 2 (integer division). The pattern 00111011 represents 59. When you shift the number to the right, you get 00011101, which is 29. If you shift the original number (59) to the left, you get 01110110, which is 118.   ■

EXAMPLE 17

Use a combination of logical and shift operations to find the value (0 or 1) of the fourth bit (from the right) in a pattern.

SOLUTION

Use the mask 00001000 to AND with the target to keep the fourth bit and clear the rest of the bits.

```
a b c d e f g h    AND
0 0 0 0 1 0 0 0
─────────────────
0 0 0 0 e 0 0 0
```

To access the value of the fourth bit (e), shift the new pattern three times to the right to move the specific bit to the rightmost position.

0000e000 ⟶ 00000e00 ⟶ 000000e0 ⟶ 0000000e

Now it is very easy to test the value of the new pattern as an unsigned integer. If the value is 1, the original bit was 1; if the value is 0, the original bit was 0.   ■

4.4   KEY TERMS

AND operator	force to 0	set
arithmetic operation	force to 1	truth table
binary operation	logical operation	two's complement
binary operator	mantissa	unary operation
carry	mask	unary operator
clear	NOT operator	unset
flip	OR operator	XOR operator
floating-point number	overflow	

4.5 SUMMARY

- You can perform arithmetic or logical operations on bits.
- Most computers use the two's complement method of integer representation.
- If there is a carry after addition of the leftmost digits, the carry is discarded.
- To subtract in two's complement, just negate the number to be subtracted and add.
- Numbers to be added must be within the range defined by the bit allocation.
- The term *overflow* describes a condition in which a number is not within the range defined by the bit allocation.
- Logical operation on bits can be unary (one input) or binary (two inputs).
- The unary NOT operator inverts its input.

- The result of the binary AND operation is true only if both inputs are true.
- The result of the binary OR operation is false only if both inputs are false.
- The result of the binary XOR operation is false only if both inputs are the same.
- A mask is a bit pattern that is applied to a target bit pattern to achieve a specific result.
- To unset (clear) a bit in a target bit pattern, set the corresponding mask bit to 0 and use the AND operator.
- To set a bit in a target bit pattern, set the corresponding mask bit to 1 and use the OR operator.
- To flip a bit in a target bit pattern, set the corresponding mask bit to 1 and use the XOR operator.

4.6 PRACTICE SET

REVIEW QUESTIONS

1. What is the difference between an arithmetic operation and a logical operation?
2. How is multiplication related to addition? Give an example.
3. What happens to a carry from the leftmost column in the final addition?
4. Can N, the bit allocation, equal 1? Why or why not?
5. Define the term *overflow*.
6. In the addition of floating-point numbers, how do you adjust the representation of numbers with different exponents?
7. What is the difference between a unary operation and a binary operation?
8. Name the logical binary operations.
9. What is a truth table?
10. What does the NOT operator do?
11. When is the result of an AND operator true?
12. When is the result of an OR operator true?
13. When is the result of an XOR operator true?

14. What is the inherent rule of the AND operator?
15. What is the inherent rule of the OR operator?
16. What is the inherent rule of the XOR operator?
17. What binary operation can be used to set bits? What bit pattern should the mask have?
18. What binary operation can be used to unset bits? What bit pattern should the mask have?
19. What binary operation can be used to flip bits? What bit pattern should the mask have?

MULTIPLE-CHOICE QUESTIONS

20. _____ is an arithmetic bit operation.
    a. The exclusive OR
    b. The unary NOT
    c. Subtraction
    d. All of the above
21. _____ is a logical bit operator.
    a. The exclusive OR
    b. The unary NOT
    c. The binary AND
    d. All of the above

22. The _____ method of integer representation is the most common method to store integers in computer memory.
    a. sign-and-magnitude
    b. one's complement
    c. two's complement
    d. unsigned integers

23. In two's complement addition, if there is a final carry after the leftmost column addition, _____.
    a. add it to the rightmost column
    b. add it to the leftmost column
    c. discard it
    d. increase the bit length

24. For an 8-bit allocation, the smallest decimal number that can be represented in two's complement form is _____.
    a. −8
    b. −127
    c. −128
    d. −256

25. For an 8-bit allocation, the largest decimal number that can be represented in two's complement form is _____.
    a. 8
    b. 127
    c. 128
    d. 256

26. In two's complement representation with a 4-bit allocation, you get _____ when you add 1 to 7.
    a. 8
    b. 1
    c. −7
    d. −8

27. In two's complement representation with a 4-bit allocation, you get _____ when you add 5 to 5.
    a. −5
    b. −6
    c. −7
    d. 10

28. If the exponent in Excess_127 is binary 10000101, the exponent in decimal is _____.
    a. 6
    b. 7
    c. 8
    d. 9

29. If you are adding two numbers, one of which has an exponent value of 7 and the other an exponent value of 9, you need to shift the decimal point of the smaller number _____.
    a. one place to the left
    b. one place to the right
    c. two places to the left
    d. two places to the right

30. The binary _____ operator takes two inputs to produce one output.
    a. AND
    b. OR
    c. XOR
    d. all of the above

31. The unary _____ operator inverts its single input.
    a. AND
    b. OR
    c. NOT
    d. XOR

32. For the binary _____ operator, if the input is two 0s, the output is 0.
    a. AND
    b. OR
    c. XOR
    d. all of the above

33. For the binary _____ operator, if the input is two 1s, the output is 0.
    a. AND
    b. OR
    c. XOR
    d. all of the above

34. For the binary AND operation, only an input of _____ gives an output of 1.
    a. two 0s
    b. two 1s
    c. one 0 and one 1
    d. any of the above

35. For the binary OR operation, only an input of _____ gives an output of 0.
    a. two 0s
    b. two 1s
    c. one 0 and one 1
    d. any of the above

36. You use a bit pattern called a _____ to modify another bit pattern.
    a. mask
    b. carry
    c. float
    d. byte

37. To flip all the bits of a bit pattern, make a mask of all 1s and then _____ the bit pattern and the mask.
    a. AND
    b. OR
    c. XOR
    d. NOT

38. To unset (force to 0) all the bits of a bit pattern, make a mask of all 0s and then _____ the bit pattern and the mask.
    a. AND
    b. OR
    c. XOR
    d. NOT

39. To set (force to 1) all the bits of a bit pattern, make a mask of all 1s and then _____ the bit pattern and the mask.
    a. AND
    b. OR
    c. XOR
    d. NOT

EXERCISES

40. Using an 8-bit allocation, first convert each of the following numbers to two's complement, do the operation, and then convert the result to decimal.
    a.   19 + 23
    b.   19 − 23
    c. −19 + 23
    d. −19 − 23

41. Using a 16-bit allocation, first convert each of the following numbers to two's complement, do the operation, and then convert the result to decimal.
    a.   161 + 1023
    b.   161 − 1023
    c. −161 + 1023
    d. −161 − 1023

42. Which of the following operations creates overflow if the numbers and the result are represented in 8-bit two's complement notation?
    a. 11000010 + 00111111
    b. 00000010 + 00111111
    c. 11000010 + 11111111
    d. 00000010 + 11111111

43. Without actually doing the problem, can you tell which of the following creates overflow if the numbers and the result are in 8-bit two's complement notation?
    a.   32 + 105
    b.   32 − 105
    c. −32 + 105
    d. −32 − 105

44. Show the result of the following operations assuming that the numbers are stored in 16-bit two's complement representation. Show the result in hexadecimal notation.
    a. x012A + x0E27
    b. x712A + x9E00
    c. x8011 + x0001
    d. xE12A + x9E27

45. Show the result of the following floating-point operations. First convert each number to binary notation and do the operation; then convert the result back to decimal notation.
    a. 34.075 + 23.12
    b. −12.00067 + 451.00
    c. 33.677 − 0.00056
    d. −344.23 − 123.8902

46. Show the result of the following floating-point operations. First convert each number to binary notation and do the operation; then convert the result back to decimal notation.
    a. 23.125 + 12.45
    b. 0.234 − 7.192
    c. −0.345 + 45.123
    d. −0.234 − 5.345

47. In which of the following situations does an overflow never occur? Justify your answer.
    a. adding two positive integers
    b. adding one positive integer to a negative integer
    c. subtracting one positive integer from a negative integer
    d. subtracting two negative integers

48. Show the result of the following operations:
    a. NOT x99
    b. NOT xFF
    c. NOT x00
    d. NOT x01

49. Show the result of the following operations:
    a. x99 AND x99
    b. x99 AND x00
    c. x99 AND xFF
    d. xFF AND xFF

50. Show the result of the following operations:
   a. x99 OR x99
   b. x99 OR x00
   c. x99 OR xFF
   d. xFF OR xFF

51. Show the result of the following operations:
   a. x99 XOR x99
   b. x99 XOR x00
   c. x99 XOR xFF
   d. xFF XOR xFF

52. Show the result of the following operations:
   a. NOT (x99 OR x99)
   b. x99 OR (NOT x00)
   c. (x99 AND x33) OR (x00 AND xFF)
   d. (x99 OR x33) AND (x00 OR xFF)

53. You need to unset (force to 0) the 4 leftmost bits of a pattern. Show the mask and the operation.

54. You need to set (force to 1) the 4 rightmost bits of a pattern. Show the mask and the operation.

55. You need to flip the 3 rightmost and the 2 leftmost bits of a pattern. Show the mask and the operation.

56. You need to unset the 3 leftmost bits and set the 2 rightmost bits of a pattern. Show the masks and operations.

57. Use the shift operation to divide an unsigned number by 4.

58. Use the shift operation to multiply an unsigned number by 8.

59. Use a combination of logical and shift operations to extract the fourth and fifth bits of an unsigned number.

Computer Hardware

Computer Organization

In this chapter, we discuss the organization of a stand-alone computer. In the next chapter, we show how to connect stand-alone computers to make a network and how to connect networks to make an internetwork (or internet).

You can divide the parts that make up a computer into three broad categories or subsystems: the CPU, main memory, and the input/output (I/O) subsystems. The next three sections discuss these subsystems and how they are connected to make a stand-alone computer. Figure 5.1 shows the three subsystems of a stand-alone computer.

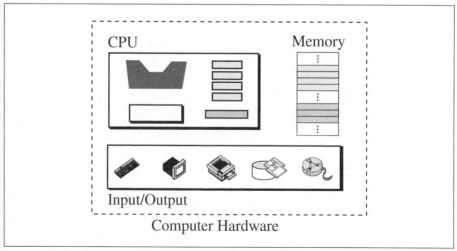

Figure 5.1 Computer hardware (subsystems)

5.1 CENTRAL PROCESSING UNIT (CPU)

The **central processing unit (CPU)** performs operations on data. It has three parts: an arithmetic logic unit (ALU), a control unit, and a set of registers (Figure 5.2).

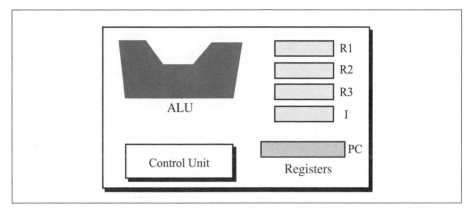

Figure 5.2   CPU

ARITHMETIC LOGIC UNIT (ALU)

The **arithmetic logic unit (ALU)** performs arithmetic and logical operations.

Arithmetic Operation

The simplest unary operations are increment (add 1) and decrement (subtract 1). The simplest binary operations are add, subtract, multiply, and divide. The control unit, as you will see shortly, is responsible for selecting one of these operations.

Logical Operation

The simplest logical unary operation is the NOT operation. The simplest logical binary operations are AND, OR, and XOR. We discussed these operations in Chapter 4. The control unit is responsible for selecting one of these operations.

REGISTERS

Registers are fast stand-alone storage locations that hold data temporarily. Multiple registers are needed to facilitate the operation of the CPU. Some of these registers are in Figure 5.2.

Data Registers

In the past, computers had only one register to alternately hold one of the input data (the other input data come directly from memory) or the result. Today, computers use dozens of registers inside the CPU to speed up the operations because, increasingly, complex operations are done using hardware (instead of using software) and there is a need for several registers to hold the intermediate results. For simplicity, we show only three general registers: two for input data and one for output data (registers R1, R2, and R3) in Figure 5.2.

Instruction Register

Today, computers store not only data but also the corresponding program inside memory. The CPU is responsible for fetching instructions, one by one, from memory, storing them in the **instruction register** (register I in Figure 5.2), interpreting them, and executing them. We will discuss this issue in a following section.

Program Counter

Another common register in the CPU is the **program counter** (register PC in Figure 5.2). The program counter keeps track of the instruction currently being executed. After execution of the instruction, the counter is incremented to point to the address of the next instruction in memory.

CONTROL UNIT

The third part of any CPU is the control unit. The **control unit** is like the part of the human brain that controls the operation of each part of the body. Controlling is achieved through wires that can be on (hot) or off (cold). For example, a simple ALU needs to perform perhaps 10 different operations. To specify these operations, you need four wires from the control unit to the ALU. Four wires can define 16 different situations (2^4). You can use 10 for arithmetic and logical operations. The rest can be used for other purposes. You can designate an off wire as 0 and an on wire as 1. The states of the wires can be designated as 0000, 0001, 0010, . . . , 1111. You can define 0000 (all wires off) to denote no operation, 0001 to denote increment, 0010 to denote decrement, and so on.

5.2   MAIN MEMORY

Main memory is another subsystem in a computer (Figure 5.3). It is a collection of storage locations, each with a unique identifier called the address. Data are transferred to and from memory in groups of bits called words. A word can be a group of 8 bits, 16 bits, 32 bits, or sometimes 64 bits. If the word is 8 bits, it is referred to as a byte. The term *byte* is so common in computer science that sometimes a 16-bit word is referred to as a 2-byte word or a 32-bit word is referred to as a 4-byte word.

ADDRESS SPACE

To access a word in memory requires an identifier. Although programmers use a name to identify a word (or a collection of words), at the hardware level, each word is identified by an address. The total number of uniquely identifiable locations in memory is called the **address space.** For example, a memory with 64 kilobytes and a word size of 1 byte has an address space that ranges from 0 to 65,535.

Table 5.1 shows the units used to refer to memory. Note that the terminology is misleading; it approximates the number of bytes in powers of 10, but the actual number of bytes is in powers of 2. The units in powers of 2 facilitate addressing.

Unit	Exact Number of Bytes	Approximation
kilobyte	2^{10} (1024) bytes	10^3 bytes
megabyte	2^{20} (1,048,576) bytes	10^6 bytes
gigabyte	2^{30} (1,073,741,824) bytes	10^9 bytes
terabyte	2^{40} bytes	10^{12} bytes
petabyte	2^{50} bytes	10^{15} bytes
exabyte	2^{60} bytes	10^{18} bytes

Table 5.1   Memory units

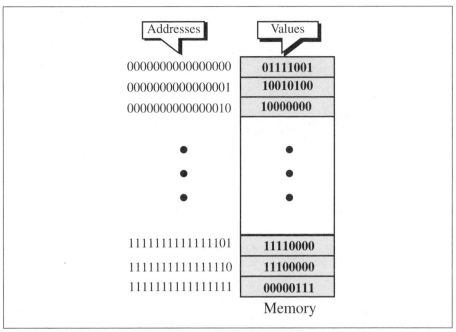

Figure 5.3   Main memory

Address as Bit Pattern

Because computers operate by storing numbers as **bit patterns,** the address itself is also represented as a bit pattern. So if a computer has 64 kilobytes (2^{16}) of memory with a word size of 1 byte, then to define an address, you need a bit pattern of 16 bits. Recall from Chapter 3 that addresses can be represented as unsigned integers (you do not have negative addresses). In other words, the first location is referred to as address 0000000000000000 (address 0), and the last location is referred to as address 1111111111111111 (address 65535). In general, if a computer has N words of memory, you need an unsigned integer of size $\log_2 N$ bits to refer to each memory location.

> Memory addresses are defined using unsigned binary integers.

EXAMPLE 1

A computer has 32 MB (megabytes) of memory. How many bits are needed to address any single byte in memory?

SOLUTION

The memory address space is 32 MB, or 2^{25} ($2^5 \times 2^{20}$). This means you need $\log_2 2^{25}$, or 25 bits, to address each byte. ∎

EXAMPLE 2

A computer has 128 MB of memory. Each word in this computer is 8 bytes. How many bits are needed to address any single word in memory?

SOLUTION

The memory address space is 128 MB, which means 2^{27}. However, each word is 8 (2^3) bytes, which means that you have 2^{24} words. This means you need $\log_2 2^{24}$, or 24 bits, to address each word.   ■

MEMORY TYPES

Two types of memory are available: RAM and ROM.

RAM

Random access memory (RAM) makes up most of the main memory in a computer. The term is confusing because ROM can also be accessed randomly. What distinguishes RAM from ROM is that RAM can be read from and written to by the user. The user can write something to RAM and later erase it simply by overwriting it. Another characteristic of RAM is that it is volatile; the information (program or data) is erased if the system is powered down. In other words, all information in RAM is deleted if you turn off the computer or if there is a power outage. RAM technology is divided into two broad categories: SRAM and DRAM.

SRAM   **Static RAM (SRAM)** technology uses the traditional flip-flop gates (a gate with two states: 0 and 1) to hold data. The gates hold their state (0 or 1), which means the data are stored as long as the power is on; there is no need for refreshing. SRAM is fast but expensive.

DRAM   **Dynamic RAM (DRAM)** technology uses capacitors. If the capacitor is charged, the state is 1; if it is uncharged, the state is 0. Because a capacitor loses some of its charge with time, memory cells need to be refreshed periodically. DRAMs are slow but inexpensive.

ROM

The contents of **read-only memory (ROM)** are written by the manufacturer; the user is allowed to read but not write to ROM. Its advantage is that it is nonvolatile; its contents are not erased if you turn off the computer. Normally, it is used for programs or data that must not be erased or changed even if you turn off the computer. For example, some computers come with a ROM that holds the booting program that runs when you switch on the computer.

PROM   One variation of ROM is **programmable read-only memory (PROM).** This type of memory is blank when the computer is shipped. The user of the computer, with some special equipment, can store programs on it. When programs are stored, it behaves like ROM and cannot be overwritten. This allows the computer user to store specific programs in PROM.

EPROM   A variation of PROM is **erasable programmable read-only memory (EPROM).** It can be programmed by the user, but it can be erased with a special device that applies ultraviolet light. To erase EPROM memory requires physical removal and reinstallation of the EPROM.

EEPROM   A variation of EPROM is **electronically erasable programmable read-only memory (EEPROM).** It can be programmed and erased using electronic impulses without being removed from the computer.

MEMORY HIERARCHY

Computer users need a lot of memory, especially memory that is very fast and very inexpensive. This demand is not always possible to satisfy. Very fast memory is usually not cheap. A compromise needs to be made. The solution is hierarchical levels of memory (Figure 5.4). The hierarchy is based on the following:

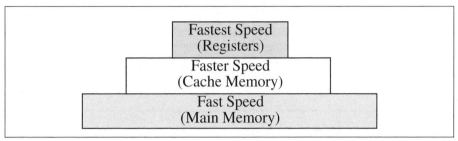

Figure 5.4 Memory hierarchy

■ Use a very small amount of high-speed memory where speed is crucial. The registers inside the CPU are of this kind.

■ Use a moderate amount of medium-speed memory to store data that are accessed often. Cache memory, discussed next, is of this kind.

■ Use a large amount of low-speed memory for data that are not accessed very often. Main memory is of this kind.

CACHE MEMORY

Cache memory is faster than main memory but slower than the CPU and the registers inside the CPU. Cache memory, which is normally small in size, is placed between the CPU and main memory (Figure 5.5).

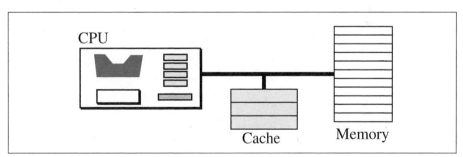

Figure 5.5 Cache

Cache memory at any time contains a copy of a portion of main memory. When the CPU needs to access a word in main memory, it follows this procedure:

1. The CPU checks the cache.

2. If the word is there, it copies the word; if not, the CPU accesses main memory and copies a block of memory starting with the desired word. The block replaces the previous contents of cache memory.

3. The CPU accesses the cache and copies the word.

This procedure can expedite operations; if the word is in the cache, it is accessed immediately. If the word is not in the cache, the word and a whole block are copied to the cache. Since it is very probable that the CPU, in its next cycle, needs to access the words following the first word, the existence of the cache speeds processing.

The reader may wonder why cache memory is so efficient despite its small size. The answer lies in the 80-20 rule. It has been observed that most computers typically spend 80 percent of the time accessing only 20 percent of the data. In other words, the same data are accessed over and over again. Cache memory, with its fast speed, can hold this 20 percent to make access faster at least 80 percent of the time.

5.3 INPUT/OUTPUT

The third subsystem in a computer is the collection of devices referred to as the **input/ output (I/O) subsystem.** This subsystem allows a computer to communicate with the outside world and to store programs and data even when the power is off. Input/output devices can be divided into two broad categories: nonstorage and storage devices.

NONSTORAGE DEVICES

Nonstorage devices allow the CPU/memory to communicate with the outside world, but they cannot store information.

Keyboard and Monitor

Two of the more common nonstorage input/output devices are the keyboard and the monitor. The **keyboard** provides input; the **monitor** displays output and at the same time echoes the input typed on the keyboard. The programs, commands, and data are input or output using strings of characters. The characters are encoded using a code such as ASCII (see Appendix A).

Printer

A **printer** is an output device that creates a permanent record. The printer is a nonstorage device because the printed material cannot be directly entered into a computer again unless someone types or scans it.

STORAGE DEVICES

Storage devices, although classified as I/O devices, can store large amounts of information to be retrieved at a later time. They are cheaper than main memory, and their contents are nonvolatile (not erased when the power is turned off). They are sometimes referred to as auxiliary storage devices. We categorize them as either magnetic or optical.

Magnetic Storage Devices

Magnetic storage devices use magnetization to store bits of data. If a spot is magnetized, it represents 1; if a spot is not magnetized, it represents 0.

Magnetic Disk   A **magnetic disk** is one or more disks stacked on top of each other. The disks are coated with a thin magnetic film. Information is stored on and retrieved from the surface of the disk using a **read/write head** for each magnetized surface of the disk. Figure 5.6 shows the physical layout of a magnetic disk.

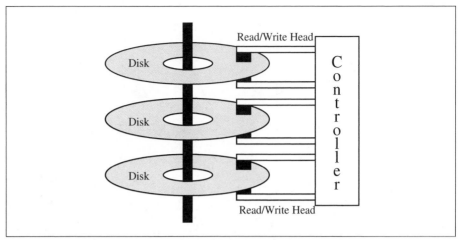

Figure 5.6 Physical layout of a magnetic disk

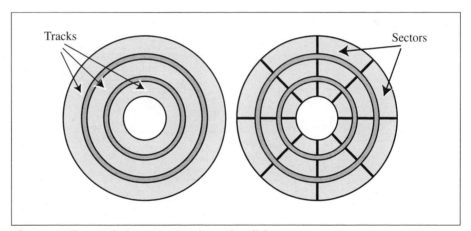

Figure 5.7 Surface organization of a disk

■ **Surface Organization.** To organize data stored on the disk, each surface is divided into **tracks,** and each track is divided into **sectors** (Figure 5.7). The tracks are separated by an **intertrack gap,** and the sectors are separated by an **intersector gap.**

■ **Data Access.** A magnetic disk is considered a random access device. However, the smallest storage area that can be accessed at one time is a sector. A block of data can be stored in one or more sectors and retrieved without the need to retrieve the rest of the information on the disk.

■ **Performance.** The performance of a disk depends on several factors; the most important are the rotational speed, the seek time, and the transfer time. The **rotational speed** defines how fast the disk is spinning. The **seek time** defines the time to move the read/write head to the desired track where the data are stored. The **transfer time** defines the time to move data from the disk to the CPU/memory.

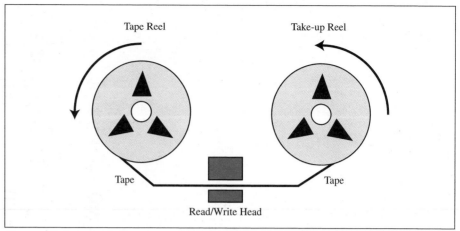

Figure 5.8   Mechanical configuration of a tape

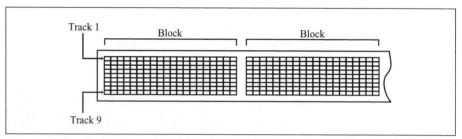

Figure 5.9   Surface Organization of a tape

Magnetic Tape   **Magnetic tape** comes in various sizes. One common type is half-inch plastic tape coated with a thick magnetic film. The tape is mounted on two reels and uses a read/write head that reads or writes information when the tape is passed through it. Figure 5.8 shows the mechanical configuration of a magnetic tape.

■ **Surface Organization.** The width of the tape is divided into nine tracks; each spot of a track can store 1 bit of information. Nine vertical spots can store 8 bits of information related to a byte plus a bit for error detection (Figure 5.9).

■ **Data Access.** A magnetic tape is considered a sequential access device. Although the surface may be divided into blocks, there is no addressing mechanism to access each block. To retrieve a specific block on the tape, you need to pass through all of the previous blocks.

■ **Performance.** Although a magnetic tape is slower than a magnetic disk, it is cheaper. Today, people use magnetic tape to backup large amounts of data.

Optical Storage Devices

Optical storage devices, a new technology, use light (laser) to store and retrieve data. The use of optical storage technology followed the invention of the CD (compact disc), used to store audio information. Today, the same technology (slightly improved) is used to store information in a computer. Devices that use this technology include CD-ROMs, CD-Rs, CD-RWs, and DVDs.

CD-ROM   The **compact disc read-only memory (CD-ROM)** uses the same technology as the CD (compact disc), originally developed by Phillips and Sony for recording music. The only difference between these two technologies is enhancement; a CD-ROM drive is more robust and checks for errors. Figure 5.10 shows the steps in creating and using a CD-ROM.

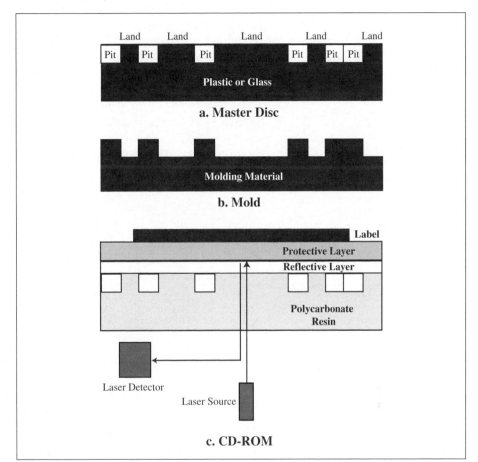

Figure 5.10   Creation and use of CD-ROM

- **Creation.** CD-ROM technology uses three steps to create a large number of discs:
    a. A **master disc** is created using a high-power infrared laser that makes bit patterns on coated plastic. The laser translates the bit patterns into a sequence of **pits** (holes) and **lands** (no holes). The pits usually represent 0s and the lands usually represent 1s. However, this is only a convention, and it can be reversed. Other schemes use a transition (pit to hole or hole to pit) to represent 1 and lack of transition to represent 0.
    b. From the master disc, a mold is made. In the mold, the pits (holes) are replaced by bumps.
    c. Molten **polycarbonate resin** is injected into the mold to produce the same pits as the master disc. A very thin layer of aluminum (serving as a reflective surface) is added to the polycarbonate. On top of this, a protective layer of lacquer is applied and a label is added. Only this step is repeated for each disk.

■ **Reading.** The CD-ROM is read using a low-power laser beam coming from the computer drive. The laser beam is reflected by the aluminum surface when passing through a land. It is reflected twice when it encounters a pit, once by the pit boundary and once by the aluminum boundary. The two reflections have a destructive effect because the depth of the pit is chosen to be exactly one-fourth of the beam wavelength. In other words, the sensor installed in the drive detects more light when the spot is a land and less light when the spot is a pit; it can read what is recorded on the original master disc.

■ **Format.** CD-ROM technology uses a different format than magnetic disk (Figure 5.11). The format of data on a CD-ROM is based on
  a. A block of 8-bit data is transformed into a 14-bit symbol using an error-correction method called the Hamming code.
  b. A frame is made of 42 symbols (14 bits/symbol).
  c. A sector is made of 96 frames (2352 bytes).

■ **Speed.** CD-ROM drives come in different speeds. Single speed is called 1x, double speed is called 2x, and so on. If the drive is single speed, it can read up to 153,600 bytes per second. Table 5.2 shows the speeds and their corresponding data rate.

Speed	Data Rate	Approximation	
1x	153,600 bytes per second	150	KB/s
2x	307,200 bytes per second	300	KB/s
4x	614,400 bytes per second	600	KB/s
6x	921,600 bytes per second	900	KB/s
8x	1,228,800 bytes per second	1.2	MB/s
12x	1,843,200 bytes per second	1.8	MB/s
16x	2,457,600 bytes per second	2.4	MB/s
24x	3,688,400 bytes per second	3.6	MB/s
32x	4,915,200 bytes per second	4.8	MB/s
40x	6,144,000 bytes per second	6	MB/s

Table 5.2 CD-ROM speeds

■ **Application.** The expenses involved in creating a master disc, mold, and the actual disc can be justified if there are a large number of potential customers. In other words, this technology is economical if the discs are mass produced.

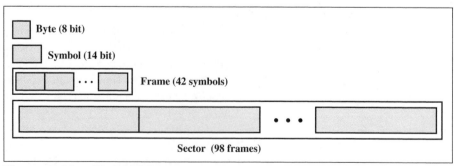

Figure 5.11 CD-ROM format

CD-R   As mentioned, CD-ROM technology is justifiable only if the manufacturer can create a large number of disks. On the other hand, the **compact disc recordable (CD-R)** allows users to create one or more disks without going through the expense involved in creating CD-ROMs. It is particularly useful for making backups. The user can write once to this disc, but it can be read many times. This is why it is sometimes called **write once, read many (WORM).**

■ **Creation.** CD-R technology uses the same principles as CD-ROM to create a disc (Figure 5.12). The following lists the differences:

   a. There is no master disc or mold.
   b. The reflective layer is made of gold instead of aluminum.
   c. There are no physical pits (holes) in the polycarbonate; the pits and lands are only simulated. To simulate pits and lands, an extra layer of dye, similar to the material used in photography, is added between the reflective layer and the polycarbonate.
   d. A high-power laser beam, created by the CD burner of the drive, makes a dark spot in the dye (changing the chemical composition) which simulates a pit. The areas not hit by the beam are lands.

■ **Reading.** CD-Rs can be read by a CD-ROM or a CD-R drive. This means that any difference should be transparent to the drive. The same low-power laser beam passes in front of the simulated pits and lands. For a land, the beam reaches the reflective layer and is reflected. For a simulated pit, the spot is opaque, so the beam cannot be reflected back.

■ **Format and Speed.** The format, capacity, and speed of CD-Rs are the same as CD-ROMs.

■ **Application.** This technology is very attractive to people who want to create and distribute a small number of disks. It is also very useful for making archive files and backups.

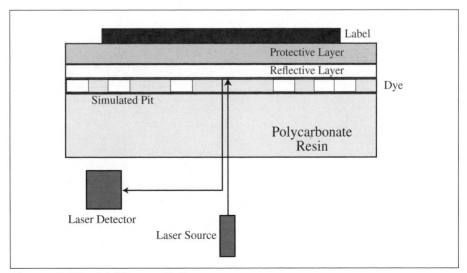

Figure 5.12   Making a CD-R

CD-RW   Although the CD-Rs have become very popular, they can be written to only once. To overwrite previous materials, there is a new technology that creates a new type of disc called **compact disc rewritable (CD-RW).** It is sometimes called an erasable optical disc.

■ **Creation.** CD-RW technology uses the same principles as CD-R to create the disc (Figure 5.13). The following lists the differences:

a. Instead of dye, the technology uses an alloy of silver, indium, antimony, and tellurium. This alloy has two stable states: crystalline (transparent) and amorphous (nontransparent).

b. The drive uses high-power lasers to create simulated pits in the alloy (changing it from crystalline to amorphous).

■ **Reading.** The drive uses the same type of low-power laser beam as CD-ROM and CD-R to detect pits and lands.

■ **Erasing.** The drive uses a medium-power laser beam to change pits to lands. The beam changes a spot from the amorphous state to the crystalline state.

■ **Format and Speed.** The format, capacity, and speed of CD-RWs are the same as CD-ROMs.

■ **Application.** The technology is definitely more attractive than CD-R technology. However, CD-Rs are more popular for two reasons. First, blank CD-R discs are less expensive than blank CD-RW discs. Second, CD-Rs are preferable in cases where the created disc must not be changed, either accidentally or intentionally.

DVD   The industry has felt the need for digital storage media with even higher capacity. The capacity of a CD-ROM (650 MB) is insufficient to store video information. The latest optical memory storage device on the market is called **digital versatile disc (DVD).** It uses a technology similar to CD-ROM but with the following differences:

1. The pits are smaller: 0.4 microns in diameter instead of the 0.8 microns used in CDs.

2. The tracks are closer to each other.

3. The beam is red laser instead of infrared.

4. DVD uses one to two recording layers, and it can be single-sided or double-sided.

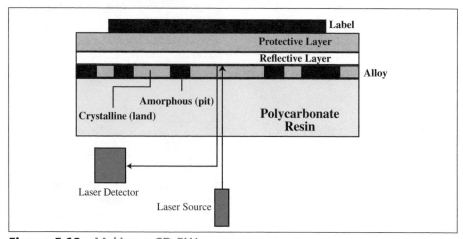

Figure 5.13   Making a CD-RW

■ **Capacity** These improvements result in higher capacities (Table 5.3).

Feature	Capacity
single-sided, single-layer	4.7 GB
single-sided, dual-layer	8.5 GB
double-sided, single-layer	9.4 GB
double-sided, dual-layer	17 GB

Table 5.3 DVD capacities

■ **Compression.** DVD technology uses MPEG (see Chapter 15) for compression. This means that a single-sided, single-layer DVD can hold 133 minutes (2 hours and 13 minutes) of video at high resolution. This also includes both audio and subtitles.

■ **Application.** Today, the high capacity of DVDs attracts many applications that need to store a high volume of data.

5.4 SUBSYSTEM INTERCONNECTION

The previous sections outlined the characteristics of the three subsystems (CPU, main memory, and I/O) in a stand-alone computer. In this section, we explore how these three subsystems are interconnected. The interconnection plays an important role because information needs to be exchanged between these three subsystems.

CONNECTING CPU AND MEMORY

The CPU and memory are normally connected by three groups of wires, each called a **bus:** data bus, address bus, and control bus (Figure 5.14).

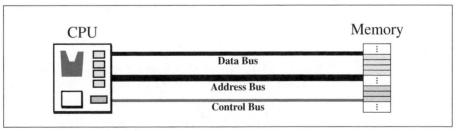

Figure 5.14 Connecting CPU and memory using three buses

Data Bus

The **data bus** is made of several wires, each carrying 1 bit at a time. The number of wires depends on the size of the word. If the word is 32 bits (4 bytes) in a computer, you need a data bus with 32 wires so that all 32 bits of a word can be transmitted at the same time.

Address Bus

The **address bus** allows access to a particular word in memory. The number of wires in the address bus depends on the address space of memory. If the memory has 2^n words, the address bus needs to carry n bits at a time. Therefore, it must have n wires.

Control Bus

The **control bus** carries communication between the CPU and memory. For example, there must be a code, sent from the CPU to memory, to specify a read or write operation. The number of wires used in the control bus depends on the total number of control commands a computer needs. If a computer has 2^m control actions, you need m wires for the control bus because m bits can define 2^m different operations.

CONNECTING I/O DEVICES

I/O devices cannot be connected directly to the buses that connect the CPU and memory because the nature of the I/O devices is different from the nature of the CPU and memory. The I/O devices are electromechanical, magnetic, or optical devices, whereas the CPU and memory are electronic devices. The I/O devices operate at a much slower speed than the CPU/memory. There is a need for an intermediary to handle this difference. The input/output devices are attached to the buses through what is called an **input/output controller** or interface. There is one specific controller for each input/output device (Figure 5.15).

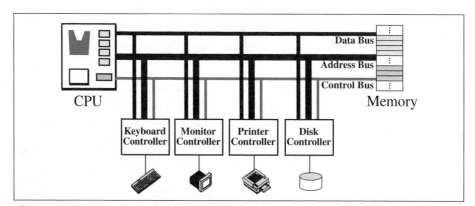

Figure 5.15   Connecting I/O devices to the buses

Controllers

Controllers or interfaces remove the obstacle between the nature of the I/O device and the CPU/memory. A controller can be a serial or parallel device. A serial controller has only one wire connection to the device. A parallel controller has several connections to the device so that several bits can be transferred at a time.

    Several kinds of controllers are in use. The most common ones today are SCSI, FireWire, and USB.

SCSI   The **small computer system interface (SCSI)** was first developed for Macintosh computers in 1984. Today, it is used in many systems. It has a parallel interface with 8, 16, or 32 wires. The SCSI interface provides a daisy chained connection as shown in Figure 5.16. Both ends of the chain must be terminated, and each device must have a unique address (target ID).

FireWire   IEEE standard 1394 defines a serial interface commonly called **FireWire.** It is a high-speed serial interface that transfers data in packets, achieving a transfer rate of up to 50 MB/sec. It can be used to connect up to 63 devices in a daisy chain or a tree connection (using only one wire). Figure 5.17 shows the connection of input/output devices to a FireWire controller. There is no need for termination as in the SCSI controller.

USB   A competitor for the FireWire controller is the **universal serial bus (USB)** controller. USB is also a serial controller used to connect slower devices such as the keyboard and mouse to a computer. It can transfer data up to 1.5 MB/sec. It has a four-wire bus; two carry power to the device. Figure 5.18 shows the connection of a USB to the buses.

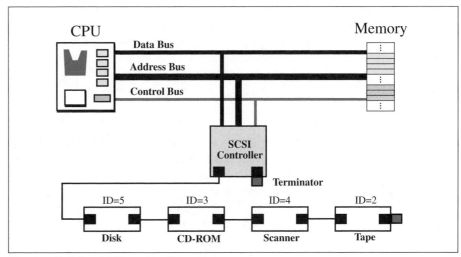

Figure 5.16 SCSI controller

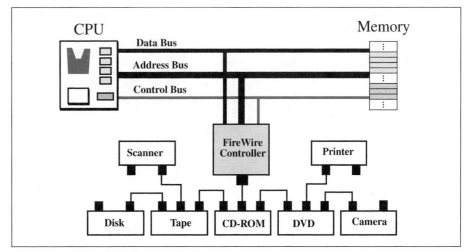

Figure 5.17 FireWire controller

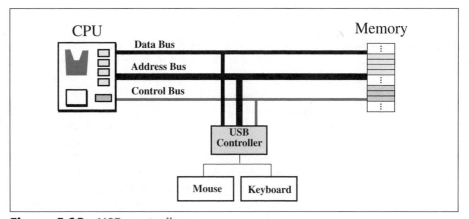

Figure 5.18 USB controller

ADDRESSING INPUT/OUTPUT DEVICES

The CPU usually uses the same bus to read data from or write data to main memory and the I/O device. The only difference is the instruction. If the instruction refers to a word in main memory, data transfer is between main memory and the CPU. If the instruction identifies an input/output device, data transfer is between the input/output device and the CPU. There are two methods to handle the addressing of I/O devices: isolated I/O and memory-mapped I/O.

Isolated I/O

In the **isolated I/O** method, the instructions used to read/write memory are totally different from the instructions used to read/write input/output devices. There are instructions to test, control, read from, and write to input/output devices. Each input/output device has its own address. The input/output addresses can overlap with memory addresses without any ambiguity because the instruction itself is different. For example, the CPU can use the command Read 05 to read from memory word 05, and it can use the command Input 05 to read from input/output device 05. There is no confusion because the Read command is for reading from memory and the Input command is for reading from an input/output device (Figure 5.19).

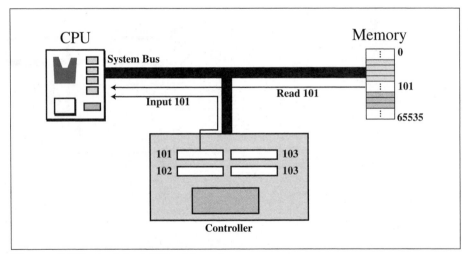

Figure 5.19   Isolated I/O addressing

Memory-Mapped I/O

In the **memory-mapped I/O** method, the CPU treats each register in the input/output controller as a word in memory. In other words, the CPU does not have separate instructions for transferring data from memory or input/output devices. For example, there is only one Read instruction. If the address defines a word from memory, the data are read from that word. If the address defines a register from an input/output device, the data are read from that register. The advantage of the memory-mapped configuration is a smaller number of instructions; all the memory instructions can be used by the input/output devices. The disadvantage is that the part of the address space used for memory is allocated to the registers in the input/output controllers. For example, if you have five input/output controllers and each has four registers, 20 addresses are used for this purpose. The size of the memory is reduced by 20 words. Figure 5.20 shows the memory-mapped I/O concept.

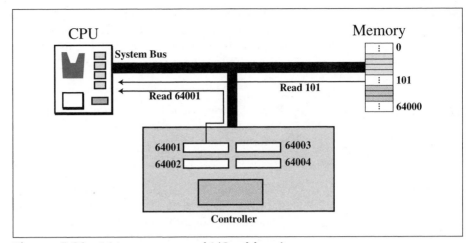

Figure 5.20 Memory-mapped I/O addressing

5.5 PROGRAM EXECUTION

Today, general-purpose computers use a set of instructions called a program to process data. A computer executes the program to create output data from input data. Both the program and the data are stored in memory.

MACHINE CYCLE

The CPU uses repeating **machine cycles** to execute instructions in the program, one by one, from beginning to end. A simplified cycle can consist of three steps: fetch, decode, and execute (Figure 5.21).

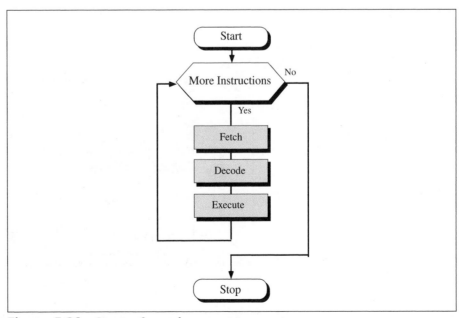

Figure 5.21 Steps of a cycle

Fetch

In the **fetch** step, the control unit orders the system to copy the next instruction into the instruction register in the CPU. The address of the instruction to be copied is held in the program counter register. After copying, the program counter is incremented to refer to the next instruction in memory.

Decode

When the instruction is in the instruction register, it gets decoded by the control unit. The result of this decode step is binary code for some operation that the system will perform.

Execute

After the instruction is decoded, the control unit sends the task order to a component in the CPU. For example, the control unit can tell the system to load (read) a data item from memory, or the CPU can tell the ALU to add the contents of two input registers and put the result in an output register. This is the **execute** step.

A MACHINE CYCLE EXAMPLE

Let us look at a very simple operation such as adding two integers. A computer with simple architecture needs at least four instructions for this job. The four instructions and the two input integers reside in memory before program execution; the result will be in memory after program execution.

Although everything is represented by bit patterns, for simplicity, assume that the numbers and addresses are in decimal. Also assume that the instructions are in memory locations 70, 71, 72, and 73. The input data are stored in locations 200 and 201. The output data will be stored in memory location 202.

Figure 5.22 shows the memory and CPU before execution of the program. R1, R2, and R3 are general registers. R1 and R2 hold input data; R3 holds output data. The I register is the instruction register, and PC is the program counter. Figure 5.23 shows the results of four operations on the memory and registers.

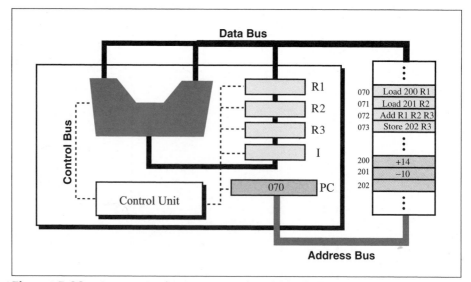

Figure 5.22   Contents of memory and register before execution

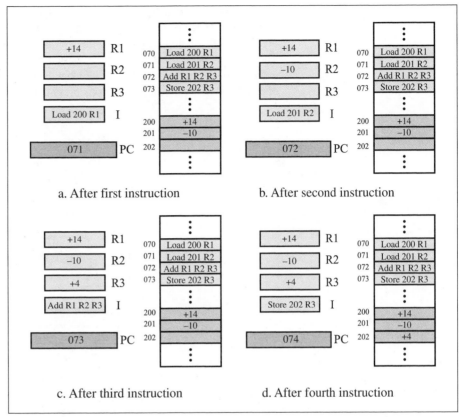

Figure 5.23   Contents of memory and register after each cycle

First Operation

In the first operation (Load 200 R1), the machine goes through the three steps of fetch, decode, and execute to load the contents of memory location 200 into data register R1.

Second Operation

In the second operation (Load 201 R2), the machine goes through the three steps of fetch, decode, and execute to load the contents of memory location 201 into data register R2.

Third Operation

In the third operation (Add R1 R2 R3), the machine goes through the three steps of fetch, decode, and execute to add the data in R1 and R2, storing the result in R3.

Fourth Operation

In the fourth operation (Store 202 R3), the machine goes through the three steps of fetch, decode, and execute to store the result of the operation in memory location 202.

INPUT/OUTPUT OPERATION

There is a need for commands to transfer data from the I/O devices to the CPU and memory. Because input/output devices operate at much slower speeds than the CPU, the operation of the CPU must be somehow synchronized with the input/output device. Three methods have been devised for this synchronization: programmed I/O, interrupt-driven I/O, and direct memory access (DMA).

Programmed I/O

In the **programmed I/O** method, synchronization is very primitive; the CPU waits for the I/O device. The transfer of data between the I/O device and the CPU is done by an instruction in the program. When the CPU encounters an I/O instruction, it does nothing else until the data transfer is complete. The CPU constantly checks the status of the I/O drive; if the device is ready to transfer, data are transferred to the CPU. If the device is not ready, the CPU continues checking the status until the I/O device is ready (Figure 5.24). The big issue here is that CPU time is wasted by checking the status of the I/O device for each unit of data to be transferred. Note that data are transferred to memory after the input operation; data are transferred from memory before the output operation.

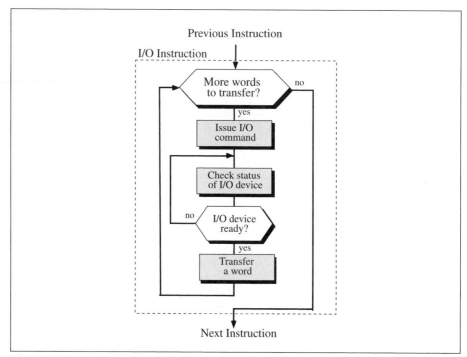

Figure 5.24   Programmed I/O

Interrupt-Driven I/O

In the **interrupt-driven I/O** method, the CPU informs the I/O device that a transfer is going to happen, but it does not test the status of the I/O device continuously. The I/O device informs (interrupts) the CPU when it is ready. During this time, the CPU can do other jobs such as running other programs or transferring data from or to other I/O devices (Figure 5.25).

In this method, CPU time is not wasted. While the slow I/O device is finishing a task, the CPU can do something else. Note that, like programmed I/O, this method also transfers data between the device and the CPU. Data are transferred to memory after the input operation; data are transferred from memory before the output operation.

Direct Memory Access (DMA)

The third method to transfer data is **direct memory access (DMA).** This method transfers a large block of data between a high-speed I/O device, such as a disk, and memory directly (without passing data through the CPU). This requires a DMA controller that relieves the CPU of some of its functions. The DMA controller has registers to hold a block of data before and after memory transfer. Figure 5.26 shows the DMA connection to the general bus. In this method, for an I/O operation, the CPU sends a message to the DMA. The message contains the type of transfer (input or output), the beginning

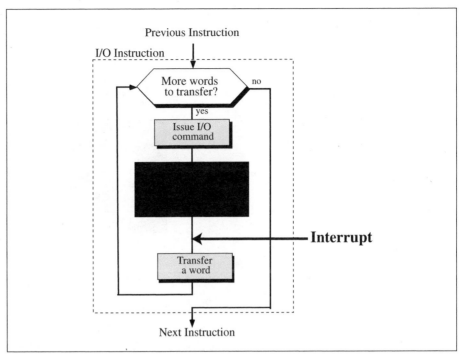

Figure 5.25 Interrupt-driven I/O

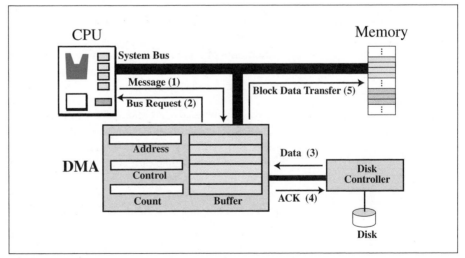

Figure 5.26 DMA connection to the general bus

address of the memory location, and the number of bytes to be transferred. The CPU is now available for other jobs.

When ready to transfer data, the DMA controller informs the CPU that it needs to take control of the buses. The CPU stops using the buses and lets the controller use them. After data transfer, directly between the DMA and memory, the CPU continues its normal operation (Figure 5.27). Note that, in this method, the CPU is idle for a short time.

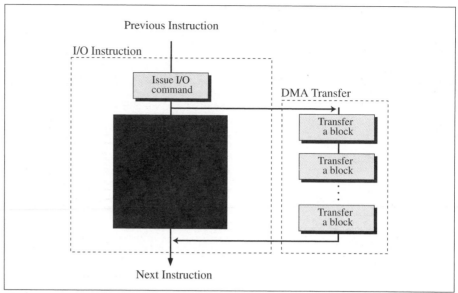

Figure 5.27   DMA input/output

However, the duration of idleness is very short compared to other methods; the CPU is idle only during the data transfer between the DMA and memory, not when the device prepares the data.

5.6   TWO DIFFERENT ARCHITECTURES

The design of computers has gone through many changes during the last decades. The two fundamental designs that dominate the market are CISC and RISC. We briefly discuss these two design methodologies.

CISC

CISC (pronounced *sisk*) stands for **complex instruction set computer.** The strategy behind CISC architecture is to have a large set of instructions, including the complex ones. Programming in CISC is easier than in the other design because there is one instruction for a simple or a complex task. Programmers do not have to write a set of instructions to do a complex task.

The complexity of the instruction set makes the circuitry of the CPU and the control unit very complicated. The designers of CISC architecture have come up with a solution to reduce this complexity. The programming is done at two levels. An instruction in the machine language is not executed directly by the CPU. The CPU performs only simple operations called microoperations. A complex instruction is transformed into a set of these simple operations and then executed by the CPU. This necessitates the addition of a special memory called micromemory that holds the set of operations for each complex instruction in the machine set. The type of programming that uses microoperations is called microprogramming.

One objection to CISC architecture is the overhead associated with microprogramming and the access of micromemory. However, proponents of the architecture argue that this compensates for smaller programs at the machine level.

An example of CISC architecture can be seen in the Pentium series of processors developed by Intel.

RISC

RISC (pronounced *risk*) stands for **reduced instruction set computer.** The strategy behind RISC architecture is to have a small set of instructions that do a minimum number of simple operations. Complex instructions are simulated using a subset of simple instructions. Programming in RISC is more difficult and longer than in the other design because most of the complex instructions are simulated using simple instructions.

An example of RISC architecture is the PowerPC series of processors used in Apple Computers.

5.7 KEY TERMS

address bus	execute	polycarbonate resin
address space	fetch	printer
arithmetic logic unit (ALU)	FireWire	program counter
arithmetic operation	frame	programmable read-only memory
bit pattern	input/output controller	(PROM)
bus	input/output (I/O) subsystem	programmed I/O
cache memory	instruction register	random access memory (RAM)
central processing unit (CPU)	interrupt-driven I/O	read-only memory (ROM)
compact disc read-only memory	intersector gap	read/write head
(CD-ROM)	intertrack gap	reduced instruction set computer (RISC)
compact disc recordable (CD-R)	isolated I/O	register
compact disc rewritable (CD-RW)	keyboard	rotational speed
complex instruction set computer	land	sector
(CISC)	logical operation	seek time
control bus	machine cycle	small computer system interface (SCSI)
control unit	magnetic disk	static RAM (SRAM)
data bus	magnetic tape	storage device
data register	main memory	track
digital versatile disc (DVD)	master disc	transfer time
direct memory access (DMA)	memory	universal serial bus (USB)
dynamic RAM (DRAM)	memory-mapped I/O	write once, read many (WORM)
electronically erasable programmable	monitor	
read-only memory (EEPROM)	nonstorage device	
erasable programmable read-only	optical storage device	
memory (EPROM)	pit	

5.8 SUMMARY

- A computer has three subsystems: the CPU, main memory, and the input/output subsystem.
- The CPU performs operations on data and has an ALU, a control unit, and a set of registers.
- The ALU performs arithmetic and logical operations.
- The registers are stand-alone storage devices that hold data temporarily. Registers can hold data, instructions, and also function as a program counter.

- The control unit oversees operations in a computer.
- Main memory is a collection of storage locations.
- Memory addresses are defined using unsigned binary integers.
- RAM provides the bulk of the memory in a computer. SRAM uses the traditional flip-flop gates to hold data, and DRAM uses capacitors.

- The contents of ROM come from the manufacturer; users are only allowed to read from it, but not write to it.
- Computers need high-speed memory for registers, medium-speed memory for cache memory, and low-speed memory for main memory.
- The input/output subsystem is a collection of devices that allows a computer to communicate with the outside world. These devices are either nonstorage devices or storage devices.
- The keyboard, monitor, and printer are examples of nonstorage devices.
- A magnetic disk is a storage device with each disk in the stack divided into tracks and sectors.
- Magnetic tape is a storage device with the tape divided into tracks. Access to the data is sequential.
- A CD-ROM is an optical storage device in which the manufacturer burns the data onto the disk. The data cannot be erased.
- A CD-R is an optical storage device in which the user burns the data onto the disk. The data cannot be erased.
- A CD-RW is an optical storage device in which the user burns the data onto the disk. The data can be erased and rewritten multiple times.
- A DVD is a high-capacity optical storage device.
- A data bus, an address bus, and a control bus connect the CPU and memory.
- A controller handles the I/O operations between the CPU/memory and the much slower I/O devices. SCSI, FireWire, and USB are common controllers.
- There are two methods to handle the addressing of I/O devices: isolated I/O and memory-mapped I/O
- To run an instruction in a program, the CPU first fetches the instruction, decodes it, and then executes it.
- There are three methods to synchronize the CPU with the I/O device: programmed I/O, interrupt-driven I/O, and DMA.
- The two designs for CPU architecture are CISC and RISC.

5.9   PRACTICE SET

REVIEW QUESTIONS

1. What are the three subsystems that make up a computer?
2. What are the parts of a CPU?
3. What is the function of the ALU?
4. Describe the different types of registers.
5. What is the function of the control unit?
6. What is the difference between a word and a byte?
7. What is the function of main memory?
8. How is the approximation of a megabyte related to the actual number of bytes?
9. What kind of number representation is used to represent memory addresses?
10. What is the difference between RAM and ROM?
11. What is the difference between SRAM and DRAM?
12. Discuss the differences between PROM, EPROM, and EEPROM.
13. What is the purpose of cache memory?
14. Discuss the levels of memory speed and the type of memory that uses each.
15. Give examples of nonstorage I/O devices.
16. What are the two main classes of storage devices?
17. Describe the physical components of a magnetic disk.
18. How is the surface of a magnetic disk organized?
19. What factors affect the performance of a magnetic disk?
20. Describe the physical components of a magnetic tape.
21. How is the surface of a magnetic tape organized?
22. How are data accessed on a magnetic tape?
23. Name five types of optical storage devices.
24. Who writes data to a CD-ROM? to a CD-R? to a CD-RW?
25. What is the advantage of CD-RW over CD-ROM and CD-R?
26. Compare and contrast pits and lands on the three types of compact discs.
27. Compare and contrast the reading of data on the three types of compact discs.
28. How are data erased on a CD-RW?
29. How does a DVD differ from a compact disc?

30. What are the functions of the three buses that connect the CPU with memory?

31. What is the function of I/O device controllers?

32. What is a SCSI controller?

33. What is the FireWire interface?

34. What is the USB controller?

35. Compare and contrast the two methods to handle the addressing of I/O devices.

36. What are the steps in a machine cycle?

37. Compare and contrast the three methods to handle the synchronization of the CPU with the I/O devices.

38. Compare and contrast CISC architecture with RISC architecture.

MULTIPLE-CHOICE QUESTIONS

39. The _____ is a computer subsystem that performs operations on data.
    a. CPU
    b. memory
    c. I/O hardware
    d. none of the above

40. _____ is a stand-alone storage location that holds data temporarily.
    a. An ALU
    b. A register
    c. A control unit
    d. A tape drive

41. _____ is a unit that can add two inputs.
    a. An ALU
    b. A register
    c. A control unit
    d. A tape drive

42. A register in a CPU can hold _____.
    a. data
    b. instructions
    c. program counter values
    d. all of the above

43. A control unit with five wires can define up to _____ operations.
    a. 5
    b. 10
    c. 16
    d. 32

44. A word is _____ bits.
    a. 8
    b. 16
    c. 32
    d. any of the above

45. If the memory address space is 16 MB and the word size is 8 bits, then _____ bits are needed to access each word.
    a. 8
    b. 16
    c. 24
    d. 32

46. The data in _____ are erased if the computer is powered down.
    a. RAM
    b. ROM
    c. a tape drive
    d. a CD-ROM

47. _____ is a memory type with capacitors that need to be refreshed periodically.
    a. SRAM
    b. DRAM
    c. ROM
    d. all of the above

48. _____ is a memory type with traditional flip-flop gates to hold data.
    a. SRAM
    b. DRAM
    c. ROM
    d. all of the above

49. There are _____ bytes in 16 terabytes.
    a. 2^{16}
    b. 2^{40}
    c. 2^{44}
    d. 2^{56}

50. _____ can be programmed and erased using electronic impulses but can remain in a computer during erasure.
    a. ROM
    b. PROM
    c. EPROM
    d. EEPROM

51. _____ is a type of memory in which the user, not the manufacturer, stores programs that cannot be overwritten.
    a. ROM
    b. PROM
    c. EPROM
    d. EEPROM

52. CPU registers should have _____ speed memory.
    a. high
    b. medium
    c. low
    d. any of the above

53. Main memory in a computer usually consists of large amounts of _____ speed memory.
    a. high
    b. medium
    c. low
    d. any of the above

54. The _____ memory contains a copy of a portion of main memory.
    a. CPU
    b. cache
    c. main
    d. ROM

55. The _____ is a nonstorage I/O device.
    a. keyboard
    b. monitor
    c. printer
    d. all of the above

56. A _____ is an optical storage device.
    a. CD-ROM
    b. CD-R
    c. CD-RW
    d. all of the above

57. The _____ is a storage device in which the manufacturer writes information to the disc.
    a. CD-ROM
    b. CD-R
    c. CD-RW
    d. all of the above

58. The _____ is a storage device in which the user can write information only once to the disc.
    a. CD-ROM
    b. CD-R
    c. CD-RW
    d. all of the above

59. The _____ is a storage device that can undergo multiple writings and erasings.
    a. CD-ROM
    b. CD-R
    c. CD-RW
    d. all of the above

60. The smallest storage area on a magnetic disk that can be accessed at one time is a _____.
    a. track
    b. sector
    c. frame
    d. head

61. For a magnetic disk, the _____ time is the time it takes for the read/write head to move to the desired track where the data are stored.
    a. rotation
    b. seek
    c. transfer
    d. location

62. Polycarbonate resin is used in _____.
    a. CD-ROMs
    b. CD-Rs
    c. CD-RWs
    d. all of the above

63. In a _____, a high-power laser beam simulates pits in an alloy of silver, indium, antimony, and tellurium.
    a. CD-ROM
    b. CD-R
    c. CD-RW
    d. all of the above

64. In a _____, a high-power laser beam simulates pits in the dye layer.
    a. CD-ROM
    b. CD-R
    c. CD-RW
    d. all of the above

65. Which optical storage device has the highest capacity?
    a. CD-ROM
    b. CD-R
    c. CD-RW
    d. DVD

66. In a DVD, a _____ beam reads the disk.
    a. high-power laser
    b. infrared
    c. red laser
    d. blue laser

67. A _____ bus connects the CPU and memory.
    a. data
    b. address
    c. control
    d. all of the above

68. If the word size is 2 bytes, a data bus with _____ wires is needed.
    a. 2
    b. 4
    c. 8
    d. 16

69. If the memory has 2^{32} words, the address bus needs to have _____ wires.
    a. 8
    b. 16
    c. 32
    d. 64

70. A control bus with eight wires can define _____ operations.
    a. 8
    b. 16
    c. 256
    d. 512

71. The _____ controller features a parallel interface and daisy-chained connection for I/O devices.
    a. SCSI
    b. FireWire
    c. USB
    d. IDE

72. The _____ controller is a serial device that connects slow devices such as the keyboard and mouse to the computer.
    a. SCSI
    b. FireWire
    c. USB
    d. IDE

73. The _____ controller is a high-speed serial interface that transfers data in packets.
    a. SCSI
    b. FireWire
    c. USB
    d. IDE

74. The three steps in the running of a program on a computer are performed _____ in this specific order.
    a. fetch, execute, and decode
    b. decode, execute, and fetch
    c. fetch, decode, and execute
    d. decode, fetch, and execute

75. In the _____ method to synchronize the operation of the CPU with the I/O device, the I/O device informs the CPU when it is ready for data transfer.
    a. programmed I/O
    b. interrupt-driven I/O
    c. DMA
    d. isolated I/O

76. In the _____ method to synchronize the operation of the CPU with the I/O device, the CPU is idle until the I/O operation is finished.
    a. programmed I/O
    b. interrupt-driven I/O
    c. DMA
    d. isolated I/O

77. In the _____ method to synchronize the operation of the CPU with the I/O device, a large block of data can be passed from an I/O device to memory directly.
    a. programmed I/O
    b. interrupt-driven I/O
    c. DMA
    d. isolated I/O

EXERCISES

78. A computer has 64 MB (megabytes) of memory. Each word is 4 bytes. How many bits are needed to address each single word in memory?

79. How many bytes of memory are needed to store a full screen of data if the screen is made of 24 lines with 80 characters in each line? The system uses ASCII code, with each ASCII character stored as a byte.

80. An imaginary computer has four data registers (R0 to R3), 1024 words in memory, and 16 different instructions (add, subtract, etc.). What is the minimum size of an instruction in bits if a typical instruction uses the following format: add 565 R2.

81. If the computer in Exercise 80 uses the same size of word for data and instructions, what is the size of each data register?

82. What is the size of the instruction register of the computer in Exercise 80?

83. What is the size of the program counter of the computer in Exercise 80?

84. What is the size of the data bus in Exercise 80?

85. What is the size of the address bus in Exercise 80?

86. What is the minimum size of the control bus in Exercise 80?

87. A computer uses isolated I/O addressing. Memory has 1024 words. If each controller has 16 registers, how many controllers can be accessed by this computer?

88. A computer uses memory-mapped I/O addressing. The address bus uses 10 lines (10 bits). If memory is made of 1000 words, how many four-register controllers can be accessed by this computer?

Computer Networks

In the previous chapter, we discussed the organization of a computer. The discussion was focused on the architecture of a stand-alone computer. Today, however, computers are often connected to form a network, and the networks are connected to form an internetwork.

In this chapter, we first define a computer network. We then discuss the OSI model that theoretically defines how the components of a network should interact with each other. Next we discuss the categories of networks such as LANs, MANs, and WANs. We show how to connect networks, using connecting devices, to make an internetwork or an internet. We then discuss the Internet and the TCP/IP protocol suite that controls it, including some of the applications on the Internet.

6.1 NETWORKS, LARGE AND SMALL

A **computer network** is a combination of systems (e.g., a computer) connected through transmission media (e.g., a wire, a cable, or air). A computer network can span a small, medium, or large geographical area. In the first case, the network is a local area network (LAN). In the second case, the network is a metropolitan area network (MAN), and in the third case, it is a wide area network (WAN). We discuss LANs, MANs, and WANs later in this chapter. These three types of networks can also be connected using connecting devices to form an internetwork (or an internet).

MODEL AND PROTOCOL

In this chapter, we frequently use two terms: model and protocol. A **model** is the specification set by a standards organization as a guideline for designing networks. A **protocol,** on the other hand, is a set of rules that controls the interaction of different devices in a network or an internetwork. The next section presents the OSI recommendation as a model. Later, we define TCP/IP as the official protocol suite of the Internet.

6.2 OSI MODEL

To make all of the components of a network or an internetwork coordinate properly, a model is needed to show the relationship between the components and the function of each component. The **Open Systems Interconnection (OSI)** is such a model. The OSI model was designed by the International Organization for Standardization (ISO). The model theoretically allows any two different systems (e.g., computers) to communicate regardless of their underlying architecture

> The Open Systems Interconnection (OSI) model is a theoretical model that shows how any two different systems can communicate with each other.

SEVEN LAYERS

The OSI model is a framework of seven layers that gives network designers an idea of the functionality of each separate but related layer. Each layer has a name: the physical (layer 1), data link (layer 2), network (layer 3), transport (layer 4), session (layer 5), presentation (layer 6), and application (layer 7) (Figure 6.1). The OSI model does not dictate that each device involved in a network must implement all seven layers. A device may need only one layer, two layers, three layers, or all layers. The number of layers depends on the functionality of the device and its location in the network.

Figure 6.2 depicts the role of the layers when a message is sent from device A to device B. As the message travels from A to B, it may pass through many intermediate **nodes** (not shown). These intermediate nodes usually involve only the first three layers of the OSI model.

As the figure shows, before data are sent to the transmission media, they move down through the seven layers until they reach the physical layer. At each layer, control information is added to the data in the form of **headers** or **trailers.** Headers are added to the message at layers 7, 6, 5, 4, 3, and 2. A trailer is added at layer 2. At the receiving machine, the header or trailer is dropped in each layer as the data move toward the seventh layer.

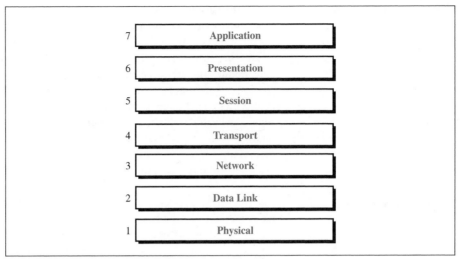

Figure 6.1 The OSI model

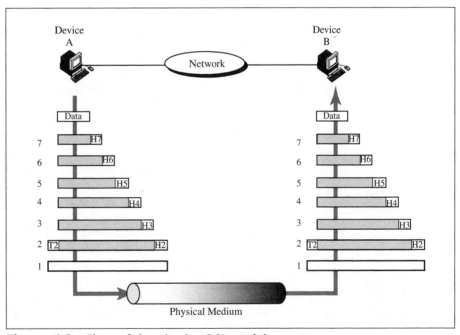

Figure 6.2 Flow of data in the OSI model

FUNCTIONS OF THE LAYERS

This section briefly describes the functions of each layer in the OSI model.

Physical Layer

The **physical layer** is responsible for transmitting a bit stream over a physical medium. It encodes and decodes bits into groups of bits. It then transforms a stream of bits into a signal. The mechanical and physical specifications of the physical devices are determined by the physical layer.

Data-Link Layer

The **data-link layer** organizes bits into logical units called **frames.** The frame contains information from the network layer. The data-link layer adds a header and trailer to define the frame for the receiving or intermediate stations. In particular, addressing information is added to the data, usually in the form of two addresses. This defines the addresses of two adjacent stations, one that sends and the other that receives. Note that the data-link layer is responsible only for **node-to-node delivery** of the frame (from one station to another). When a station receives a frame (not destined for itself), it changes the source address to its own address and the destination address to the address of the next station. The data-link layer is often responsible for error handling between two adjacent stations. Redundant data are added in the trailer to either correct or detect errors.

Network Layer

The data-link layer is responsible for node-to-node delivery of a frame between two adjacent stations; the **network layer** is responsible for delivery of a packet (the data unit handled by the network layer is called a *packet*) between the original source and final destination. To do this task, the network layer adds a header to the data unit coming from the upper layer that includes, among other things, a source address and a destination address. These addresses are often called logical addresses (or as you will see later, IP addresses) to distinguish them from physical addresses. For global communication, logical addresses should be unique. Note that when a packet moves from a source to a destination, the **physical address** (added at the data-link layer) changes from station to station, but the logical address remains unchanged from the source to the destination.

Transport Layer

The **transport layer** is responsible for **source-to-destination** (end-to-end) **delivery** of the entire message. Note the difference in the responsibility between the network layer and the transport layer. The network layer is responsible for end-to-end delivery of individual packets. The transport layer, in constrast, is responsible for end-to-end delivery of the whole message. A message can be made of one or more packets. The transport layer is responsible for breaking the entire message into several packets and delivering them to the network layer. The network layer sends the packets out one by one, each one independent of the other. Some packets may arrive out of order at the destination. Other packets may be lost. The transport layer is responsible for ensuring that the whole message is transmitted from the source to destination. If packets are lost, they must be retransmitted. If packets arrive out of order, they must be reorganized. In summary, the transport layer sees the message as an integral entity that must be delivered to the transport layer at the destination.

Session Layer

The **session layer** is designed to control the dialog between users. It establishes, maintains, and synchronizes the dialog between communicating systems. It also adds what are called **synchronization points** for backup delivery in case of system or network failure. The synchronization points divide a long message into smaller ones and ensure that each section is received and acknowledged by the receiver. In this case, if the system or network fails, the sender does not have to resend the entire message. The sender can move to the last synchronization point and resend the message from that point. Most network implementations today do not use a separate session layer. If the services of a session layer are needed, they are usually included in the application layer.

Presentation Layer

The **presentation layer** is concerned with the syntax (format) and semantics (meaning) of the information exchanged between two systems. It deals with the fact that different systems use different coding methods (e.g., ASCII and Unicode). It compresses and decompresses data for efficiency. It encrypts and decrypts data for security (see Chapter 16). As with the case of the session layer, most implementations do not use a presentation layer today. This does not mean that functions defined for the presentation layer are not needed; it simply means that networks today have assigned these responsibilities to other layers. For example, encryption/decryption is done both at the network layer and application layer.

Application Layer

The **application layer** enables the user, whether human or software, to access the network. It defines common applications that can be implemented to make the job of the user simpler. We discuss some of these applications in the section on the Internet later in this chapter.

6.3 CATEGORIES OF NETWORKS

Now that you have a model for communication, we can divide the networks into three broad categories: local area networks (LANs), metropolitan area networks (MANs), and wide area networks (WANs) (Figure 6.3).

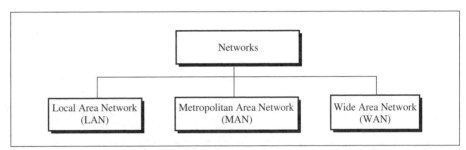

Figure 6.3 Categories of networks

LOCAL AREA NETWORK (LAN)

A **local area network (LAN)** is designed to allow resource sharing (hardware, software, and data) between computers. A LAN can be simply defined as a combination of computers and peripheral devices (e.g., printers) connected through a transmission medium (e.g., cable). Figure 6.4 shows three examples of LANs.

The first LAN in the figure uses a **bus topology** in which computers are connected through a common medium called a bus. In this configuration, when a station sends a frame to another computer, all computers receive the frame and check its destination address. If the destination address in the frame header matches the physical address of the station, the frame is accepted and the data contained in the frame are processed; otherwise, the frame is discarded. One important issue in this type of **topology** is the removal of the frame. A bus topology uses cable terminators that are designed to electronically kill the signal they receive. If the cable terminators are not functioning, the signal will bounce back and forth between two ends to be received by each station again and again; this is an undesirable situation.

The second LAN in the figure uses a **star topology** in which computers are connected via a hub (a device that facilitates connection) or a switch (a sophisticated hub that controls the forwarding of the frame). When a hub is used, the LAN acts logically

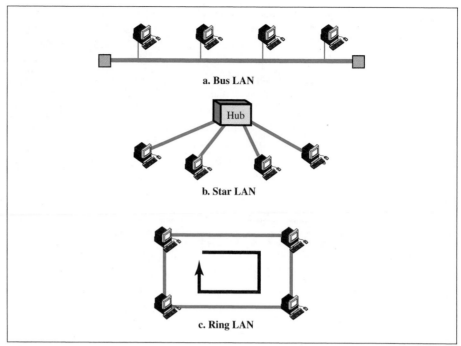

Figure 6.4 LANs

like a bus. The hub just sends data out of all its interfaces. When a switch is used, the address in the frame is checked by the switch, and the frame is sent out only through the interface of the destination. In a star topology, each station that receives a frame is responsible for removing the frame from the network.

The third LAN uses a **ring topology.** In this topology, when a computer needs to send a frame to another computer, it sends it to its neighbor. Here the frame is regenerated and sent to the next neighbor until it reaches the final destination. The destination opens the frame, copies the data, and either removes the frame from the ring or adds an acknowledgment and sends the frame (via the ring) back to the original sender. In the latter case, the frame is then removed by the sender.

LANs installed in the past were configured in any of the foregoing topologies, but the dominant topology today is the star.

METROPOLITAN AREA NETWORK (MAN)

A **metropolitan area network (MAN)** uses services provided by a common carrier (network service provider) such as a telephone company. It spans a city or a town and provides services to individual users or organizations. Individual users can connect their computers to the network, and organizations can connect their LANs to the network (Figure 6.5). Many telephone companies provide a popular MAN service called Switched Multimegabit Data Services (SMDS).

WIDE AREA NETWORK (WAN)

A **wide area network (WAN)** is the connection of individual computers or LANs over a large area (state, country, world). WANs, like MANs, are installed and run by common carriers (Figure 6.6). Note that a person using a telephone line to connect to an Internet service provider (ISP) is using a WAN. The ISP negotiates fees directly with the telephone company for services and receives payment from its customers (Internet users).

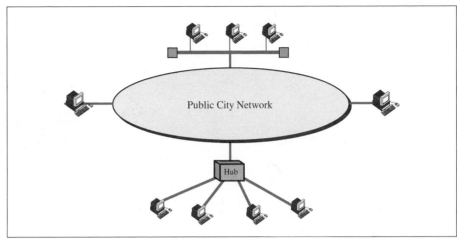

Figure 6.5 MAN

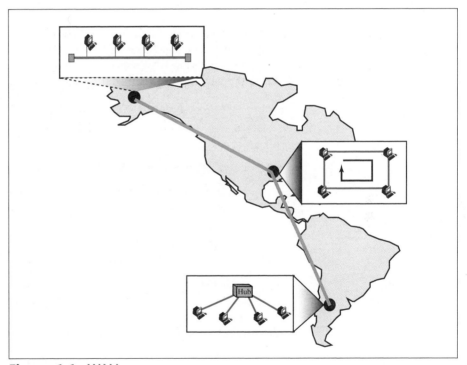

Figure 6.6 WAN

6.4 CONNECTING DEVICES

The three network types just presented can be connected using **connecting devices.** The interconnection of networks makes global communication from one side of the world to the other possible. Connecting devices can be divided into four types based on their functionality as related to the layers in the OSI model: repeaters, bridges, routers, and gateways. Repeaters and bridges typically connect devices in a network. Routers and gateways typically connect networks into internetworks (Figure 6.7).

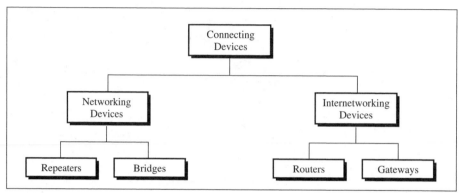

Figure 6.7   Connecting devices

REPEATERS

A **repeater** is an electronic device that regenerates data. It extends the physical length of a network. As a signal is transmitted, it may lose strength, and a weak signal may be interpreted erroneously by a receiver. A repeater can regenerate the signal and send it to the rest of the network. Figure 6.8 shows a network with and without a repeater.

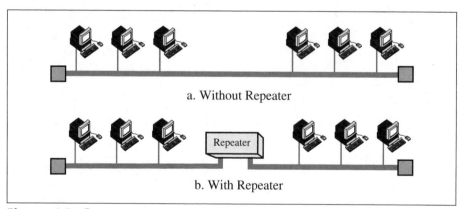

Figure 6.8   Repeater

Repeaters operate only in the physical layer of the OSI model. They do not recognize physical or logical addresses. They simply regenerate every signal they receive. Repeaters, popular when the dominant topology was the bus topology, often connected two buses to increase the length of the network.

Repeaters operate at the first layer of the OSI model.

BRIDGES

When a network uses a bus topology, the medium is shared between all stations. In other words, when a station sends a frame, the common bus is occupied by this one station, and no other station is allowed to send a frame (if it does, the two frames collide). This implies a degradation of performance. Stations need to wait until the bus is free. This is similar to an airport that has only one runway. When the runway is used by one aircraft, the other aircraft ready for takeoff must wait.

A **bridge** is a traffic controller. It can divide a long bus into smaller segments so that each segment is independent trafficwise. A bridge installed between two segments can pass or block frames based on the destination address in the frame. If a frame originates in one segment and the destination is in the same segment, there is no reason for the frame to pass the bridge and go to the other segments. The bridge uses a table to decide if the frame needs to be forwarded to another segment. With a bridge, two or more pairs of stations can communicate at the same time (Figure 6.9).

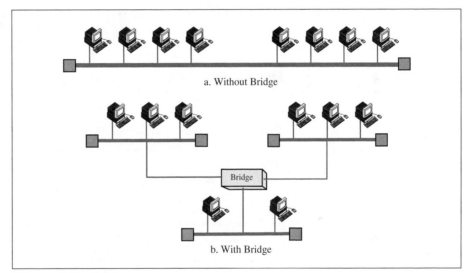

a. Without Bridge

Bridge

b. With Bridge

Figure 6.9 Bridge

In addition to its traffic controlling duties, a bridge also functions as a repeater by regenerating the frame. As discussed previously, this means that a bridge operates at the physical layer. But because a bridge needs to interpret the address embedded in the frame to make filtering decisions, it also operates at the data-link layer of the OSI model.

> Bridges operate at the first two layers of the OSI model.

In recent years, the need for better performance has led to the design of a new device referred to as a second-layer **switch,** which is simply a sophisticated bridge with multiple interfaces. For example, a network with 20 stations can be divided into four segments using a four-interface bridge. Or the same network can be divided into 20 segments (with one station per segment) using a 20-interface switch. A switch in this case increases performance; a station that needs to send a frame sends it directly to the switch. The media are not shared; each station is directly connected to the switch (Figure 6.10).

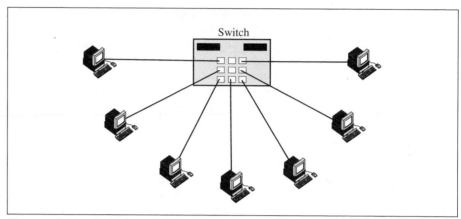

Figure 6.10   Switch

ROUTERS

Routers are devices that connect LANs, MANs, and WANs. A router operates at the third layer of the OSI model. Whereas a bridge filters a frame based on the physical (data-link layer) address of the frame, a router routes a packet based on the logical (network layer) address of the packet.

> Routers operate at the first three layers of the OSI model.

Whereas a bridge may connect two segments of a LAN or two LANs belonging to the same organization, a router can connect two independent networks: a LAN to a WAN, a LAN to a MAN, a WAN to another WAN, and so on. The result is an internetwork (or an internet). You will see shortly that the Internet (the unique global internet) that connects the whole world together is an example of an internetwork where many networks are connected together through routers. Figure 6.11 shows an example of an internetwork.

GATEWAYS

Traditionally, a **gateway** is a connecting device that acts as a protocol converter. It allows two networks, each with a different set of protocols for all seven OSI layers, to be connected to each other and communicate. A gateway is usually a computer installed with the necessary software. The gateway understands the protocols used by each connected network and is therefore able to translate from one to another. For example, a gateway can connect a network using the AppleTalk protocol to a network using the Novell Netware protocol.

Today, however, the term *gateway* is used interchangeably with the term *router*. Some people refer to the gateway as a router, and others refer to a router as a gateway. The distinction between the two terms is disappearing.

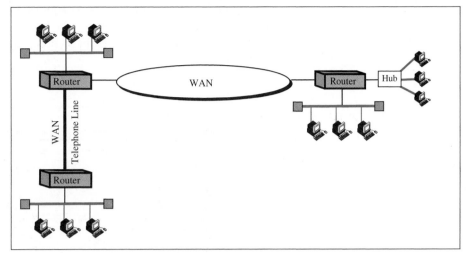

Figure 6.11   Routers in an internet

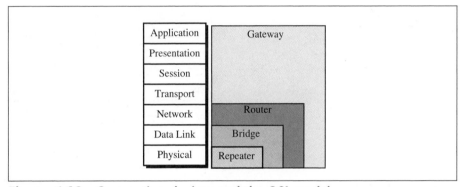

Figure 6.12   Connecting devices and the OSI model

**OSI MODEL
AND CONNECTING
DEVICES**

Figure 6.12 presents the relationship between the connecting devices and the OSI model.

6.5   THE INTERNET AND TCP/IP

As mentioned earlier, you can connect individual LANs, MANs, and WANs (using routers or gateways) to form a network of networks, called an **internetwork,** or an internet. Today, there are many private and public internets. However, the most famous is the **Internet** (with an uppercase I). The Internet was originally a research internetwork designed to connect several different heterogeneous networks. It was sponsored by the Defense Advanced Research Projects Agency (DARPA). Today, however, the Internet is an internetwork that connects millions of computers throughout the world.

The **Transmission Control Protocol/Internet Protocol (TCP/IP)** is a suite or a stack of protocols that officially controls the Internet. TCP/IP was developed before the OSI model. Therefore, the layers in the TCP/IP protocol do not exactly match those in the OSI model (Figure 6.13).

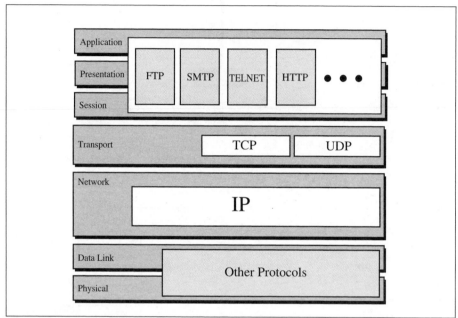

Figure 6.13   TCP/IP and OSI model

PHYSICAL AND DATA-LINK LAYERS

At the physical and data-link layers, TCP/IP does not define any specific protocol. It supports all of the standard and proprietary protocols.

NETWORK LAYER

At the network layer (or more accurately, the internetwork layer or the internet layer), TCP/IP supports the **Internet Protocol (IP).** IP is an unreliable protocol and a best-effort delivery service. The term *best-effort* means that IP provides no error checking or tracking. The data unit at the IP layer is called an **IP datagram,** an independent packet that travels from the source to the destination. **Datagrams** belonging to the same message or different messages may travel along different routes and may arrive out of sequence or duplicated. IP does not keep track of the routes and has no facility for reordering datagrams once they arrive.

Addressing

TCP/IP requires that every computer connected to the Internet be identified by a unique international address. This address is sometimes referred to as the Internet address, or **IP address.**

Each **Internet address** consists of 4 bytes (32 bits). To make the 32-bit form shorter and easier to read, Internet addresses are usually written in decimal form with decimal points separating the bytes: **dotted-decimal notation.** Figure 6.14 shows the bit pattern and decimal format of a possible address.

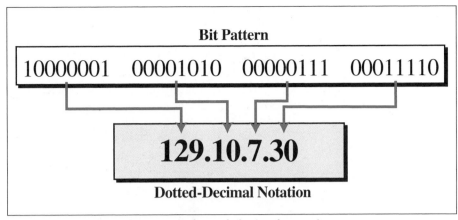

Figure 6.14 IP addresses in dotted-decimal notation

TRANSPORT LAYER

At the transport layer, TCP/IP defines two protocols: **Transmission Control Protocol (TCP)** and **User Datagram Protocol (UDP).** The User Datagram Protocol is the simpler of the two. It is an end-to-end transport level protocol that provides only the basic necessities for end-to-end delivery of a transmission.

The Transmission Control Protocol provides full transport layer services to applications. TCP is a reliable transport protocol. It divides a message into a sequence of segments that are numbered sequentially. If one segment is lost, it is sent again. If a segment is received out of order, it is ordered with the help of the sequence numbering mechanism.

APPLICATION LAYER

The TCP/IP application layer is equivalent to the combined session, presentation, and application layers of the OSI model. This means that all of the functionalities associated with those three layers are handled in one single layer, the application layer.

Communication on the Internet uses the **client-server model** (Figure 6.15). A **client,** an application program running on a local machine, requests a service from a **server,** an application program running on a remote machine. Usually, the server program is always running, and the client program runs only when needed.

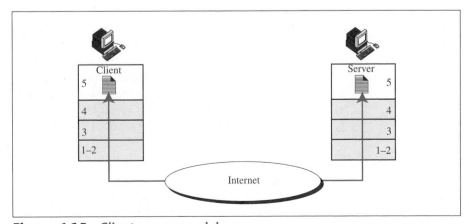

Figure 6.15 Client-server model

File Transfer Protocol (FTP)

The standard protocol on the Internet for transferring a file from one machine to another is the **File Transfer Protocol (FTP).** FTP was designed to respond to traditional problems related to file transfer. One problem is the different coding systems in use; one machine may use ASCII, and the other may use Unicode. Another problem is the different file formats in use. FTP was designed to resolve these problems.

FTP establishes two connections between the communicating computers: one for data transfer and the other for control information (commands and responses). The control connection is present during the entire FTP session; the data connection is present only when there are data to be transferred (Figure 6.16).

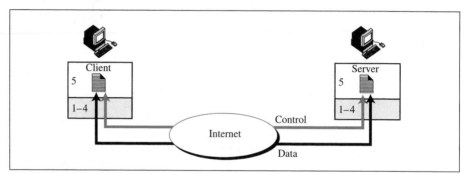

Figure 6.16   FTP

Simple Mail Transfer Protocol (SMTP)

By far the most popular application on the Internet today is **electronic mail (email).** The protocol that supports email on the Internet is **Simple Mail Transfer Protocol (SMTP)** (Figure 6.17). Email service by nature is different from other applications. To send and receive email, the user must install both client and server SMTP software on a computer. In addition, SMTP must always be running to receive email. A machine that is turned off will not receive email. To solve this problem, SMTP is often used with another protocol such as **Post Office Protocol (POP).** The user still uses the SMTP client to send email messages. However, email messages are not received directly but instead go to another computer (which is running all the time). The SMTP server is running on this computer and receives the messages and stores them in the user's mailbox (a special file). When the user wants to retrieve email, he or she uses the POP client to contact the POP server (on the same computer that is running the SMTP server) and downloads the email. There is normally a user interface called the user agent (UA) that facilitates these transactions.

Addresses   SMTP uses a unique addressing system that consists of two parts: a *local part* and a *domain name* separated by an @ sign (Figure 6.18). The local part defines the name of a special file, called the user mailbox, where all the mail received for a user is stored for retrieval by the user agent. The domain name defines the computer (often symbolically) that serves as the SMTP server.

TELNET

FTP and SMTP provide specific services for the user. FTP is used for transferring files; SMTP is used for sending email. There are other services that a user needs on the Internet. For example, students taking a programming course need to access a computer in the university lab to do the programming. They need to create a program, compile the program, and run the program (see Chapter 9). All of these tasks must be done remotely.

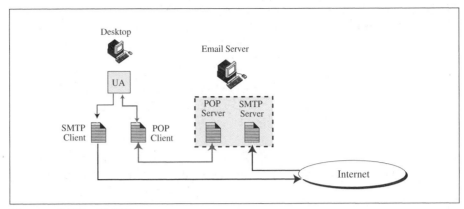

Figure 6.17   SMTP

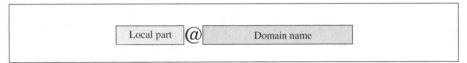

Figure 6.18   Email address

But there is no client-server program on the Internet called "creating a program" or "compiling a program" or "running a program". Today, there are many different tasks a user needs to do on a remote computer. There is no way to have a specific client-server program for each task.

The solution is a general-purpose client-server program that allows a user to run an application program on a remote computer as though the user is accessing that computer locally. When a user goes to a computer lab and directly accesses a computer, it is called **local login.** On the other hand, when the user stays at home and accesses the same computer remotely, it is called **remote login.**

TELNET (TErminaL NETwork) is a general client-server program on the Internet that allows remote login. TELNET enables the establishment of a connection from a local system to a remote system in such a way that the local terminal appears to be a terminal at the remote system (Figure 6.19).

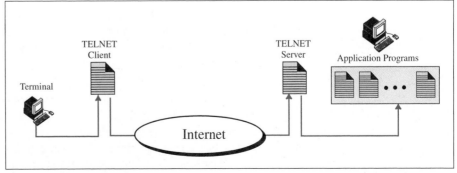

Figure 6.19   TELNET

Hypertext Transfer Protocol (HTTP)

Hypertext Transfer Protocol (HTTP) is a client-server program that is used to access and transfer documents on the World Wide Web. Although it transfers data in the form of plain text, hypertext, audio, video, and so on, it is particularly designed to transfer hypertext documents (see the next section).

A client HTTP sends a request to the server. The server sends the response to the client. The commands from the client to the server are embedded in a letterlike request message. The contents of the requested file or other information is embedded in a letterlike response message.

Uniform Resource Locator (URL)   HTTP uses a special kind of addressing called the **Uniform Resource Locator (URL),** which is a standard for specifying any kind of information on the Internet. The URL defines four things: method, host computer, port, and path (Figure 6.20).

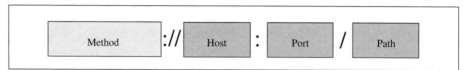

Figure 6.20   URL

The *method* is the client-server program used for transferring the documents, HTTP in this case (the URL can be used by other application programs). The *host* is the computer where the information is located, although the name of the computer can be an alias. Web pages are usually stored in computers, and computers are given alias names that usually begin with the characters "www."

The *port,* which defines the port number of the server, is optional. The *path* is the pathname of the file where the information is located. Note that the path can itself contain slashes that, in the UNIX operating system, separate the directories from the subdirectories and files.

World Wide Web (WWW)

The **World Wide Web (WWW),** or the **Web,** is based on the idea of distributed information. Instead of holding all information in one place, each entity (individual or organization) that has information to share stores that information on its own computer and allows Internet users to access it. The WWW is a collection of multimedia documents.

Hypertext   The WWW uses the concept of hypertext, which is a document containing special text, words, and phrases that can create a link to other documents containing text, images, audio, or video. A document of hypertext available on the Web is called a *page*. The main page for an organization or an individual is known as a **home page.**

Browser   To access a page on the WWW, one needs a **browser** that usually consists of three parts: a controller, a method, and an interpreter (Figure 6.21). The controller is the heart of the browser; it coordinates all activities. The method is a client application program that retrieves the document. Although it can be any of the application programs we have discussed, it is usually HTTP. The interpreter displays the document on the screen.

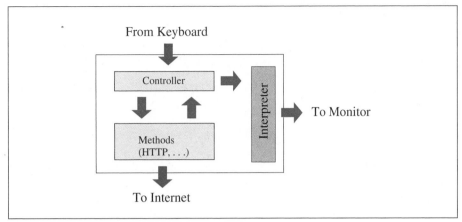

Figure 6.21   Browser

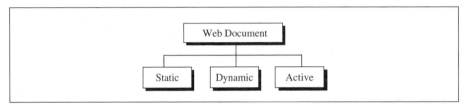

Figure 6.22   Categories of Web documents

Document Types   Generally, there are three different types of documents on the Internet: static, dynamic, and active (Figure 6.22).

■ **Static documents** have fixed contents. They are created at the server site and can only be copied. The static document normally uses Hypertext Markup Language (HTML) for screen formatting and links in the document. We discuss HTML in Chapter 9.

■ **Dynamic documents** are programs residing at the server site. When a browser sends a request, the server runs the program and sends the result (not the program itself) to the browser. For example, the browser can request the server to run the date program and send the result of the program to the client. Dynamic documents use a technology called Common Gateway Interface (CGI) that includes programming languages such as Perl (see Chapter 9) and HTML to handle the document creation and interpretation.

■ **Active documents** are also programs, but they cannot be run at the server site. Instead, the browser needs to request the transfer of the program. After transfer, it is run at the browser site. The difference between a dynamic document and an active document is that the former is run at the server site with the result transferred to the browser, and the latter is first transferred to the browser site and then run. An active document is needed when the program cannot be run at the server site. For example, when a program involves animation, it needs to be run at the browser site. An active document is usually written in the Java language (see Chapter 9). The browser needs a Java interpreter to interpret (run) an active document.

6.6 KEY TERMS

active document

application layer

bridge

browser

bus topology

client

client-server model

computer network

connecting devices

data-link layer

datagram

dotted-decimal notation

dynamic document

electronic mail (email)

File Transfer Protocol (FTP)

frame

gateway

header

home page

Hypertext Markup Language (HTML)

Hypertext Transfer Protocol (HTTP)

Internet

Internet address

internetwork

Internet Protocol (IP)

IP address

IP datagram

local area network (LAN)

local login

metropolitan area network (MAN)

model

network layer

node

node-to-node delivery

Open Systems Interconnection (OSI)

physical address

physical layer

presentation layer

protocol

remote login

repeater

ring topology

router

segment

server

session layer

Simple Mail Transfer Protocol
    (SMTP)

source-to-destination delivery

star topology

static document

switch

synchronization point

TELNET (TErminaL NETwork)

topology

trailer

Transmission Control Protocol (TCP)

Transmission Control Protocol /
    Internet Protocol (TCP/IP)

transport layer

Uniform Resource Locator (URL)

User Datagram Protocol (UDP)

Web

wide area network (WAN)

World Wide Web (WWW)

6.7 SUMMARY

■ A computer network is a combination of devices connected by transmission media.

■ The Open Systems Interconnection (OSI) model is a theoretical model that shows how any two different systems can communicate with each other.

■ The seven layers of the OSI model are the physical layer, data-link layer, network layer, transport layer, session layer, presentation layer, and application layer.

■ A local area network (LAN) allows resource sharing (hardware, software, and data) between computers.

■ A LAN can be configured in a bus, ring, or star topology.

■ A metropolitan area network (MAN) uses the services provided by a common carrier.

■ A wide area network (WAN) is the connection of individual computers or LANs over a large area. WANs are installed and run by common carriers.

■ A repeater is a connecting device that regenerates data and extends the physical length of a network.

■ A bridge is a connecting device that filters traffic.

■ A router is a connecting device that routes packets.

■ A gateway allows two networks, each with a completely different protocol suite, to communicate.

■ An internetwork is two or more LANs, MANs, or WANs.

■ Transmission Control Protocol/Internet Protocol (TCP/IP) is the set of protocols used by the Internet, a worldwide internetwork of computers.

■ The Internet Protocol (IP) is TCP/IP's unreliable protocol at the internet layer.

■ An IP address identifies each computer connected to the Internet.

■ User Datagram Protocol (UDP) and Transmission Control Protocol (TCP) are TCP/IP's protocols at the transport layer.

■ File Transfer Protocol (FTP) is a TCP/IP client-server application for copying files from one host to another.

- The protocol that supports electronic mail (email) on the Internet is Simple Mail Transfer Protocol (SMTP).
- TELNET is a client-server application that allows a user to log on to a remote machine, giving the user access to the remote system.
- Hypertext Transfer Protocol (HTTP) is a client-server program for accessing and transferring documents on the World Wide Web (WWW), a collection of multimedia documents.

- The Uniform Resource Locator (URL) is a standard identifier for specifying information on the Internet.
- A browser is needed to access a page on the WWW.
- A document on the Internet can be classified as static, dynamic, or active.

6.8   PRACTICE SET

REVIEW QUESTIONS

1. What is the difference between a model and a protocol? Give an example of each.

2. Name the layers of the OSI model.

3. Name the layers of the TCP/IP protocol suite.

4. What is the function of each layer of the OSI model?

5. What is the difference between node-to-node delivery and source-to-destination delivery?

6. What is the difference between a frame and a packet?

7. What is the purpose of a synchronization point?

8. What are the three common topologies? Which is most popular today?

9. Name four types of connecting devices and their functions.

10. What's the difference between TCP and UDP?

11. Why are Internet addresses needed?

12. How does the application layer of TCP/IP differ from that of the OSI model?

13. What is the purpose of FTP?

14. What is the purpose of TELNET?

15. What is the purpose of SMTP?

16. What is the difference between local login and remote login?

17. Compare and contrast the three Internet document types.

MULTIPLE-CHOICE QUESTIONS

18. A _____ is a set of rules that controls the interaction of different devices in a network or internetwork.
    a. model
    b. protocol
    c. dialog
    d. synchronization point

19. The OSI model has _____ layers.
    a. five
    b. six
    c. seven
    d. any of the above

20. The _____ layer of the OSI model organizes bits into logical data units called frames.
    a. physical
    b. data-link
    c. network
    d. transport

21. The _____ layer of the OSI model enables a person to access the network.
    a. data-link
    b. transport
    c. application
    d. physical

22. The _____ layer of the OSI model compresses and decompresses data.
    a. physical
    b. data-link
    c. session
    d. presentation

23. The _____ layer of the OSI model encrypts data.
    a. physical
    b. data-link
    c. session
    d. presentation

24. The _____ layer of the OSI model transmits a bit stream over a physical medium.
    a. physical
    b. data-link
    c. network
    d. transport

25. The _____ layer of the OSI model is responsible for node-to-node delivery of a frame between two adjacent stations.
    a. transport
    b. network
    c. data-link
    d. session

26. The _____ layer of the OSI model is responsible for source-to-destination delivery of the entire message.
    a. transport
    b. network
    c. data-link
    d. session

27. The _____ layer of the OSI model is responsible for source-to-destination delivery of an individual packet.
    a. transport
    b. network
    c. data-link
    d. session

28. The _____ layer of the OSI model controls the dialog between users.
    a. transport
    b. session
    c. presentation
    d. application

29. Through the _____ layer of the OSI model, mail services and directory services are available to network users.
    a. data connection
    b. session
    c. transport
    d. application

30. Cindy's Dessert Heaven is a bakery with four outlets in San Francisco. The outlets need to communicate with each other. This type of network is probably a _____.
    a. LAN
    b. MAN
    c. WAN
    d. none of the above

31. Kate's Irish Potato Company is based in Ireland but has branches in Boston and San Francisco. The branches communicate with each other through a _____.
    a. LAN
    b. MAN
    c. WAN
    d. none of the above

32. Vecchiarelli Consultants occupies two adjacent rooms in the Coffland Building. The network, consisting of four workstations and a printer, is probably a _____.
    a. LAN
    b. MAN
    c. WAN
    d. none of the above

33. What is the domain name in the email address kayla@pit.arc.nasa.gov?
    a. kayla
    b. pit.arc.nasa.gov
    c. kayla@pit.arc.nasa.gov
    d. nasa.gov

34. Which topology uses a hub or switch?
    a. bus
    b. ring
    c. star
    d. all of the above

35. Which topology needs cable terminators?
    a. bus
    b. ring
    c. star
    d. all of the above

36. A _____ is a connecting device that only regenerates the signal.
    a. repeater
    b. bridge
    c. router
    d. gateway

37. A _____ is a connecting device that acts as a proto-col converter.
    a. repeater
    b. bridge
    c. router
    d. gateway

38. A _____ is a connecting device that segments traffic.
    a. repeater
    b. bridge
    c. router
    d. gateway

39. A _____ is a device that can route a packet based on its network layer address.
    a. bridge
    b. router
    c. repeater
    d. all of the above

40. A bridge operates at _____ of the OSI model.
    a. the first layer
    b. the first two layers
    c. the first three layers
    d. all layers

41. A gateway operates at _____ of the OSI model.
    a. the first layer
    b. the first two layers
    c. the first three layers
    d. all layers

42. The _____ layer of TCP/IP has functions similar to those of the application, presentation, and session lay-ers of the OSI model.
    a. transport
    b. network
    c. application
    d. session

43. The IP address is currently _____ bits in length.
    a. 4
    b. 8
    c. 32
    d. any of the above

44. The transport layer protocol of TCP/IP is called _____.
    a. TCP
    b. UDP
    c. IP
    d. a and b

45. _____ is a protocol for file transfer.
    a. FTP
    b. SMTP
    c. TELNET
    d. HTTP

46. _____ is a protocol for mail services.
    a. FTP
    b. SMTP
    c. TELNET
    d. HTTP

47. _____ is a protocol for accessing and transferring documents on the WWW.
    a. FTP
    b. SMTP
    c. TELNET
    d. HTTP

48. A _____ document has fixed contents.
    a. static
    b. dynamic
    c. active
    d. all of the above

EXERCISES

49. Which of the OSI layers is (are) involved in each of the following activities:
    a. sending a frame to the next station
    b. sending a packet from the source to the destination
    c. sending a long message from the source to the destination
    d. logging into a remote computer
    e. encrypting and decrypting data
    f. changing the data from the machine code to Unicode

50. A small part of a bus LAN with 200 stations is dam-aged. How many stations are affected by this damage?

51. A small part of a star LAN with 200 stations is dam-aged. How many stations are affected by this damage?

52. A small part of a ring LAN with 200 stations is dam-aged. How many stations are affected by this damage?

53. If you have a square room with a computer in each corner, which topology needs less cabling? Justify your answer.
    a. a bus LAN
    b. a ring LAN
    c. a star LAN with a hub at the center of the room

54. If you have a square room with a computer in each corner, which topology is more reliable? Justify your answer.

    a. a bus LAN

    b. a ring LAN

    c. a star LAN with a hub at the center of the room

55. An engineer notices that the data received by computers at the two ends of a bus LAN contain many errors. What do you think is the problem? What can be done to solve the problem?

56. An engineer notices a large amount of traffic on a long bus LAN. What can be done to alleviate the situation?

57. What is the advantage of having two transport protocols in the TCP/IP?

58. What are the advantages and disadvantages of having one application layer in the TCP/IP protocol suite instead of three layers (session, presentation, and application) as in the OSI model?

59. Change the following IP addresses from dotted-decimal notation to binary notation:

    a. 112.32.7.28

    b. 129.4.6.8

    c. 208.3.54.12

    d. 38.34.2.1

    e. 255.255.255.255

60. Change the following IP addresses from binary notation to dotted-decimal notation:

    a. 01111110 11110001 01100111 01111111

    b. 10111111 11011100 11100000 00000101

    c. 00011111 11110000 00111111 11011101

    d. 10001111 11110101 11000011 00011101

    e. 11110111 10010011 11100111 01011101

61. Explain the client-server model on the Internet. In which layer of the TCP/IP protocol suite is the model implemented?

62. Separate the local part and the domain name in the following email addresses:

    a. madeline@belle.gov

    b. lindsey@jasmine.com

    c. wuteh@hunan.int

    d. honoris@queen.org

63. Explain the difference between an email address and an IP address. Is there a one-to-one relationship between the two addresses?

64. Explain the difference between FTP and TELNET. When do you use FTP and when do you use TELNET?

65. A user uses a browser to download a game. What type of document is downloaded?

66. A user uses a browser to download a technical document. What type of document is downloaded?

67. Write a URL that uses HTTP. It accesses a file with the path/user/general in a computer with the alias name www.hadb.

Computer Software

III

7 Operating Systems

A computer is a system made of two major components: hardware and software. Computer hardware is the physical equipment. Software is the collection of programs that allows the hardware to do its job.

Computer **software** is divided into two broad categories: the operating system and application programs (Figure 7.1). The application programs use the computer hardware to solve users' problems. The operating system, on the other hand, controls the access of hardware by users.

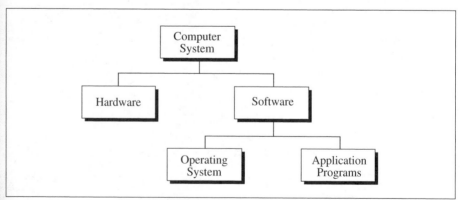

Figure 7.1 Computer system

7.1 DEFINITION

An **operating system** is so complex that it is difficult to give a simple universal definition. Instead, here are some common definitions:

- An operating system is an interface between the hardware of a computer and the user (programs or humans).
- An operating system is a **program** (or a set of programs) that facilitates the execution of other programs.
- An operating system acts as a general manager supervising the activity of each component in the computer system. As a general manager, the operating system checks that hardware and software resources are used efficiently, and when there is a conflict in using a resource, the operating system mediates to solve it.

> An operating system is an interface between the hardware of a computer and the user (programs or humans) that facilitates the execution of other programs and the access to hardware and software resources.

Two major design goals of an operating system are

1. Efficient use of hardware.
2. Easy to use resources.

7.2 EVOLUTION

Operating systems have gone through a long history of evolution, which we summarize next.

BATCH SYSTEMS

Batch operating systems were designed in the 1950s to control mainframe computers. At that time, a computer was a large machine using punched cards for input, line printers for output, and tape drives for secondary storage media.

Each program to be executed was called a **job.** A programmer who wished to execute a job sent a request to the operating room along with punched cards for the program and data. The programmer did not have any control or interaction with the system. The punched cards were processed by an operator. If the program was successful, the result was sent to the programmer; if not, a printout of the error was sent.

Operating systems during this era were very simple; they only ensured that all of the resources were transferred from one job to the next.

TIME-SHARING SYSTEMS

To use computer system resources efficiently, **multiprogramming** was introduced. The idea is to hold several jobs in memory and only assign a resource to a job that needs it on the condition that the resource is available. For example, when one program is using an input/output device, the CPU is free and can be used by another program. We discuss multiprogramming later in this chapter.

Multiprogramming brought the idea of **time sharing:** Resources can be shared between different jobs. Each job can be allocated a portion of time to use the resource. Because a computer is much faster than a human, time sharing is transparent to the user. Each user has the impression that the whole system is serving him or her.

Multiprogramming, and eventually time sharing, tremendously improved the efficiency of a computer system. However, it required a more complex operating system. The operating system now had to do **scheduling:** allocating the resources to different programs and deciding which program should use which resource when.

During this era, the relationship between a computer and a user also changed. The user could directly interact with the system without going through an operator. A new term was also coined: **process.** A job is a program to be run; a process is a program that is in memory and waiting for resources.

PERSONAL SYSTEMS

When personal computers were introduced, there was a need for an operating system for this type of computer. During this era, **single-user operating systems** such as DOS (disk operating system) were introduced.

PARALLEL SYSTEMS

The need for more speed and efficiency led to the design of **parallel systems:** multiple CPUs on the same machine. Each CPU can be used to serve one program or a part of a program, which means that many tasks can be accomplished in parallel instead of serially. The operating system for these systems is more complex than the ones with single CPUs.

DISTRIBUTED SYSTEMS

Networking and internetworking, as you saw in Chapter 6, have created a new dimension in operating systems. A job that was previously done all on one computer can now be shared between computers that may be thousands of miles apart. A program can be run partially on one computer and partially on another computer if they are connected through an internetwork such as the Internet. In addition, resources can be distributed. A program may need files located in different parts of the world. **Distributed systems** combine features of the previous generation with new duties such as controlling security.

7.3 COMPONENTS

Today, operating systems are very complex. An operating system needs to manage different resources in a computer system. It resembles an organization with several managers at the top level. Each manager is responsible for managing his or her department but also needs to cooperate with others and coordinate activities. A modern operating system has at least four duties: memory manager, process manager, device manager, and file manager. Like many organizations that have a department not necessarily under any manager, an operating system also has such a component, which is usually called a user interface or a shell. The user interface is responsible for communication outside the operating system (like a public relations department). Figure 7.2 shows the components of an operating system.

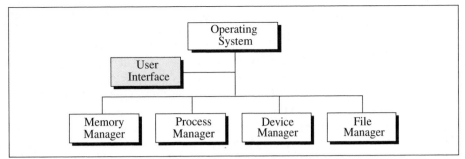

Figure 7.2 Components of an operating system

MEMORY MANAGER One of the responsibilities of a modern computer system is memory management. Although the memory size of computers has increased tremendously in recent years, so has the size of the programs and data to be processed. Memory allocation must be managed to prevent the "running out of memory" syndrome. Operating systems can be divided into two broad categories of memory management: monoprogramming and multiprogramming.

Monoprogramming **Monoprogramming** belongs to the past, but it is worth mentioning because it helps you to understand multiprogramming. In monoprogramming, most of the memory capacity is dedicated to one single program; only a small part is needed to hold the operating system. In this configuration, the whole program is in memory for execution. When the program finishes running, it is replaced by another program (Figure 7.3).

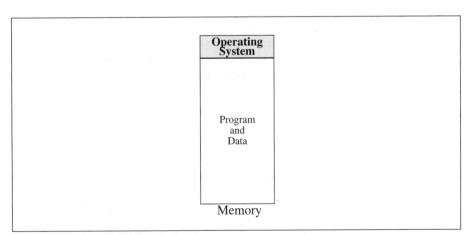

Figure 7.3 Monoprogramming

The job of the **memory manager** is straightforward here. It loads the program into memory, runs it, and replaces it with the next program. However, there are several problems with this technique:

■ The program must fit in memory. If the size of memory is less than the size of the program, the program cannot be run.

■ When one program is being run, no other program can be executed. A program, during its execution, often needs to receive data from input devices and needs to send data to output devices. The input/output devices are really slow compared with the CPU. So when the input/output operations are being carried out, the CPU is idle. It cannot serve another program because this program is not in memory. This is a very inefficient use of memory and CPU.

Multiprogramming

In multiprogramming, more than one program is in memory at the same time, and they are executed concurrently. The CPU switches between the programs. Figure 7.4 shows memory in a multiprogramming environment.

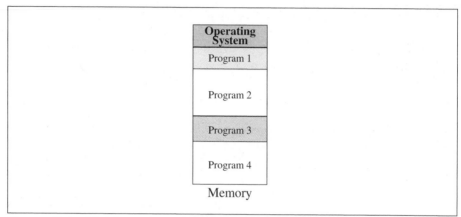

Figure 7.4   Multiprogramming

Since the 1960s, multiprogramming has gone through several improvements that can be seen in the taxonomy in Figure 7.5. We discuss each scheme very briefly in the next few sections. Two techniques belong to the nonswapping category. This means that the program remains in memory for the duration of execution. The other two techniques belong to the swapping category. This means that, during execution, the program can be swapped between memory and disk one or more times.

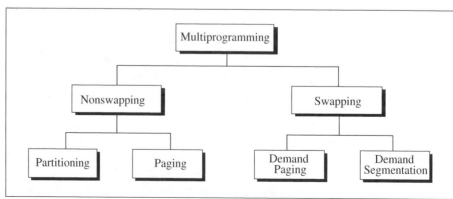

Figure 7.5   Categories of multiprogramming

Partitioning   The first technique used in multiprogramming is called **partitioning.** In this scheme, memory is divided into variable length sections. Each section or partition holds one program. The CPU switches between programs. It starts with one program. It executes some instructions until it either encounters an input/output operation or the time allocated for that program has expired. The CPU saves the address of the memory location where the last instruction was executed and moves to the next program. The same procedure is repeated with the second program. After all of the programs have been served, the CPU moves back to the first program. Of course, there can be priority levels in accessing the CPU (Figure 7.6).

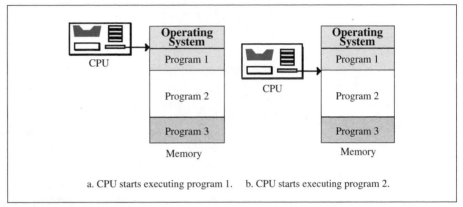

a. CPU starts executing program 1.   b. CPU starts executing program 2.

Figure 7.6   **Partitioning**

With this technique, each program is entirely in memory and occupying contiguous locations. Partitioning improves the efficiency of the CPU, but there are still some issues:

■ The size of the partitions has to be determined beforehand by the memory manager. If partition sizes are small, some programs cannot be loaded into memory. If partition sizes are large, there might be some holes (unused locations) in memory.

■ Even if partitioning is perfect when the computer is started, there may be some holes after programs are replaced by new ones.

■ When there are many holes, the memory manager can compact the partitions to remove the holes and create new partitions, but this creates extra overhead on the system.

Paging   **Paging** improves the efficiency of the partitioning. In paging, memory is divided into equally sized sections called **frames.** The program is divided into equally sized sections called **pages.** The size of a page and a frame is usually the same and equal to the size of the block used by the system to retrieve information from a storage device (Figure 7.7).

A page is loaded into a frame in memory. If a program has three pages, it occupies three frames in memory. With this technique, the program does not have to be contiguous in memory. Two consecutive pages can occupy noncontiguous frames in memory.

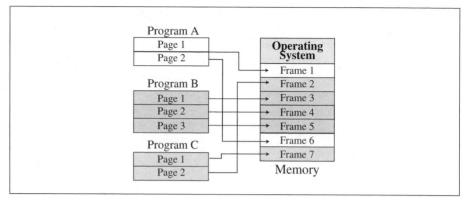

Figure 7.7   Paging

The advantage of paging over partitioning is that two programs, each using three non-contiguous frames, can be replaced by one program that needs six frames. There is no need for the new program to wait until six contiguous frames are free before being loaded into memory.

Paging improves efficiency to some extent, but the whole program still needs to be in memory before being executed. This means that a program that needs six frames cannot be loaded into memory if there are only four nonoccupied frames.

Demand Paging   Paging does not require that the program be in contiguous memory locations, but it does require that the entire program be in memory for execution. Demand paging has removed this last restriction. In **demand paging,** the program is divided into pages, but the pages can be loaded into memory one by one, executed, and replaced by another page. In other words, memory can hold one page from multiple programs at the same time. In addition, consecutive pages from the same program do not have to be loaded into the same frame. A page can be loaded into any free frame.

Demand Segmentation   A technique similar to paging is segmentation. In paging, a program is divided into equally sized pages, which is not the way a programmer thinks. A programmer thinks in terms of modules, not equally sized pages. As you will see in later chapters, a program is usually made of a main program and subprograms. In **demand segmentation,** the program is divided into segments that match the programmer's view. These are loaded into memory, executed, and replaced by another module from the same or a different program.

Demand Paging and Segmentation   **Demand paging and segmentation** can even be combined to further improve the efficiency of the system. A segment may be too large to fit any available free space in memory. Memory can be divided into frames, and a module can be divided into pages. The pages of a module can then be loaded into memory one by one and executed.

Virtual Memory

Demand paging and demand segmentation mean that part of the program is in main memory and part is on the disk when a program is being executed. This means that, for example, a memory size of 10 MB can execute 10 programs, each of size 3 MB, for a total of 30 MB. At any moment, 10 MB of the 10 programs are in memory and 20 MB are on disk. There is an actual memory size of 10 MB but a **virtual memory** size of 30 MB. Figure 7.8 shows the concept. Virtual memory, which implies demand paging, demand segmentation, or both, is used in almost all operating systems today.

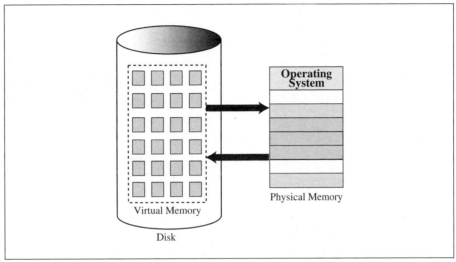

Figure 7.8 Virtual memory

PROCESS MANAGER

A second function of an operating system is process management, but before discussing this concept, we define some terms.

Program, Job, and Process

Modern operating systems use three terms that refer to a set of instructions: program, job, and process. Although the terminology is vague and varies from one operating system to another, we can define these terms informally.

Program   A program is a nonactive set of instructions written by a programmer and stored on disk (or tape). It may or may not become a job.

Job   A program becomes a job from the moment it is selected for execution until it has finished running and becomes a program again. During this duration, a job may or may not be executed. It may be residing on disk waiting to be loaded to memory, or it may be residing in memory waiting for execution by the CPU. It may be residing on disk or in memory waiting for an input/output event, or it may be residing in memory while being executed by the CPU. The program is a job in all of these situations. When a job has finished executing (either normally or abnormally), it becomes a program and once again resides on the disk. The operating system no longer governs the program. Note that every job is a program, but not every program is a job.

Process   A process is a program in execution. It is a program that has started but has not finished. In other words, a process is a job that is residing in memory. It has been selected among other waiting jobs and loaded into memory. A process may be executing at the moment or it may be waiting for CPU time. As long as the job is in memory, it is a process. Note that every process is a job, but not every job is a process.

State Diagram

The relationship between a program, a job, and a process becomes clearer if you consider how a program becomes a job and how a job becomes a process. This can be illustrated with a **state diagram** that shows the different states of each of these entities. Figure 7.9 is a state diagram using broken lines for the boundaries between a program, a job, and a process.

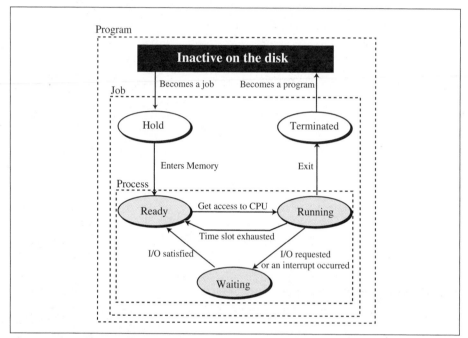

Figure 7.9 State diagram with the boundaries between a program, a job, and a process

A program becomes a job when selected by the operating system and brought to the **hold state.** It remains in this state until it can be loaded into memory. When there is memory space available to load the program totally or partially, the job moves to the **ready state.** It now becomes a process. It remains in memory and in this state until the CPU can execute it; it moves to the **running state** at this time. When in the running state, one of three things can happen:

■ The process executes until it needs I/O.

■ The process exhausts its allocated slot of time.

■ The process terminates.

In the first case, the process goes to the **waiting state** and waits until I/O is complete. In the second case, it goes directly to the ready state. In the third case, it goes to the **terminated state** and is no longer a process. A process can move between the running, waiting, and ready states multiple times before it goes to the terminated state. Note that the diagram can be much more complex if the system uses virtual memory and swaps programs in and out of main memory.

Schedulers

To move a job or process from one state to another, the **process manager** uses two schedulers: the job scheduler and the process scheduler.

Job Scheduler The **job scheduler** moves a job from the hold state to the ready state or from the running state to the terminated state. In other words, a job scheduler is responsible for creating a process from a job and terminating a process. Figure 7.10 shows the job scheduler with respect to a state diagram.

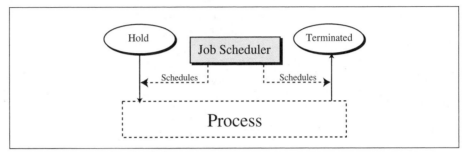

Figure 7.10 Job scheduler

Process Scheduler The **process scheduler** moves a process from one state to another. It moves a process from the running state to the waiting state when the process is waiting for some event to happen. It moves a process from the running state to the ready state if the time allotment has expired. It moves the process from the waiting state to the ready state when the event has occurred. When the CPU is ready to run the process, the process scheduler moves the process from the ready state to the running state. Figure 7.11 shows the process scheduler with respect to a state diagram.

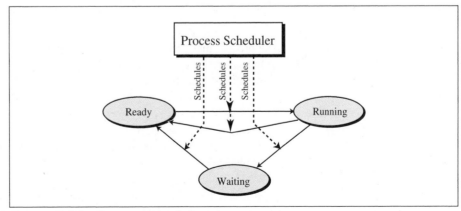

Figure 7.11 Process scheduler

Other Schedulers Some operating systems use other types of schedulers to make switching between processes more efficient.

Queuing

Our state diagram shows one job or process moving from one state to another. In reality, there are many jobs and many processes competing with each other for computer resources. For example, when some jobs are in memory, others must wait until space is available. Or when a process is running using the CPU, others must wait until the CPU is free. To handle multiple processes and jobs, the process manager uses **queues** (waiting lists). Associated with each job or process is a *job control block* or *process control block* that stores information about that job or process. The process manager stores the job or process control block in the queues instead of the job or process itself. The job or process remains in memory or disk; it is too big to be duplicated in a queue. The job control block or process control block is the representative of the waiting job or process.

An operating system can have several queues. For example, Figure 7.12 shows the circulation of jobs and processes through three queues: the job queue, the ready queue, and the I/O queue. The job queue holds the jobs that are waiting for memory. The ready queue holds the processes that are in memory, ready to be run, and waiting for the CPU. The I/O queue holds the processes that are waiting for an I/O device (there can be several I/O queues, one for each input/output device, but we show only one for simplicity).

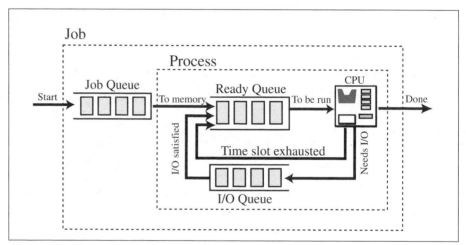

Figure 7.12 Queues for process management

The process manager can have different policies for selecting the next job or process from a queue; it could be first in, first out (FIFO), shortest length first, the one with highest priority, and so on.

Process Synchronization

The whole idea behind process management is to synchronize different processes with different resources. Whenever resources can be used by more than one user (processes in this case), you can have two situations: deadlock and starvation. A brief discussion of these two situations follows.

Deadlock   Instead of a formal definition of **deadlock,** we give an example. Assume that there are two processes called A and B. Process A is holding a file called File1 (File1 is assigned to A) and cannot release it until it has another file called File2 (A has requested File2). Process B is holding File2 (File2 is assigned to B) and cannot release it until it has File1 (B has requested File1). The files in most systems are not sharable; when used by one process, the file cannot be used by another process. If there is no provision in this situation to force a process to release a file, deadlock is created (Figure 7.13).

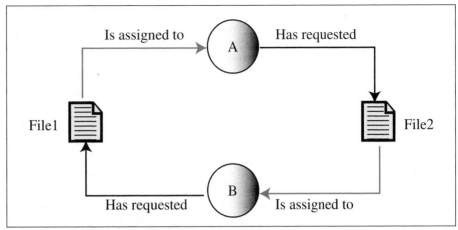

Figure 7.13 Deadlock

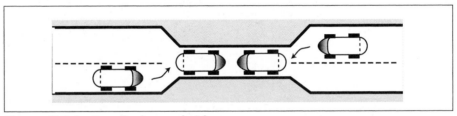

Figure 7.14 Deadlock on a bridge

As an analogy, Figure 7.14 shows deadlock on a narrow bridge. The situation is similar because the resource (part of the bridge) is held by a vehicle that does not release it until it gets the other part of the bridge, which is held by the other vehicle, and vice versa.

Deadlock occurs if the operating system allows a process to start running without first checking to see if the required resources are ready and allows the process to hold it as long as it wants. There should be some provision in the system to prevent deadlock. One solution is not to allow a process to start running until the resources are free, but you will see later that this creates another problem. The second solution is to limit the time a process can hold a resource.

> Deadlock occurs when the operating system does not put resource restrictions on processes.

Deadlock does not always occur. There are four necessary conditions for deadlock: *mutual exclusion* (only one process can hold a resource), *resource holding* (a process holds a resource even though it cannot use it until other resources are available), *no preemption* (the operating system cannot temporarily reallocate a resource), and *circular waiting* (all processes and resources involved form a loop, as in Figure 7.13). All four conditions are required for deadlock to occur. However, these conditions are only necessary conditions (not sufficient), which means that they must be present for deadlock, but they might not be enough. In other words, if one of these conditions is missing, deadlock never occurs. This gives you a method for preventing or avoiding deadlock: Do not allow one of these conditions to happen.

Starvation **Starvation** is the opposite of deadlock. It can happen when the operating system puts too many resource restrictions on a process. For example, imagine an operating system that specifies possession of all the required resources before a process can be run. In Figure 7.15, imagine process A needs two files, File1 and File2. File1 is being used by process B and File2 is being used by process E. Process B terminates first and releases File1. Process A cannot be started because File2 is still not available. At this moment, process C, which needs only File1, is allowed to run. Now process E terminates and releases File2, but process A still cannot run because File1 is unavailable.

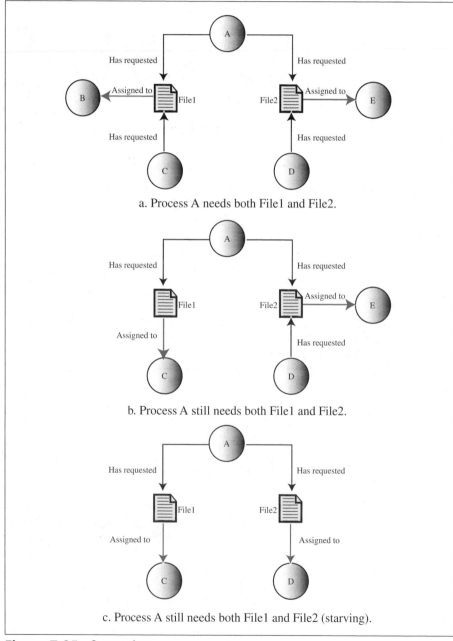

a. Process A needs both File1 and File2.

b. Process A still needs both File1 and File2.

c. Process A still needs both File1 and File2 (starving).

Figure 7.15 Starvation

Figure 7.16 Dining philosophers

A classic starvation problem is the one introduced by Dijkstra. Five philosophers are sitting at a round table (Figure 7.16). Each philosopher needs two chopsticks to eat a bowl of rice. However, one or both chopsticks could be used by a neighbor. A philosopher could "starve" if two chopsticks are not available at the same time.

DEVICE MANAGER

The **device manager,** or input/output manager, is responsible for access to input/output devices. There are limitations on the number and speed of input/output devices in a computer system. Because these devices are slower in speed compared with the CPU and memory, when a process accesses an input/output device, it is not available to other processes for a period of time. The device manager is responsible for the efficient use of input/output devices.

A detailed discussion of the device manager requires advanced knowledge of operating system principles and is beyond the scope of this book. However, we can briefly list the responsibilities of a device manager:

■ The device manager monitors every input/output device constantly to assure that the device is functioning properly. The manager also needs to know when a device has finished serving one process and is ready to serve the next process in the queue.

■ The manager maintains a queue for each input/output device or one or more queues for similar input/output devices. For example, if there are two fast printers in the system, the manager can have one queue for each or one queue for both.

■ The manager controls the different policies for accessing input/output devices. For example, it may use FIFO for one device and shortest length first for another.

FILE MANAGER

An operating system today uses a **file manager** to control access to the files. A detailed discussion of the file manager also requires advanced knowledge of operating system principles and file access concepts that are beyond the scope of this book. We discuss some issues related to file access in Chapter 13, but this is not adequate to understand the actual operation of a file manager. Here is a brief list of the responsibilities of a file manager:

■ The file manager controls access to files. Access is permitted only by those that are allowed, and the type of access can vary. For example, a process (or a user that calls a process) may be allowed to read a file but is not allowed to write (change). Another process may be allowed to execute a file but is not allowed even to look at the contents.

- The file manager supervises the creation, deletion, and modification of files.
- The file manager can control the naming of files.
- The file manager supervises the storage of files: how they are stored, where they are stored, and so on.
- The file manager is responsible for archiving and backups.

USER INTERFACE

Each operating system has a **user interface,** which is a program that accepts requests from users (processes) and interprets them for the rest of the operating system. A user interface in some operating systems, such as UNIX, is called a **shell.** In some others, it is called a **window** to denote that it is menu driven and has a GUI (graphical user interface) component.

7.4 POPULAR OPERATING SYSTEMS

In this section, we introduce some popular operating systems as a motivation for further study. We have chosen three operating systems that are familiar to most computer users.

WINDOWS 2000

Windows 2000 (from Microsoft) is a good example of an operating system that has gone a long way in its evolution. It started as an interface to be run with DOS (disk operating system). Now it is a complex menu-driven operating system that includes a full-fledged GUI. It uses virtual memory that allows multiprogramming. It has an integral networking capability that makes it a networking operating system. Windows 2000 also includes a security feature that makes it suitable for situations where security is an issue.

UNIX

UNIX is a popular operating system among computer programmers and computer scientists. It is a very powerful operating system with three outstanding features. First, UNIX is a portable operating system that can be moved from one platform to another without many changes. The reason is that it is written mostly in the C language (instead of a machine language for a specific system). Second, UNIX has a powerful set of utilities (commands) that can be combined (in an executable file called a *script*) to solve many problems that require programming in other operating systems. Third, it is device independent because it includes the device drivers in the operating system itself, which means that it can be easily configured to run any device. In summary, UNIX has every feature that a powerful operating system has, including multiprogramming, virtual memory, and very well-designed file and directory systems. The only criticism heard often about UNIX is that its commands are short and esoteric for normal users; in fact, it is very convenient for programmers who need short commands.

LINUX

Linux, which was developed by Linus Torvalds in Finland, is based on UNIX. As a matter of fact, it is so close to UNIX that some people call it a UNIX clone. The whole idea was to make UNIX more efficient when run on an Intel microprocessor. Linux is now available for every platform and becoming more and more popular both among programmers and commercial users.

7.5   KEY TERMS

batch operating system
deadlock
demand paging
demand paging and segmentation
demand segmentation
device manager
distributed system
file manager
frame
hold state
job
job scheduler
Linux
memory manager

monoprogramming
multiprogramming
operating system
page
paging
parallel system
partitioning
process
process manager
process scheduler
process synchronization
program
queue
ready state

running state
multiprogramming
scheduling
single-user operating system
software
starvation
state diagram
terminated state
time sharing
UNIX
user interface
virtual memory
waiting state

7.6   SUMMARY

■ An operating system facilitates the execution of other software, acts as the general manager of a computer system, and ensures the efficient use of hardware and software resources.

■ The evolution of operating systems has included batch operating systems, time-sharing systems, single-user operating systems, parallel systems, and distributed systems.

■ The operating system oversees the memory manager, the process manager, the device manager, the file manager, and the user interface.

■ In monoprogramming, most of memory capacity is dedicated to one single program.

■ In multiprogramming, more than one program is in memory at the same time.

■ In partitioning, memory is divided into variable length sections, each of which holds one program.

■ In paging, memory is divided into equally sized sections called frames and the program is divided into equally sized sections called pages. Pages of a program need not be contiguous, but all pages must be present in memory for execution.

■ Demand paging is similar to paging except that all pages need not be in memory.

■ Demand segmentation is similar to paging except that, instead of equally sized sections, the program is divided to match the program divisions.

■ Demand paging and demand segmentation can be combined to further improve the efficiency of a computer system.

■ The sum of the sizes of all the programs in memory is virtual memory.

■ A program is a nonactive set of instructions written by a programmer and stored on disk or tape.

■ A job is a program that is selected for execution.

■ A process is a job residing in memory.

■ A state diagram shows the relationship between a program, job, and process. A job can be in the hold, terminated, ready, running, or waiting state. A process can be in one of the latter three states.

■ The job scheduler creates a process from a job and changes a process back to a job.

■ The process scheduler moves a process from one state to another.

■ Jobs and processes wait in queues.

■ Deadlock is a situation in which a process is unable to execute due to unrestricted use of resources by other processes.

- Starvation is a situation in which a process is unable to execute due to too many restrictions on resources.
- The device manager controls access to I/O devices.
- The file manager controls access to files.
- The user interface is software that accepts requests from processes and interprets them for the rest of the operating system.
- Windows 2000, UNIX, and Linux are three popular operating systems.

7.7   PRACTICE SET

REVIEW QUESTIONS

1. What is the difference between an application program and an operating system?

2. How has networking and internetworking changed the operating system?

3. What is the difference between monoprogramming and multiprogramming?

4. What are the components of an operating system?

5. How is paging different from partitioning?

6. What is the difference between a page and a frame?

7. How is demand paging more efficient than regular paging?

8. What is demand segmentation?

9. How is virtual memory related to physical memory?

10. How is a program related to a job? How is a job related to a process? How is a program related to a process?

11. Where does a program reside? Where does a job reside? Where does a process reside?

12. What is the purpose of a state diagram?

13. What kinds of states can a process be in?

14. What kinds of states can a job be in?

15. If a process is in the running state, what states can it go to next?

16. What is the difference between a job scheduler and a process scheduler?

17. Why does an operating system need queues?

18. How is deadlock different from starvation?

19. What are the functions of a device manager?

20. What are the functions of a file manager?

MULTIPLE-CHOICE QUESTIONS

21. _____ is a program that facilitates the execution of other programs.
    a. An operating system
    b. Hardware
    c. A queue
    d. An application program

22. _____ supervises the activity of each component in a computer system.
    a. An operating system
    b. Hardware
    c. A queue
    d. An application program

23. The earliest operating system, called _____ operating systems, only had to ensure that resources were transferred from one job to the next.
    a. batch
    b. time-sharing
    c. personal
    d. parallel

24. A _____ operating system is needed for jobs shared between distant connected computers.
    a. batch
    b. time-sharing
    c. parallel
    d. distributed

25. Multiprogramming requires a _____ operating system.
    a. batch
    b. time-sharing
    c. parallel
    d. distributed

26. DOS is considered a _____ operating system.
    a. batch
    b. time-sharing
    c. parallel
    d. personal

27. A system with more than one CPU requires a _____ operating system.
    a. batch
    b. time-sharing
    c. parallel
    d. distributed

28. _____ is multiprogramming with swapping.
    a. Partitioning
    b. Paging
    c. Demand paging
    d. Queuing

29. _____ is multiprogramming without swapping.
    a. Partitioning
    b. Virtual memory
    c. Demand paging
    d. Queuing

30. In _____, only one program can reside in memory for execution.
    a. monoprogramming
    b. multiprogramming
    c. partitioning
    d. paging

31. _____ is a multiprogramming method in which multiple programs are entirely in memory with each program occupying a contiguous space.
    a. Partitioning
    b. Paging
    c. Demand paging
    d. Demand segmentation

32. In paging, a program is divided into equally sized sections called _____.
    a. pages
    b. frames
    c. segments
    d. partitions

33. In _____, the program can be divided into differently sized sections.
    a. partitioning
    b. paging
    c. demand paging
    d. demand segmentation

34. In _____, the program can be divided into equally sized sections called pages, but the pages need not be in memory at the same time for execution.
    a. partitioning
    b. paging
    c. demand paging
    d. demand segmentation

35. A process in the _____ state can go to either the ready, terminated, or waiting state.
    a. hold
    b. virtual
    c. running
    d. a and c

36. A process in the ready state goes to the running state when _____.
    a. it enters memory
    b. it requests I/O
    c. it gets access to the CPU
    d. it finishes running

37. A program becomes a _____ when it is selected by the operating system and brought to the hold state.
    a. job
    b. process
    c. deadlock
    d. partition

38. Every process is a _____.
    a. job
    b. program
    c. partition
    d. a and b

39. The _____ scheduler creates a process from a job and changes a process back to a job.
    a. job
    b. process
    c. virtual
    d. queue

40. The _____ scheduler moves a process from one process state to another.
    a. job
    b. process
    c. virtual
    d. queue

41. To prevent _____, an operating system can put resource restrictions on processes.
    a. starvation
    b. synchronization
    c. paging
    d. deadlock

42. _____ can occur if a process has too many resource restrictions.
    a. Starvation
    b. Synchronization
    c. Paging
    d. Deadlock

43. The _____ manager is responsible for archiving and backup.
    a. memory
    b. process
    c. device
    d. file

44. The _____ manager is responsible for access to I/O devices.
    a. memory
    b. process
    c. device
    d. file

45. The job scheduler and the process scheduler are under the control of the _____ manager.
    a. memory
    b. process
    c. device
    d. file

EXERCISES

46. A computer has a monoprogramming operating system. If the size of memory is 64 MB and the residing operating system needs 4 MB, what is the maximum size of a program that can be run by this computer?

47. Redo Exercise 46 if the operating system automatically allocates 10 MB of memory to data.

48. A monoprogramming operating system runs programs that on average need 10 microseconds access to the CPU and 70 microseconds access to the I/O devices. What percentage of time is the CPU idle?

49. A multiprogramming operating system uses an apportioning scheme and divides the 60 MB of available memory into four partitions of 10 MB, 12 MB, 18 MB, and 20 MB. The first program to be run needs 17 MB and occupies the third partition. The second program needs 8 MB and occupies the first partition. The third program needs 10.5 MB and occupies the second partition. Finally, the fourth program needs 20 MB and occupies the fourth partition. What is the total memory used? What is the total memory wasted? What percentage of memory is wasted?

50. Redo Exercise 49 if all programs need 10 MB of memory.

51. A multiprogramming operating system uses paging. The available memory is 60 MB divided into 15 pages, each of 4 MB. The first program needs 13 MB. The second program needs 12 MB. The third program needs 27 MB.
    a. How many pages are used by the first program?
    b. How many pages are used by the second program?
    c. How many pages are used by the third program?
    d. How many pages are unused?
    e. What is the total memory wasted?
    f. What percentage of memory is wasted?

52. An operating system uses 0 virtual memory but requires the whole program to be in physical memory during execution (no paging or segmentation). The size of physical memory is 100 MB. The size of virtual memory is 1 GB. How many programs of size 10 MB can be run concurrently by this operating system? How many of them can be in memory at any time? How many of them must be on disk?

53. What is the status of a process in each of the following situations (according to Figure 7.9)?
    a. The process is using the CPU.
    b. The process has finished printing and needs the attention of the CPU again.
    c. The process has been stopped because its time slot is over.
    d. The process is reading data from the keyboard.
    e. The process is printing data.

54. Three processes (A, B, and C) are running concurrently. Process A has File1, but needs File2. Process B has File3, but needs File1. Process C has File2, but needs File3. Draw a diagram similar to Figure 7.13 for these processes. Is this a deadlock situation?

55. Three processes (A, B, and C) are running concurrently. Process A has File1. Process B has File2, but needs File1. Process C has File3, but needs File2. Draw a diagram similar to Figure 7.13 for these processes. Is this a deadlock situation? If your answer is "no," show how the processes can eventually finish their tasks.

Algorithms

In this chapter, we introduce the concept of algorithms, step-by-step procedures for solving a problem. We then discuss the tools used to develop algorithms. Finally, we give some examples of common iterative and recursive algorithms.

8.1 CONCEPT

In this section, we informally define an **algorithm** and elaborate on the concept using an example.

An informal definition of an algorithm is:

> **Algorithm:** a step-by-step method for solving a problem or doing a task.

In this definition, an algorithm is independent of the computer system. More specifically, we should also note that the algorithm accepts a list of **input data** and creates a list of **output data** (Figure 8.1).

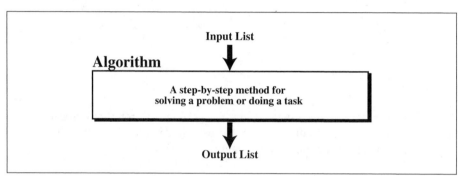

Figure 8.1   Informal definition of an algorithm used in a computer

Let us elaborate on this simple definition with an example. We want to develop an algorithm for finding the largest integer among a list of positive integers. The algorithm should find the largest integer among a list of integers of any value (5, 1000, 10,000, 1,000,000, etc.). The algorithm should be general and not depend on the number of integers.

It is obvious that finding the largest integer among many integers (e. g., 1 million) is a task that cannot be done in one step (by a human or a computer). The algorithm needs to test each integer one by one.

To solve this problem, you need an intuitive approach. First use a small number of integers (e.g., five) and then extend the solution to any number of integers. Your solution for five integers follows the same principles and restrictions for 1000 or 1,000,000 integers. Assume, even for a five-integer case, that the algorithm handles the integers one by one. It looks at the first integer without knowing the values of the remaining integers. After it handles the first, it looks at the second integer and so on. Figure 8.2 shows one way to solve this problem.

We call the algorithm **FindLargest.** Each algorithm has a name to distinguish it from other algorithms. The algorithm receives a list of five integers (as input) and gives the largest integer as output.

The algorithm accepts the list of five integers as input.

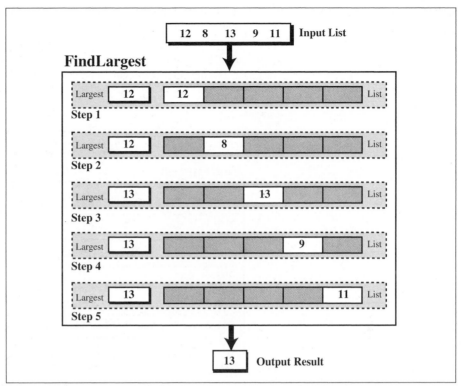

Figure 8.2 Finding the largest integer among five integers

Processing

The algorithm uses the following five steps to find the largest integer.

STEP 1 In this step, the algorithm inspects the first integer (12). Since it has not handled the rest of the integers yet (note that we do not reveal the remaining integers because the algorithm does not inspect them at this moment), it decides that the largest integer (so far) is the first integer. The algorithm defines a data item, called Largest, and sets its value to the first integer (12).

STEP 2 The largest integer so far is 12, but the new number may change the situation. The algorithm makes a comparison between the value of Largest (12) and the value of the second integer (8). It finds that Largest is larger than the second integer, which means that Largest is still holding the largest integer. There is no need to change the value of Largest.

STEP 3 The largest integer so far is 12, but the new number (13) is larger than Largest. This means than the value of Largest is no longer valid. The value of Largest should be replaced by the third number (13). The algorithm changes the value of Largest to 13 and moves to the next step.

STEP 4 Nothing is changed in this step because Largest is larger than the fourth integer (9).

STEP 5 Again nothing is changed because Largest is larger than the fifth integer (11).

Output

Because there are no more integers to be processed, the algorithm outputs the value of Largest, which is 13.

DEFINING ACTIONS

Figure 8.2 does not show what should be done in each step. You can modify the figure to show more details. In step 1, set Largest to the value of the first integer. In steps 2 to 5, however, additional actions are needed to compare the value of Largest with the current integer being processed. If the current integer is larger than Largest, set the value of Largest to the current integer (Figure 8.3).

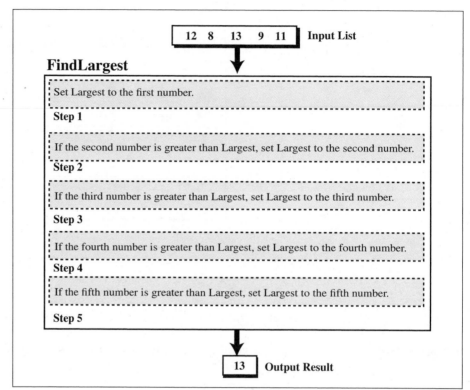

Figure 8.3 Defining actions in FindLargest algorithm

REFINEMENT

This algorithm needs refinement to be acceptable to the programming community. There are two problems. First, the action in the first step is different from the ones for the other steps. Second, the wording is not the same in steps 2 to 5. You can easily redefine the algorithm to remove these two inconveniences. Change the wording in steps 2 to 5 to "If the current number is greater than Largest, set Largest to the current number." The reason that the first step is different from the other steps is because Largest is not initialized. If you initialize Largest to 0 (no positive integer can be less than 0), then the first step can be the same as the other steps. Add a new step (call it step 0 to show that it should be done before processing any numbers). Figure 8.4 shows the result of this refinement. Note that you do not have to show all of the steps because they are now the same.

GENERALIZATION

Is it possible to generalize the algorithm? You want to find the largest of N positive integers, where N can be 1000, 1,000,000, or even more. Of course, you can follow Figure 8.4 and repeat each step. But if you change the algorithm to a program, then you need to actually type the actions for N steps! There is a better way to do this. You can tell the computer to repeat the steps N times. We now include this feature in our pictorial algorithm (Figure 8.5).

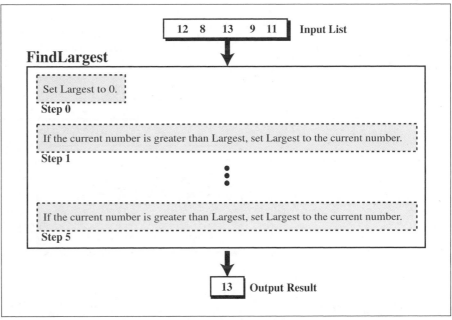

Figure 8.4   FindLargest refined

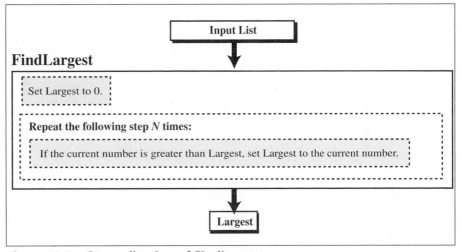

Figure 8.5   Generalization of FindLargest

8.2 THREE CONSTRUCTS

Computer scientists have defined three constructs for a structured program or algorithm. The idea is that a program must be made of a combination of only these three constructs: sequence, decision (selection), and repetition (Figure 8.6). It has been proved there is no need for any other constructs. Using only these constructs makes a program or an algorithm easy to understand, debug, or change.

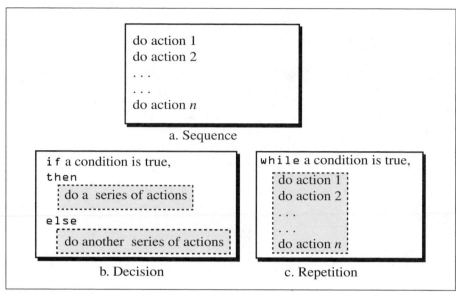

Figure 8.6   Three constructs

SEQUENCE

The first construct is called the sequence. An algorithm, and eventually a program, is a sequence of instructions, which can be a simple instruction or either of the other two constructs.

DECISION

Some problems cannot be solved with only a sequence of simple instructions. Sometimes you need to test a condition. If the result of testing is true, you follow a sequence of instructions; if it is false, you follow a different sequence of instructions. This is called the decision (selection) construct.

REPETITION

In some problems, the same sequence of instructions must be repeated. You handle this with the repetition construct. Finding the largest number among a set of numbers (that you saw at the beginning of the chapter) is a construct of this kind.

8.3   ALGORITHM REPRESENTATION

So far, we have used figures to convey the concept of an algorithm. During the last few decades, tools have been designed for this purpose. Two of these tools, the flowchart and pseudocode, are presented here.

FLOWCHART

A **flowchart** is a pictorial representation of an algorithm. It hides all of the details of an algorithm in an attempt to give the big picture; it shows how the algorithm flows from beginning to end. Flowcharts are covered in detail in Appendix C. Here we show only how the three constructs are represented in flowcharts (Figure 8.7).

PSEUDOCODE

Pseudocode is an Englishlike representation of an algorithm. There is no standard for pseudocode; some people use a lot of details, and others use less. Some use a type of code that is close to English, and others use a syntax like the Pascal language. Pseudocode is covered in detail in Appendix D. Here we show only how the three constructs can be represented by pseudocode (Figure 8.8).

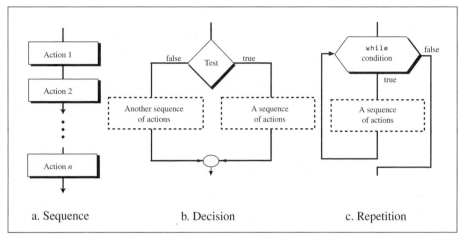

Figure 8.7 Flowchart for three constructs

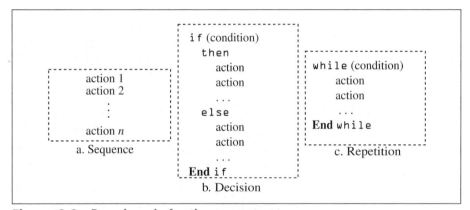

Figure 8.8 Pseudocode for three constructs

EXAMPLE 1

Write an algorithm in pseudocode that finds the average of two numbers.

SOLUTION

This is a simple problem that can be solved using only the sequence construct. Note that we number the instructions for easy reference (see Algorithm 8.1). Note also that we name the algorithm, define the input to the algorithm, and at the end, show the output using a return instruction.

Algorithm 8.1 Average of two

AverageOfTwo
Input: Two numbers

1. Add the two numbers
2. Divide the result by 2
3. Return the result of step 2
End

EXAMPLE 2

Write an algorithm to change a numeric grade to a pass/no pass grade.

SOLUTION

This problem cannot be solved with only the sequence construct. You also need the decision construct. The computer is given a number between 0 and 100. It returns "pass" if the number is greater than or equal to 70; it returns "no pass" if the number is less than 70. Algorithm 8.2 shows the pseudocode for this algorithm. Note the numbering. The decision instruction is numbered 1, and its subinstruction is numbered 1.1 (the first subinstruction inside the first instruction).

Algorithm 8.2 Pass/no pass grade

```
    Pass/NoPassGrade
    Input: One number
1.  if (the number is greater than or equal to 70)
        then
            1.1  Set the grade to "pass"
        else
            1.2  Set the grade to "nopass"
    End if
2.  Return the grade
    End
```

EXAMPLE 3

Write an algorithm to change a numeric grade to a letter grade.

SOLUTION

This problem needs more than one decision. The pseudocode in Algorithm 8.3 shows one way (not the best one, but an easy one to understand) to solve the problem. Again, a number is given between 0 and 100, and you want to change it to a letter grade (A, B, C, D, or F).

Algorithm 8.3 Letter grade

```
    LetterGrade
    Input: One number
1.  if (the number is between 90 and 100, inclusive)
        then
            1.1  Set the grade to "A"
    End if
2.  if (the number is between 80 and 89, inclusive)
        then
            2.1  Set the grade to "B"
    End if
3.  if (the number is between 70 and 79, inclusive)
        then
            3.1  Set the grade to "C"
    End if
```

4. **if** (the number is between 60 and 69, inclusive)
      then
         4.1   Set the grade to "D"
      End if
5. **if** (the number is less than 60, inclusive)
      then
         5.1   Set the grade to "F"
      End if
6. Return the grade
      End

Note that the **if** instructions do not need an **else** because you do nothing if the condition is false.

EXAMPLE 4

Write an algorithm to find the largest of a set of integers. You do not know the number of integers.

SOLUTION

Use the concept in Figure 8.5 to write an algorithm for this problem (see Algorithm 8.4).

Algorithm 8.4 Find largest

FindLargest
Input: A list of positive integers

1. Set Largest to 0
2. **while** (more integers)
         2.1 **if** (the integer is greater than Largest)
               then
                  2.1.1   Set Largest to the value of the integer
            End if
      End while
3. Return Largest
      End

EXAMPLE 5

Write an algorithm to find the largest of 1000 numbers.

SOLUTION

Here you need a counter to count the number of integers. Initialize the counter to 0 and increment it in each repetition. When the counter is 1000, exit from the loop (see Algorithm 8.5).

Algorithm 8.5 Find largest of 1000 numbers

FindLargest
Input: 1000 positive integers

1. Set Largest to 0
2. Set Counter to 0

```
3. while (Counter less than 1000)
      3.1 if (the integer is greater than Largest)
             then
                   3.1.1   Set Largest to the value of the integer
             End if
      3.2 Increment the Counter
   End while
4. Return Largest
   End
```

8.4   MORE FORMAL DEFINITION

Now that we have discussed the concept of an algorithm and have shown its representation, here is a more formal definition:

Algorithm: an ordered set of unambiguous steps that produces a result and terminates in a finite time.

Let us elaborate on this definition.

ORDERED SET

An algorithm must be a well-defined, ordered set of instructions.

UNAMBIGUOUS STEPS

Each step in an algorithm must be clearly and unambiguously defined. If one step is to *add two numbers,* you must define both numbers as well as the add operation. You cannot use the same symbol to mean addition in one place and multiplication somewhere else.

PRODUCE A RESULT

An algorithm must produce a result; otherwise, it is useless. The result can be data that are returned to the calling algorithm or some other effect (e.g., printing).

TERMINATE IN A FINITE TIME

An algorithm must terminate (halt). If it does not (e.g., has an infinite loop), you have not created an algorithm. In Chapter 17, we will discuss solvable and unsolvable problems, and you will see that a solvable problem has a solution in the form of an algorithm that terminates.

8.5   SUBALGORITHMS

With the three constructs that have been described, you can create an algorithm for any solvable problem. The principles of structured programming, however, require that an algorithm be broken into small units called **subalgorithms** (the terms **subprograms, subroutines, procedures, functions, methods,** and **modules** are also used). Each subalgorithm is in turn divided into smaller subalgorithms. The process continues until the subalgorithms become intrinsic (understood immediately).

You can divide Algorithm 8.4 into a main algorithm and a subalgorithm. This algorithm is a good candidate for this purpose because it repeats a task many times. In each **iteration,** the algorithm finds the larger of two integers. You can separate this part of the task and create a small subtask out of it (Figure 8.9).

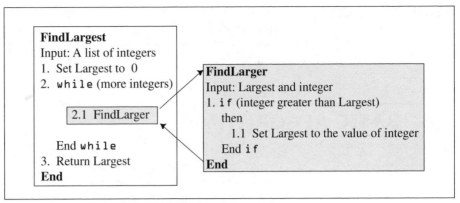

Figure 8.9   Concept of a subalgorithm

The algorithm FindLargest executes each instruction until it encounters the name of another algorithm, FindLarger, at line 2.1. In this line, FindLargest is suspended and FindLarger begins. FindLarger finds the larger number between the current Largest value and the current integer value. This is known as a function call. Note that in each iteration, FindLarger is called once. You may think this design is longer than the original design. In this case, it is true. But using subalgorithms has advantages that more than compensate the extra effort of writing a few more lines of code:

■ It is more understandable. Looking at the FindLargest algorithm, you can immediately see that a task (finding the larger of two numbers) is repeated.

■ A subalgorithm can be called many times in different parts of the main algorithm without being rewritten.

Algorithm 8.6 shows in pseudocode how to use a subalgorithm inside an algorithm.

Algorithm 8.6 Find largest

```
   FindLargest
   Input: A list of positive integers
1. Set Largest to  0
2. while (more integers)
        2.1   FindLarger
   End while
3. Return Largest
   End
```

```
   FindLarger
   Input: Largest and current integer
1. if (the integer is greater than Largest)
        then
            1.1   Set Largest to the value of the integer
        End if
   End
```

STRUCTURE CHART   Another tool programmers use is the **structure chart.** A structure chart is a high-level design tool that shows the relationship between different modules in an algorithm. It is used mostly at the design level rather than at the programming level. We discuss the structure chart in Appendix E.

8.6 BASIC ALGORITHMS

Several algorithms are used in computer science so prevalently that they are considered basic. We discuss the most common here. This discussion is very general; implementation depends on the language.

SUMMATION   One of the commonly used algorithms in computer science is **summation.** You can add two or three numbers very easily, but how can you add many numbers or a variable series of numbers? The solution is simple: Use the add operator in a loop (Figure 8.10). A summing algorithm has three logical parts:

1. Initialization of the sum at the beginning.
2. The loop, which in each iteration adds a new number to the sum.
3. Returning the result after exiting from the loop.

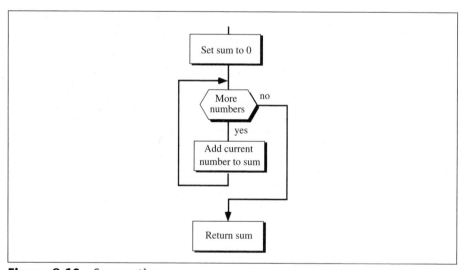

Figure 8.10   Summation

PRODUCT   Another common algorithm is finding the product of a list of numbers. The solution is simple: Use the multiplication operator in a loop (Figure 8.11). A product algorithm has three logical parts:

1. Initialization of the product at the beginning.
2. The loop, which in each iteration multiplies a new number with the product.
3. Returning the result after exiting from the loop.

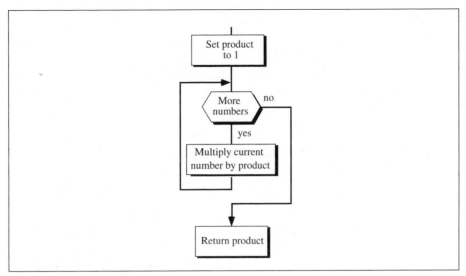

Figure 8.11   Product

For example, the preceding algorithm can be used to calculate x^n using a minor modification (left as an exercise). As another example, the same algorithm can be used to calculate the factorial of a number (left as an exercise).

SMALLEST AND LARGEST

We discussed the algorithm for finding the largest among a list of numbers at the beginning of the chapter. The idea was to write a decision construct to find the larger of two numbers. If you put this construct in a loop, you can find the largest of a list of numbers.

Finding the smallest number among a list of numbers is similar with two minor differences. First, use a decision construct to find the smaller of two numbers. Second, initialize with a very large number instead of a very small one.

SORTING

One of the most common applications in computer science is **sorting,** which is the process by which data are arranged according to their values. People are surrounded by data. If the data were not ordered, it would take hours and hours to find a single piece of information. Imagine the difficulty of finding someone's telephone number in a telephone book that was not ordered.

In this section, we introduce three sorting algorithms: selection sort, bubble sort, and insertion sort. These three sorting algorithms are the foundation of the faster sorts used in computer science today.

Selection Sort

In **selection sort,** the list is divided into two sublists—sorted and unsorted—which are divided by an imaginary wall. You find the smallest element from the unsorted sublist and swap it with the element at the beginning of the unsorted data. After each selection and swapping, the imaginary wall between the two sublists moves one element ahead, increasing the number of sorted elements and decreasing the number of unsorted ones. Each time you move one element from the unsorted sublist to the sorted sublist, you have completed a **sort pass.** A list of n elements requires $n - 1$ passes to completely rearrange the data. Selection sort is presented graphically in Figure 8.12.

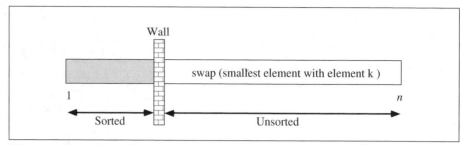

Figure 8.12   Selection sort

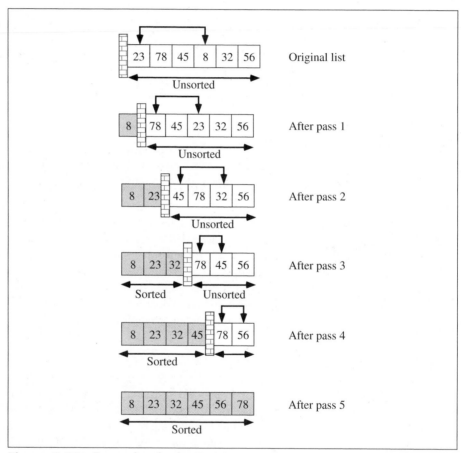

Figure 8.13   Example of selection sort

Figure 8.13 traces a set of six integers as we sort them. It shows how the wall between the sorted and unsorted sublists moves in each pass. As you study the figure, you will see that the list is sorted after five passes, which is one less than the number of elements in the list. Thus, if you use a loop to control the sorting, the loop will have one less iteration than the number of elements in the list.

Selection Sort Algorithm

The algorithm uses two loops, one inside the other. The outer loop is iterated for each pass; the inner loop finds the smallest element in the unsorted list. Figure 8.14 shows the flowchart for the selection sort algorithm. We leave the pseudocode as an exercise.

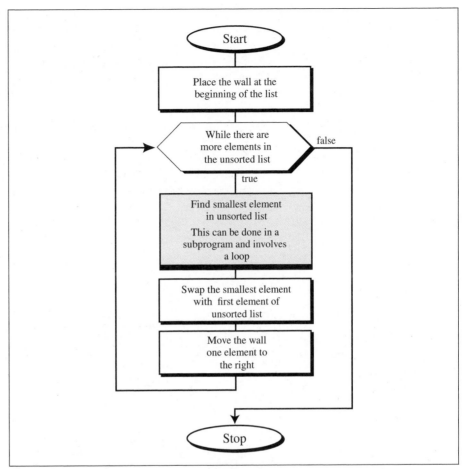

Figure 8.14   Selection sort algorithm

Bubble Sort

In the **bubble sort** method, the list is divided into two sublists: sorted and unsorted. The smallest element is *bubbled* from the unsorted sublist and moved to the sorted sublist. After the smallest element has been moved to the sorted list, the wall moves one element ahead, increasing the number of sorted elements and decreasing the number of unsorted ones. Each time an element moves from the unsorted sublist to the sorted sublist, one sort pass is completed (Figure 8.15). Given a list of n elements, bubble sort requires up to $n - 1$ passes to sort the data.

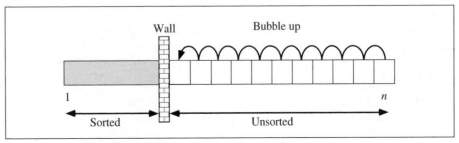

Figure 8.15   Bubble sort

Figure 8.16 shows how the wall moves one element in each pass. Looking at the first pass, you start with 56 and compare it to 32. Since 56 is not less than 32, it is not moved, and you step down one element. No exchanges take place until you compare 45 to 8. Since 8 is less than 45, the two elements are exchanged, and you step down one element. Because 8 was moved down, it is now compared to 78, and these two elements are exchanged. Finally, 8 is compared to 23 and exchanged. This series of exchanges places 8 in the first location, and the wall is moved up one position.

Bubble sort was originally written to "bubble down" the highest element in the list. From an efficiency point of view, it makes no difference whether the high element is bubbled or the low element is bubbled. From a consistency point of view, however, it makes comparisons between the sorts easier if all three of them work in the same manner. For that reason, we have chosen to bubble the lowest value in each pass.

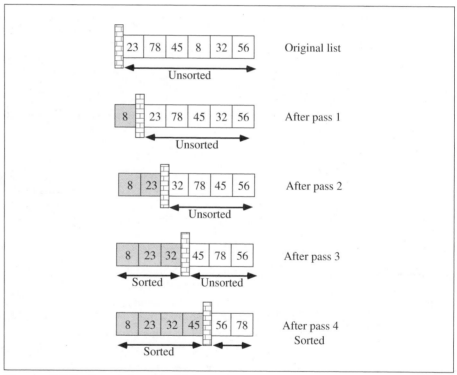

Figure 8.16 Example of bubble sort

Bubble Sort Algorithm   Bubble sort also uses two loops, one inside the other. The outer loop is iterated for each pass; each iteration of the inner loop tries to bubble one element to the top (left). We leave the flowchart and pseudocode as exercises.

Insertion Sort

The **insertion sort** algorithm is one of the most common sorting techniques, and it is often used by card players. Each card a player picks up is inserted into the proper place in his or her hand to maintain a particular sequence. (Card sorting is an example of a sort that uses two criteria for sorting: suit and rank.)

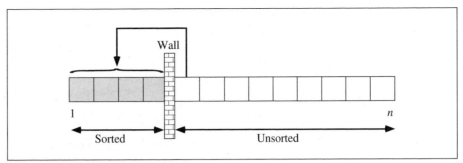

Figure 8.17 Insertion sort

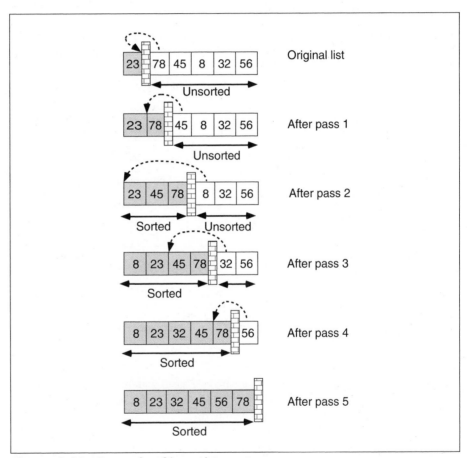

Figure 8.18 Example of insertion sort

In insertion sort, as in the other two sorting algorithms discussed in this chapter, the list is divided into two parts: sorted and unsorted. In each pass, the first element of the unsorted sublist is picked up, transferred to the sorted sublist, and inserted at the appropriate place (Figure 8.17). Note that a list of n elements will take at most $n - 1$ passes to sort the data.

Figure 8.18 traces insertion sort through our list of six numbers. The wall moves with each pass as an element is removed from the unsorted sublist and inserted into the sorted sublist.

Insertion Sort Algorithm   The design of insertion sort follows the same pattern seen in both selection sort and bubble sort. The outer loop is iterated for each pass, and the inner loop finds the position of insertion. We leave the flowchart and pseudocode as exercises.

Other Sorting Algorithms

There are other sorting algorithms: quicksort, heap sort, Shell sort, bucket sort, merge sort, and so on. Most of these advanced sorting algorithms are discussed in books on data structures.[1]

You may ask why there are so many sorting algorithms. The reason lies in the type of data that needs to be sorted. One algorithm is more efficient for a list that is mostly sorted, whereas another algorithm is more efficient for a list that is completely unsorted. To decide which algorithm is suitable for a particular application, a measurement called the *complexity of algorithms* is needed. We discuss this issue in Chapter 17, but a thorough understanding requires additional courses in programming and data structures.

SEARCHING

Another common algorithm in computer science is **searching,** which is the process of finding the location of a target among a list of objects. In the case of a list, searching means that given a value, you want to find the location (index) of the first element in the list that contains that value. The search concept is illustrated in Figure 8.19.

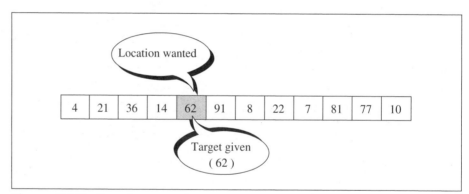

Figure 8.19   Search concept

There are two basic searches for lists: sequential search and binary search. Sequential search can be used to locate an item in any list, whereas binary search requires the list to be sorted.

Sequential Search

Sequential search is used if the list being searched is not ordered. Generally, you use this technique only for small lists or lists that are not searched often. In other cases, the best approach is to first sort the list and then search it using the binary search discussed later.

In a sequential search, you start searching for the target from the beginning of the list. You continue until you either find the target or you are sure that it is not in the list (because you have reached the end of the list). Figure 8.20 traces the steps to find the value 62.

---

[1]See Richard F. Gilberg and Behrouz A. Forouzan, *Data Structures: A Pseudocode Approach with C++,* (Pacific Grove, CA: Brooks/Cole, 2001), pp. 502–559.

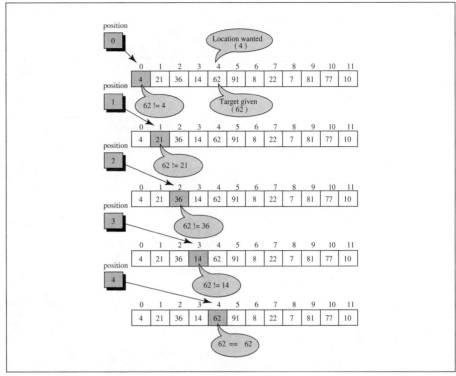

Figure 8.20 Example of a sequential search

Binary Search

The sequential search algorithm is very slow. If you have a list of 1 million elements, you must do 1 million comparisons in the worst case. If the list is not sorted, this is the only solution. If the list is sorted, however, you can use a more efficient algorithm called **binary search.** Generally speaking, programmers use a binary search when a list is large.

A binary search starts by testing the data in the element at the middle of the list. This determines if the target is in the first half or the second half of the list. If it is in the first half, there is no need to further check the second half. If it is in the second half, there is no need to further check the first half. In other words, you eliminate half the list from further consideration. Repeat this process until you either find the target or satisfy yourself that it is not in the list. Figure 8.21 shows how to find the target, 22, in the list using three references: *first, mid,* and *last.*

1. At the beginning, *first* shows 0 and *last* shows 11. Let *mid* show the middle position, (0 + 11) / 2, or 5. Now compare the target (22) with data at position 5 (21). The target is greater than this value, so ignore the first half.

2. Move *first* after *mid,* to position 6. Let *mid* show the middle of the second half, (6 + 11) / 2, or 8. Now compare the target (22) with data at position 8 (62). The target is smaller than this value, so ignore the numbers from this value (62) to the end.

3. Move *last* before *mid* to position 7. Recalculate *mid* again, (7 + 6) / 2, or 6. Compare the target (22) with the value at this position (22). You have found the target and can quit.

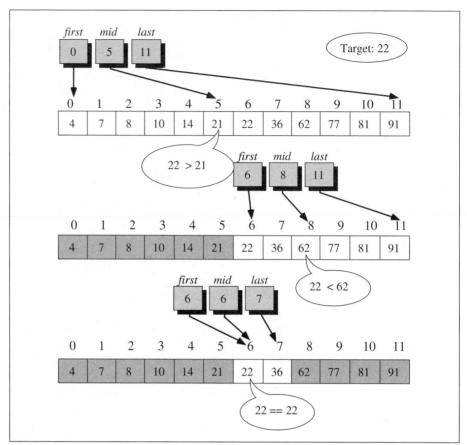

Figure 8.21 Example of a binary search

8.7 RECURSION

In general, there are two approaches to writing algorithms for solving a problem. One uses iterations; the other uses recursion. **Recursion** is a process in which an algorithm calls itself.

ITERATIVE DEFINITION

To study a simple example, consider the calculation of a factorial. The factorial of a number is the product of the integral values from 1 to the number. The definition is iterative (Figure 8.22). An algorithm is iterative whenever the definition does not involve the algorithm itself.

$$\text{Factorial }(n) = \begin{bmatrix} 1 & \text{if } n = 0 \\ n \times (n-1) \times (n-2) \times \ldots \times 3 \times 2 \times 1 & \text{if } n > 0 \end{bmatrix}$$

Figure 8.22 Iterative definition of factorial

$$
\text{Factorial } (n) = \begin{bmatrix} 1 & \text{if } n = 0 \\ n \times \text{Factorial } (n-1) & \text{if } n > 0 \end{bmatrix}
$$

Figure 8.23   Recursive definition of factorial

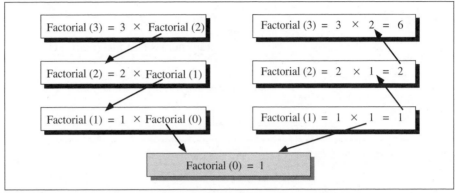

Figure 8.24   Tracing recursive solution to factorial problem

RECURSIVE DEFINITION

An algorithm is defined recursively whenever the algorithm appears within the definition itself. For example, the factorial function can be defined recursively as in Figure 8.23.

The decomposition of factorial (3), using recursion, is shown in Figure 8.24. If you study the figure carefully, you will note that the recursive solution for a problem involves a two-way journey. First you decompose the problem from top to bottom, and then you solve it from bottom to top.

Judging by this example, it looks as if the recursive calculation is much longer and more difficult. So why would you want to use the recursive method? Although the recursive calculation looks more difficult when using paper and pencil, it is often a much easier and more elegant solution when using computers. Additionally, it offers a conceptual simplicity to the creator and the reader.

Iterative Solution

Let us write an algorithm to solve the factorial problem iteratively. This solution usually involves a loop such as seen in Algorithm 8.7.

Algorithm 8.7 Iterative factorial

Factorial
Input: A positive integer *num*

1. Set FactN to 1
2. Set i to 1
3. **while** (i less than or equal to num)
   3.1 Set FactN to FactN × i
   3.2 Increment i
   End while
4. Return FactN
   End

Recursive Solution

The recursive solution to factorial is seen in Algorithm 8.8. It does not need a loop; the concept itself involves repetition. In the recursive version, you let the algorithm *factorial* call itself.

Algorithm 8.8 Recursive factorial

> **Factorial**
> **Input:** A positive integer *num*
>
> 1. `if` (num is equal to 0)
>   **then**
>   1.1 return 1
>   **else**
>   1.2 return num × Factorial (num − 1)
>   **End** `if`
>   End

8.8 KEY TERMS

algorithm	module	sort pass
binary search	output data	sorting
bubble sort	procedure	structure chart
flowchart	pseudocode	subalgorithm
function	recursion	subprogram
input data	searching	subroutine
insertion sort	selection sort	summation
iteration	sequential search	

8.9 SUMMARY

- Informally, an algorithm is a step-by-step method for solving a problem or doing a task.

- An algorithm accepts an input list of data and creates an output list of data.

- A program is a combination of sequence constructs, decision constructs, and repetition constructs.

- A flowchart is a pictorial representation of an algorithm.

- Pseudocode is an Englishlike representation of an algorithm.

- Formally, an algorithm is an ordered set of unambiguous steps that produces a result and terminates in a finite time.

- An algorithm can be broken into smaller units called subalgorithms.

- A structure chart is a high-level design tool that shows the relationship between different modules of a program.

- Summation is a basic algorithm in which numbers are added.

- Product is a basic algorithm in which numbers are multiplied.

- Finding the minimum or the maximum in a list of numbers is a basic algorithm.

- Sorting, a process to order data, is a basic algorithm.

- Selection sort, bubble sort, and insertion sort are commonly used sorting algorithms.

- Searching, a process to locate a target in a list of data, is a basic algorithm.

- Sequential search is used for unordered lists.
- Binary search is used for ordered lists.

- An iterative algorithm involves only the parameters and not the algorithm itself.
- A recursive algorithm involves the algorithm itself.

8.10   PRACTICE SET

REVIEW QUESTIONS

1. What is the formal definition of an algorithm?
2. Define the three constructs used in structured programming.
3. How is a flowchart related to an algorithm?
4. How is pseudocode related to an algorithm?
5. What are the alternative terms for the units that make up an algorithm?
6. How do programmers use the structure chart?
7. What is the purpose of the summation algorithm?
8. What is the purpose of the product algorithm?
9. What is the purpose of a sorting algorithm?
10. What are the three types of sorting algorithms?
11. How are the three sorting algorithms the same? How are they different?
12. What is the purpose of a searching algorithm?
13. What are the two major types of searches? How are they different?
14. Give a definition and an example of an iterative process.
15. Give a definition and an example of a recursive process.

MULTIPLE-CHOICE QUESTIONS

16. _____ is a step-by-step method for solving a problem or doing a task.
    a. A construct
    b. A recursion
    c. An iteration
    d. An algorithm
17. To set the value of a variable before any processing occurs, you _____ the variable.
    a. construct
    b. iterate
    c. initialize
    d. increase

18. There are _____ basic constructs in computer science.
    a. one
    b. two
    c. three
    d. four
19. The _____ construct tests a condition.
    a. sequence
    b. decision
    c. repetition
    d. logical
20. The _____ construct is any action.
    a. sequence
    b. decision
    c. repetition
    d. logical
21. The _____ construct handles repeated actions.
    a. sequence
    b. decision
    c. repetition
    d. logical
22. _____ is a pictorial representation of an algorithm.
    a. A flowchart
    b. A structure chart
    c. Pseudocode
    d. An algorithm
23. _____ is an Englishlike representation of the code.
    a. A flowchart
    b. A structure chart
    c. Pseudocode
    d. An algorithm
24. _____ is a high-level design tool that shows the relationship between different modules of a program.
    a. A flowchart
    b. A structure chart
    c. Pseudocode
    d. An algorithm

25. A subalgorithm is also known as a _____.
   a. function
   b. subroutine
   c. module
   d. all of the above

26. _____ is a basic algorithm that finds the product of a list of numbers.
   a. Summation
   b. Product
   c. Smallest
   d. Largest

27. _____ is a basic algorithm that arranges data according to their values.
   a. Inquiry
   b. Sorting
   c. Searching
   d. Recursion

28. _____ is a basic algorithm that adds a list of numbers.
   a. Summation
   b. Product
   c. Smallest
   d. Largest

29. _____ is a basic algorithm that finds the smallest of a list of numbers.
   a. Summation
   b. Product
   c. Smallest
   d. Largest

30. In _____ sort, the items are divided into two lists: sorted and unsorted.
   a. selection
   b. bubble
   c. insertion
   d. all of the above

31. For _____ sort, $n - 1$ passes are needed to sort the data.
   a. selection
   b. bubble
   c. insertion
   d. all of the above

32. For _____ sort, two loops are needed.
   a. selection
   b. bubble
   c. insertion
   d. all of the above

33. In _____ sort, the item that goes to the sorted list is always the first item in the unsorted list.
   a. selection
   b. bubble
   c. insertion
   d. all of the above

34. In _____ sort, the smallest item from the unsorted list is swapped with the item at the beginning of the unsorted list.
   a. selection
   b. bubble
   c. insertion
   d. all of the above

35. In _____ sort, the smallest item moves to the beginning of the unsorted list. There is no one-to-one swapping.
   a. selection
   b. bubble
   c. insertion
   d. all of the above

36. _____ is a basic algorithm in which you want to find the location of a target in a list of items.
   a. Sorting
   b. Searching
   c. Product
   d. Summation

37. Use a _____ search for an unordered list.
   a. sequential
   b. binary
   c. bubble
   d. insertion

38. Use a _____ search for an ordered list.
   a. sequential
   b. binary
   c. bubble
   d. insertion

39. _____ is a process in which an algorithm calls itself.
   a. Insertion
   b. Searching
   c. Recursion
   d. Iteration

EXERCISES

40. Write pseudocode for the summation algorithm defined in Figure 8.10.

41. Write pseudocode for the product algorithm defined in Figure 8.11.

42. Draw a flowchart for an algorithm that finds the smallest number among N numbers.

43. Write pseudocode for the smallest algorithm in Exercise 42.

44. Draw a flowchart for an algorithm that finds the largest number among N numbers.

45. Write pseudocode for the largest algorithm in Exercise 44.

46. Write pseudocode for the selection sort algorithm.

47. Draw a flowchart and write pseudocode for the bubble sort algorithm.

48. Draw a flowchart and write pseudocode for the insertion sort algorithm.

49. Using the selection sort algorithm, manually sort the following list and show your work in each pass:

14 7 23 31 40 56 78 9 2

50. Using the bubble sort algorithm, manually sort the following list and show your work in each pass:

14 7 23 31 40 56 78 9 2

51. Using the insertion sort algorithm, manually sort the following list and show your work in each pass:

14 7 23 31 40 56 78 9 2

52. A list contains the following elements. The first two elements have been sorted using the selection sort algorithm. What is the value of the elements in the list after three more passes of selection sort?

7 8 26 44 13 23 98 57

53. A list contains the following elements. The first two elements have been sorted using the bubble sort algorithm. What is the value of the elements in the list after three more passes of bubble sort?

7 8 26 44 13 23 57 98

54. A list contains the following elements. The first two elements have been sorted using the insertion sort algorithm. What is the value of the elements in the list after three more passes of insertion sort?

3 13 7 26 44 23 98 57

55. A list contains the following elements. Using the binary search algorithm, trace the steps followed to find 88. At each step, show the values of *first, last,* and *mid.*

8 13 17 26 44 56 88 97

56. A list contains the following elements. Using the binary search algorithm, trace the steps followed to find 20. At each step, show the values of *first, last,* and *mid.*

8 13 17 26 44 56 88 97

57. Write a recursive algorithm to find the greatest common divisor (gcd) of two integers using the definition in Figure 8.25.

$$\text{gcd}(x, y) = \begin{bmatrix} \text{gcd}(y, x) & \text{if } x < y \\ x & \text{if } y = 0 \\ \text{gcd}(y, x \bmod y) & \text{otherwise} \end{bmatrix}$$

Figure 8.25 Exercise 57

58. Write a recursive algorithm to find the combination of n objects taken k at a time using the definition in Figure 8.26.

$$C(n, k) = \begin{bmatrix} 1 & \text{if } k = 0 \text{ or } n = k \\ C(n-1, k) + C(n-1, k-1) & \text{if } n > k > 0 \end{bmatrix}$$

Figure 8.26 Exercise 58

Programming Languages

In this chapter, we do a quick survey of **programming languages** to give the student an idea about the different languages and when they are used. First, we discuss the evolution of languages. We then categorize the languages according to their approach to problem solving and the types of problems they can solve. Then we survey one popular language and discuss its elements and capabilities.

9.1 EVOLUTION

To write a program for a computer, you must use a computer language. A **computer language** is a set of predefined words that are combined into a program according to predefined rules **(syntax).**

Over the years, computer languages have evolved from machine language to natural languages. A time line for computer languages is presented in Figure 9.1.

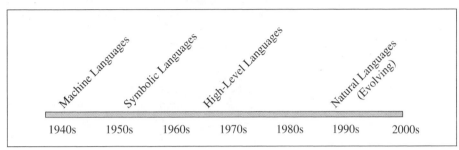

Figure 9.1 Evolution of computer languages

MACHINE LANGUAGES

In the earliest days of computers, the only programming languages available were **machine languages.** Each computer has its own machine language, which is made of streams of 0s and 1s. Program 9.1 shows an example of a machine language program. This program multiplies two numbers and prints the results.

```
1  00000000   00000100   000000000000000
2  01011110   00001100   11000010   0000000000000010
3             11101111   00010110   0000000000000101
4             11101111   10011110   0000000000001011
5  11111000   10101101   11011111   0000000000010010
6             01100010   11011111   0000000000010101
7  11101111   00000010   11111011   0000000000010111
8  11110100   10101101   11011111   0000000000011110
9  00000011   10100010   11011111   0000000000100001
10 11101111   00000010   11111011   0000000000100100
11 01111110   11110100   10101101
12 11111000   10101110   11000101   0000000000101011
13 00000110   10100010   11111011   0000000000110001
14 11101111   00000010   11111011   0000000000110100
15                       00000100   0000000000111101
16                       00000100   0000000000111101
```

Program 9.1 Program in machine language

The instructions in machine language must be in streams of 0s and 1s because the internal circuit of a computer is made of switches, transistors, and other electronic devices that can be in one of two states: off or on. The off state is represented by 0; the on state is represented by 1.

> The only language understood by a computer is machine language.

SYMBOLIC LANGUAGES

It became obvious that not many programs would be written if programmers continued to work in machine language. In the early 1950s, Grace Hopper, a mathematician and a member of the U.S. Navy, developed the concept of a language that simply mirrored the machine languages using symbols, or mnemonics, to represent the various machine language instructions. Because they used symbols, these languages were known as **symbolic languages.** Program 9.2 shows the multiplication program in a symbolic language.

```
 1 entry  main,^m<r2>
 2 subl2  #12,sp
 3 jsb    C$MAIN_ARGS
 4 movab  $CHAR_STRING_CON
 5
 6 pushal  -8(fp)
 7 pushal  (r2)
 8 calls   #2,read
 9 pushal  -12(fp)
10 pushal  3(r2)
11 calls   #2,read
12 mull3   -8(fp),-12(fp),-
13 pusha   6(r2)
14 calls   #2,print
15 clrl             r0
16 ret
```

Program 9.2   Program in symbolic language

A special program called an **assembler** is used to translate symbolic code into machine language. Because symbolic languages had to be assembled into machine language, they soon became known as **assembly languages.** This name is still used today for symbolic languages that closely represent machine language.

HIGH-LEVEL LANGUAGES

Although symbolic languages greatly improved programming efficiency, they still required programmers to concentrate on the hardware they were using. Working with symbolic languages was also very tedious because each machine instruction had to be individually coded. The desire to improve programmer efficiency and to change the focus from the computer to the problem being solved led to the development of **high-level languages.**

High-level languages are portable to many different computers, allowing the programmer to concentrate on the application rather than the intricacies of the computer. They are designed to relieve the programmer from the details of assembly language. High-level languages share one characteristic with symbolic languages: They must be converted to machine language. This process is called *compilation.*

Over the years, various languages, most notably BASIC, COBOL, Pascal, Ada, C, C++, and Java, were developed. Program 9.3 shows the Program 9.2 multiplication program as it would appear in the C++ language.

```
1 /* This program reads two integer numbers from the
2 keyboard and prints their product.
3 Written by:
4 Date:
5 */
6 #include <iostream.h>
7
8 int main (void)
9 {
10 // Local Declarations
11        int number1;
12        int number2;
13        int result;
14
15 // Statements
16        cin >> number1;
17        cin >> number2;
18        result = number1 * number2;
19        cout << result;
20        return 0;
21 }      // main
```

Program 9.3 Program in C++ language

NATURAL LANGUAGES

Ideally, you could use your **natural language** (e.g., English, French, or Chinese), and the computer would understand it and execute your requests immediately. Although this may sound like something out of science fiction, considerable work on natural languages is being done in labs today. So far, its use in industry is still quite limited.

9.2 BUILDING A PROGRAM

As you learned in the previous section, a computer understands a program only if the program is translated to its machine language. In this section, we explain the procedure for turning a program in a high-level language into machine language.

It is the job of the programmer to write the program and then to turn it into an **executable** (machine language) **file.** There are three steps in this process:

1. Writing and editing the program
2. Compiling the program
3. Linking the program with the required library modules

Figure 9.2 shows these three processes.

WRITING AND EDITING PROGRAMS

The software used to write programs is known as a **text editor.** A text editor helps you enter, change, and store character data. Depending on the editor on your system, you could use it for writing letters, creating reports, or writing programs. The big difference

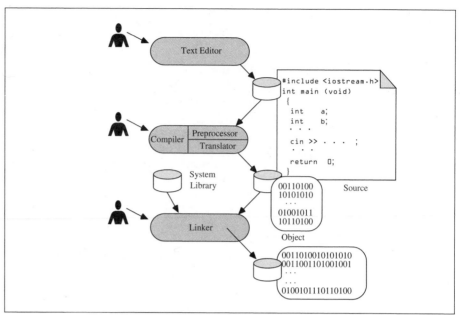

Figure 9.2   Building a program

between the other forms of text processing and writing programs is that programs are oriented around lines of code, whereas most text processing is oriented around characters and lines. After you complete a program, you save your file to disk. This file will be input to the compiler; it is known as a **source file.**

COMPILING PROGRAMS

The information in a source file stored on disk must be translated into machine language so the computer can understand it. Most high-level languages use a compiler to do this. The compiler is actually two separate programs: the **preprocessor** and the **translator.**

The preprocessor reads the source code and prepares it for the translator. While preparing the code, it scans for special commands known as **preprocessor directives.** These directives tell the preprocessor to look for special code libraries, make substitutions in the code, and in other ways prepare the code for translation into machine language. The result of preprocessing is called the **translation unit.**

After the preprocessor has prepared the code for compilation, the translator does the work of converting the translation unit into machine language. The translator reads the translation unit and writes the resulting **object module** to a file that can then be combined with other precompiled units to form the final program. An object module is the code in machine language. Even though the output of the compiler is machine language code, it is not yet ready to run; that is, it is not yet executable because it does not have all the required parts.

LINKING PROGRAMS

A high-level language has many **subprograms.** Some of these subprograms are written by you and are a part of your source program. However, there are other subprograms, such as input/output processes and mathematical library subroutines, that exist elsewhere and must be attached to your program. The **linker** assembles all of these functions, yours and the system's, into your final executable program.

9.3 PROGRAM EXECUTION

Once your program has been linked, it is ready for execution. To execute your program you use an operating system command, such as *run,* to load your program into primary memory and execute it. Getting the program into memory is the function of an operating system program known as the **loader.** It locates the executable program and reads it into memory. When everything is ready, control is given to the program, and it begins execution.

In a typical program execution, the program reads data for processing either from the user or from a file. After the program processes the data, it prepares the output. Data can be output to the user's monitor or to a file. When the program is finished, it tells the operating system, which removes the program from memory. A program execution in a personal computer environment is seen in Figure 9.3.

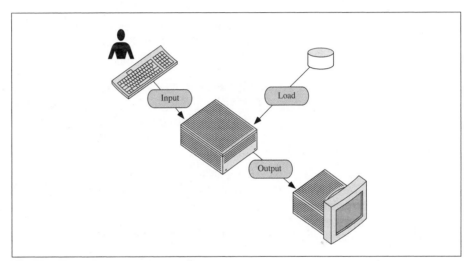

Figure 9.3   Program execution

9.4 CATEGORIES OF LANGUAGES

Today, computer languages are categorized according to the approach they use in solving a problem and the category of problems they solve. We divide computer languages into five categories: procedural (imperative) languages, object-oriented languages, functional languages, declarative languages, and special languages (Figure 9.4).

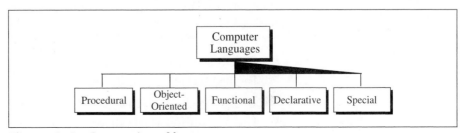

Figure 9.4   Categories of languages

PROCEDURAL (IMPERATIVE) LANGUAGES

A procedural, or imperative, language uses the traditional approach to programming. It follows the same approach used by the computer hardware to execute a program (fetch, decode, execute). A **procedural language** is a set of instructions that are executed one by one from beginning to end unless an instruction forces the control elsewhere. Even in this case, the program is still a series of instructions that are executed one after another, although some may be executed more than once or some may be skipped.

When programmers need to solve a problem using one of the procedural languages, they should know the *procedure* to follow. In other words, for each problem, the programmer should carefully design an algorithm, and the algorithm should be carefully translated to instructions.

Each instruction in a procedural language either manipulates data items (changing the values stored in memory locations or moving them somewhere else) or is a control instruction that locates the next instruction to be executed. That is why a procedural language is sometimes called an **imperative language:** Each instruction is a command to the computer system to do some specific task.

Several high-level procedural languages have been developed during the last few decades: FORTRAN, COBOL, Pascal, C, and Ada. We briefly present characteristics of each language here. Later in this chapter, we discuss the elements of C in more detail.

FORTRAN

FORTRAN (FORmula TRANslation), designed by a group of IBM engineers under the supervision of Jack Backus, was commercially available in 1957. FORTRAN was the first high-level language. It has some features that, after four decades, still make it an ideal language for scientific and engineering applications. These features can be summarized as

- High-precision arithmetic
- Capability of handling complex numbers
- Exponentiation computation (a^b)

During the last 40 years, FORTRAN has gone through several versions:

1. FORTRAN
2. FORTRAN II
3. FORTRAN IV
4. FORTRAN 77
5. FORTRAN 99
6. HPF (High Performance FORTRAN)

The newest version (HPF) is used in high-speed multiprocessor computers.

COBOL

COBOL (COmmon Business-Oriented Language) was designed by a group of computer scientists under the direction of Grace Hopper of the U.S. Navy. COBOL had a specific design goal: to be used as a business programming language. The problems to be solved in a business environment are totally different from those in an engineering environment. Business programs do not need the precise calculations required by engineering programs. The programming needs of the business world can be summarized as follows:

- Fast access to files and databases
- Fast updating of files and databases
- Large amounts of generated reports
- User-friendly formatted output

COBOL was designed to fulfill all of these goals.

Pascal

Pascal was invented by Niklaus Wirth in 1971 in Zurich, Switzerland. It was named after Blaise Pascal, the 17th-century French mathematician and philosopher who invented the Pascaline calculator.

Pascal was designed with a specific goal in mind: to teach programming to novices by emphasizing the structured programming approach. Although Pascal became the most popular language in academia, it never attained the same popularity in industry. Today's procedural languages owe a lot to this language.

C

The **C language** was developed in the early 1970s by Dennis Ritchie at Bell Laboratories. It was originally intended for writing operating systems and system software (most of the UNIX operating system is written in C). Later, it became popular among programmers for several reasons:

- C has all the high-level instructions a structured high-level programming language should have; it hides the hardware details from the programmer.

- C also has some low-level instructions that allow the programmer to access the hardware directly and quickly; C is closer to assembly language than any other language. This makes it a good language for system programmers.

- C is a very efficient language; its instructions are short. Sometimes one symbol in C can do the same job as a long word in a language like COBOL. This conciseness attracts programmers who want to write short programs.

- C has been standardized by ANSI and ISO.

We discuss some C language elements at the end of this chapter.

Ada

Ada was named after Augusta Ada Byron, the daughter of Lord Byron and the assistant to Charles Babbage (the inventor of the Analytical Engine). It was created for the U.S. Department of Defense (DoD) to be the uniform language used by all DoD contractors.

Ada has three features that make it very popular for DoD, jumbo computers, and industry:

- Ada has high-level instructions like other procedural languages.

- Ada has instructions to allow real-time processing. This makes it suitable for process control.

- Ada has parallel-processing capabilities. It can be run on mainframe computers with multiple processors.

OBJECT-ORIENTED LANGUAGES

Object-oriented programming uses an approach to problem solving that is totally different from procedural programming. You can think of a data item in both languages as an object. A program can be thought of as a series of operations that you want to perform on the object.

In procedural programming, the objects are totally separate and independent from the operations. The objects can be stored on a computer, and different programs using different operations are applied on them. In other words, in procedural programming, the objects are *passive*. They do not have any operations defined for them. The programmers define the operations and apply them to the objects.

In object-oriented programming, the objects and the operations to be applied to them are tied together. The programmer first defines an object and the types of operations that can be applied to this object. The programmer (or another programmer) can then use this combination and invokes some or all of the operations defined to solve a problem. In other words, the objects in object-oriented programming are *active*.

The idea is similar to objects in real life. There are objects that are passive, such as a stone. There is no operation included with the stone. If someone wants to perform an operation on a stone, he or she defines the operation and does it. On the other hand, a car is an active object. Several operations are already defined for a car. The driver needs only invoke one of these operations.

Several **object-oriented languages** have been developed. We briefly discuss the characteristics of two: C++ and Java.

C++

The **C++ language** was developed by Bjarne Stroustrup at Bell Laboratory as a better C language. It uses **classes** to define the general characteristics of similar objects and the operations that can be applied to them. For example, a programmer can define a `Geometrical_Shapes` class and all the characteristics common to two-dimensional geometrical shapes such as center, number of sides, and so on. The class can also define operations (functions or methods) that can be applied to a geometrical shape such as calculating and printing the area, calculating and printing the perimeter, printing the coordinate of the center point, and so on. A program can then be written to create different objects of type `Geometrical_Shapes`. Each object can have a center located at a different point and a different number of sides. The program can then calculate and print the area, perimeter, and the location of the center for each object.

Three principles were used in the design of the C++ language: encapsulation, inheritance, and polymorphism.

Encapsulation **Encapsulation** is the idea of hiding the data and some operations that can be performed on the data inside the object. The user of objects would normally not directly access the data. Instead, the data are accessed through an interface (a call to a particular set of operations). In other words, the user knows what to do with the data without knowing how it is done.

Inheritance In C++, as in nature, an object can inherit from another object. This concept is called **inheritance.** When a general class is defined, you can define a more specific class that inherits some of the characteristics of the general class but also has some new characteristics. For example, when an object of type `Geometrical_Shapes` is defined, you can define a class called `Rectangles`. Rectangles are geometrical shapes with additional characteristics. In C++, multiple inheritance is allowed. A class can inherit from more than one class.

Polymorphism Polymorphism means "many forms." **Polymorphism** in C++ means that you can define several operations with the same name that can do different things in related classes. For example, assume that you define two classes, `Rectangles` and `Circles`, both inherited from the class `Geometrical_Shapes`. You define two operations both named *area,* one in `Rectangles` and one in `Circles`, that calculate the area of a rectangle or a circle. The two operations have the same name but do different things; calculating the area of a rectangle and the area of a circle need different operands and operations.

Java

Java was developed at Sun Microsystems, Inc. It is based on C and C++, but some features of C++, such as multiple inheritance, are removed to make the language more robust. In addition, the language is totally class oriented. In C++, one can solve a problem without even defining a class. In Java, every data item belongs to a class.

A program in Java can either be an application or an applet. An application is a complete stand-alone program that can be run independently (like a C++ program).

An applet, on the other hand, is embedded in HTM language, stored on a server, and run by a browser. The browser can download the applet and run it locally.

In Java, an application program (or an applet) is a collection of classes and instances of those classes. One interesting feature of Java is the class library, a collection of classes. Although C++ also provides a class library, in Java the user can build new classes based on the ones provided by the library.

The execution of a program in Java is also unique. You create a class and pass it to the interpreter that calls the class methods.

Another interesting feature in Java is multithreading. A thread is a sequence of actions executed one after another. C++ allows only single threading (the whole program is executed as a single thread), but Java allows multithreading (concurrent execution of several lines of codes).

FUNCTIONAL LANGUAGES

In functional programming, a program is considered a mathematical function. In this context, a **function** is a black box that maps a list of inputs to a list of outputs (Figure 9.5).

For example, *summation* can be considered a function with n inputs and only one output. The function takes the n inputs, adds them, and creates the sum. A **functional language** does the following:

1. It predefines a set of primitive (atomic) functions that can be used by any programmer.

2. It allows the programmer to combine primitive functions to create new functions.

For example, you can define a primitive function called `first` that extracts the first element of a list. It may also have a function called `rest` that extracts all the elements except the first. A program can define a function that extracts the third element of a list by combining these two functions as shown in Figure 9.6.

Figure 9.5 Function in a functional language

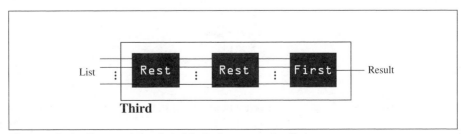

Figure 9.6 Extracting the third element of a list

A functional language has two advantages over a procedural language: It encourages modular programming and allows the programmer to make new functions out of existing ones. These two factors help a programmer create large and less error-prone programs from already-tested programs.

We briefly discuss LISP and Scheme as examples of functional languages.

LISP

LISP (LISt Programming) was designed by a team of researchers at MIT in the early 1960s. It is a list-processing programming language in which everything is considered a list.

Scheme

The LISP language suffered from a lack of standardization. After a while, there were different versions of LISP everywhere; the de facto standard is the one developed by MIT in the early 1970s called **Scheme.**

The Scheme language defines a set of primitive functions that solves problems. The function name and the list of inputs to the function are enclosed in parentheses. The result is an output list, which can be used as the input list to another function. For example, there is a function, car, that extracts the first element of a list. There is a function, called cdr, that extracts the rest of the elements in a list except the first one. In other words, you have

```
(car  2 3 7 8 11 17 20)  ====>  2
(cdr  2 3 7 8 11 17 20) ====>   3 7 8 11 17 20
```

Now you can combine these two functions to extract the third element of any list.

```
(car (cdr (cdr  list)))
```

If you apply the above function to 2 3 7 8 11 17 20, it extracts 7 because the result of the innermost parentheses is 3 7 8 11 17 20. This becomes the input to the middle parentheses with the result 7 8 11 17 20. This list now becomes the input to the car function, which takes out the first element, 7.

DECLARATIVE (LOGIC) LANGUAGES

A **declarative language** uses the principle of logical reasoning to answer queries. It is based on formal logic defined by Greek mathematicians and later developed into what is called *first-order predicate calculus.*

Logical reasoning is based on deduction. Some statements (facts) are given that are assumed to be true; the logician uses solid rules of logical reasoning to deduce new statements (facts).

For example, the famous rule of deduction in logic is

```
If (A is B) and (B is C), then (A is C)
```

Using this rule and the two following facts,

```
Fact 1: Socrates is a human    ⟶    A is B
Fact 2: A human is mortal       ⟶    B is C
```

we can deduce a new fact

```
Fact 3: Socrates is mortal      ⟶    A is C
```

Programmers should study the domain of their subject (know all the facts in this domain) or get the facts from experts in the field. Programmers should also be expert in logic to carefully define the rules. Then the program can deduce and create new facts.

One problem associated with declarative languages is that a program is specific to a particular domain because collecting all the facts into one program makes it huge. This is the reason declarative programming is limited so far to only specific fields such as artificial intelligence.

Prolog

One of the famous declarative languages is **Prolog** (PROgramming in LOGic), developed by A. Colmerauer in France in 1972. A program in Prolog is made of facts and rules. For example, the previous facts about human beings can be stated as

```
human (John)
mortal (human)
```

The user can then ask

```
?-mortal (John)
```

and the program will respond with *yes*.

SPECIAL LANGUAGES

During the last decades, some new languages have emerged that cannot be placed in the four categories just discussed. Some are a mixture of two or more models and others belong to a specific task. We categorize them under special languages.

HTML

HTML (Hypertext Markup Language) is a pseudolanguage that includes marks that serve as formatting hints and links to other files. An HTML file is made of text and tags. A tag is enclosed in two angle brackets and usually comes in pairs. An HTML file (page) is stored on the server and can be downloaded by a browser. The browser removes the tags and interprets them as either formatting hints or links to other files. A markup language such as HTML allows you to embed formatting instructions in the file itself. The instructions are stored with the text. In this way, any browser can read the instructions and format the text according to the workstation being used.

One might ask: Why not use the formatting capabilities of word processors to create and save formatted text? The answer is that different word processors use different techniques or procedures for formatting text. HTML lets you use only ASCII characters for both the main text and formatting instructions. In this way, every computer can receive the entire document as an ASCII document. The main text is the data, and the formatting instructions can be used by the browser to format the data. An HTML program is made up of two parts: the head and body.

Head The head is the first part that contains the title of the page and other parameters that the browser will use.

Body The actual contents of a page are in the body, which includes the text and the tags. Whereas the text is the actual information contained in a page, the tags define the appearance of the document. Every HTML tag is a name followed by an optional list of attributes, all enclosed between angle brackets (< and >).

Tags The browser makes a decision about the structure of the text based on the tags, which are marks that are embedded into the text. A tag is enclosed in two angle brackets and usually comes in pairs. A tag can have a list of attributes, each of which can be followed by an equal sign and a value associated with the attribute. Table 9.1 shows some of the most common tags.

Beginning Tag	Ending Tag	Meaning
<HTML>	</HTML>	Defines an HTML document
<HEAD>	</HEAD>	Defines the head of the document
<BODY>	</BODY>	Defines the body of the document
<TITLE>	</TITLE>	Defines the title of the document
<Hi>	</Hi>	Defines different headers (i is an integer)
<B>	</B>	Boldface
<I>	</I>	Italic
<U>	</U>	Underlined
_		Subscript
[	]	Superscript
<CENTER>	</CENTER>	Centered
 		Line break
<OL>	</OL>	Ordered list
<UL>	</UL>	Unordered list
<LI>	</LI>	An item in a list
<IMG>		Defines an image
<A>	</A>	Defines an address (hyperlink)

Table 9.1   Common tags

The following shows an example of an HTML program (Web page). When it is run, it shows the picture that is linked to it.

```
<HTML>
     <HEAD>
          <TITLE> Sample Document </TITLE>
     </HEAD>
     <BODY>
        This is the picture of a book:
        <IMG SRC="Pictures/book1.gif"    ALIGN=MIDDLE>
     </BODY>
</HTML>
```

Program 9.4   HTML program

PERL

Practical Extraction and Report Language (**PERL**) is a high-level language with a syntax similar to the C language but more efficient. The power of PERL lies in its well-designed use of *regular expressions* that allow the programmer to parse a string of characters into its components and extract the needed information.

SQL

Structured Query Language (**SQL**) is a language used to answer queries about databases. We will see some examples of SQL in Chapter 14 when we discuss relational databases.

9.5   A PROCEDURAL LANGUAGE: C

In this section, we do a quick navigation through a common procedural language that is considered by most programmers to be the mother of several modern languages such as C++, Java, and PERL. We discuss the structure of the language and describe its elements. This journey is not by any means a complete coverage of the language syntax. It is a bird's-eye view that shows the different aspects of the language for students who will take programming languages in the future.[1]

IDENTIFIERS

One feature present in all computer languages is the **identifier.** Identifiers allow you to name data and other objects in the program. Each piece of data in a computer is stored at a unique address. If there were no identifiers to symbolically represent data locations, you would have to know and use data addresses to manipulate them. Instead, you simply give data identifier names and let the **compiler** keep track of where they are physically located.

Different programming languages use different rules to form identifiers. In C, the rules for identifiers are very simple. The only valid name symbols are the capital letters *A* through *Z,* the lowercase letters *a* through *z,* the digits 0 through 9, and the underscore. The first character of the identifier cannot be a digit. By custom, applications do not use the underscore for the first character either because many of the identifiers in the system libraries that support C start with an underscore. In this way, you make sure that your names do not duplicate system names, which could become very confusing. The last rule is that the name you create cannot be any of about 50 special names, known as **reserved words** or **keywords,** that are contained in the language itself.

DATA TYPES

A **data type** defines a set of **values** and a set of **operations** that can be applied to those values. The set of values for each type is known as the domain for the type. For example, a light switch can be compared to a computer type. It has a set of two values: on and off. Since the domain of a light switch consists of only these two values, its size is two. There are only two operations that can be applied to a light switch: turn on and turn off.

C contains three **standard types:** int (short for integer), char (short for character), float (short for floating-point). Standard types are atomic: They cannot be broken down. They also serve as the basic building blocks for the derived types. **Derived types** are complex structures that are built using the standard types. The derived types are *pointer, enumerated type, union, array,* and *structure.*

integer

An int **(integer)** type is a number without a fraction part. It is also known as an integral number. C supports three different sizes of the integer data type: short int, int, and long int. A short int can also be referred to as short, and long int can be referred to as long. We already defined an integer in Chapter 3; the designations short and long define the number of bytes allocated for an integer by the compiler.

char

The second type is char (character). Although we think of characters as the letters of the alphabet, the C language has another definition. To C, a character is any value that can be represented in the computer's alphabet. C uses the American Standard Code for Information Interchange (ASCII, pronounced "a-skey") alphabet. ASCII characters are tabulated in Appendix A.

---

[1]For a complete discussion, see Behrouz A. Forouzan and Richard F. Gilberg, *An Introduction to Computer Science: A Structured Programming Approach Using C,* 2nd ed. (Pacific Grove, CA: Brooks/Cole, 2001).

float

A `float` type is a number with a fractional part, such as 43.32. We defined the floating types in Chapter 3. The C language supports three different sizes of floating-point data types: `float`, `double`, and `long double`. As was the case for `int`, `float` types are defined from smallest to largest.

VARIABLES

Variables are names for memory locations. As discussed in Chapter 5, each memory location (or word) in a computer has an address. Although the addresses are used by the computer internally, it is very inconvenient for the programmer to use addresses because the programmer does not know where the program and data are stored in memory. Names, as a substitute for addresses, free the programmer to think at the level at which the program is executed. A programmer can use a variable, such as `score`, to store the integer value of a score received in a test (97). The computer can use memory location 245,876 to store this value. Whenever a reference is made to `score` during execution of the program, the computer knows it means location 245,876. Figure 9.7 shows the concept of a variable.

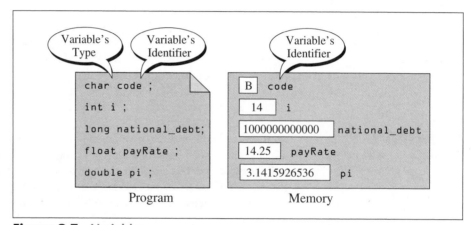

Figure 9.7   Variables

C requires the programmer to define a type for the variable. The reason is that the type defines the range of the data that can be stored in the variable and defines the number of bytes that can be allocated for that variable.

Variable Declaration and Definition

C requires that a variable be declared and defined before being used. A **declaration** is used to name a variable. **Definitions** are used to create the variable and to allocate a memory location for it.

When you create a variable, the declaration gives it a symbolic name, and the definition reserves memory for it. Once defined, variables are used to hold the data that are required by the program for its operation.

A variable's type can be any of the data types, such as `char`, `int`, or `float`. To create a variable, specify the type and the name. For example, the following can be used to declare and define a variable called `price` in C. The name of the variable is `price`, and its type is `float` (floating-point number).

```
float    price  ;
```

After this, the computer allocates some memory locations (the number depends on the computer system) and collectively calls them `price`. Note that this variable is defined, but nothing is stored in it yet.

Variable Initialization

C allows a variable to be initialized at the time it is declared and defined. The **initializer** establishes the first value that the variable will contain. To initialize a variable when it is defined, the name is followed by the assignment operator (the equal sign) and then the initializer. This simple initialization format is

```
float price = 23.45 ;
```

CONSTANTS

Constants are data values that cannot be changed during the execution of a program. For example, a programmer may need to use the value of *pi* (3.14) several times. It is very convenient to define a constant at the top of the program and use it. On some occasions, the value can be changed, but not each time the program is run. For example, the tax rate may change every year, but it is fixed during the year. A programmer can define a constant for the tax rate and check each year to see if it has changed.

Constants can appear in a program in one of three ways: literal constant, named constant, or symbolic constant.

Literal Constant

A **literal constant** is an unnamed value that is used in a program as is. For example, the following shows how a literal constant is used in an instruction in C. The value 2 is a literal constant. The variables are length, width, and circumference.

```
circumference = 2  *  length  *  width
```

Named Constant

A **named constant** is a value that you store in memory; you do not want the program to change it. The following shows how the C language creates a named constant:

```
const  pi = 3.14 ;
```

Symbolic Constant

A **symbolic constant** is a value that has only a symbolic name. The compiler can replace the name with the value. In most programming languages, the value is not stored in memory. The symbolic constant is defined at the beginning of the program to be conspicuous. It is used for a constant that changes its value occasionally. The following shows how the C language defines a symbolic constant:

```
#define  taxRate  0.0825
```

Constants and Types

Like variables, constants have a type. Most programming languages use integer constant, floating-point constant, character constant, and string constant. For example, the following shows different constants in the C language. The character literals are stored in single quotes; the string literals are in double quotes. Note that the text enclosed between /* and */ is a comment that is ignored by the compiler.

```
23        /*  Integer literal         */
23.12     /*  Floating-point literal  */
'A'       /*  Character literal       */
"Hello"   /*  String literal          */
```

INPUT AND OUTPUT

Almost every program needs to read and/or write data. These operations can be quite complex, especially when you read and write large files. Most programming languages use a predefined function for input and output.

Input

Data are input by either a statement or a predefined function. The C language has several input functions. For example, the `scanf` function reads data from the keyboard and stores it in a variable. The following is an example:

```
scanf ("%d", &num) ;
```

When the program encounters this instruction, it waits for the user to type an integer. It then stores the value in the variable `num`. The `%d` tells the program to expect an integer.

Output

Data are output by either a statement or a predefined function. The C language has several output functions. For example, the `printf` function displays a string on the monitor. The programmer can include the value of a variable or variables as part of the string. The following displays the value of a variable at the end of a literal string.

```
printf ("The value of the number is : %d" , num );
```

EXPRESSIONS

An **expression** is a sequence of operands and operators that reduces to a single value. For example, the following is an expression with a value of 10.

```
2  *  5
```

Operator

An **operator** is a language-specific syntactical token that requires an action to be taken. The most familiar operators are drawn from mathematics. For example, multiply (*) is an operator. It indicates that two numbers are to be multiplied. Every language has operators, and their use is rigorously specified in the syntax, or rules, of the language.

Arithmetic Operators   The C language defines several **arithmetic operators,** some of which are shown in Table 9.2.

Operator	Definition	Example
+	Addition	3 + 5
−	Subtraction	2 − 4
*	Multiplication	Num * 5
/	Division (quotient)	Sum/
%	Division (remainder)	Count
		Count % 4
++	Increment (add 1 to the value of the variable)	Count++
−−	Decrement (Subtract 1 from the value of the variable)	Count−−

Table 9.2   Arithmetic operators

Relational Operators   **Relational operators** compare data to see if a value is greater than, less than, or equal to another value. The result of applying relational operators is the logical value true or false. The C language uses six relational operators (Table 9.3).

Operator	Definition	Example
<	Less than	Num1 < 5
<=	Less than or equal to	Num1 <= 5
>	Greater than	Num2 > 3
>=	Greater than or equal to	Num2 >= 3
==	Equal to	Num1 == Num2
!=	Not equal to	Num1 != Num2

Table 9.3 Relational operators

Logical Operators **Logical operators** combine logical values (true or false) to get a new value. The C language uses three logical operators as shown in Table 9.4.

Operator	Definition	Example
!	NOT	! (Num1 < Num2)
&&	AND	(Num1 < 5) && (Num2 > 10)
||	OR	(Num1 < 5) || (Num2 > 10)

Table 9.4 Logical operators

Assignment Operators An **assignment operator** stores a value in a variable. The C language defines several assignment operators, some of which are shown in Table 9.5.

Operator	Example	Meaning
=	num = 5 ;	Store 5 in variable num
+=	num += 5 ;	Same as num = num + 5
-=	num -= 5 ;	Same as num = num - 5
*=	num *= 5 ;	Same as num = num * 5
/=	num /= 5 ;	Same as num = num / 5
%=	num %= 5 ;	Same as num = num % 5

Table 9.5 Assignment operators

Operand

An **operand** receives an operator's action. For any given operator, there may be one, two, or more operands. In our arithmetic example, the operands of multiply are the multiplier and the multiplicand.

STATEMENTS

A **statement** causes an action to be performed by the program. It translates directly into one or more executable computer instructions. For example, the C language defines six types of statements: expression statement, compound statement, labeled statement, selection statement, iterative statement, and jump statement (Figure 9.8). We discuss some of these in this section.

Expression Statements

An expression is turned into a statement by placing a semicolon (;) after it. When C sees the semicolon, it performs the evaluation on the expression. If there is an assignment involved (existence of an assignment operator or ++ or --) the value is stored in the variable. If there is no assignment, the value is discarded. The following are some examples of **expression statements:**

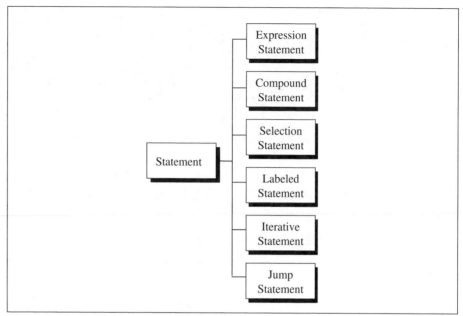

Figure 9.8   Statements

```
a++ ;
b = 4 ;
c = b + c * 4 ;
```

Compound Statements

A **compound statement** is a unit of code consisting of zero or more statements. It is also known as a **block.** The compound statement allows a group of statements to become one single entity. A compound statement consists of an opening brace, an optional statement section, followed by a closing brace. The following shows the makeup of a compound statement.

```
{
x = 1 ;
y = 20;
}
```

FUNCTIONS

In C, a subroutine is called a **function.** A C program is made of one or more functions, one and only one of which must be called main. The execution of the program always starts and ends with main, but this function can call other functions to do special tasks.

A function in C (including main) is an independent module that is called to do a specific task. The function main is called by the operating system; main in turn calls other functions. When main is complete, control returns to the operating system.

In general, the purpose of a function is to receive zero or more pieces of data, operate on them, and return at most one piece of data. At the same time, a function can have a **side effect.** A function's side effect is an action that results in a change in the state of the program. If there is a side effect, it occurs while the function is executing and before the function returns. The side effect can involve accepting data from outside the

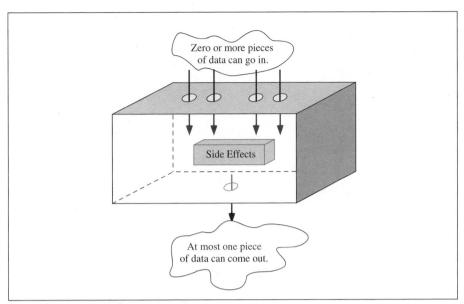

Figure 9.9   Side effect of a function

program, sending data out of the program to the monitor or a file, or changing the value of a variable in the calling function. The function concept is shown in Figure 9.9.

Function Declaration

Functions in C must be both declared and defined. The **function declaration** is done with a prototype declaration. You use the function by calling it. The function definition contains the code required to complete the task. Figure 9.10 shows the interrelationships among these function components. Note that the function name is used three times: when the function is declared, when it is called, and when it is defined.

Function Definition

The **function definition** contains the code for a function. The definition is made up of two parts: the function header and the function body, which is a compound statement.

Function Header   A **function header** consists of three parts: the return type, the function name, and the **formal parameter** list.

Function Body   The **function body** contains the declarations and statements for the function. The body starts with local definitions that specify the variables required by the function. After the local declarations, the function statements, terminating with a `return` statement, are coded. If a function return type is `void`, it may be written without a `return` statement.

Function Call

A **function call** is used to call the function. The call contains the **actual parameters,** which identify the values that are to be sent to the called function. They match the function's formal parameters in type and order in the parameter list. If there are multiple actual parameters, they are separated by commas.

Parameter Passing

In C, you can pass a parameter to a function in one of two ways: pass by value and pass by reference.

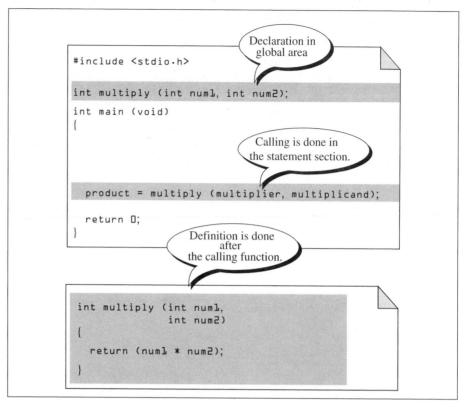

Figure 9.10   Function declaration

Pass by Value   When you **pass by value,** a copy of the data is created and placed in a local variable in the called function. This means of passing data ensures that regardless of how the data are manipulated and changed in the called function, the original data in the calling function are safe and unchanged. Because passing by value protects the data, it is the preferred passing technique.

Pass by Reference   There are times, however, when it is necessary to pass by reference. **Pass by reference** sends the address of a variable to the called function rather than sending its value. When you want to change the contents in a variable in the calling function, you must pass by reference.

Consider the case in which you need to write a function that processes two data values and returns them to the calling function; that is, it stores their values in the calling program. Since a function can return only one value, you have a problem. The solution is to pass by reference.

SELECTION

As you saw in Chapter 8, to solve a problem using an algorithm, you need selection constructs.

if-else

To implement a two-way selection in C, one can use the **if-else statement.** Figure 9.11 shows the logic flow for an if-else. The expression can be any C expression. After it has been evaluated, if its value is true (not 0), statement1 is executed; otherwise, statement2 is executed. It is impossible for both statements to be executed in the

a. Logical Flow

```
if (expression)
   statement1
else
   statement2
```

b. Code

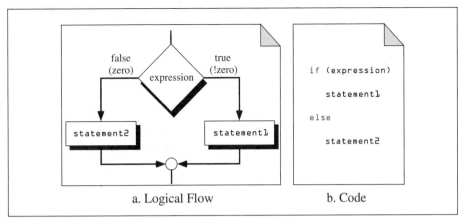

Figure 9.11 `if-else` statement

```
switch  ( expression )
 {
 case  constant-1 : statement
                    statement
 case  constant-2 : statement
                    statement
 case  constant-n : statement
                    statement
 default          : statement
                    statement
 }
```

Figure 9.12 `switch` statement

same evaluation. An `if-else` statement can be nested (one inside another) to create multiway selection.

switch

Although you can use nested `if-else` statements for multiway selection, there is another statement in C for this purpose: the **`switch` statement** (Figure 9.12). The selection condition must be one of the C integral types.

REPETITION

You saw in Chapter 8 that you need repetition constructs. The C language defines three types of loop statements: `while`, `for`, and `do-while`.

while Loop

The main repetition construct in the C language is the `while` loop (Figure 9.13). A **`while` loop** is a pretest loop. It checks the value of a testing expression. If the value is

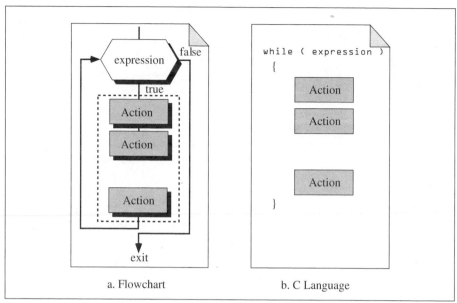

Figure 9.13   while loop

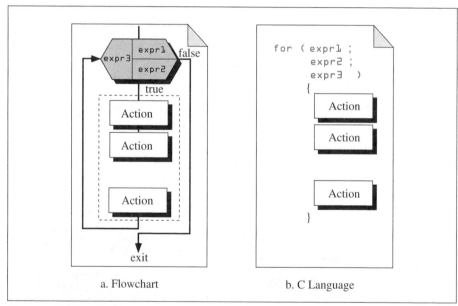

Figure 9.14   for loop

true (nonzero), it goes through one iteration of the loop and tests the value again. The while loop is considered an event-controlled loop. The loop continues in iteration until an event happens that changes the value of the test expression from true to false.

for Loop

The **for loop** is also a pretest loop (Figure 9.14). However, in contrast to the while loop, it is a counter-controlled loop. A counter is set to an initial value and is incremented (or decremented) in each iteration. The loop is terminated when the value of the counter matches a predetermined value.

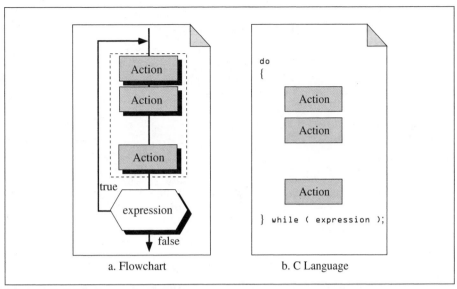

Figure 9.15 `do-while` loop

do-while Loop

The `do-while` **loop** is also an event-controlled loop; however, in contrast to the `while` loop, it is a posttest loop (Figure 9.15). The loop does one iteration and tests the value of an expression. If it is false, it terminates. If it is true, it does one more iteration and tests again.

DERIVED DATA TYPES

In addition to the simple data types discussed earlier, the C language also allows derived data types: arrays, pointers, unions, and structures. We will discuss some of these data types in Chapter 11 on data structures.

RECURSION

The C language supports **recursion** (discussed in Chapter 8). A function in C can call itself.

9.6 KEY TERMS

acrual parameters
Ada
arithmetic operator
assembler
assembly language
assignment operator
block
C language
C++ language
char
class
COBOL
compiler
compound statement
computer language

constant
data type
declaration
declarative language
definition
derived types
do-while loop
encapsulation
executable file
expression
expression statement
float
for loop
formal parameter
FORTRAN

function
function body
function call
function declaration
function definition
function header
functional language
high-level language
HTML
identifier
if-else statement
imperative language
inheritance
initializer
integer

Java   Pascal   source file
keyword   pass by reference   SQL
linker   pass by value   standard types
LISP   PERL   statement
literal constant   polymorphism   subprogram
loader   preprocessor   `switch` statement
logical operator   preprocessor directive   symbolic constant
machine language   procedural language   symbolic language
named constant   programming language   syntax
natural language   Prolog   text editor
object module   recursion   translation unit
object-oriented language relational operator   translator
operand   reserved word   variable
operation   Scheme   `while` loop
operator   side effect

9.7 SUMMARY

■ The only language understood by a computer is machine language.

■ A symbolic language uses symbols to represent various machine language instructions. Symbolic languages are also called assembly languages.

■ A high-level language is portable from one computer type to another and frees the programmer from hardware concerns. BASIC, Pascal, Ada, C, C++, and Java are high-level languages.

■ The steps to building a program include writing, editing, compiling, and linking code.

■ There are five categories of computer languages: procedural, object-oriented, functional, declarative, and special.

■ In a procedural language, an algorithm is translated into code. The code manipulates data and controls the execution of instructions. FORTRAN, COBOL, Pascal, C, and Ada are all procedural languages.

■ In an object-oriented language such as C++ and Java, the objects and the operations applied to the objects are tied together.

■ C++ uses the concepts of encapsulation, inheritance, and polymorphism.

■ In a functional language, the algorithm is mathematical in nature. LISP and Scheme are functional languages.

■ A declarative language uses the principles of logical reasoning. Prolog is a declarative language.

■ A special language cannot be categorized into one of the other four groups. HTML, PERL, and SQL are special languages.

■ C is considered the mother of languages such as C++, Java, and PERL.

■ An identifier names data and other objects in a program.

■ A data type defines a set of values and a set of operations that can be applied on those values.

■ Standard data types for the C language are `int` (integer), `char` (character), and `float` (floating-point).

■ A constant is a data value that cannot be changed during the execution of a program.

■ A variable is a name for a memory location.

■ Data are usually input and/or output with predefined functions.

■ An expression is a sequence of operands and operators that reduces to a single value.

■ A statement causes an action to be performed by a program.

■ A function is an independent module that performs a specific task.

■ A C program has a function called `main` and zero or more other functions.

■ An `if-else` statement or a `switch` statement can implement a decision in C.

■ Repetition in C can be handled with a `while` loop, a `for` loop, or a `do-while` loop.

9.8 PRACTICE SET

REVIEW QUESTIONS

1. How is a symbolic language different from a machine language?

2. Why is symbolic language also known as assembly language?

3. What are the advantages of a high-level language over a machine language?

4. Name some high-level languages.

5. What is a natural language?

6. What is a source file? What is an executable file? How are these two file types related?

7. What is the function of a compiler?

8. What is the function of a linker?

9. What are the five categories of computer languages? Give an example of each.

10. How is Java related to C and C++?

11. Why is C a popular language among programmers?

12. What are some of the groups that use Ada?

13. How is procedural programming different from object-oriented programming?

14. What are three concepts intrinsic to programs in C++?

15. What is a functional language? Give an example of a function.

16. What is a declarative language?

17. What is a special language?

18. Name the three standard data types in the C language.

19. What is the purpose of an initializer in the C language?

20. What are the differences between a literal constant, a named constant, and a symbolic constant?

21. What is a variable?

22. What is an efficient way to handle often-used functions such as reading input from a file?

23. What are the relational operators in the C language?

24. What are the logical operators in the C language?

25. What are the assignment operators in the C language?

26. Describe the function `main` in the C language.

27. Name the parts of a function definition in C and their duties.

28. What is the purpose of a decision (selection) statement?

29. How does an `if-else` statement differ from a `switch` statement? Is one the subset of the other? Explain why or why not.

30. Discuss the three loop statements.

MULTIPLE-CHOICE QUESTIONS

31. The only language understood by computer hardware is a _____ language.
    a. machine
    b. symbolic
    c. high-level
    d. natural

32. _____ languages are also known as assembly languages.
    a. Machine
    b. Symbolic
    c. High-level
    d. Natural

33. Norwegian, Farsi, and Russian can be classified as _____ languages.
    a. machine
    b. symbolic
    c. high-level
    d. natural

34. C, C++, and Java can be classified as _____ languages.
    a. machine
    b. symbolic
    c. high-level
    d. natural

35. The software used to write a program is called a _____.
    a. preprocessor
    b. text editor
    c. translator
    d. source file

36. The _____ assembles precompiled units from different sources into an executable program.
    a. preprocessor
    b. text editor
    c. linker
    d. loader

37. The compiler consists of a _____ and a _____.
    a. preprocessor; loader
    b. text editor; loader
    c. preprocessor; translator
    d. linker; preprocessor

38. _____ is the code in machine language.
    a. A translation unit
    b. An object module
    c. A source file
    d. A subprogram

39. An operating system program called the _____ gets the program into memory.
    a. loader
    b. linker
    c. translator
    d. processor

40. A _____ language uses the traditional approach to programming and is also referred to as an imperative language.
    a. procedural
    b. functional
    c. declarative
    d. object-oriented

41. FORTRAN is a(n) _____ language.
    a. procedural
    b. functional
    c. declarative
    d. object-oriented

42. Pascal is a(n) _____ language.
    a. procedural
    b. functional
    c. declarative
    d. object-oriented

43. C++ is a(n) _____ language.
    a. procedural
    b. functional
    c. declarative
    d. object-oriented

44. LISP is a(n) _____ language.
    a. procedural
    b. functional
    c. declarative
    d. object-oriented

45. _____ is a common language in the business environment.
    a. FORTRAN
    b. C++
    c. C
    d. COBOL

46. _____, the first high-level language, is still popular with the scientific and engineering communities.
    a. FORTRAN
    b. C++
    c. C
    d. COBOL

47. _____ is a program designed to teach programming to novices that emphasizes the structured programming approach.
    a. C++
    b. C
    c. Pascal
    d. Scheme

48. The UNIX operating system is written in a language called _____.
    a. C++
    b. C
    c. Pascal
    d. LISP

49. A procedural language that is very popular with the DoD is _____.
    a. Ada
    b. Java
    c. C++
    d. Scheme

50. A popular object-oriented language is _____.
    a. FORTRAN
    b. COBOL
    c. C++
    d. LISP

51. In C++, _____ is the hiding of data and operations from the user.
    a. encapsulation
    b. inheritance
    c. polymorphism
    d. modularity

52. A _____ program can be either an application or an applet.
    a. FORTRAN
    b. C++
    c. C
    d. Java

53. LISP and Scheme are both _____ languages.
    a. procedural
    b. functional
    c. declarative
    d. object-oriented

54. An example of a(n) _____ language is Prolog.
    a. procedural
    b. functional
    c. declarative
    d. object-oriented

55. HTML, PERL, and SQL fall under the classification of _____ languages.
    a. modern
    b. special
    c. declarative
    d. object-oriented

56. A standard data type in the C language is _____.
    a. int
    b. char
    c. float
    d. all of the above

57. The standard data type _____ describes a number with a fractional part.
    a. int
    b. char
    c. float
    d. all of the above

58. The standard data type _____ describes a number without a fractional part.
    a. int
    b. char
    c. float
    d. all of the above

59. The standard data type _____ describes any value that can be represented in the computer's alphabet.
    a. int
    b. char
    c. float
    d. all of the above

EXERCISES

60. Do some research and find the arithmetic operators in FORTRAN, COBOL, and Pascal. Compare and contrast them with the arithmetic operators defined for the C language in this chapter. Use a table for comparison.

61. Do some research and find the relational operators in FORTRAN, COBOL, and Pascal. Compare and contrast them with the arithmetic operators defined for the C language in this chapter. Use a table for comparison.

62. Do some research and find the format of the compound statement in FORTRAN, COBOL, and Pascal. Compare and contrast them with the format defined for the C language in this chapter. Use a table for comparison.

63. Do some research and find the format of iterative statements (`for` loop, `while` loop, `do-while` loop, etc.) in FORTRAN, COBOL, and Pascal. Compare and contrast them with the format defined for the C language in this chapter. Use a table for comparison.

64. Do some research and find the format of decision statements (`if` and `switch`) in FORTRAN, COBOL, and Pascal. Compare and contrast them with the format defined for the C language in this chapter. Use a table for comparison.

65. Do some research and find the jump statement (e.g., `goto` and `continue`) in FORTRAN, COBOL, and Pascal. Compare and contrast them with the format defined for the C language in this chapter. Use a table for comparison.

66. Do some research and find how functions are handled in FORTRAN, COBOL, and Pascal. Compare and contrast them with the functions defined for the C language in this chapter. Use a table for comparison.

67. Do some research and find if recursion is supported in FORTRAN, COBOL, and Pascal.

68. Identify each of the following identifiers in C as valid or not valid. Justify your answer.
    a. 2AB
    b. A2B
    c. A C
    d. 999

69. Declare and define the following variables in the C language:
    a. An `int` variable named i.
    b. A `float` variable named f.
    c. A `char` variable named c.

70. Redo Exercise 69 but initialize each variable to an appropriate value.

71. In the C language, show how to read two integers from the keyboard using only one statement.

72. In the C language, show how to print the value of two integer variables using only one statement.

73. Write the following statements in the C language:

   a. Multiply the value of variable x by the value of variable y and store the result in variable z.

   b. Increment the value of variable x.

   c. Decrement the value of variable y.

   d. Compare the value of variable x and y for equality.

74. Write a `for` loop in C to print the message "Hello World!" 10 times.

75. Repeat Exercise 74 using a `while` loop.

76. Repeat Exercise 74 using a `do-while` loop.

77. Write a statement in Scheme to make a new list out of the existing list containing only the third and the fourth elements.

Software Engineering

In this chapter, we introduce the concept of software engineering. We begin with the idea of the software life cycle. We then show two models used for the development process: the waterfall model and the incremental model. Finally, we discuss issues related to software engineering, such as modularity, quality, and documentation.

Software engineering is the establishment and use of sound engineering methods and principles to obtain reliable software that works on real machines. This definition, from the first international conference on software engineering in 1969, was proposed 30 years after the first computer was built. During that period, software was more of an art than a science. In fact, one of the most authoritative treatments of programming describes it as an art: *The Art of Computer Programming.* This three-volume series, originally written by Donald E. Knuth in the late 1960s and early 1970s, is considered the most complete discussion of many computer science concepts.

10.1 SOFTWARE LIFE CYCLE

A fundamental concept in **software engineering** is the **software life cycle.** Software, like many other products, goes through a cycle of repeating phases (Figure 10.1).

Software is first developed by a group of developers/programmers. Usually, it is in use for a while before modifications are necessary. Modification is often needed due to errors found in the software, changes in the rules or laws, or changes in the company itself. The software should be modified before further use. These two steps, use and modify, continue until the software becomes obsolete. By "obsolete," we mean the software loses its validity because of inefficiency, obsolescence of the language, major changes in the company, or other factors. Some examples of software developments that normally go through this cycle are student registration systems, billing systems, and accounting systems.

The development process in the software life cycle involves four phases: analysis, design, implementation, and testing. Figure 10.2 shows these phases as part of the development process.

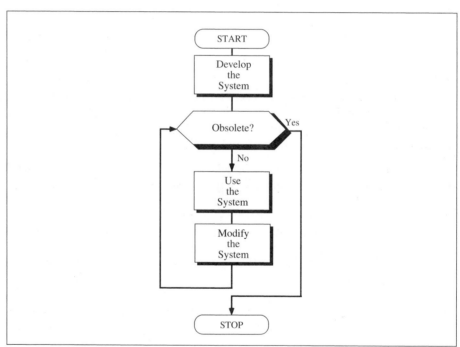

Figure 10.1 System life cycle

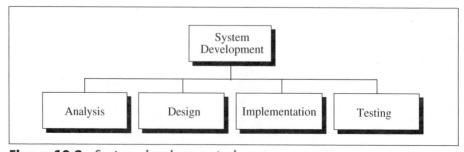

Figure 10.2 System development phases

ANALYSIS PHASE

The development process starts with the **analysis phase,** which shows what the package should do. In this phase, the systems analyst defines requirements that specify what the proposed system is to accomplish. The requirements are usually stated in terms that the user understands. There are four steps in the analysis phase: define the user, define the needs, define the requirements, and define the methods.

Define the User

A software package may be designed for a generic user or a specific user. For example, an accounting package may be created for use by any firm. On the other hand, a customized banking package may be created for a specific bank. The user of the package must be clearly defined.

Define the Needs

After the user has been identified, the analysts clearly define the needs. In this step, the best answer comes from the user. The user, or the representative of the user, clearly defines his/her expectations of the package.

Define the Requirements

Based on the needs of the user, the analyst can exactly define the requirements for the system. For example, if a package is to print checks at the end of the month for each employee, what level of security and accuracy should be implemented?

Define the Methods

Finally, after the requirements are defined in clear terms, the analyst can choose the appropriate methods to meet those requirements.

DESIGN PHASE

The **design phase** defines *how* the system will accomplish *what* was defined in the analysis phase. In the design phase, the systems are determined, and the design of the files and/or the databases is completed.

Modularity

Today, the design phase uses a very well-established principle called **modularity.** The whole package is divided into small **modules.** Each module is designed and tested and is linked to other modules through a main program. We discuss modularity later in this chapter.

Tools

The design phase uses several tools, the most common being a structure chart (discussed in Chapter 8). A structure chart shows how to break your package into logical steps; each step is a separate module. The structure chart also shows the interaction between all the parts (modules).

IMPLEMENTATION PHASE

In the **implementation phase,** you create the actual programs.

Tools

This phase uses several tools to show the logical flow of the programs before the actual writing of code. One tool, still popular, is the flowchart (discussed in Chapter 8). A **flowchart** uses standard graphical symbols to represent the logical flow of data through a module.

The second tool used by programmers is pseudocode (also discussed in Chapter 8). **Pseudocode** is part English and part program logic that describes, in precise algorithmic detail, what the program is to do. This requires defining the steps in sufficient detail so that conversion to a computer program can be accomplished easily.

Coding

After production of a flowchart, pseudocode, or both, the programmer actually writes the code in a language specific for the project. The choice of the language is based on the efficiency of the language for that particular application.

TESTING PHASE

Once the programs have been written, they must be tested. The **testing phase** can be a very tedious and time-consuming part of program development. The programmers are completely responsible for testing their programs. In large development projects, there are often specialists known as test engineers who are responsible for testing the system as a whole—that is, for testing to make sure all the programs work together.

There are two types of testing: black box and white box. Black box testing is done by the system test engineer and the user. White box testing is the responsibility of the programmer.

Black Box Testing

Black box testing gets its name from the concept of testing a program without knowing what is inside it and without knowing how it works. In other words, the program is like a black box that you can't see into.

Simply stated, black box test plans are developed by looking only at the requirements statement. This is why it is so important to have a good set of requirements. The test engineer uses these requirements and his or her knowledge of systems development and the user working environment to create a test plan. This plan will then be used when the system is tested as a whole. You should ask to see these test plans before you write your program.

White Box Testing

Whereas black box testing assumes that nothing is known about the program, **white box testing** assumes that you know everything about the program. In this case, the program is like a glass house in which everything is visible.

White box testing is the responsibility of the programmer, who knows exactly what is going on inside the program. You must make sure that every instruction and every possible situation have been tested. That is not a simple task!

Experience will help a programmer design good test data, but one thing that she can do from the start is to get in the habit of writing test plans. She should start her test plan when she is in the design stage. As she builds her structure chart, she should ask herself what situations, especially unusual situations, she needs to test for and make a note of them immediately. She may not remember an hour later.

When she is writing her flowcharts or pseudocode, she should review them with an eye toward test cases and make notes of the cases she needs.

When it comes time to construct her test cases, she should review her notes and organize them into logical sets. Except for very simple student programs, one set of test data will not completely validate a program. For large-scale development projects, 20, 30, or more test cases may need to be run to validate a program.

Finally, while she is testing, she will think of more test cases. Again, she should write them down and incorporate them into her test plan. After her program is finished and in production, she will need the test plans again when she modifies the program.

10.2 DEVELOPMENT PROCESS MODELS

There are several models for the development process. We discuss the two most common: the waterfall model and the incremental model.

WATERFALL MODEL

One very popular model for the development process is known as the **waterfall model** (Figure 10.3). In this model, the development process flows in only one direction. This means that a phase cannot be started until the previous phase is completed. For example,

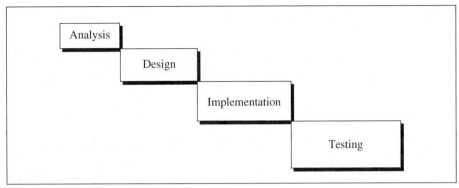

Figure 10.3   Waterfall model

the analysis phase of the whole project should be completed before its design phase is started. The entire design phase should be finished before the implementation phase can be started.

There are advantages and disadvantages to the waterfall model. An advantage is that each phase is completed before the next phase starts. The group that works on the design phase, for example, knows exactly what to do because they have the complete analysis phase. The testing phase can test the whole package because the entire project is ready.

A disadvantage of the waterfall model is the difficulty in locating a problem. The entire process must be investigated.

INCREMENTAL MODEL

In the **incremental model,** the process is developed in a series of steps. The software group first completes a simplified version of the whole package. The version represents the entire package but does not include the details.

This first version usually consists of only the main modules with calls to empty submodules. For example, if the package has 10 submodules, the main module calls each of them, with each submodule returning just a message that it was called.

In the second version, one or more submodules are completed, while the rest are left unfinished (they just communicate). The package is tested again to prove that the main module can use these submodules without problems. If there is a problem here, the developer knows that the problem is with these submodules and not with the main module. They do not add more submodules until the package works properly.

This process continues until all submodules are added. Figure 10.4 shows the incremental model concept.

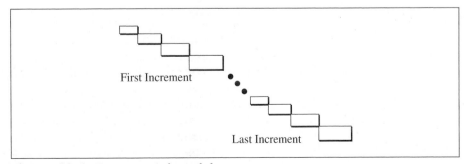

Figure 10.4   Incremental model

10.3 MODULARITY

Modularity means breaking a large project into smaller parts that can be understood and handled easily. In other words, modularity means to divide a large program into small programs that can communicate with each other.

TOOLS

Two types of tools can be used in programming to achieve modularity: the structure chart or the class diagram. A **structure chart** is used in procedural programming to show the relationship between procedures or functions. A **class diagram** is used in object-oriented programming to show the relationships between classes.

A new standard has been developed called **Unified Modeling Language (UML)**, which includes tools and diagrams to help in this respect.

COUPLING

Coupling is a measure of how tightly two modules are bound to each other. The more tightly coupled, the less independent they are. Since the objective is to make the modules as independent as possible, you want them to be loosely coupled. There are several reasons **loose coupling** is desirable.

1. Independent, that is loosely coupled, functions are more likely to be reusable.
2. Loosely coupled functions are less likely to create errors in related functions; conversely, the tighter the coupling, the higher the probability that an error in one function will generate an error in a related function.
3. Maintenance modifications—modifications required to implement new user requirements—are easier and less apt to create errors with loosely coupled functions.

We will discuss a few types of coupling.

Data Coupling

Data coupling passes only the minimum required data from the calling function to the called function. All required data are passed as parameters, and no extra data are passed. This is the best form of coupling and should be used whenever possible.

Stamp Coupling

Functions are **stamp coupled** if the parameters are composite objects such as arrays or structures. Stamp coupling is not bad and is often necessary. The danger with stamp coupling is that it is often too easy to send a structure when all the data in the structure are not required. When extra data are sent, you begin to open the door for errors and undesired side effects.

Control Coupling

Control coupling is the passing of **flags** that may be used to direct the logic flow of a function. It closely resembles data coupling except that a flag is being passed rather than data.

Properly used, control coupling is a necessary and valid method of communicating between two functions. Like stamp coupling, however, it can be misused. Properly used, it communicates status: The end of the file has been reached. The search value was found.

Poor flag usage is usually an indication of poor program design, such as a process that is divided between two or more independent functions. Flags used to communicate horizontally across several functions in the structure chart are often an indication of poor design. Action flags, as opposed to status flags, that require the receiving function to perform some special processing are also highly suspect. An example of an action flag is one that turns down a customer's purchase request rather than simply reporting that the credit limit has been exceeded or that no payment was received last month.

Global Coupling

Global coupling uses global variables to communicate between two or more functions. This is not a good coupling technique. In fact, it should *never* be used. There are several reasons you should never use global coupling. We will cite only the top two.

1. Global coupling makes it virtually impossible to determine which modules are communicating with each other. When a change needs to be made to a program, therefore, it is not possible to evaluate and isolate the impact of the change. This often causes functions that were not changed to suddenly fail.
2. Global coupling tightly binds a function to the program. This means that it cannot be easily transported to another program.

Content Coupling

The last type of coupling, **content coupling,** occurs when one function refers directly to the data or statements in another function. Obviously, this concept breaks all the tenets of structured programming. Referring to the data in another function requires that the data be made externally visible outside the function.

COHESION

Another issue in modularity is cohesion. **Cohesion** is a measure of how closely the processes in a program are related. There are several levels of cohesion.

Functional Cohesion

A module with **functional cohesion** contain only one process. This is the highest level of cohesion and the level that you should try to model. For example, in printing a report, the report function should call three lower level functions: one to get the data, one to format and print the report header, and one to format and print the data.

Only One Thing   Each function should do only one thing. Furthermore, all of the statements in the function should contribute only to that one thing. For example, let us assume that you are writing a program that requires the statistical measures of average and standard deviation. The two statistical measures are obviously related, if for no other reason than they are both measures of the same series of numbers. But you would not calculate both measures in one function. That would be calculating two things, and each function should do only one thing.

In One Place   The corollary rule is that the one thing a function does should be done in only one place. If the code for a process is scattered in several different and unrelated parts of the program, it is very difficult to change. Therefore, all the processing for a task should be placed in one function and, if necessary, its subfunctions.

Sequential Cohesion

A module with **sequential cohesion** contains two or more related tasks that are closely tied together, usually with the output of one flowing as input to the other. An example of sequential cohesion is the calculations for a sale. The design for this function might be the following:

1. Extend item prices
2. Sum items
3. Calculate sales tax
4. Calculate total

In this example, the first process multiplies the quantity purchased by the price. The extended prices are used by the process that calculates the sum of the purchased items. This sum is then used to calculate the sales tax, which is finally added to the sum to get the sale total. In each case, the output of one process was used as the input of the next process.

Although it is quite common to find the detailed code for these processes combined into a single function, it does make the function more complex and less reusable. Reusability is a concern if the same or similar calculations occur in different parts of one program.

Communicational Cohesion

Communicational cohesion combines processes that work on the same data. It is natural to have communicational cohesion in the higher modules in a program, but you should never find it at the primitive level. For example, consider a function that reads an inventory file, prints the current status of the parts, and then checks to see if any parts need to be ordered.

The first three levels of cohesion are all considered good structured programming principles. Beyond this point, however, ease of understanding and implementation, maintainability, and accuracy begin to drop rapidly. The next levels should be used only at the higher levels of a structure chart, and then only rarely.

Procedural Cohesion

The fourth level, **procedural cohesion,** combines unrelated processes that are linked by a control flow. (This differs from sequential cohesion, where data flow from one process to the next.)

Temporal Cohesion

The fifth level, **temporal cohesion,** is acceptable only over a limited range of processes. It combines unrelated processes that always occur together. Two temporally cohesive functions are initialization and end of job. They are acceptable because they are used only once in the program and because they are never portable. Recognize, however, that they should still contain calls to functionally cohesive primitive functions whenever practical.

Logical Cohesion and Coincidental Cohesion

The last two levels are seldom found in programs today. **Logical cohesion** combines processes that are related only by the entity that controls them. A function that conditionally opened different sets of files based on a flag passed as a parameter would be logically cohesive. Finally, **coincidental cohesion** combines processes that are unrelated. Coincidental cohesion exists only in theory. We have never seen a professional program that contained coincidental cohesion.

10.4   QUALITY

You will find no one who would even consider minimizing software quality, at least not publicly. Everyone wants the best software available, and to listen to the creators of systems on the market, their systems are all perfect. Yet, as users of software, we often feel that **quality software** is a contradiction in terms. We all have our favorite software products, but not one of them is without a flaw or two.

People moving into the world to be one of those software creators need to be aware of the basic concepts of software quality. In this section, we discuss some of the attributes of a quality product and how you go about achieving quality.

QUALITY DEFINED

Quality software is defined as

Software that satisfies the user's explicit and implicit requirements, is well documented, meets the operating standards of the organization, and runs efficiently on the hardware for which it was developed.

Every one of these attributes of good software falls squarely on the system designer and programmer. Note that we place on the programmer the burden of satisfying not only the users' explicit requirements but also their implicit needs. Often, users don't fully know what they need. When this happens, it is the programmer's job to determine their implicit requirements, which are hidden in the background. This is a formidable task indeed.

But quality software is not just a vague concept. If you want to attain it, you have to be able to measure it. Whenever possible, these measurements should be quantitative; that is, they should be numerically measurable. For example, if an organization is serious about quality, it should be able to tell you the number of errors (bugs) per thousand lines of code and the mean time between failures for every software system it maintains. These are measurable statistics.

On the other hand, some of the measurements may be qualitative, meaning that they cannot be numerically measured. Flexibility and testability are examples of qualitative software measurements. This does not mean that they can't be measured, but rather that they rely on someone's judgment in assessing the quality of a system.

QUALITY FACTORS

Software quality can be divided into three broad measures: operability, maintainability, and transferability. Each of these measures can be further broken down as shown in Figure 10.5.

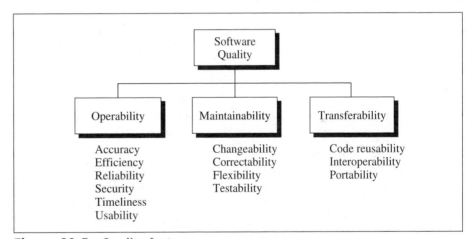

Figure 10.5 Quality factors

Operability

Operability refers to the basic operation of a system. The first things a user notices about a system are its look and feel. This means, especially for an online interactive system, how easy and intuitive it is to use. Does it fit well into the operating system it is running under? For example, if it is running in a Windows environment, its pull-down and pop-up menus should work the same way the operating system's menus do. In short, operability answers the question: "How does it drive?"

But these factors are subjective; they are not measurable. So here are the factors that comprise operability. They are listed alphabetically.

Accuracy   A system that is not accurate is worse than no system at all. Most workers would rather rely on intuition and experience than on a system that they know gives false and misleading information.

Any system that is developed, therefore, must be thoroughly tested both by a system's test engineer and the user. **Accuracy** can be measured by such metrics as mean time between failures, number of bugs per thousand lines of code, and number of user requests for change.

Efficiency   **Efficiency** is, by and large, a subjective term. In some cases, the user will specify a performance standard, such as a real-time response that must be received within 1 second 95 percent of the time. This is certainly measurable.

Reliability   **Reliability** is really the sum of the other factors. If users count on the system to get their job done and are confident in it, then it is most likely reliable. On the other hand, some measures speak directly to a system's reliability, most notably, mean time between failures.

Security   How secure a system is refers to how easy it is for unauthorized persons to get at the system's data. Although this is a subjective area, there are checklists that assist in assessing the system's **security.** For example, does the system have and require passwords to identify users?

Timeliness   **Timeliness** in software engineering can mean several different things. Does the system deliver its output in a timely fashion? For online systems, does the response time satisfy the users' requirements? For batch systems, are the reports delivered in a timely fashion? It is also possible, if the system has good auditability, to determine if the data in the system are timely. That is, are data recorded within a reasonable time after the activity that creates them takes place?

Usability   This is another area that is highly subjective. The best measure of usability is to watch the users and see if they are using the system. User interviews will often reveal problems with the usability of a system.

Maintainability

Maintainability refers to keeping a system running correctly and up to date. Many systems require regular changes, not because they were poorly implemented but because of changes in external factors. For example, the payroll system for a company must be changed yearly, if not more often, to meet changes in government laws and regulations.

Changeability   How easy it is to change a system is a subjective factor. Experienced project leaders, however, are able to estimate how long a requested change will take. If it takes too long, it may be because the system is difficult to change. This is especially true of older systems.

There are software measurement tools in the field today that will estimate a program's complexity and structure. They should be used regularly, and if a program's complexity is high, rewriting the program should be considered. Programs that have been changed many times over the years have often lost their structured focus and are difficult to change. They also should be rewritten.

Correctability   One measure of **correctability** is mean time to recovery, which is the time it takes to get a program back in operation after it fails. Although this is a reactive definition, there are currently no predictors of how long it will take to correct a program when it fails.

Flexibility   Users are constantly requesting changes in systems. **Flexibility** is a qualitative attribute that attempts to measure how easy it is to make these changes. If a program needs to be completely rewritten to effect a change, it is not flexible. Fortunately, this factor became less of a problem with the advent of structured programming.

Testability   You might think that this is a highly subjective area, but a test engineer has a checklist of factors that can assess a program's **testability.**

Transferability

Transferability refers to the ability to move data and/or a system from one platform to another and to reuse code. In many situations, it is not an important factor. On the other hand, if you are writing generalized software, it can be critical.

Code Reusability   If functions are written so that they can be reused in different programs and on different projects, then they have high reusablility. Good programmers build libraries of functions that they can reuse for solving similar problems.

Interoperability   **Interoperability** is the capability of sending data to other systems. In today's highly integrated systems, it is a desirable attribute. In fact, it has become so important that operating systems now support the ability to move data between systems, such as between a word processor and a spreadsheet.

Portability   **Portability** is the ability to move software from one hardware platform to another—for example, from a Macintosh to a Windows environment or from an IBM mainframe to a VAX environment.

THE QUALITY CIRCLE

The first and most important point to recognize is that quality must be designed into a system. It can't be added as an afterthought. It begins at step 1, determining the user requirements, and continues throughout the life of the system. Since quality is a continuous concept that, like a circle, never ends, we refer to it as the **quality circle.** There are six steps to quality software: quality tools, technical reviews, formal testing, change controls, standards, and measurement and reporting (Figure 10.6).

No one can deny that quality begins with the software engineers assigned to the team, and they need quality tools to develop a quality product. Fortunately, today's development tools are excellent. A whole suite of quality tools known as computer-aided software engineering (CASE) guides software development through requirements, design, programming, and testing and into production. For the programmer, there are workstations that not only assist in writing the program but also in testing and debugging. For example, it is possible to track tests through a program and then determine which statements were executed and which were not. Tools such as this are invaluable for white box testing.

Another major step in quality software is the technical review. These reviews should be conducted at every step in the development process, including requirements, design, programming, and testing. A typical program review begins after the programmer has designed the data structures and structure chart for a program. A design review board consisting of the systems analyst, test engineer, user representative, and one or two peers is then convened. Note that no one from management is allowed to attend a technical review. During the review, the programmer explains the approach and discusses interfaces to other programs while the reviewers ask questions and make suggestions.

Quality also requires formal testing. Formal testing ensures that the programs work together as a system and meet the defined requirements. After the programmer has completed unit testing, the program is turned over to another software engineer for

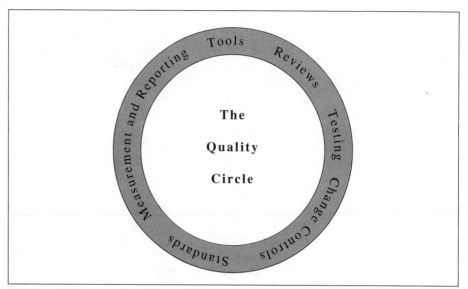

Figure 10.6 Quality circle

integration and system testing. On a small project, this is most likely the systems analyst and/or the user. On a large project, there is a separate testing team.

Large systems take months and sometimes years to develop. It is only natural that over extended periods of time, changes to the requirements and design occur. To ensure quality, each change should be reviewed and approved by a change control board. The impact of a requested change on each program needs to be assessed and properly planned. Uncontrolled change causes schedule and budget overruns and poor-quality products.

Finally, a good-quality environment measures all aspects of quality and regularly reports the results. Without measurement, you cannot tell if quality is good or bad, improving or deteriorating. At the same time, published standards provide the yardstick for many quality measurements.

10.5 DOCUMENTATION

For a software package to be used properly and maintained efficiently, documentation is needed. Usually, two separate sets of documentation are prepared for a software package: user documentation and system documentation.

USER DOCUMENTATION

To run the package properly, the user needs documentation, traditionally called a manual, that shows how to use the package step by step. It usually contains a tutorial section to guide the user through each feature of the package.

A good user manual can be a very powerful marketing tool. It should be written for both the novice and the expert user. The importance of user documentation in marketing cannot be overemphasized. A software package with good user documentation will definitely increase sales.

SYSTEM DOCUMENTATION

System documentation defines the package itself. It should be written so that the package can be maintained and modified by people other than the original developers. There should be system documentation for all four phases of system development.

| **Documentation in the Analysis Phase** | In this phase, the information collected should be carefully documented. In addition, the analyst should define the source of information. The requirements and methods chosen must be clearly stated with the rationale behind them. |

Documentation in the Analysis Phase

In this phase, the information collected should be carefully documented. In addition, the analyst should define the source of information. The requirements and methods chosen must be clearly stated with the rationale behind them.

Documentation in the Design Phase

In this phase, the tools used in the final copy must be documented. For example, if a structural chart undergoes several changes, the final copy should be documented with complete explanations.

Documentation in the Implementation Phase

In this phase, every tool and every program should be documented. In addition, the program should usually be self-documented. There are two levels of program documentation. The first is the general documentation at the start of the program. The second level is found within each block.

General Documentation   Each program should start with a general description of the program. Following this is the name of the author and the date the program was written. Next is the program's change history. For a production program that spans several years, the change history can become quite extensive.

Function Documentation   In addition, whenever necessary, you should include a brief comment for blocks of code. A block of code is much like a paragraph in a report. It contains one thought—that is, one set of statements that accomplishes a specific task. Blocks of code in your program should be separated by blank lines, just as you insert blank lines in your reports between paragraphs.

Documentation in the Testing Phase

Finally, the developers must carefully document the testing phase. Each type of test applied to the final product should be mentioned along with the result. Even unfavorable results and the data that produced them must be documented.

DOCUMENTATION AS AN ONGOING PROCESS

Note that documentation is an ongoing process. If the package has problems after release, they must be documented. If the package is modified, all modifications and their relationships with the original package must also be documented. Documentation stops when the package becomes obsolete.

10.6   KEY TERMS

accuracy	design phase	modules
analysis phase	efficiency	operability
black box testing	flag	portability
changeability	flexibility	procedural cohesion
class diagram	flowchart	pseudocode
cohesion	functional cohesion	quality circle
coincidental cohesion	global coupling	quality software
communicational cohesion	implementation phase	reliability
content coupling	incremental model	reusability
control coupling	interoperability	security
correctability	logical cohesion	sequential cohesion
coupling	loose coupling	software engineering
data coupling	modularity	software life cycle

stamp coupling   temporal cohesion   timeliness
structure chart   testability   waterfall model
system documentation   testing phase   white box testing

10.7   SUMMARY

- Software engineering is the establishment and use of sound engineering methods and principles to obtain reliable software that works on real machines.

- The development process for a software package involves four phases: analysis, design, implementation, and testing.

- The analysis phase of the development process consists of defining the users, needs, requirements, and methods.

- The design phase of the development process consists of determining the systems and designing the files and/or the databases.

- In the implementation phase of the development process, the actual code is written.

- In the testing phase of the development process, black box testing and white box testing must be performed.

- There are two models of software development: the waterfall model and the incremental model.

- In the waterfall model, each module is completely finished before the next module is started.

- In the incremental model, the entire package is constructed, with each module consisting of only a shell; the modules gain complexity with each iteration of the package.

- Modularity is the division of a large program into smaller parts that can communicate with each other.

- Coupling is a measure of how tightly two modules are bound to each other. The types of coupling include data, control, global, and content.

- Cohesion is a measure of how closely the processes in a program are related. The types of cohesion include functional, sequential, communicational, procedural, temporal, logical, and coincidental.

- Software quality can be divided into three broad measures: operability, maintainability, and transferability.

- Factors important to the operability of software are accuracy, efficiency, reliability, security, timeliness, and usability.

- Factors important to the maintainability of software are changeability, correctability, flexibility, and testability.

- Factors important to the transferability of software are code reusability, interoperability, and portability.

- There are six steps to quality software: standards, measurement and reporting, quality tools, technical reviews, formal testing, and change controls.

- User documentation and system documentation are necessary for a software package to be used properly and maintained efficiently.

10.8   PRACTICE SET

REVIEW QUESTIONS

1. Define software engineering.

2. What is meant by the software life cycle?

3. When does software become obsolete?

4. What are the four phases in software development?

5. What does the analysis phase of system development entail?

6. What is black box testing?

7. What is white box testing?

8. What is the difference between cohesion and coupling?

MULTIPLE-CHOICE QUESTIONS

9. Software engineering principles were first established _____ years ago.
   a. 10
   b. 30
   c. 100
   d. 1,000

10. A software system becomes obsolete when _____.
    a. an error is found in the code
    b. the language in which it is written is no longer used
    c. the head programmer quits
    d. a and b

11. One phase in system development is _____.
    a. analysis
    b. testing
    c. design
    d. all of the above

12. Defining the users, needs, requirements, and methods is part of the _____ phase.
    a. analysis
    b. design
    c. implementation
    d. testing

13. In the system development process, writing the code is part of the _____ phase.
    a. analysis
    b. design
    c. implementation
    d. testing

14. In the system development process, the structure chart is a tool used in the _____ phase.
    a. analysis
    b. design
    c. implementation
    d. testing

15. In the system development process, the flowchart is a tool used in the _____ phase.
    a. analysis
    b. design
    c. implementation
    d. testing

16. In the system development process, pseudocode is a tool used in the _____ phase.
    a. analysis
    b. design
    c. implementation
    d. testing

17. Testing a software package can involve _____ testing.
    a. black box
    b. white box
    c. breadbox
    d. a and b

18. Black box testing is done by _____.
    a. the user
    b. the system test engineer
    c. the programmer
    d. a and b

19. White box testing is done by _____.
    a. the programmer
    b. the user
    c. the system test engineer
    d. the CTO

20. In the first version of the _____ model, each called module just returns a message that it was called.
    a. waterfall
    b. incremental
    c. instrumental
    d. black box

21. In the _____ model, an entire phase of the project is completed before the next phase starts.
    a. waterfall
    b. incremental
    c. instrumental
    d. black box

22. _____ is the breaking up of a large program into smaller parts.
    a. Coupling
    b. Incrementing
    c. Obsolescence
    d. Modularity

23. Modularity is made more visible through tools such as _____.
    a. the structure chart
    b. the class diagram
    c. the incremental waterfall
    d. a and b

24. _____ is a measure of how tightly two modules are bound to each other.
    a. Modularity
    b. Coupling
    c. Interoperability
    d. Cohesion

25. _____ is a measure of how closely the processes in a program are related.
    a. Modularity
    b. Coupling
    c. Interoperability
    d. Cohesion

26. _____ coupling passes only the minimum required data from the calling function to the called function.
    a. Data
    b. Stamp
    c. Control
    d. Global

27. _____ coupling occurs when one function refers directly to the data or statements in another function.
    a. Data
    b. Stamp
    c. Content
    d. Control

28. _____ coupling uses global variables to communicate between two or more functions.
    a. Data
    b. Stamp
    c. Control
    d. Global

29. _____ coupling passes flags that may direct the logic flow of a function.
    a. Data
    b. Stamp
    c. Content
    d. Control

30. _____ coupling passes parameters that are composite objects such as arrays or structures.
    a. Data
    b. Stamp
    c. Content
    d. Control

31. _____ cohesion is the highest level of cohesion.
    a. Functional
    b. Sequential
    c. Communicational
    d. Logical

32. _____ cohesion combines unrelated processes that always occur together.
    a. Logical
    b. Procedural
    c. Temporal
    d. Functional

33. _____ cohesion combines processes that are related only by the entity that controls them.
    a. Logical
    b. Procedural
    c. Temporal
    d. Functional

34. _____ cohesion combines two or more related tasks that are closely tied together.
    a. Functional
    b. Sequential
    c. Communicational
    d. Logical

35. _____ cohesion combines unrelated processes that are linked by a control flow.
    a. Functional
    b. Sequential
    c. Procedural
    d. Logical

36. _____ cohesion combines processes that work on the same data.
    a. Functional
    b. Sequential
    c. Communicational
    d. Logical

37. Accuracy, efficiency, reliability, security, timeliness, and usability are factors important to the _____ of software.
    a. operability
    b. maintainability
    c. transferability
    d. longevity

38. Changeability, correctability, flexibility, and testability are factors important to the _____ of software.
    a. operability
    b. maintainability
    c. transferability
    d. longevity

39. Code reusability, interoperability, and portability are factors important to the _____ of software.
    a. operability
    b. maintainability
    c. transferability
    d. longevity

EXERCISES

40. A function is written to find the smallest number among a list of numbers. The list is passed as an array to the function. The smallest number is returned to the caller. What type(s) of coupling is used between the caller and the called function?

41. A function is written to sort a list of numbers. The function uses the list in the caller, but returns a flag to show if the sorting is successful or not. What type(s) of coupling is used between the caller and the called function?

42. A function is written to exchange data between two variables. The function directly uses a variable defined in the caller. What type of coupling is used?

43. A programmer writes a program that includes a summation function. Later she writes another program that also requires summation. When she tries to use the previous function, she finds that she should write a whole new one. What quality principle is violated here?

44. Imagine you are assigned to do system documentation in the analysis phase for a big project. Devise the appropriate template sheet to be used for the four steps involved in this phase.

45. Repeat Exercise 44 for the design phase.

46. Repeat Exercise 44 for the implementation phase.

47. Repeat Exercise 44 for the testing phase.

Data Organization

IV

11 Data Structures

In the preceding chapters, we used variables that store a single entity. Although single variables are used extensively in programming languages, they cannot be used to solve complex problems efficiently.

In this chapter, we introduce data structures. A **data structure** uses a collection of related variables that can be accessed individually or as a whole. In other words, a data structure represents a set of data items with a specific relationship between them.

We discuss three data structures in this chapter: arrays, records, and linked lists. Most programming languages have an implicit implementation of the first two. The third, however, is simulated using pointers and records.

This chapter is a prelude to the next chapter, in which we introduce abstract data types (ADTs).

11.1 ARRAYS

Imagine you have a problem that requires 20 numbers to be processed. You need to read them, process them, and print them. You must also keep these 20 numbers in memory for the duration of the program. You can define 20 **variables,** each with a different name, as shown in Figure 11.1.

But having 20 different names creates another problem. How can you read 20 numbers from the keyboard and store them? To read 20 numbers from the keyboard, you need 20 references, one to each variable. Furthermore, once you have them in memory, how can you print them? To print them, you need another 20 references. In other words, you need the flowchart in Figure 11.2 to read, process, and print these 20 numbers.

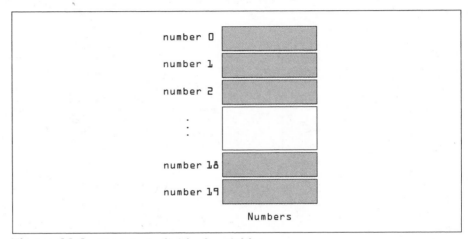

Figure 11.1   Twenty individual variables

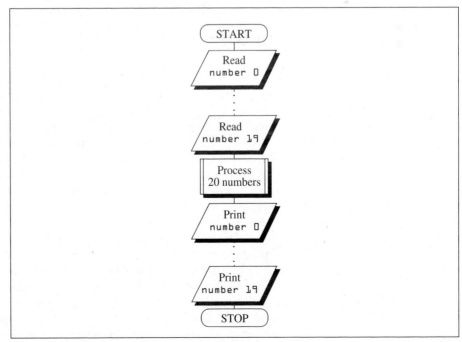

Figure 11.2   Processing individual variables

Although this may be acceptable for 20 numbers, it is definitely not acceptable for 200 or 2000 or 20,000 numbers. To process large amounts of data, you need a powerful data structure such as an array. An **array** is a fixed-size, sequenced collection of elements of the same data type. Since an array is a sequenced collection, you can refer to the elements in the array as the first element, the second element, and so forth until you get to the last element. If you were to put your 20 numbers into an array, you could designate the first element $number_0$ as shown in Figure 11.1. In a similar fashion, you could refer to the second number as $number_1$ and the third number as $number_2$. Continuing the series, the last number would be $number_{19}$. The **subscripts** indicate the ordinal number of the element counting from the beginning of the array.

What you have seen is that the elements of the array are individually addressed through their subscripts (Figure 11.3). The array as a whole has a name, number, but each member can be accessed individually using its subscript.

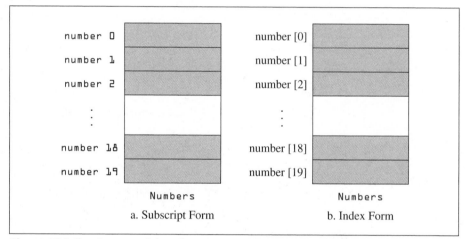

Figure 11.3   Arrays with subscripts and indexes

The advantages of the array would be limited if you didn't also have programming constructs that allow you to process the data more conveniently. Fortunately, there is a powerful set of programming constructs, **loops,** that makes array processing easy.

You can use loops to read and write the elements in an array. You can use loops to add, subtract, multiply, and divide the elements. You can also use loops for more complex processing such as calculating averages. Now it does not matter if there are 2, 20, 200, 2000, or 20,000 elements to be processed. Loops make it easy to handle them all.

But one question still remains: How can you write an instruction so that one time it refers to the first element of an array and the next time it refers to another element? It is really quite simple: You simply borrow from the subscript concept you have been using. Rather than using subscripts, however, you place the subscript value in square brackets. Using this notation, you refer to $number_0$ as number[0].

Following the convention, $number_1$ becomes number[1] and $number_{19}$ becomes number[19]. This is known as indexing. Using a typical reference, you now refer to your array using the variable. The flowchart to process your 20 numbers using an array and looping is in Figure 11.4.

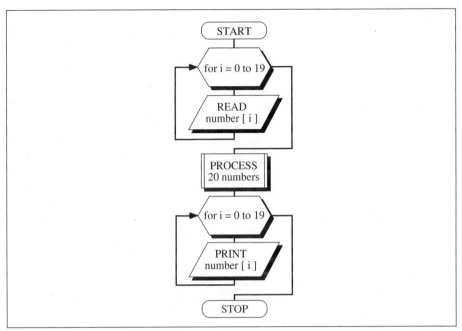

Figure 11.4 Processing an array

ARRAY APPLICATIONS

In this section, we study one array application: the frequency array and its graphical representation.

Frequency Arrays

A **frequency array** shows the number of elements with the same value found in a series of numbers. For example, suppose you have taken a sample of 100 values between 0 and 19. You want to know how many of the values are 0, how many are 1, how many are 2, and so forth up through 19.

You can read these values into an array called numbers. Then you create an array of 20 elements that will show the frequency of each value in the series (Figure 11.5).

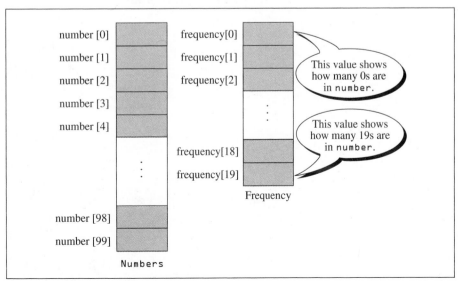

Figure 11.5 Frequency array

Histograms

A **histogram** is a pictorial representation of a frequency array. Instead of printing the values of the elements to show the frequency of each number, you print a histogram in the form of a **bar chart.** For example, Figure 11.6 is a histogram for a set of numbers in the range 0 to 19. In this example, asterisks (*) are used to build the bar. Each asterisk represents one occurrence of the data value.

TWO-DIMENSIONAL ARRAYS

The arrays discussed so far are known as **one-dimensional arrays** because the data are organized linearly in only one direction. Many applications require that data be stored in more than one dimension. One common example is a table, which is an array that consists of rows and columns. Figure 11.7 shows a table, which is commonly called a **two-dimensional array.** Note that arrays can have three, four, or more dimensions. However, the discussion of **multidimensional arrays** is beyond the scope of this book.

Memory Layout

The indexes in the definition of a two-dimensional array represent rows and columns. This format maps the way the data are laid out in **memory.** If you were to consider memory as a row of bytes with the lowest address on the left and the highest address on the right, then an array would be placed in memory with the first element to the left and the last element to the right. Similarly, if the array is two-dimensional, then the first dimension is a row of elements that is stored to the left. This is known as **"row-major" storage** (Figure 11.8).

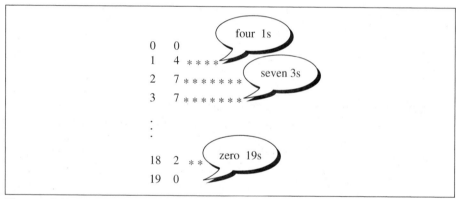

Figure 11.6   Histogram

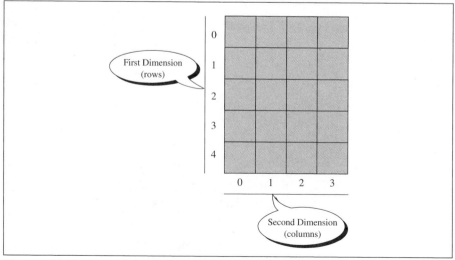

Figure 11.7   Two-dimensional array

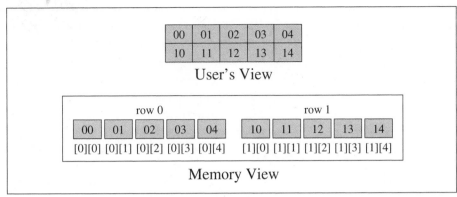

Figure 11.8   Memory layout

11.2   RECORDS

A **record** is a collection of related elements, possibly of different types, having a single name. Each element in a record is called a field. A **field** is the smallest element of named data that has meaning. It has a type, and it exists in memory. It can be assigned values, which in turn can be accessed for selection or manipulation. A field differs from a variable primarily in that it is part of a record.

The difference between an array and a record is that all elements in an array must be of the same type, whereas the elements in a record can be of the *same or different types*.

Figure 11.9 contains two examples of records. The first example, fraction, has two fields, both of which are integers. The second example, student, has three fields made up of two different types.

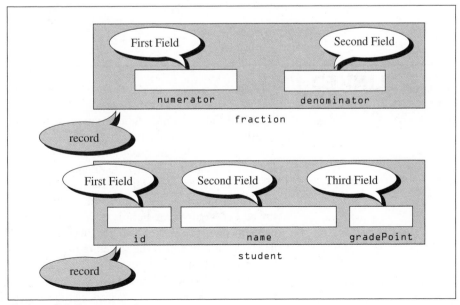

Figure 11.9   Records

> The elements in a record can be of the same or different types. But all elements in the record must be related.

One design caution, however. The data in a record should all be related to one object. In Figure 11.9, the integers in the fraction both belong to the same fraction, and the data in the second example all relate to one student. Do not combine unrelated data for programming expediency.

ACCESSING RECORDS

We first describe how to access individual components of a record and then examine the assignment of whole records.

Accessing Individual Fields

Each field in a record can be accessed and manipulated using expressions and operators. Anything you can do with an individual variable can be done with a record field. The only problem is to identify the individual fields you are interested in.

Since each field in a record has a name, you could simply use the name. The problem with such a simple approach is that if you wanted to compare a student's id in one record to a student's id in another record, the statement would be ambiguous. Therefore, you need some way to identify the records that contain the field identifiers, in this case, id. Many programming languages use a period (.) to separate the record name from the field name.

For example, if you have two records (Student1 and Student2) of the type *student*, you can refer to individual fields in these records as follows:

```
Student1.id, Student1.name, and Student1.gradePoint
Student2.id, Student2.name, and Student2.gradePoint
```

You can also read data into and write data from record members just as you can from individual variables.

11.3 LINKED LISTS

A **linked list** is an ordered collection of data in which each element contains the location of the next element; that is, each element contains two parts: data and **link.** The data part holds the useful information, the data to be processed. The link is used to chain the data together. It contains a **pointer** (an address) that identifies the next element in the list. In addition, a pointer variable identifies the first element in the list. The name of the list is the same as the name of this pointer variable. The simple linked list we describe here is commonly known as a **singly linked list** because it contains only one link to a single successor. A linked list is an example of a derived data structure in which the structure does not exist in the language but is simulated by other available structures.

Figure 11.10 shows a linked list, pList (for pointer to the head of the list), that contains four elements. The link in each element except the last points to its successor. The link in the last element contains a **null pointer,** indicating the end of the list. We define

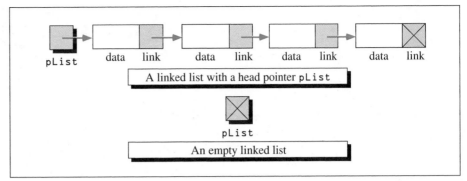

Figure 11.10   Linked lists

Figure 11.11   Node

an empty linked list to be a null head pointer. Figure 11.10 also contains an example of an empty linked list.

NODES

The elements in a linked list are traditionally called nodes. A **node** in a linked list is a record that has at least two fields: One contains the data, and the other contains the address of the next node in the sequence (Figure 11.11).

The nodes in a linked list are called **self-referential records.** In a self-referential record, each instance of the record contains a pointer to another instance of the same structural type.

POINTERS TO LINKED LISTS

A linked list must always have a head pointer. Depending on how you will use the list, you may have several other pointers as well. For example, if you are going to search a linked list, you will undoubtedly have a pointer to the location (pLoc) where you found the data for which you were looking. In many records, programming is more efficient if there is a pointer to the last node in the list as well as a head pointer. This last pointer is often called either pLast (for pointer to last) or pRear (for pointer to rear).

OPERATIONS ON LINKED LISTS

We define five operations for a linked list, which should be sufficient to solve any sequential list problem. If an application requires additional list operations, they can be easily added.

Inserting a Node

To insert a node in a linked list, follow these three steps (Figure 11.12):

1. Allocate memory for the new node and write data.
2. Make the new node point to its successor.
3. Make the predecessor point to the new node.

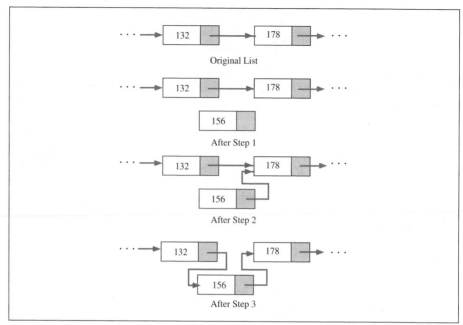

Figure 11.12　Inserting a node

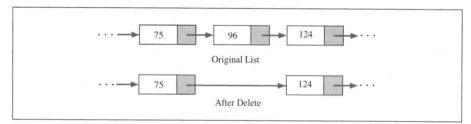

Figure 11.13　Deleting a node

Note that in some special cases (adding to the end of a list, adding to the beginning of a list, or adding to an empty list), these three steps should be modified accordingly.

Deleting a Node

To delete a node, you must first locate the node itself. Once you locate the node to be deleted, simply change its predecessor's link field to point to the deleted node's successor (Figure 11.13). You need to be concerned, however, about deleting the only node in a list because this results in an empty list. Note that deleting the first node or the only node are special cases that need special handling.

Searching a List

A list search is used by other operations to locate data in a list. For example, to insert data, you need to know the logical predecessor to the new data. To delete data, you need to find the node to be deleted and identify its logical predecessor. To retrieve data from a list, you need to search the list and find the data. In addition, many user applications require that lists be searched to locate data.

To **search a list** on a key, you need a key field. For simple lists, the key and the data can be the same field. For more complex records, you need a separate key field.

Given a target key, the ordered list search attempts to locate the requested node in the linked list. If a node in the list matches the target value, the search returns true; if there are no key matches, it returns false.

Retrieving a Node

Now that you know how to locate a node in the list, we can discuss retrieving a node. To retrieve a node, search the list to locate the data. If the data are found, they are moved to the output area in the calling module. If the data are not found, nothing is retrieved.

Traversing a List

Algorithms that traverse a list start at the first node and examine each node in succession until the last node has been processed. Traversal logic is used by several types of algorithms, such as changing a value in each node, printing the list, summing a field in the list, or calculating the average of a field. Any application that requires the entire list to be processed uses a traversal.

To traverse the list, you need a walking pointer, which is a pointer that moves from node to node as each element is processed. Begin by setting the walking pointer to the first node in the list. Then, using a loop, continue until all of the data have been processed. Each loop calls a process module and passes it the data and then advances the walking pointer to the next node. When the last node has been processed, the walking pointer becomes null and the loop terminates (Figure 11.14).

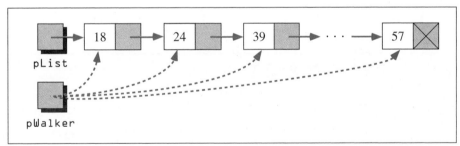

Figure 11.14 Traversing a list

11.4 KEY TERMS

array
bar chart
data structure
field
frequency array
histogram
link
linked list

loop
memory
multidimensional array
node
null pointer
one-dimensional array
pointer
record

row-major storage
search a list
self-referential record
singly linked list
subscript
two-dimensional array
variable

11.5 SUMMARY

- Arrays, records, and linked lists are data structures studied in this chapter.
- A one-dimensional array is a fixed-size sequence of elements of the same type.
- You can access the individual elements of an array using the array name and the index.
- You can process the values of an array using a loop.
- A frequency array is an array whose elements show the number of occurrences of data values in another array.
- A histogram is a pictorial representation of a frequency array.
- A two-dimensional array is a representation of a table with rows and columns.
- A multidimensional array is an extension of a two-dimensional array to three, four, or more dimensions.
- A record is a collection of related elements, possibly of different types, having a single name.
- Each element in a record is called a field.

- One difference between an array and a record is that all elements in an array must be of the same type, whereas the elements in a record can be of the same or different types.
- A linked list is an ordered collection of data in which each element contains the location (address) of the next element; that is, each element contains two parts: data and link.
- The node in a singly linked list contains only one link to a single successor unless it is the last, in which case it is not linked to any other node.
- When you want to insert into a linked list, you must consider four cases: adding to the empty list, adding at the beginning, adding to the middle, and adding at the end.
- Traversing a linked list means going through the list, node by node, and processing each node. Three examples of list traversals are counting the number of nodes, printing the contents of nodes, and summing the values of one or more fields.

11.6 PRACTICE SET

REVIEW QUESTIONS

1. Why is there a need for data structures?
2. Name three types of data structures.
3. What is an array?
4. How is an element in an array different from an element in a record?
5. How is an element in an array different from an element in a linked list?
6. Why should you use indexes rather than subscripts to identify array elements?
7. What is a frequency array?
8. How is a histogram related to a frequency array?
9. How are the elements of an array stored in memory?
10. What is the definition of a field in a record?
11. What are the fields of a node in a linked list?
12. What is the function of the pointer in a linked list?

13. How do you point to the first node in a linked list?
14. To what does the pointer in the last node of a linked list point?
15. What is a singly linked list?
16. Describe the predecessor's pointer when you add a node to
    a. the beginning of a linked list,
    b. the middle of a linked list,
    c. the end of a linked list, and
    d. an empty list.

MULTIPLE-CHOICE QUESTIONS

17. A data structure can be _____.
    a. an array
    b. a record
    c. a linked list
    d. all of the above

18. _____ is a fixed-size, sequenced collection of elements of the same data type.
    a. An array
    b. A record
    c. A linked list
    d. A variable

19. Given the array called `object` with 20 elements, if you see the term $object_{10}$, you know the array is in _____ form.
    a. variable
    b. record
    c. index
    d. subscript

20. Given the array called `object` with 20 elements, if you see the term object[10], you know the array is in _____ form.
    a. variable
    b. record
    c. index
    d. subscript

21. A _____ is a pictorial representation of a frequency array.
    a. linked list
    b. histogram
    c. record
    d. node

22. An array that consists of just rows and columns is probably a _____ array.
    a. one-dimensional
    b. two-dimensional
    c. three-dimensional
    d. multidimensional

23. In a two-dimensional array with four rows, the row with the highest addresses in memory is the _____ row.
    a. first
    b. second
    c. third
    d. fourth

24. _____ is a collection of related elements, possibly of different types, having a single name.
    a. An array
    b. A record
    c. A linked list
    d. All of the above

25. Each element in a record is called _____.
    a. a variable
    b. an index
    c. a field
    d. a node

26. All the members of an array must be of _____.
    a. the same type
    b. different types
    c. integer type
    d. character type

27. All the members of a record must be _____.
    a. the same type
    b. related types
    c. integer type
    d. character type

28. _____ is an ordered collection of data in which each element contains the location of the next element.
    a. An array
    b. A record
    c. A linked list
    d. A node

29. In a linked list, each element contains _____.
    a. data
    b. a link
    c. a record
    d. a and b

30. The _____ is a pointer that identifies the next element in the linked list.
    a. link
    b. node
    c. array
    d. a or b

31. Given a linked list called `children`, the pointer variable `children` identifies _____ element of the linked list.
    a. the first
    b. the second
    c. the last
    d. any

32. An empty linked list consists of _____.
    a. a variable
    b. two nodes
    c. data and a link
    d. a null head pointer

33. In a self-referential record, each instance of the record contains a pointer to another instance of _____ type.
    a. the same
    b. a different
    c. a similar
    d. a or b

34. Given a node to insert into a linked list, if the predecessor node has a null pointer, then you are adding to _____.
    a. an empty list
    b. the beginning of the list
    c. the end of the list
    d. a or b

35. Given a node to insert into a linked list, if the predecessor node has a nonnull pointer, then you are adding to _____.
    a. the beginning of the list
    b. the body of the list
    c. the end of the list
    d. a or b

36. To traverse a list, you need a _____ pointer.
    a. null
    b. walking
    c. beginning
    d. insertion

EXERCISES

37. You have two arrays, A and B, each of 10 integers. Write an algorithm that tests if every element of array A is equal to its corresponding element in array B.

38. Write an algorithm that reverses the elements of an array so that the last element becomes the first, the second to the last becomes the second, and so forth.

39. Write an algorithm to print the contents of a two-dimensional array of *I* rows and *J* columns.

40. Using Figure 11.9, what is the result of the following statements, assuming that `Fr1` is of type fraction?
    ```
    Fr1.numerator = 7;
    Fr1.denominator = 8;
    ```

41. Using Figure 11.9, write an algorithm to add a fraction (`Fr1`) to another fraction (`Fr2`).

42. Using Figure 11.9, write an algorithm to subtract a fraction (`Fr1`) from another fraction (`Fr2`).

43. Using Figure 11.9, write an algorithm to multiply a fraction (`Fr1`) by another fraction (`Fr2`).

44. Using Figure 11.9, write an algorithm to divide a fraction (`Fr1`) by another fraction (`Fr2`).

45. You can have an array of records. Show pictorially an array of fractions (use Figure 11.9).

46. You can have a linked list in which the data part can be a record. Show pictorially a linked list of student records (use Figure 11.9).

47. In most programming languages, an array is a static data structure. When you define an array, the size is fixed. What problem will this restriction create?

48. A linked list is a dynamic data structure. The size of a linked list can be changed dynamically (during program execution). How does this feature benefit the programmer?

49. Which operation do you think is easier, adding an element to an array or adding an element to a linked list? Justify your answer.

50. Which operation do you think is easier, deleting an element from an array or deleting an element from a linked list? Justify your answer.

51. Which operation do you think is easier, accessing an element of an array or accessing an element of a linked list? Justify your answer.

52. Which operation do you think is easier, searching an array or searching a linked list? Justify your answer.

53. Which operation do you think is easier, sorting an array or sorting a linked list? Justify your answer.

Abstract Data Types

We begin this chapter with a brief background on the abstract type (ADT). We then give a definition and propose a model. The remainder of the chapter discusses various ADTs, such as the linear list, the stack, the queue, the tree, the binary tree, and the graph.

12.1 BACKGROUND

In the earlier days of programming, there were no abstract data types. If we wanted to read a file, we wrote the code to read the physical file device. It did not take long to realize that we were writing the same code over and over again. So computer scientists created what is known today as an **abstract data type (ADT).** We wrote the code to read a file and placed it in a library for all programmers to use.

This concept is found in modern languages today. The code to read the keyboard is an ADT. It has a data structure, character, and a set of operations that can be used to read that data structure. The rules allow you to not only read the structure but also convert it into different data structures such as integers and strings.

With an ADT, users are not concerned with *how* the task is done but rather with *what* it can do. In other words, the ADT consists of a set of definitions that allow programmers to use the functions while hiding the implementation. This generalization of operations with unspecified implementations is known as **abstraction.** You abstract the essence of the process and leave the implementation details hidden.

The concept of abstraction means:
1. You know what a data type can do.
2. How it is done is hidden.

As an example, consider the system analyst who needs to simulate the waiting line of a bank to determine how many tellers are needed to serve customers efficiently. This analysis requires the simulation of a **queue.** However, queues are not generally available in programming languages. Even if a queue type were available, the analyst would still need some basic operations, such as enqueuing (insertion) and dequeuing (deleting), for the **queue simulation.**

There are two potential solutions to this problem: (1) you can write a program that simulates the queue your analyst needs (in this case, your solution is good only for the one application at hand) or (2) you can write a queue ADT that can be used to solve any queue problem. If you choose the latter course, your analyst will still need to write a program to simulate the banking application, but doing so will be much easier and faster because he or she will be able to concentrate on the application rather than the queue.

DEFINITION

Let us now formally define an ADT. An abstract data type is a data declaration packaged together with the operations that are meaningful for the data type. You then encapsulate the data and the operations on the data and hide them from the user.

Abstract Data Type

1. Declaration of data
2. Declaration of operations
3. Encapsulation of data and operations

We cannot overstress the importance of hiding the implementation. The user should not have to know the **data structure** to use the ADT. Referring to the queue example, the application program should have no knowledge of the data structure. All references to and manipulation of the data in the queue must be handled through defined interfaces to the structure. Allowing the application program to directly reference the data structure is a common fault in many implementations that keeps the ADT from being fully portable to other applications.

MODEL FOR AN ABSTRACT DATA TYPE

The ADT model is shown in Figure 12.1. The light shaded area with an irregular outline represents the model. Inside the abstract area are two aspects of the model: the data structure and the operational functions. Both are entirely contained in the model and are not within the user's scope. However, the data structure is available to all of the ADT's operations as needed, and an operation may call on other functions to accomplish its task. In other words, the data structure and the functions are within the scope of each other.

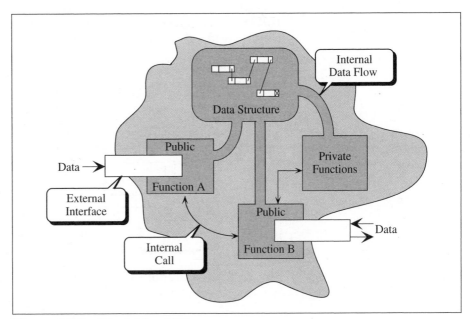

Figure 12.1 Model for ADT

OPERATIONS ON ADTS

Data are entered, accessed, modified, and deleted through the operational interfaces drawn as rectangles partially in and partially out of the structure. For each operation header, there is an algorithm that performs its specific operation. Only the operation name and its parameters are visible to the user, and they provide the only interface to the ADT. Additional operations may be created to satisfy specific requirements.

12.2 LINEAR LISTS

We start defining a few ADTs beginning with the linear list. A **linear list** is a **list** in which each element has a unique successor. In other words, a linear list has a sequential structure. The sequentiality of a linear list is diagramed in Figure 12.2.

Figure 12.2 Linear list

Linear lists can be divided into two categories: general and restricted. In a **general list,** data can be inserted and deleted anywhere, and there are no restrictions on the operations that can be used to process the list. General structures can be further described by their data as either random or ordered lists. In a **random list,** there is no ordering of the data. In an **ordered list,** the data are arranged according to a key. A **key** is one or more fields within a structure that are used to identify the data or otherwise control their use. In a simple array, the data are also the keys.

In a **restricted list,** data can only be added or deleted at the ends of the structure, and processing is restricted to operations on the data at the ends of the list. We describe two restricted list structures: the **first in, first out (FIFO)** list and the **last in, first out (LIFO)** list. The FIFO list is generally called a queue; the LIFO list is generally called a stack. Figure 12.3 shows the types of linear lists.

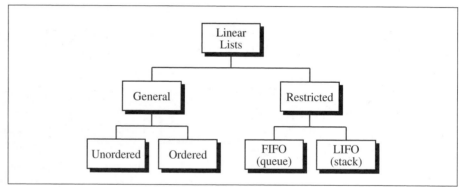

Figure 12.3 Categories of linear lists

In this section, we concentrate on one kind of linear list: the general linear list with ordered data. Restricted linear lists will be discussed later in the chapter.

OPERATIONS ON LINEAR LISTS

Although we can define many operations on a general linear list, we discuss only four common operations: insertion, deletion, retrieval, and traversal.

Insertion

Data must be inserted into ordered lists so that the ordering of the list is maintained. Maintaining the order may require inserting the data at the beginning or at the end of the list, but most of the time, data are inserted somewhere in the middle of the list. To determine where the data are to be placed, computer scientists use a search algorithm. The only potential problem with this simple operation is running out of room for the new item. If there is not enough room, the list is in an overflow state and the item cannot be added. Insertion is graphically shown in Figure 12.4. The inserted data are identified by the shaded element, in this case the third element of the revised list.

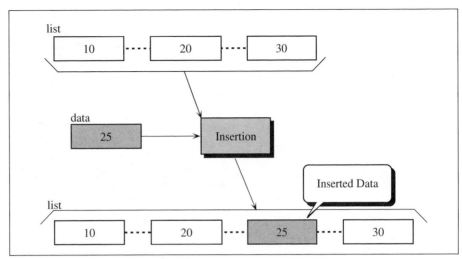

Figure 12.4 Insertion in a linear list

Deletion

Deletion from a general list (Figure 12.5) requires that the list be searched to locate the data being deleted. Any sequential search algorithm can be used to locate the data. Once located, the data are removed from the list. The only potential problem with this simple operation is the empty list. If the list is empty, the list is in an **underflow** state and the operation fails.

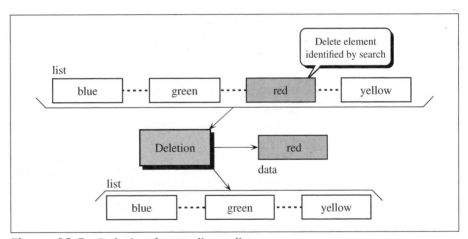

Figure 12.5 Deletion from a linear list

Retrieval

List **retrieval** requires that data be located in a list (Figure 12.6). A copy of the data should be retrieved without changing the contents of the list. As with both insertion and deletion, any sequential search algorithm can be used to locate the data to be retrieved from a general list. The only potential problem with this simple operation is an empty list. You cannot retrieve an item from an empty linear list.

Traversal

List **traversal** is an operation in which all elements in the list are processed sequentially, one by one (Figure 12.7). In this figure, the variable called Walker points to the element that must be processed. Processing here can be retrieval, storing, and so on. List traversal requires a looping algorithm rather than a search. Each iteration of a loop processes one element in the list. The loop terminates when all elements have been processed.

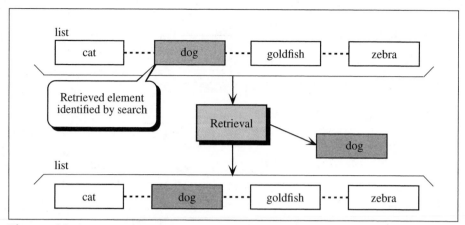

Figure 12.6 Retrieval from a linear list

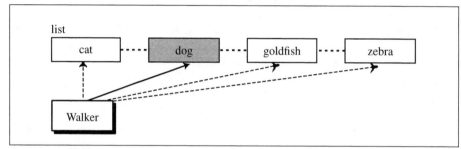

Figure 12.7 Traversal of a linear list

IMPLEMENTATION OF A GENERAL LINEAR LIST

Two common methods of implementing a general linear list are an **array** and a **linked list.**

LINEAR LIST APPLICATIONS

Linear lists are used in situations where the elements are accessed randomly. For example, in a college, a linear list can be used to store information about the students who are enrolled in each semester. The information can be accessed randomly.

12.3 STACKS

A **stack** is a restricted linear list in which all additions and deletions are made at one end, called the top. If you inserted a series of data into a stack and then removed it, the order of the data would be reversed. Data input as 5, 10, 15, 20 would be removed as 20, 15, 10, and 5. This reversing attribute is why stacks are known as a last in, first out (LIFO) data structure.

You use many different types of stacks in your daily lives. We often talk of a stack of coins or a stack of dishes. Any situation in which you can only add or remove an object at the top is a stack. If you want to remove any object other than the one at the top, you must first remove all objects above it. Three representations of a stack are shown in Figure 12.8.

Figure 12.8   Three representations of a stack

OPERATIONS ON STACKS

Although we can define many operations for a stack, three are basic: push, pop, and empty.

Push

Push adds an item at the top of the stack (Figure 12.9). After the push, the new item becomes the top. The only potential problem with this simple operation is running out of room for the new item. If there is not enough room, the stack is in an overflow state and the item cannot be added.

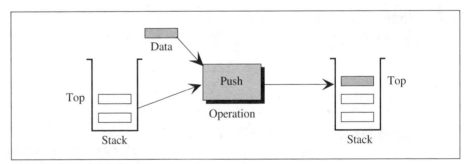

Figure 12.9   Push operation in a stack

Pop

When you **pop** a stack, you remove the item at the top of the stack and return it to the user (Figure 12.10). When the last item in the stack is deleted, the stack must be set to its empty state. If pop is called when the stack is empty, it is in an underflow state.

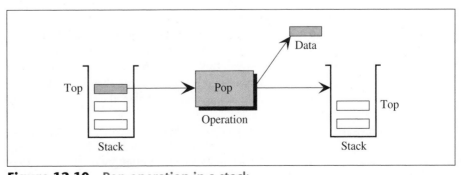

Figure 12.10   Pop operation in a stack

Empty

This operation checks to see if a stack is empty or not. The response is either true or false.

EXAMPLE 1

Show the result of the following operations on a stack S.

```
push (S, 10)
push (S, 12)
push (S, 8)
if not empty (S), then pop (S)
push (S, 2)
```

SOLUTION

Figure 12.11 shows the operations and the final result.

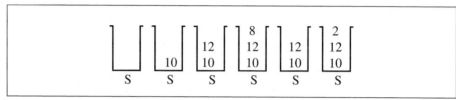

Figure 12.11   Example 1   ■

IMPLEMENTATION OF A STACK

Although a stack can be implemented either as an array or a linked list, the more common is a linked list because the pop and the push operations can be implemented much more easily in a linked list.

STACK APPLICATIONS

Stack applications can be classified into four broad categories: reversing data, parsing data, postponing data usage, and backtracking steps.

Reversing Data

Reversing data requires that a given set of data be reordered so that the first and last elements are exchanged, with all of the positions between the first and last being relatively exchanged also. For example, 1 2 3 4 becomes 4 3 2 1.

Parsing

Another application of stacks is **parsing.** Parsing is any logic that breaks data into independent pieces for further processing. For example, to translate a source program to machine language, a compiler must parse the program into individual parts such as keywords, names, and tokens.

One common programming problem is unmatched parentheses in an algebraic expression. When parentheses are unmatched, two types of errors can occur: The opening parenthesis can be missing, or the closing parenthesis can be missing. Whenever an opening parenthesis is encountered, it is pushed onto the stack. When a closing parenthesis is encountered, one opening parenthesis (from the top of the stack) is popped and discarded. If the stack is not empty at the end, it means that there are more opening than closing parentheses. An error also occurs when a closing parenthesis is encountered and there are no opening parentheses at the top of the stack.

Postponement

When you use a stack to reverse a list, the entire list is read before you begin to output the results. Often, the logic of an application requires that the usage of the data be deferred until some later point. A stack can be useful when the application requires the postponement of the use of data.

Backtracking

Backtracking, going back to previous data, is a stack use found in applications such as computer gaming, decision analysis, and expert systems.

12.4 QUEUES

A queue is a linear list in which data can only be inserted at one end, called the rear, and deleted from the other end, called the front. These restrictions ensure that the data are processed through the queue in the order in which they are received. In other words, a queue is a first in, first out (FIFO) structure.

A queue is the same as a line. In fact, if you were in England, you would not get into a line; you would get into a queue. A line of people waiting for the bus in a station is a queue, a list of calls put on hold to be answered by a telephone operator is a queue, and a list of waiting jobs to be processed by a computer is a queue.

Figure 12.12 shows two representations of a queue: one a queue of people and the other a computer queue. Both people and data enter the queue at the rear and progress through the queue until they arrive at the front. Once they are at the front of the queue, they leave the queue and are served.

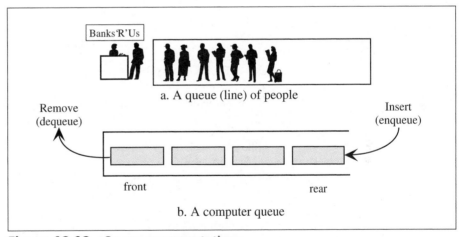

Figure 12.12 Queue representations

OPERATIONS ON QUEUES

Although we can define many operations for a queue, three are basic: enqueue, dequeue, and empty.

Enqueue

The queue insert operation is known as **enqueue** (Figure 12.13). After the data have been inserted into the queue, the new element becomes the rear. As you saw with stacks, the only potential problem with enqueue is running out of room for the data. If there is not enough room for another element in the queue, the queue is in an overflow state.

Dequeue

The queue delete operation is known as **dequeue** (Figure 12.14). The data at the front of the queue are removed from the queue and returned to the user. If there are no data in the queue when a dequeue is attempted, the queue is in an underflow state.

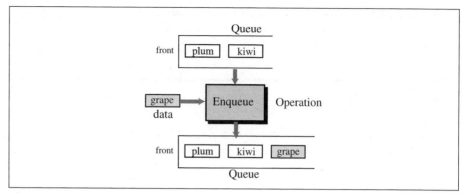

Figure 12.13   Enqueue operation

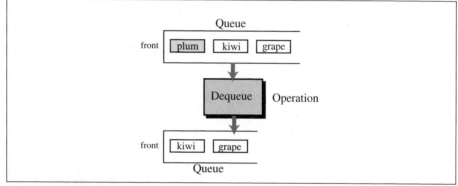

Figure 12.14   Dequeue operation

Empty

This operation checks to see if a queue is empty or not. The result is true or false.

EXAMPLE 2

Show the result of the following operations on a queue Q.

```
enqueue (Q, 23)
if not empty (Q), dequeue (Q)
enqueue (Q, 20)
enqueue (Q, 19)
if not empty (Q), dequeue (Q)
```

SOLUTION

Figure 12.15 shows the operations and the final result.

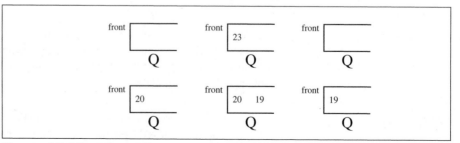

Figure 12.15   Example 2

IMPLEMENTATION OF A QUEUE

A queue can be implemented as either an array or a linked list.

QUEUE APPLICATIONS

Queues are one of the most common of all data processing structures. They are found in virtually every operating system and network and in countless other areas. For example, queues are used in business online applications such as processing customer requests, jobs, and orders. In a computer system, a queue is needed to process jobs and for system services such as print spools.

Queues can become quite complex; we give one simple queue implementation: an application that is useful for categorizing data. A queue preserves the order of data. For example, you have a list of numbers and need to categorize them into groups (100 or less, between 100 and 201, etc.). You can read the data and create several queues. A number is enqueued in the appropriate queue and can be retrieved in the order it is read but in its own group. For example, all the numbers in the 100 or less category can be printed first in the order they were read. Then all numbers between 100 and 201 can be printed in the order they were read and so on.

12.5 TREES

Trees are used extensively in computer science as an efficient structure for searching large, dynamic lists and for such diverse applications as artificial intelligence systems and encoding algorithms. In this section, we discuss the basic concept of a tree. In the next section, we present a special kind of a tree, called a binary tree, which is a common structure in computer science.

BASIC TREE CONCEPTS

A **tree** consists of a finite set of elements, called **nodes,** and a finite set of directed lines, called **branches,** that connect the nodes. The number of branches associated with a node is the **degree** of the node. When the branch is directed toward the node, it is an **indegree** branch; when the branch is directed away from the node, it is an **outdegree** branch. The sum of the indegree and outdegree branches is the degree of the node. In Figure 12.16, the degree of node B is 3.

If the tree is not empty, the first node is called the **root.** The indegree of the root is, by definition, zero. With the exception of the root, all of the nodes in a tree must have an indegree of exactly one. All nodes in the tree can have zero, one, or more branches leaving them; that is, they may have an outdegree of zero, one, or more.

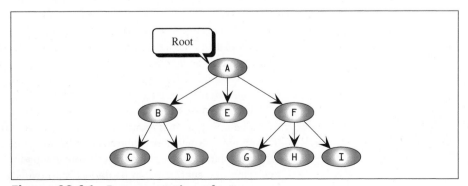

Figure 12.16 Representation of a tree

Terminology

In addition to *root,* many different terms are used to describe the attributes of a tree. A **leaf** is any node with an outdegree of zero. In Figure 12.16, node E is a leaf. A node that is not a root or a leaf is known as an **internal node** because it is found in the middle portion of a tree. In Figure 12.16, node B is an internal node.

A node is a **parent** if it has successor nodes—that is, if it has an outdegree greater than zero. Conversely, a node with a predecessor is a **child.** A child node has an indegree of one. Two or more nodes with the same parent are **siblings.** Fortunately, you don't have to worry about aunts, uncles, nieces, nephews, and cousins. Although some literature uses the term *grandparent,* we do not. We prefer the more general term *ancestor.* An **ancestor** is any node in the path from the root to the node. A **descendant** is any node in the path below the parent node; that is, all nodes in the paths from a given node to a leaf are descendents of the node. Figure 12.17 shows the usage of these terms.

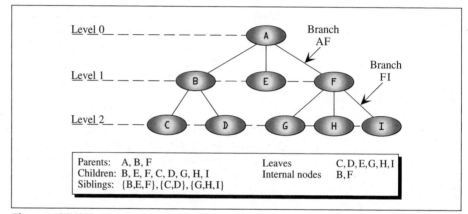

Figure 12.17   Tree terminology

Several terms drawn from mathematics or created by computer scientists describe attributes of trees and their nodes. A **path** is a sequence of nodes in which each node is adjacent to the next one. Every node in the tree can be reached by following a unique path starting from the root. In Figure 12.17, the path from the root to the leaf I is designated as AFI. It includes two distinct branches: AF and FI.

The **level** of a node is its distance from the root. Because the root has a zero distance from itself, the root is at level 0. The children of the root are at level 1, their children are at level 2, and so forth. Note the relationship between levels and siblings in Figure 12.17. Siblings are always at the same level, but all nodes in a level are not necessarily siblings. For example, at level 2, C and D are siblings, as are G, H, and I. However, D and G are not siblings because they have different parents.

The **height** of the tree is the level of the leaf in the longest path from the root plus 1. By definition, the height of an empty tree is -1. Figure 12.17 contains nodes at three levels: 0, 1, and 2. Its height is 3. Because the tree is drawn upside down, some texts refer to the **depth** of a tree rather than its height.

A tree may be divided into subtrees. A **subtree** is any connected structure below the root. The first node in a subtree is known as the root of the subtree and is used to name the subtree. Furthermore, subtrees can be subdivided into subtrees. In Figure 12.18, BCD is a subtree, as are E and FGHI. Note that by this definition, a single node is a subtree. Thus, the subtree B can be divided into two subtrees, C and D, and the subtree F contains the subtrees G, H, and I.

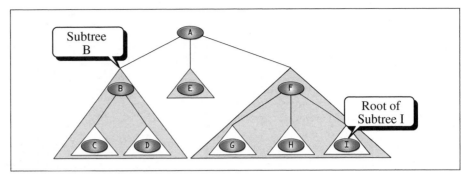

Figure 12.18 Subtrees

OPERATIONS ON TREES

Operations on a tree are complex and beyond the scope of this book. They are discussed in a data structures course.

12.6 BINARY TREES

A **binary tree** is a tree in which no node can have more than two subtrees. In other words, a node can have zero, one, or two subtrees. These subtrees are designated as the left subtree and right subtree. Figure 12.19 shows a binary tree with its two subtrees. Note that each subtree is itself a binary tree.

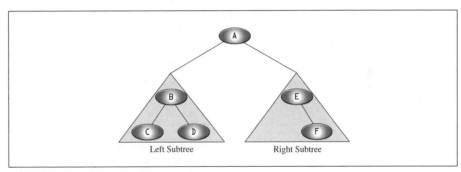

Figure 12.19 Binary tree

To better understand the structure of binary trees, study Figure 12.20. It contains eight trees, the first of which is a null tree. A **null tree** is a tree with no nodes (Figure 12.20[a]). As you study this figure, note that symmetry is not a tree requirement.

Properties

We now define several properties for binary trees that distinguish them from general trees.

Height of Binary Trees   The height of binary trees can be mathematically predicted. Given that you need to store N nodes in a binary tree, the maximum height, H_{max}, can be defined as

$$H_{max} = N$$

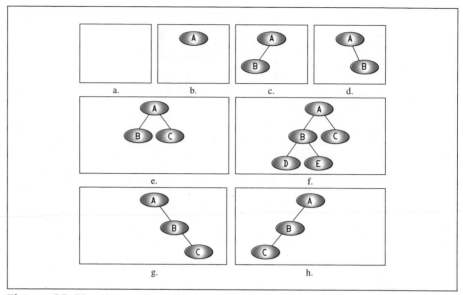

Figure 12.20   Examples of binary trees

A tree with a maximum height is rare. It occurs when the entire tree is built in one direction, as shown in Figure 12.20(g) and Figure 12.20(h). The minimum height of the tree, H_{min}, is determined by the following formula:

$$H_{min} = \lceil \log_2 N \rceil + 1$$

Given a height of the binary tree, H, the minimum and maximum number of nodes in the tree are given as

$$N_{min} = H$$

$$N_{max} = 2^H - 1$$

Balance   The distance of a node from the root determines how efficiently it can be located. For example, the children of any node in a tree can be accessed by following only one branch path, the one that leads to the desired node. For example, the nodes at level 2 of a tree can all be accessed by following only two branches from the root. It stands to reason, therefore, that the shorter the tree, the easier it is to locate any desired node in the tree.

This concept leads us to a very important characteristic of a binary tree: its **balance.** To determine whether a tree is balanced, calculate its balance factor. The **balance factor** of a binary tree is the difference in height between its left and right subtrees. If you define the height of the left subtree as H_L and the height of the right subtree as H_R, then the balance factor of the tree, B, is determined by the following formula:

$$B = H_L - H_R$$

Using this formula, the balances of the eight trees in Figure 12.20 are (a) 0 by definition, (b) 0, (c) 1, (d) –1, (e) 0, (f) 1, (g) –2, and (h) 2.

A tree is balanced if its balance factor is 0 and its subtrees are also balanced. Because this definition occurs so seldom, an alternative definition is more generally applied: A binary tree is balanced if the height of its subtrees differs by no more than 1 (its balance factor is –1, 0, or +1) and its subtrees are also balanced. This definition was created by Adelson-Velskii and Landis in their definition of an AVL tree.

OPERATIONS ON BINARY TREES

The three most common operations defined for a binary tree are add, delete, and traversal. Add and delete operations are complex and beyond the scope of this book. We discuss binary tree traversal in this section.

Binary Tree Traversals

A **binary tree traversal** requires that each node of the tree be processed once and only once in a predetermined sequence. The two general approaches to the traversal sequence are depth first and breadth first.

Depth-First Traversals   Given that a binary tree consists of a root, a left subtree, and a right subtree, we can define six different **depth-first traversal** sequences. Computer scientists have assigned three of these sequences standard names in the literature; the other three are unnamed but are easily derived. The standard traversals are shown in Figure 12.21.

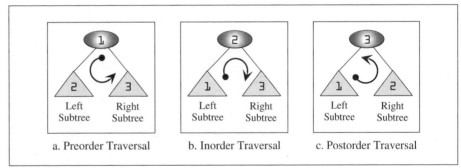

Figure 12.21   Depth-first traversal of a binary tree

The traditional designation of the traversals uses a designation of `node` (N) for the root, `left` (L) for the left subtree, and `right` (R) for the right subtree.

■ **Preorder Traversal (NLR).** In the **preorder traversal,** the root node is processed first, followed by the left subtree and then the right subtree. It draws its name from the Latin prefix *pre,* which means "to go before." Thus, the root goes before the subtrees. Figure 12.22 shows another way to visualize the traversal of the tree. Imagine that you are walking around the tree, starting on the left of the root and keeping as close to the nodes as possible. In the preorder traversal, you process the node when you are to its left. This is shown as a black box to the left of the node. The path is shown as a line following a route completely around the tree and back to the root.

■ **Inorder Traversal (LNR).** The **inorder traversal** processes the left subtree first, then the root node, and finally the right subtree. The meaning of the prefix *in* is that the root is processed "in between" the subtrees. Figure 12.23 shows another way to visualize the traversal of the tree. Imagine that you are walking around the tree, starting on the left of the root and keeping as close to the nodes as possible. In the inorder traversal, you process the node when you are under it. This is shown as a black box under the node. The path is shown as a line following a route completely around the tree and back to the root.

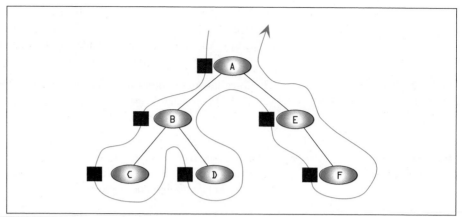

Figure 12.22   Preorder traversal of a binary tree

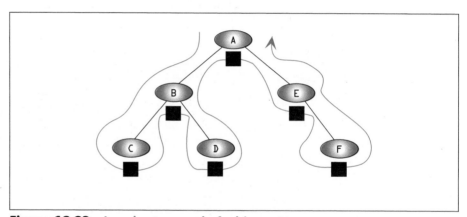

Figure 12.23   Inorder traversal of a binary tree

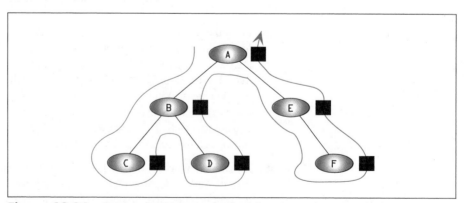

Figure 12.24   Postorder traversal of a binary tree

■   **Postorder Traversal (LRN).** The last of the standard traversals is the **postorder traversal.** It processes the root node after *(post)* the left and right subtrees have been processed. It starts by locating the leftmost leaf and processing it. It then processes its right sibling, including its subtrees (if any). Finally, it processes the root node. Figure 12.24 shows another way to visualize the traversal of the tree. Imagine that you are walking around the tree, starting on the left of the root and keeping as close to the nodes as possible. In the postorder traversal, you process the node when you are to its right. This is shown as a black box to the right of the node. The path is shown as a line following a route completely around the tree and back to the root.

Breadth-First Traversals

In the **breadth-first traversal** of a binary tree, you process all of the children of a node before proceeding with the next level. In other words, given a root at level n, you process all nodes at level n before proceeding with the nodes at level $n + 1$. To traverse a tree in depth-first order, you use a stack. On the other hand, to traverse a tree in breadth-first order, you use a queue.

As with depth-first traversals, you can trace the traversal with a walk. This time, however, the walk proceeds in a stairlike fashion, first across the root level, then across level 1, next at level 2, and so forth until the entire tree is traversed (Figure 12.25).

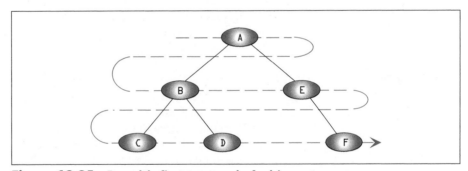

Figure 12.25 Breadth-first traversal of a binary tree

IMPLEMENTATION OF A BINARY TREE

A binary tree is normally implemented as a linked list.

BINARY TREE APPLICATIONS

One interesting binary tree application is the expression tree. An expression is a sequence of tokens that follow prescribed rules. A **token** may be either an operand or an operator. In this discussion, we consider only binary arithmetic operators in the form operand-operator-operand. To simplify the discussion, we use only four operators: addition, subtraction, multiplication, and division.

An **expression tree** is a binary tree with the following properties:

1. Each leaf is an operand.
2. The root and internal nodes are operators.
3. Subtrees are subexpressions, with the root being an operator.

For an expression tree, the three standard traversals represent the three different expression formats: **infix, postfix,** and **prefix.** The inorder traversal produces the infix expression, the postorder traversal produces the postfix expression, and the preorder traversal produces the prefix expression. Figure 12.26 is an infix expression and its expression tree.

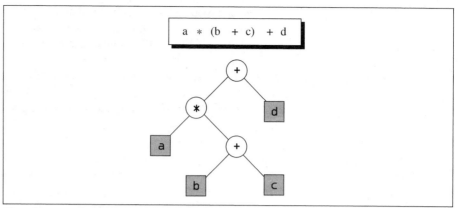

Figure 12.26   Expression tree

12.7   GRAPHS

A graph can also be classified as an abstract data type. Graphs can be used to solve complex routing problems, such as designing and routing airlines among the airports they serve. Similarly, they can be used to route messages over a computer network from one node to another.

TERMINOLOGY

A **graph** is a collection of nodes, called vertices (sing. *vertex*), and a collection of line segments, called **lines,** connecting pairs of vertices. In other words, a graph consists of two sets: a set of vertices and a set of lines. Graphs may be either directed or undirected. In a **directed graph,** or **digraph** for short, each line has a direction (arrowhead) to its successor. The lines in a directed graph are known as **arcs.** In a directed graph, the flow along the arcs between two vertices can follow only the indicated direction. In an **undirected graph,** there is no direction (arrowhead) on any of the lines, which are known as **edges.** In an undirected graph, the flow between two vertices can go in either direction. Figure 12.27 contains an example of both a directed graph (a) and an undirected graph (b).

Two vertices in a graph are said to be **adjacent vertices** (or neighbors) if a line directly connects them. In Figure 12.27, A and B are adjacent, whereas D and F are not.

A **path** is a sequence of vertices in which each vertex is adjacent to the next one. In Figure 12.27, {A, B, C, E} is one path and {A, B, E, F} is another. Note that both directed and undirected graphs have paths. In an undirected graph, you may travel in either direction.

A **cycle** is a path consisting of at least three vertices that starts and ends with the same vertex. In Figure 12.27(b), B, C, D, E, B is a cycle. Note, however, that the same vertices in Figure 12.27(a) do not constitute a cycle because in a digraph, a path can only follow the direction of the arc, whereas in an undirected graph, a path can move in either direction along the edge. A **loop** is a special case of a cycle in which a single arc begins and ends at the same vertex.

Two vertices are said to be connected if there is a path between them. A graph is said to be connected if, suppressing direction, there is a path from any vertex to any other vertex. Furthermore, a directed graph is **strongly connected** if there is a path from each vertex to every other vertex in the digraph. A directed graph is **weakly connected** if at least two vertices are not connected. (A connected undirected graph would always be strongly connected, so the concept is not normally used with undirected graphs.) A **disjoint graph** is not connected.

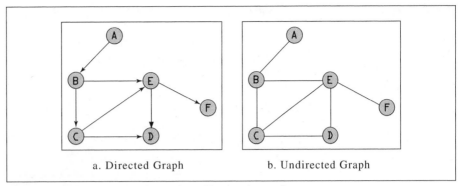

Figure 12.27 Directed and undirected graphs

The *degree* of a vertex is the number of lines incident to it. The *outdegree* of a vertex in a digraph is the number of arcs leaving the vertex; the *indegree* is the number of arcs entering the vertex.

**OPERATIONS
ON GRAPHS**

In this section, we define six primitive graph operations that provide the basic modules needed to maintain a graph: add a vertex, delete a vertex, add an edge, delete an edge, find a vertex, and traverse a graph. As you will see, there are two graph traversal methods.

Add Vertex

Add vertex inserts a new vertex into a graph. When a vertex is added, it is disjoint; that is, it is not connected to any other vertices in the list. Obviously, adding a vertex is only the first step in an insertion process. After a vertex is added, it must be connected. Figure 12.28 shows a graph before and after a new vertex is added.

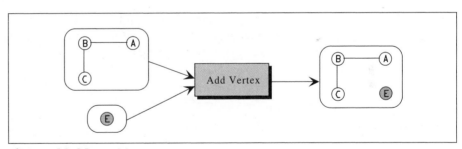

Figure 12.28 Add vertex

Delete Vertex

Delete vertex removes a vertex from a graph. When a vertex is deleted, all connecting edges are also removed. Figure 12.29 contains an example of deleting a vertex.

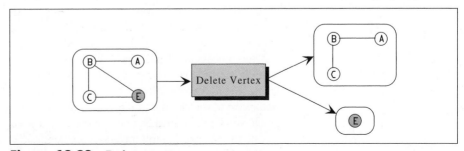

Figure 12.29 Delete vertex

Add Edge

Add edge connects a vertex to a destination vertex. If a vertex requires multiple edges, then add edge must be called once for each adjacent vertex. To add an edge, two vertices must be specified. If the graph is a digraph, one of the vertices must be specified as the source and one as the destination. Figure 12.30 contains an example of adding the edge {A, E} to a graph.

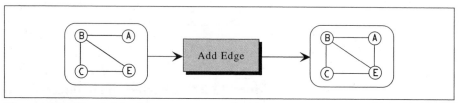

Figure 12.30   Add edge

Delete Edge

Delete edge removes one edge from a graph. Figure 12.31 contains an example of deleting the edge {A, E} from a graph.

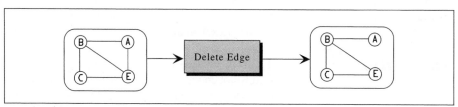

Figure 12.31   Delete edge

Find Vertex

Find vertex traverses a graph looking for a specified vertex. If the vertex is found, its data are returned. If it is not found, an error is indicated. In Figure 12.32, find vertex traverses the graph looking for the vertex C.

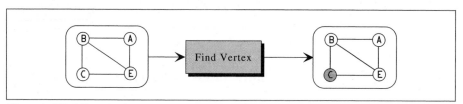

Figure 12.32   Find vertex

Traverse Graph

There is always at least one application that requires that all vertices in a given graph be visited; that is, at least one application requires that the graph be traversed. Because a vertex in a graph can have multiple parents, the traversal of a graph presents some problems not found in the traversal of linear lists and trees. Specifically, you must somehow ensure that you process the data in each vertex only once. However, because there are multiple paths to a vertex, you may arrive at it from more than one direction as you traverse the graph. The traditional solution to this problem is to include a visited flag at each vertex. Before the traversal, you set the visited flag in each vertex off. Then, as you traverse the graph, you set the visited flag on to indicate that the data have been processed.

The two standard graph traversals are depth first and breadth first. Both use the visited flag.

Depth-First Traversal   In the **depth-first traversal,** you process a vertex's descendants before you move to an adjacent vertex. This concept is most easily seen when the graph is a tree. In Figure 12.33, we show preorder traversal, one of the standard depth-first traversals.

The depth-first traversal of a graph starts by processing the first vertex of the graph. After processing the first vertex, select any vertex adjacent to the first vertex and process it. As you process each vertex, select an adjacent vertex until you reach a vertex with no adjacent entries. This is similar to reaching a leaf in a tree. Then back out of the structure, processing adjacent vertices as you go. It should be obvious that this logic requires a stack (or recursion) to complete the traversal.

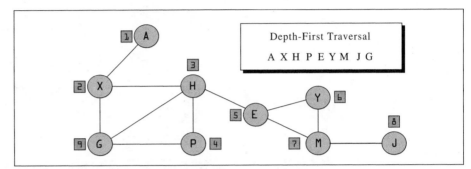

Figure 12.33   Depth-first traversal of a graph

Breadth-First Traversal   In the **breadth-first traversal** of a graph, you process all adjacent vertices of a vertex before going to the next level. Looking at the tree in Figure 12.34, you see that its breadth-first traversal starts at level 0 and then processes all the vertices in level 1 before going on to process the vertices in level 2.

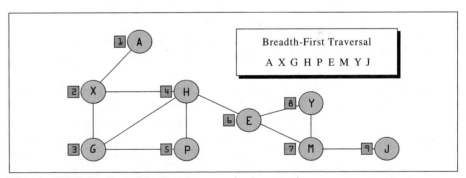

Figure 12.34   Breadth-first traversal of a graph

The breadth-first traversal of a graph follows the same concept. Begin by picking a starting vertex; after processing it, process all of its adjacent vertices. After you process all of the first vertex's adjacent vertices, pick the first adjacent vertex and process all of its vertices, then the second adjacent vertex and process all of its vertices, and so forth until you are finished.

IMPLEMENTATION OF A GRAPH

To represent a graph, you need two sets of data. The first set represents the vertices of the graph, and the second set represents the edges or arcs. The two most common structures used to store these sets are the array **(adjacency matrix)** and the linked list **(adjacency list).** Figure 12.35 shows these two implementations for a simple graph. The numbers between the vertices are weights (e.g., the distance between networks in an internetwork).

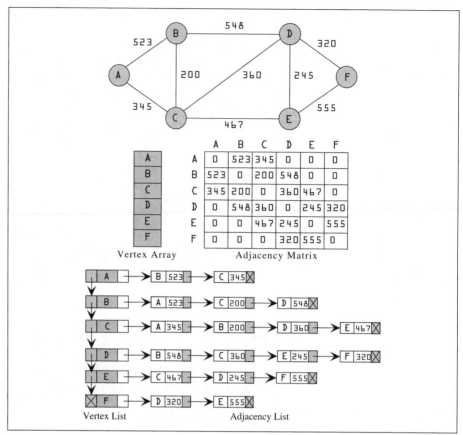

Figure 12.35   Graph implementations

GRAPH APPLICATIONS

Graphs have many applications in computer science. We mention two here: networks and minimum spanning trees.

Networks

A **network** is a graph with weighted lines. It is also known as a **weighted graph.** The meaning of the weights depends on the application. For example, an airline might use a graph to represent the routes between cities that it serves. In this example, the vertices represent the cities, and the edge is a route between two cities. The edge's weight could represent the flight miles between the two cities or the price of the flight. A network for a small hypothetical airline is shown in Figure 12.35. In this case, the weights represent the mileage between the cities.

Because the weight is an attribute of an edge, it is stored in the structure that contains the edge. In an adjacency matrix, the weight would be stored as the intersection value. In an adjacency list, it would be stored as the value in the adjacency linked list.

Minimum Spanning Tree

We can derive one or more spanning trees from a connected network. A **spanning tree** is a tree that contains all of the vertices in the graph. A **minimum spanning tree** is a spanning tree such that the sum of its weights is the minimum. There are many applications for minimum spanning trees, all with the requirement to minimize some aspect of the graph, such as the distance between all of the vertices in the graph. For example, given a network of computers, you could create a tree that connects all of the computers. The minimum spanning tree gives the shortest length of cable that can be used to connect all of the computers while ensuring that there is a path between any two computers.

12.8 KEY TERMS

abstract data type (ADT)
abstraction
adjacency list
adjacency matrix
adjacent vertices
ancestor
arc
array
backtracking
balance
balance factor
binary tree
binary tree traversal
branch
breadth-first traversal
child
cycle
degree
depth
depth-first traversal
dequeue
descendant
digraph
directed graph
disjoint graph
edge
enqueue

expression tree
first in, first out (FIFO)
general list
graph
height
indegree
infix
inorder traversal (LNR)
internal node
key
last in, first out (LIFO)
leaf
level
line
linear list
list
loop
minimum spanning tree
network
node
null tree
ordered list
outdegree
parent
parsing
path
pop

postfix
postorder traversal
postponement
prefix
preorder traversal
push
queue
queue simulation
random list
restricted list
retrieval
root
siblings
spanning tree
stack
strongly connected graph
subtree
token
traversal
tree
underflow
undirected graph
vertex
weakly connected graph
weighted graph

12.9 SUMMARY

- In a linear list, each element has a unique successor.

- Linear lists can be divided into two categories: general and restricted.

- In a general list, data can be inserted and deleted anywhere, and there are no restrictions on the operations that can be used to process the list.

- In a restricted list, data can be added or deleted at the ends of the structure, and processing is restricted to the operations on the data at the ends of the list.

- Two common restricted list structures are stacks (last in, first out [LIFO] lists) and queues (first in, first out [FIFO] lists).

- Four common operations are associated with linear lists: insertion, deletion, retrieval, and traversal.

- A stack is a linear list in which all additions and deletions are restricted to one end, called the top. A stack is also called an LIFO list.

- We defined two operations for a stack: push and pop.

- Push adds an item to the top of the stack. After the push, the new item becomes the top.

- Pop removes the item at the top of the stack. After the pop, the next item, if any, becomes the top.

- Four stack applications were discussed in this chapter: reversing, parsing, postponing, and backtracking.

- A queue is a linear list in which data can only be inserted at one end, called the rear, and deleted from the other end, called the front. A queue is a first in, first out (FIFO) structure.

■ We discussed two queue operations in this chapter: enqueue and dequeue.

■ A queue can be used to categorize data.

■ A tree consists of a finite set of elements called nodes and a finite set of directed lines called branches that connect the nodes. The number of branches associated with a node is the degree of the node. When the branch is directed toward the node, it is an indegree branch; when the branch is directed away from the node, it is an outdegree branch. The sum of indegree and outdegree branches is the degree of the node.

■ If the tree is not empty, the first node is called the root, which has the indegree of zero. All nodes in the tree, except the root, must have an indegree of one.

■ A leaf is a node with an outdegree of zero.

■ An internal node is neither the root nor a leaf.

■ A node can be a parent, a child, or both. Two or more nodes with the same parent are called siblings.

■ A path is a sequence of nodes in which each node is adjacent to the next one.

■ An ancestor is any node in the path from the root of a given node. A descendent is any node in all of the paths from a given node to a leaf.

■ The level of a node is its distance from the root.

■ The height of a tree is the level of the leaf in the longest path from the root plus 1; the height of an empty tree is −1.

■ A subtree is any connected structure below the root.

■ A tree can be defined recursively as a set of nodes that either (1) is empty or (2) has a designated node called the root from which hierarchically descend zero or more subtrees, which are also trees.

■ In a binary tree, no node can have more than two children.

■ A binary tree traversal visits each node of the tree once and only once in a predetermined sequence.

■ The two approaches to binary tree traversal are depth first and breadth first.

■ Using the depth-first approach, you traverse a binary tree in six different sequences; however, only three of these sequences are given standard names: preorder, inorder, and postorder.

a. In the preorder traversal, you process the root first, followed by the left subtree and then the right subtree.

b. In the inorder traversal, you process the left subtree first, followed by the root and then the right subtree.

c. In the postorder traversal, you process the left subtree first, followed by the right subtree and then the root.

■ In the breadth-first approach, you process all nodes in a level before proceeding to the next level.

■ We defined one application for a binary tree in this chapter: expression tree.

■ A graph is a collection of nodes, called vertices, and a collection of line segments connecting pairs of nodes, called edges or arcs.

■ Graphs may be directed or undirected. In a directed graph, or digraph, each line has a direction. In an undirected graph, there is no direction on the lines. A line in a directed graph is called an arc. A line in an undirected graph is called an edge.

■ In a graph, two vertices are said to be adjacent if an edge directly connects them.

■ A path is a sequence of vertices in which each vertex is adjacent to the next one.

■ A cycle is a path of at least three vertices that starts and ends with the same vertex.

■ A loop is a special case of a cycle in which a single arc begins and ends with the same node.

■ A graph is said to be connected if, for any two vertices, there is a path from one to the other. A graph is disjointed if it is not connected.

■ The degree of a vertex is the number of vertices adjacent to it. The outdegree of a vertex is the number of arcs leaving the node; the indegree of a vertex is the number of arcs entering the node.

■ Six operations were defined for a graph: add a vertex, delete a vertex, add an edge, delete an edge, find a node, and traverse the graph.

■ There are two standard graph traversals: depth first and breadth first.

■ In the depth-first traversal, all of a node's descendants are processed before moving to an adjacent node.

■ In the breadth-first traversal, all of the adjacent vertices are processed before processing the descendants of a vertex.

■ To represent a graph in a computer, you need to store two sets of information: The first set represents the vertices, and the second set represents the edges.

■ The most common methods used to store a graph are the adjacency matrix method and the adjacency list method.

■ In the adjacency matrix method, you use an array to store the vertices and a matrix to store the edges.

■ In the adjacency list method, you use a linked list to store the vertices and a matrix to store the edges.

■ We defined two applications for a graph in this chapter: a network and a minimal spanning tree.

12.10   PRACTICE SET

REVIEW QUESTIONS

1. What is an abstract data type?

2. In an ADT, what is known and what is hidden?

3. What is a linear list?

4. What is the difference between a general list and a restricted list?

5. What are two common implementations of a general list?

6. What is an advantage of the linked list implementation of a general linear list over an array implementation of a general linear list?

7. What is the difference between the push operation and the pop operation?

8. What are three common stack operations?

9. Describe the enqueue and dequeue operations.

10. What does it mean when a binary tree is balanced?

11. What is the difference between a depth-first traversal and a breadth-first traversal of a binary tree?

12. What is the relationship between a path and a cycle?

13. What is the difference between a depth-first traversal and a breadth-first traversal of a graph?

14. What is the major limitation of using an array to implement a graph? Why is this a problem?

15. What is the difference between a graph and a network?

MULTIPLE-CHOICE QUESTIONS

16. In an abstract data type, _____.
    a. the ADT implementation is known
    b. the ADT implementation is hidden
    c. the ADT functions are hidden
    d. none of the above

17. A _____ could be an ADT.
    a. matrix
    b. linked list
    c. tree
    d. all of the above

18. In an ADT, the _____.
    a. data are declared
    b. operations are declared
    c. data and operations are encapsulated
    d. all of the above

19. A _____ is a list in which each element has a unique successor.
    a. matrix
    b. network
    c. linear list
    d. linked list

20. An FIFO list is a _____ linear list.
    a. general
    b. restricted
    c. unordered
    d. a or b

21. _____ linear list can be ordered or unordered.
    a. A general
    b. A restricted
    c. A FIFO
    d. A LIFO

22. A(n) _____ list is also known as a queue.
    a. LIFO
    b. FIFO
    c. unordered
    d. ordered

23. A(n) _____ list is also known as a stack.
    a. LIFO
    b. FIFO
    c. unordered
    d. ordered

24. When there is not enough room for insertion, an ordered list is in _____ state.
    a. an overflow
    b. an underflow
    c. a slow
    d. a restricted

25. When an ordered list is in _____ state, the list is empty.
    a. an overflow
    b. an underflow
    c. a slow
    d. a restricted

26. In list _____ for an ordered list, the data in the list and the number of list elements remain unchanged.
    a. insertion
    b. deletion
    c. retrieval
    d. all of the above

27. In list _____ for an ordered list, each element in the list is processed sequentially.
    a. insertion
    b. deletion
    c. retrieval
    d. traversal

28. If A is the first data element input into a stack followed by B, C, and D, _____ is the first element to be removed.
    a. A
    b. B
    c. C
    d. D

29. If A is the first data element input into a queue followed by B, C, and D, _____ is the first element to be removed.
    a. A
    b. B
    c. C
    d. D

30. The pop operation _____ of the stack.
    a. removes an item from the top
    b. removes an item from the bottom
    c. adds an item to the top
    d. adds an item to the bottom

31. The push operation _____ of the stack.
    a. removes an item from the top
    b. removes an item from the bottom
    c. adds an item to the top
    d. adds an item to the bottom

32. When data are broken into independent pieces for further processing, it is called _____.
    a. reversing the data
    b. postponement of data
    c. parsing the data
    d. backtracking the data

33. In a queue, data are inserted only at the _____ and deleted only at the _____.
    a. rear; front or rear
    b. front; rear
    c. rear; front
    d. rear or front; front

34. The indegree of _____ of a tree is always zero.
    a. any node
    b. a branch
    c. the root
    d. a leaf

35. If an internal node has 4 outdegree branches, its degree is _____.
    a. 9
    b. 1
    c. 4
    d. 5

36. A node of a tree has a degree of 3. This means its outdegree is _____.
    a. 0
    b. 2
    c. 4
    d. none of the above

37. A _____ is a sequence of nodes in which each node is adjacent to the next one.
    a. leaf
    b. root
    c. descendant
    d. path

38. If the height of a tree is 10, the highest level of the tree is _____.
    a. 10
    b. 9
    c. 5
    d. 1

39. In a binary tree, each node has _____ two subtrees.
    a. more than
    b. less than
    c. at most
    d. at least

40. If there are 22 nodes to be stored in a binary tree, the maximum height of the tree is _____.
a. greater than 22
b. less than 22
c. equal to 22
d. none of the above

41. If there are 16 nodes to be stored in a binary tree, the minimum height of the tree is _____.
a. 16
b. 5
c. 4
d. 1

42. A binary tree has a height of 5. What is the minimum number of nodes?
a. 31
b. 15
c. 5
d. 1

43. A binary tree has a height of 5. What is the maximum number of nodes?
a. 31
b. 15
c. 5
d. 1

44. In a preorder traversal, the _____ is processed first.
a. left subtree
b. right subtree
c. root
d. a or b

45. In _____ traversal, the right subtree is processed last.
a. a preorder
b. an inorder
c. a postorder
d. a or b

46. In a postorder traversal, the root is processed _____.
a. first
b. second
c. last
d. a or b

47. In a postorder traversal, the left subtree is processed _____.
a. first
b. second
c. last
d. a or b

48. In _____ traversal, the left subtree is processed last.
a. a preorder
b. an inorder
c. a postorder
d. none of the above

49. In an inorder traversal, the root is processed _____.
a. first
b. second
c. last
d. a or b

50. In a breadth-first traversal of a binary tree with three levels (0, 1, and 2), which level is processed last?
a. 0
b. 1
c. 2
d. any of the above

51. _____ is a line between two vertices in a digraph.
a. A node
b. An arc
c. An edge
d. A path

52. An edge is _____ between two vertices in an undirected graph.
a. a node
b. an arc
c. a line
d. a path

53. If C and D are two adjacent vertices in an undirected graph, then _____.
a. there are two paths
b. there is just one path {C, D}
c. there is just one path {D, C}
d. there are no paths

54. A vertex in a digraph has four arcs entering and three arcs leaving. The outdegree of the vertex is _____.
a. 4
b. 3
c. 2
d. 1

EXERCISES

55. Show the contents of stack s1 after the following operations:

```
push (s1, 5)
push (s1, 3)
push (s1, 2)
pop (s1)
pop (s1)
push (s1, 6)
```

56. Use a `while` loop to empty the contents of stack s2.

57. Use a `while` loop to move the contents of stack s1 to s2. After the operation, stack s1 should be empty.

58. Use a `while` loop to copy the contents of stack s1 to s2. After the operation, the contents of stacks s1 and s2 should be the same.

59. Use a `while` loop to concatenate the contents of stack s2 to the contents of stack s1. After the concatenation, the elements of stack s2 should be at the top of the elements of stack s1. Stack s2 should be empty.

60. A palindrome is a string that can be read backward and forward with the same result. For example, the following is a palindrome:

        Able was I ere I saw Elba

    Write an algorithm using a stack to test if a string is a palindrome.

61. Write an algorithm to compare the contents of two stacks.

62. Show the contents of stack s1 and queue q1 after the following operations:

    ```
    push (s1, 3)
    push (s1, 5)
    enqueue (q1, 6)
    enqueue (q1, 9)
    pop (s1)
    enqueue (q1, 9)
    dequeue (q1)
    ```

63. Use a `while` loop to empty the contents of queue q3.

64. Use a `while` loop to move the contents of queue q2 to queue q3. After the operation, queue q2 should be empty.

65. Use a `while` loop to copy the contents of queue q2 to queue q3. After the operation, the contents of queue q1 and queue q2 should be the same.

66. Use a `while` loop to concatenate the contents of queue q2 to the contents of queue q1. After the concatenation, the elements of queue q2 should be at the end of the elements of queue q1. Queue q2 should be empty.

67. Write an algorithm to compare the contents of two queues.

68. Find the root of each of the following binary trees:
    a. Tree with postorder traversal: FCBDG
    b. Tree with preorder traversal: IBCDFEN
    c. Tree with postorder traversal: CBIDFGE

69. A binary tree has 10 nodes. The inorder and preorder traversal of the tree follow. Draw the tree:

    Preorder: JCBADEFIGH

    Inorder: ABCEDFJGIH

70. A binary tree has eight nodes. The inorder and postorder traversal of the tree follow. Draw the tree:

    Postorder: FECHGDBA

    Inorder: FECABHDG

71. A binary tree has seven nodes. The inorder and postorder traversal of the tree follow. Can you draw the tree? If not, explain.

    Postorder: GFDABEC

    Inorder: ABDCEFG

72. Draw all possible nonsimilar trees with three nodes (A, B, and C).

73. Give the depth-first traversal of the graph in Figure 12.36 starting from vertex A.

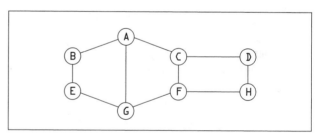

Figure 12.36 Exercises 73 and 74

74. Give the breadth-first traversal of the graph in Figure 12.36 starting from vertex A.

75. Give the adjacency matrix representation of the graph in Figure 12.37.

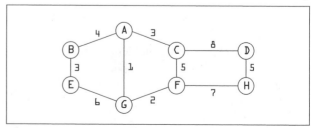

Figure 12.37 Exercise 75 and 76

76. Give the adjacency list representation of the graph in Figure 12.37.

77. Draw a graph for the adjacency matrix representation in Figure 12.38.

	A	B	C	D	E	F
A	0	3	4	0	2	1
B	0	0	2	0	0	3
C	0	0	0	2	6	1
D	2	6	1	0	1	2
E	0	0	0	0	0	3
F	0	0	0	0	0	0

Figure 12.38 Exercise 77

File Structures

A **file** is an external collection of related data treated as a unit. The primary purpose of a file is to store data. Since the contents of primary memory are lost when the computer is shut down, you need files to store data in a more permanent form. Additionally, the collection of data is often too large to reside entirely in main memory at one time. Therefore, you must have the ability to read and write portions of the data while the rest remain in the file.

Files are stored in what are known as **auxiliary** or **secondary storage devices.** The two most common forms of secondary storage are disk and tape. Files in secondary storage can be both read and written. Files can also exist in forms that the computer can write but not read. For example, the display of information on the system monitor is a form of a file as are data sent to a printer. In a general sense, the keyboard is also a file, although it cannot store data.

For our purposes, a file is a collection of data records with each record consisting of one or more fields, as defined in Chapter 11.

13.1 ACCESS METHODS

When you design a file, the question is not how you should store the file. The question is how you can retrieve the information (a specific record) from the file. Sometimes you need to process records one after another. Sometimes you need to quickly access a specific record without retrieving the previous records. The **access method** determines how records can be retrieved: sequentially or randomly.

SEQUENTIAL ACCESS

If you need to access a file sequentially (one record after another, from beginning to end), you use a **sequential file** structure.

RANDOM ACCESS

If you need to access one specific record without having to retrieve all records before it, you use a file structure that allows **random access.** Two file structures allow this: the indexed file and the hashed file. The taxonomy of file structures is shown in Figure 13.1.

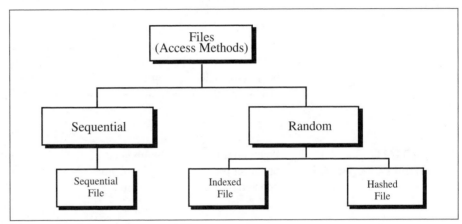

Figure 13.1 Taxonomy of file structures

13.2 SEQUENTIAL FILES

A sequential file is one in which records can only be accessed sequentially, one after another, from beginning to end. Figure 13.2 shows the layout of a sequential file. Records are stored one after another in auxiliary storage (**tape** or **disk**), and there is an EOF (end-of-file) marker after the last record. The operating system has no information about the record addresses. The only thing known to the operating system is that the records are one after the other.

Figure 13.2 Sequential file

The following code shows how to access all records in a sequential file.

```
while Not EOF
{
    Read the next record
    Process the record
}
```

Program 13.1   Processing records in a sequential file

You use a loop to read and process records one by one. After the operating system processes the last record, the EOF is detected and the loop is exited.

The sequential file is used in applications that need to access all records from beginning to end. For example, if personal information about each employee in a company is stored in a file, you can use **sequential access** to retrieve each record at the end of the month to print the paychecks. Here, because you have to process each record, sequential access is more efficient and easier than random access.

However, the sequential file is not efficient for random access. For example, if all customer records in a bank can only be accessed sequentially, a customer who needs to get money from an ATM would have to wait as the system checks each record from the beginning of the file until it reaches the customer's record. If this bank has a million customers, the system, on average, would retrieve half a million records before reaching the customer's record. This is very inefficient.

UPDATING SEQUENTIAL FILES

Sequential files must be updated periodically to reflect changes in information. The updating process is very involved because all of the records need to be checked and updated (if necessary) sequentially.

Files Involved in Updating

There are four files associated with an update program: the new master file, the old master file, the transaction file, and the error report file.

- **New Master File.** First there is the new permanent data file or, as it is commonly known, the **new master file.** The new master file contains the most current data.

- **Old Master File.** The **old master file** is the permanent file that should be updated. Even after updating, the old master file should be kept for reference.

- **Transaction File.** The third file is the **transaction file.** It contains changes to be applied to the master file. There are three basic types of changes in all file updates. *Add transactions* contain data about a new record to be added in the master file. *Delete transactions* identify records to be deleted from the file. And *change transactions* contain revisions to specific records in the file. To process any of these transactions, you need a key. A **key** is one or more fields that uniquely identify the data in the file. For example, in a file of students, the key could be student ID. In an employee file, the key could be social security number.

- **Error Report File.** The fourth file needed in an update program is an **error report file.** It is very rare that an update process does not produce at least one error. When an error occurs, you need to report it to the user. The *error report* contains a listing of all errors discovered during the update process and is presented to the user for corrective action.

Process

Figure 13.3 is a pictorial representation of a sequential file update. In this figure, you see the four files that have been discussed. Although we use the tape symbol for the files, we could just as easily have represented them with the disk symbol. Note that after the update program completes, the new master file is sent to offline storage where it is kept until it is needed again. When the file is to be updated, the master file is retrieved from offline storage and becomes the old master.

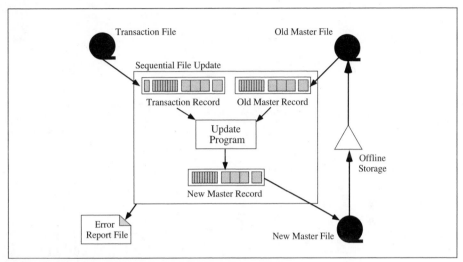

Figure 13.3   Updating a sequential file

To make the updating process efficient, all files are sorted on the same key. The update process requires that you compare the keys on the transaction and master files and, assuming that there are no errors, follow one of three actions:

1. If the transaction file key is less than the master file key, add the transaction to the new master.
2. If the transaction file key is equal to the master file key, either
   a. Change the contents of the master file data if the transaction is a revision (R)
   b. Remove the data from the master file if the transaction is a deletion (D).
3. If the transaction file key is greater than the master file key, write the old master file record to the new master file. In this case, the transaction code should be addition (A), or there is an error.

This updating process is seen in Figure 13.4. In the transaction file, the transaction codes are A for add, D for delete, and R for revise. The process begins by comparing the keys for the first record of each file.

13.3   INDEXED FILES

To access a record in a file randomly, you need to know the address of the record. For example, suppose a customer wants to check her bank account. Neither the customer nor the teller knows the address of the customer's record. The customer can only give the teller her account number (key). Here, an indexed file can relate the account number (key) to the record address (Figure 13.5).

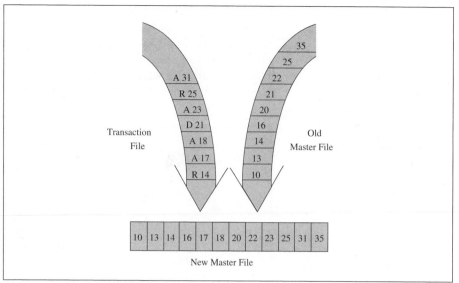

Figure 13.4   Updating process

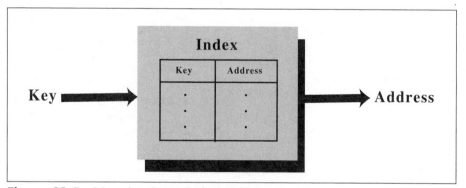

Figure 13.5   Mapping in an indexed file

An **indexed file** is made of a **data file,** which is a sequential file, and an **index.** The index itself is a very small file with only two fields: the key of the sequential file and the address of the corresponding record on the disk. Figure 13.6 shows the logical view of an indexed file. To access a record in the file, follow these steps:

1. The entire index file is loaded into main memory (the file is small and uses little memory).

2. The entries are searched, using an efficient search algorithm such as a binary search, to find the desired key.

3. The address of the record is retrieved.

4. Using the address, the data record is retrieved and passed to the user.

INVERTED FILES

One of the advantages of the indexed file is that you can have more than one index, each with a different key. For example, an employee file can be retrieved based on either social security number or last name. This type of indexed file is usually called an **inverted file.**

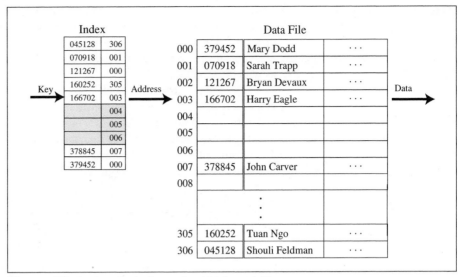

Figure 13.6   Logical view of an indexed file

13.4   HASHED FILES

In an indexed file, the index maps the key to the address. A **hashed file** uses a function to accomplish this mapping. The user gives the key, the function maps the key to the address and passes it to the operating system, and the record is retrieved (Figure 13.7).

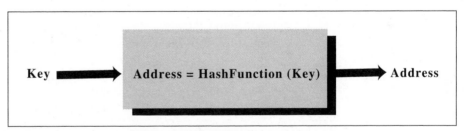

Figure 13.7   Mapping in a hashed file

The hashed file eliminates the need for an extra file (index). In an indexed file, you must keep this index on file in the disk, and when you need to process the data file, you must first load the index into memory, search it to find the address of the data record, and then access the data file to access the record. In a hashed file, finding the address is done through the use of a function. There is no need for an index and all of the overhead associated with it. However, you will see that hashed files have their own problems.

HASHING METHODS   For key-address mapping, you can select one of several hashing methods. We discuss a few of them here.

Direct Method

In **direct hashing,** the key is the address without any algorithmic manipulation. The file must therefore contain a record for every possible key. Although the situations for direct hashing are limited, it can be very powerful because it guarantees that there are no synonyms or collisions (synonyms and collisions are discussed later in this chapter) as with other methods.

Let's look at a trivial example. Imagine that an organization has fewer than 100 employees. Each employee is assigned a number between 1 and 100 (employee ID). In this case, if you create a file of 100 employee records, the employee number can be directly used as the address of any individual record. This concept is shown in Figure 13.8. The record with key 025 (Vu Nguyen . . .) is hashed to address (sector) 025. Note that not every element in the file contains an employee record. Some of the space is wasted.

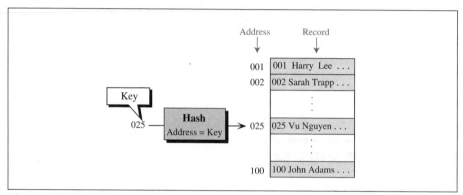

Figure 13.8   Direct hashing

Although this is the ideal method, its application is very limited. For example, it is very inefficient to use social security number as the key because social security numbers have nine digits. You need a huge file with 999,999,999 records, but you would use less than 100. Let's turn our attention, therefore, to hashing techniques that map a large population of possible keys into a small address space.

Modulo Division Method

Also known as **division remainder hashing,** the **modulo division** method divides the key by the file size and uses the remainder plus 1 for the address. This gives the simple hashing algorithm that follows, where `list_size` is the number of elements in the file.

```
address = key % list_size + 1
```

Although this algorithm works with any list size, a list size that is a prime number produces fewer collisions than other list sizes. Therefore, whenever possible, try to make the file size a prime number.

As your little company begins to grow, you realize that soon you will have more than 100 employees. Planning for the future, you create a new employee numbering system that will handle 1 million employees. You also decide that you want to provide data space for up to 300 employees. The first prime number greater than 300 is 307. You therefore choose 307 as your list (file) size. Your new employee list and some of its hashed addresses are shown in Figure 13.9. In this case, Vu Nguyen, with key 121267, is hashed to address 003 because 121267 % 307 = 2, and you add 1 to the result to get the address (003).

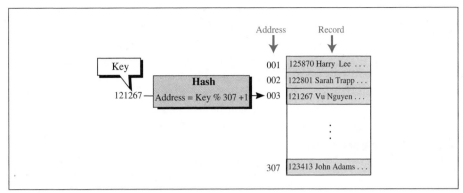

Figure 13.9 Modulo division

Digit Extraction Method

Using **digit extraction hashing,** selected digits are extracted from the key and used as the address. For example, using your six-digit employee number to hash to a three-digit address (000–999), you could select the first, third, and fourth digits (from the left) and use them as the address. Using the keys from Figure 13.9, hash them to the following addresses:

```
125870  ⟶  158
122801  ⟶  128
121267  ⟶  112
   ⋮
123413  ⟶  134
```

Other Methods

There are other popular methods, such as the midsquare method, folding methods, the rotational method, and the pseudorandom method. We leave the exploration of these as exercises.

COLLISION

Generally, the population of keys for a hashed list is greater than the number of records in the data file. For example, if you have a file of 50 students for a class in which the students are identified by the last four digits of their social security number, then there are 200 possible keys for each element in the file (10,000 / 50). Because there are many keys for each address in the file, there is a possibility that more than one key will hash to the same address in the file. We call the set of keys that hash to the same address in our list **synonyms.** The collision concept is seen in Figure 13.10.

In the figure, when you calculate the address for two different records, you obtain the same address (4). Obviously, the two records cannot be stored in the same address. You need to resolve the situation as discussed in the next section.

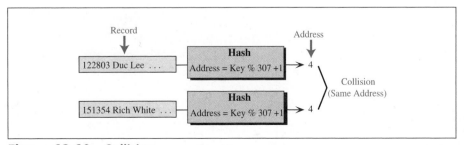

Figure 13.10 Collision

If the actual data that you insert into your list contain two or more synonyms, you will have collisions. A **collision** is the event that occurs when a hashing algorithm produces an address for an insertion key, and that address is already occupied. The address produced by the hashing algorithm is known as the **home address.** The part of the file that contains all of the home addresses is known as the **prime area.** When two keys collide at a home address, you must resolve the collision by placing one of the keys and its data in another location.

Collision Resolution

With the exception of the direct method, none of the methods we discussed for hashing creates one-to-one mapping. This means that when you hash a new key to an address, you may create a collision. There are several methods for handling collisions, each of them independent of the hashing algorithm. That is, any hashing method can be used with any **collision resolution** method. In this section, we discuss some of these methods.

Open Addressing   The first collision resolution method, **open addressing resolution,** resolves collisions in the prime area. When a collision occurs, the prime area addresses are searched for an open or unoccupied record where the new data can be placed. One simple strategy for data that cannot be stored in the home address is to store them in the next address (home address + 1). Figure 13.11 shows how to solve the collision in Figure 13.10 using this method. The first record is stored in address 4, and the second is stored in address 5.

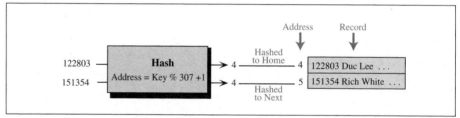

Figure 13.11   Open addressing resolution

Linked List Resolution   A major disadvantage to open addressing is that each collision resolution increases the probability of future collisions. This disadvantage is eliminated in another approach to collision resolution, **linked list resolution.** In this method, the first record is stored in the home address, but it contains a pointer to the second record. Figure 13.12 shows how to resolve the situation in Figure 13.10.

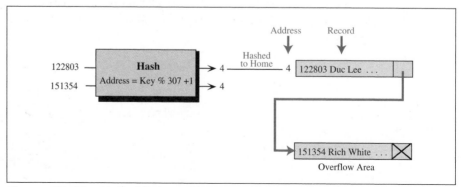

Figure 13.12   Linked list resolution

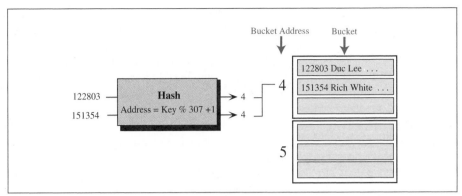

Figure 13.13 Bucket hashing resolution

Bucket Hashing   Another approach to handling the problem of collision is to hash to **buckets.** Figure 13.13 shows how to solve the collision in Figure 13.10 using **bucket hashing.** A bucket is a node that can accommodate more than one record.

Combination Approaches   There are several approaches to resolving collisions. As you saw with the hashing methods, a complex implementation will often use multiple approaches.

13.5   TEXT VERSUS BINARY

Before closing this chapter, we discuss two terms used to categorize files: text files and binary files. A file stored on a storage device is a sequence of bits that can be interpreted by an application program as a text file or a binary file as shown in Figure 13.14 and explained next.

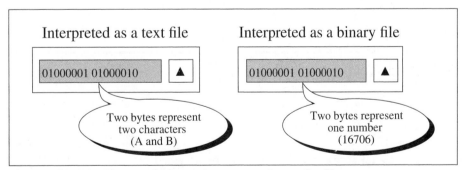

Figure 13.14 Text and binary interpretations of a file

TEXT FILES

A **text file** is a file of characters. It cannot contain integers, floating-point numbers, or any other data structures in their internal memory format. To store these data types, they must be converted to their character equivalent formats.

Some files can only use character data types. Most notable are file streams for keyboards, monitors, and printers. This is why you need special functions to format data that are input from or output to these devices.

Let's look at an example. When data (a file stream) are sent to the printer, the printer takes 8 bits, interprets them as 1 byte, and decodes them into the encoding system of the printer (ASCII or EBCDIC). If the character belongs to the printable category, it will be printed; otherwise, some other activity takes place, such as printing a space. The printer takes the next 8 bits and repeats the process. This is done until the file stream is exhausted.

BINARY FILES

A **binary file** is a collection of data stored in the internal format of the computer. In this definition, data can be an integer, a floating-point number, a character, or any other structured data (except a file).

Unlike text files, binary files contain data that are meaningful only if they are properly interpreted by a program. If the data are textual, 1 byte is used to represent one character. But if the data are numeric, 2 or more bytes are considered a data item. For example, assume you are using a personal computer that uses 2 bytes to store an integer. In this case, when you read or write an integer, 2 bytes are interpreted as one integer.

13.6 KEY TERMS

access method	error report file	old master file
auxiliary storage device	file	open addressing resolution
binary file	hashed file	prime area
bucket	home address	random access
bucket hashing	index	secondary storage device
collision	indexed file	sequential access
collision resolution	inverted file	sequential file
data file	key	storage device
digit extraction hashing	linked list	synonym
direct hashing	linked list resolution	tape
disk	modulo division	text file
division remainder hashing	new master file	transaction file

13.7 SUMMARY

- A file is a collection of related data treated as a unit.

- A record in a file can be accessed sequentially or randomly.

- In sequential access, each record must be accessed sequentially, one after the other, from beginning to end.

- The update of a sequential file requires a new master file, an old master file, a transaction file, and an error report file.

- In random access, a record can be accessed without having to retrieve any records before it. The address of the record must be known.

- For random access of a record, an indexed file, consisting of a data file and an index, can be used.

- In random file access, the index maps a key to an address, which is then used to retrieve the record from the data file.

- A hashed file is a random-access file in which a function maps a key to an address.

- In direct hashing, the key is the address, and no algorithm manipulation is necessary.

- In modulo division hashing, the key is divided by the file size. The address is the remainder plus 1.

- In digit extraction hashing, the address is composed of digits selected from the key.
- Keys that hash to the same address are called synonyms.
- A collision is an event that occurs when a hashing algorithm produces an address for an insertion, and that address is already occupied.
- Collision resolution methods move the hashed data that cannot be inserted to a new address.
- The open addressing collision resolution method searches the prime area for an open address for the data to be inserted.
- The linked list resolution method uses a separate area to store collisions and chains all synonyms together in a linked list.
- Bucket hashing is a collision resolution method that uses buckets, nodes that accommodate multiple data occurrences.
- A text file is a file of characters.
- A binary file is data stored in the internal format of the computer.

13.8 PRACTICE SET

REVIEW QUESTIONS

1. What is a file and what is its function?
2. What are the two general types of file access methods?
3. Why do you need an EOF marker when you process files sequentially?
4. What is the relationship between the new master file and the old master file?
5. What is the purpose of the transaction file in the updating of a sequential file?
6. Give your own example of a situation in which a file should be accessed randomly.
7. Give your own example of a situation in which a file should be accessed sequentially.
8. Describe the function of the address in a randomly accessed file.
9. How is the index related to the data file in indexed files?
10. What is the relationship between the key and the address in direct hashing of a file?
11. What is the relationship between the key and the address in modulo division hashing of a file?
12. What is the relationship between the key and the address in digit extraction hashing of a file?
13. What is a collision?
14. Give three collision resolution methods.
15. How does the open addressing collision resolution method work?
16. Discuss the two storage areas required for the linked list collision resolution method.
17. What is the difference between a text file and a binary file?

MULTIPLE-CHOICE QUESTIONS

18. _____ file can be accessed randomly.
    a. A sequential
    b. An indexed
    c. A hashed
    d. b and c

19. _____ file can be accessed sequentially.
    a. A sequential
    b. An indexed
    c. A hashed
    d. b and c

20. When a sequential file is updated, the _____ file gets the actual update.
    a. new master
    b. old master
    c. transaction
    d. error report

21. When a sequential file is updated, the _____ file contains a list of all errors occurring during the update process.
    a. new master
    b. old master
    c. transaction
    d. error report

22. When a sequential file is updated, the _____ file contains the changes to be applied.
    a. new master
    b. old master
    c. transaction
    d. error report

23. After a sequential file is updated, the _____ file contains the most current data.
    a. new master
    b. old master
    c. transaction
    d. error report

24. When a sequential file needs to be updated, the _____ file in storage becomes the _____ file.
    a. new master; old master
    b. old master; new master
    c. transaction; new master
    d. transaction; old master

25. If the transaction file key is 20 and the first master file key is 25, then you _____.
    a. add the new record to the new master file
    b. revise the contents of the old master file
    c. delete the data
    d. write the old master file record to the new master file

26. If the transaction file key is 20 with a delete code and the master file key is 20, then you _____.
    a. add the transaction to the new master file
    b. revise the contents of the old master file
    c. delete the data
    d. write the old master file record to the new master file

27. If a record needs to be accessed _____, an indexed file is the most efficient file type to use.
    a. sequentially
    b. randomly
    c. in order
    d. none of the above

28. An indexed file consists of _____.
    a. a sequential data file
    b. an index
    c. a random data file
    d. b and c

29. The index of an indexed file has _____ fields.
    a. two
    b. three
    c. four
    d. any number of

30. To access a record randomly, you use a(n) _____ in the index to find an address.
    a. address
    b. key
    c. synonym
    d. a or b

31. In the _____ hashing method, selected digits are extracted from the key and used as the address.
    a. direct
    b. division remainder
    c. modulo division
    d. digit extraction

32. In the _____ hashing method, the key is divided by the file size, and the address is the remainder plus 1.
    a. direct
    b. modulo division
    c. division remainder
    d. digit extraction

33. In the _____ hashing method, there are no synonyms or collisions.
    a. direct
    b. modulo division
    c. division remainder
    d. digit extraction

34. _____ are keys that hash to the same location in the data file.
    a. Collisions
    b. Buckets
    c. Synonyms
    d. Linked lists

35. When a hashing algorithm produces an address for an insertion key and that address is already occupied, it is called a _____.
    a. collision
    b. probe
    c. synonym
    d. linked list

36. The address produced by a hashing algorithm is the _____ address.
    a. probe
    b. synonym
    c. collision
    d. home

37. The _____ area is the file area that contains all the home addresses.
    a. probe
    b. linked
    c. hash
    d. prime

38. In the _____ collision resolution method, you try to put data that cannot be placed in location 123 in location 124.
    a. open addressing
    b. linked list
    c. bucket hashing
    d. a and b

39. In the _____ collision resolution method, a node can hold multiple pieces of data.
    a. open addressing
    b. linked list
    c. bucket hashing
    d. a and b

40. In the _____ collision resolution method, both the prime area and the overflow area store data.
    a. open addressing
    b. linked list
    c. bucket hashing
    d. a and b

41. A _____ file is a file of characters.
    a. text
    b. binary
    c. character
    d. hash

EXERCISES

42. Given the old master file and the transaction file in Figure 13.15, find the new master file. If there is any error, create an error file too.

```
        Old Master File                   Transaction File

   14  John  Wu        17.00      A  17  Martha Kent   17.00
   16  George Brown    18.00      D  20
   17  Duc Lee         11.00      R  31                28.00
   20  Li Nguyen       12.00      D  45
   26  Ted White       23.00      A  89  Orva Gilbert  20.00
   31  Joanne King     27.00
   45  Bruce Wu        12.00
   89  Mark Black      19.00
   92  Betsy Yellow    14.00
```

Figure 13.15   Exercise 42

43. Create an index file for Table 13.1.

Key	Name	Dept.
123453	John Adam	CIS
114237	Ted White	MATH
156734	Jimmy Lions	ENG
093245	Sophie Grands	BUS
077654	Eve Primary	CIS
256743	Eva Lindens	ENG
423458	Bob Bauer	ECO

Table 13.1   Exercise 43

44. A hash file uses a modulo division method with 41 as the divisor. What is the address for each of the following keys?
    a. 14232
    b. 12560
    c. 13450
    d. 15341

45. In the midsquare hashing method, the key is squared and the address is selected from the middle of the result. Use this method to select the address from each of the following keys. Use the digits 3, 4, and 5 (from the left).
    a. 142
    b. 125
    c. 134
    d. 153

46. In the fold shift hashing method, the key is divided into parts. The parts are added to obtain the address. Use this method to find the address from the following keys. Divide the key into two-digit parts and add them to find the address.
    a. 1422
    b. 1257
    c. 1349
    d. 1532

47. In the fold boundary hashing method, the key is divided into parts. The left and right parts are reversed and added to the middle part to obtain the address. Use this method to find the address from the following keys. Divide the key into three two-digit parts, reverse the digits in the first and the third part, and then add the parts to obtain the address.
    a. 142234
    b. 125711
    c. 134919
    d. 153213

48. Find the address of the following keys using the modulo division method and a file of size 411. If there is a collision, use open addressing to resolve it. Draw a figure to show the position of the records.
    a. 10278
    b. 08222
    c. 20553
    d. 17256

49. Redo Exercise 48 using linked list resolution.

14

Databases

We begin by defining a database management system (DBMS) and discussing its components. Next we present the three-level architecture for a DBMS. We focus on the relational database model with examples of its operations. Then we discuss a language (Standard Query Language) that operates on relational databases. Finally, we briefly discuss other database models.

A **database** is a collection of data that is logically, but not necessarily physically, coherent. Normally, there should be some meaning inherent in the data to justify the creation of the database.

14.1   DATABASE MANAGEMENT SYSTEM

A **database management system (DBMS)** defines, creates, and maintains a database. The DBMS also allows users controlled access to data in the database. A DBMS is a combination of five components: hardware, software, data, users, and procedures (Figure 14.1).

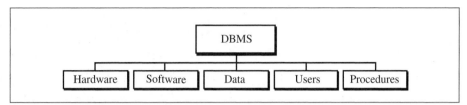

Figure 14.1   DBMS components

Hardware

The **hardware** is the physical computer system that allows physical access to data. For example, the user terminals, the hard disk, the main computer, and workstations are considered part of the hardware in a DBMS.

Software

The **software** is the actual program that allows users to access, maintain, and update physical data. In addition, the software controls which user can access which part of the data in the database.

Data

The data in a database are stored physically on the storage devices. In a database, data are a separate entity from the software that accesses them. This separation allows the organization to change the software without having to change the physical data or the way it is stored. If an organization has decided to use a DBMS, then all the information needed by the organization should be kept under one entity, to be accessible by the software in the DBMS.

Users

The term **users** in a DBMS has a broad meaning. We can divide the users into two categories: end users and application programs.

End Users   The **end users** are those humans who can access the database directly to get information. There are two types of end users: the database administrator (DBA) and the normal user. The database administrator has the maximum level of privileges. She can control the other users and their access to the DBMS. She can grant some of her privileges to somebody else but retains the ability to revoke them at any time. A normal user, on the other hand, can only use part of the database and has limited access.

Application Programs   The other users of data in a database are **application programs.** Applications need to access and process data. For example, a payroll application program needs to access part of the data in a database to create paychecks at the end of the month.

Procedures

The last component of a DBMS is a set of **procedures** or rules that should be clearly defined and followed by the users of the database.

14.2   ARCHITECTURE

The American National Standards Institute **Standards Planning and Requirements Committee** (ANSI/SPARC) has established a three-level architecture for a DBMS: internal, conceptual, and external (Figure 14.2).

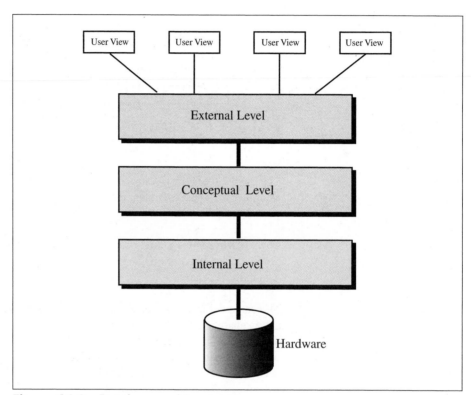

Figure 14.2   Database architecture

INTERNAL LEVEL

The **internal level** determines where data are actually stored on the storage device. This level deals with low-level access methods and how bytes are transferred to and from the storage device. In other words, the internal level interacts directly with the hardware.

CONCEPTUAL LEVEL

The **conceptual,** or community, **level** defines the logical view of the data. In this level, the data model and the schema diagrams are defined. The main functions of the DBMS are in this level. The DBMS changes the internal view of data to the external view of data that the users need to see. The conceptual level is an intermediary and frees the users from dealing with the internal level.

EXTERNAL LEVEL

The **external level** interacts directly with the user (end users or application programs). It changes the data coming from the conceptual level to a format and view that are familiar to the users.

14.3 DATABASE MODELS

A database model defines the logical design of data. The model also describes the relationships between different parts of data. In the history of database design, three models have been in use: the hierarchical model, the network model, and the relational model.

HIERARCHICAL MODEL

In a **hierarchical model,** data are organized as an upside down tree. Each entity has only one parent but can have several children. At the top of the hierarchy, there is one entity, which is called the root. Figure 14.3 shows a logical view of the hierarchical model. As the hierarchical model is obsolete, no further discussion of this model is necessary.

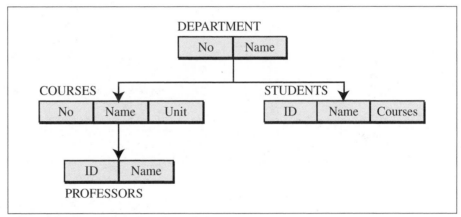

Figure 14.3   Hierarchical model

NETWORK MODEL

In a **network model,** the entities are organized in a graph, where some entities can be accessed through several paths (Figure 14.4). There is no hierarchy. This model is also obsolete and needs no further discussion.

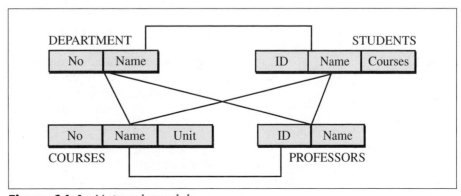

Figure 14.4   Network model

RELATIONAL MODEL

In a **relational model,** data are organized in two-dimensional tables called relations. There is no hierarchical or network structure imposed on the data. The tables or relations are, however, related to each other, as you will see shortly (Figure 14.5).

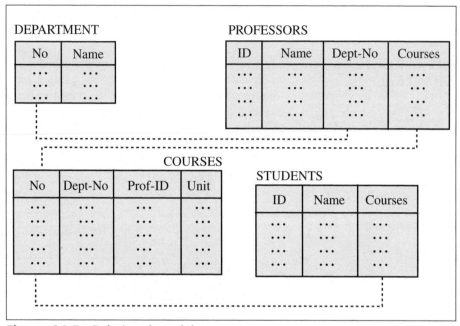

Figure 14.5   Relational model

The relational model is one of the common models in use today, and we devote most of this chapter to it. In the last section, we briefly discuss the other two common models that are derived from the relational model: the distributed model and the object-oriented model.

14.4   RELATIONAL MODEL

We continue the discussion of databases with the most popular model, the **relational database management system (RDBMS).** In this model, the data (universe of discourse) are represented as a set of **relations.**

RELATION

A relation, in appearance, is a two-dimensional table. The RDBMS organizes the data so that the external view is a set of relations or tables. This does not mean that data are stored as tables; the physical storage of the data is independent of the way the data are logically organized. Figure 14.6 shows an example of a relation.

A relation in an RDBMS has the following features:

■ **Name.** Each relation in a relational database should have a name that is unique among other relations.

■ **Attributes.** Each column in a relation is called an attribute. The attributes are the column headings in the table. Each attribute gives meaning to the data stored under it.

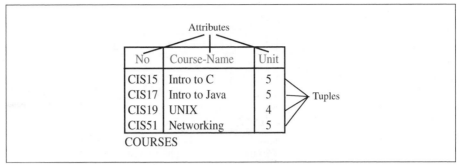

Figure 14.6 Relation

Each column in the table must have a name that is unique in the scope of the relation. The total number of attributes for a relation is called the degree of the relation. For example, in Figure 14.6, the relation has a degree of 3. Note that the attribute names are not stored in the database; the conceptual level uses the attributes to give meaning to each column.

■ **Tuples.** Each row in a relation is called a **tuple.** A tuple defines a collection of attribute values. The total number of rows in a relation is called the **cardinality** of the relation. Note that the cardinality of a relation changes when tuples are added or deleted. This make the database dynamic.

14.5 OPERATIONS ON RELATIONS

In a relational database, we can define several operations to create new relations out of the existing ones. We define nine operations in this section: insert, delete, update, select, project, join, union, intersection, and difference.

INSERT

The insert operation is a unary operation; it is applied to one single relation. The operation inserts a new tuple into the relation. Figure 14.7 shows an example of the insert operation. A new course (CIS52) has been inserted (added) to the relation.

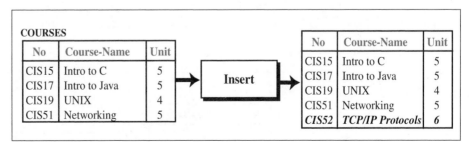

Figure 14.7 Insert operation

DELETE

The delete operation is also a unary operation. The operation deletes a tuple defined by a criterion from the relation. Figure 14.8 shows an example of the delete operation. The course CIS19 has been deleted.

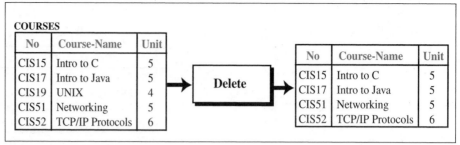

Figure 14.8   Delete operation

UPDATE

The **update operation** is also a unary operation; it is applied to one single relation. The operation changes the value of some attributes of a tuple. Figure 14.9 shows an example of the update operation. The number of units for CIS51 has been updated (changed) from 5 to 6.

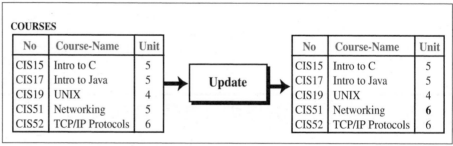

Figure 14.9   Update operation

SELECT

The **select operation** is a unary operation; it is applied to one single relation and creates another relation. The tuples (rows) in the resulting relation are a subset of the tuples in the original relation. The select operation uses some criteria to select some of the tuples from the original relation. The number of attributes (columns) in this operation remains the same. Figure 14.10 shows an example of the select operation. In this figure, there is a relation that shows courses offered by a small department. The select operation allows the user to select only the five-unit courses.

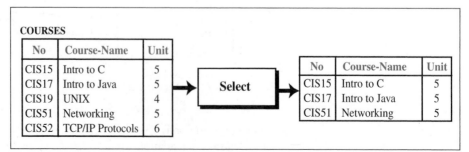

Figure 14.10   Select operation

PROJECT

The **project operation** is also a unary operation; it is applied to one single relation and creates another relation. The attributes (columns) in the resulting relation are a subset of the attributes in the original relation. The project operation creates a relation in which each tuple has fewer attributes. The number of tuples (rows) in this operation remains the same. Figure 14.11 shows an example of the project operation that creates a relation with only two columns.

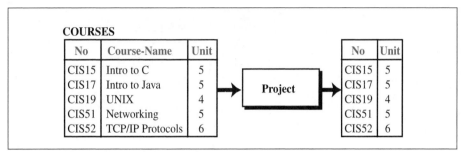

Figure 14.11   Project operation

JOIN

The **join operation** is a binary operation; it takes two relations and combines them based on common attributes. The join operation is very complex and has many variations. In Figure 14.12, we show a very simple example in which the COURSES relation is combined with the TAUGHT-BY relation to create a relation that shows full information about the courses, including the names of the professors that teach them. In this case, the common attribute is the course number (No).

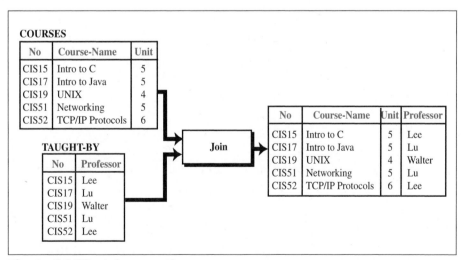

Figure 14.12   Join operation

UNION

The **union operation** is also a binary operation; it takes two relations and creates a new relation. However, there is a restriction on the two relations; they must have the same attributes. The union operation, as defined in set theory, creates a new relation in which each tuple is either in the first relation, in the second, or in both. For example,

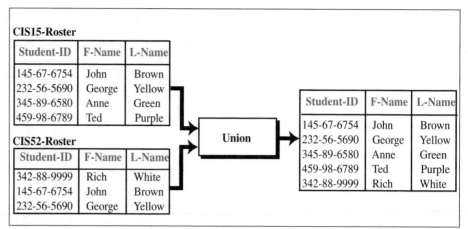

Figure 14.13 Union operation

Figure 14.13 shows two relations. On the upper left is the roster for CIS15; on the lower left is the roster for CIS52. The result is a relation with information about students that take either CIS15, CIS52, or both.

INTERSECTION

The **intersection operation** is also a binary operation; it takes two relations and creates a new relation. Just like the union operation, the two relations must have the same attributes. The intersection operation, as defined in set theory, creates a new relation in which each tuple is a member in both relations. For example, Figure 14.14 shows two input relations. The result of the intersection operation is a relation with information about students taking both CIS15 and CIS52.

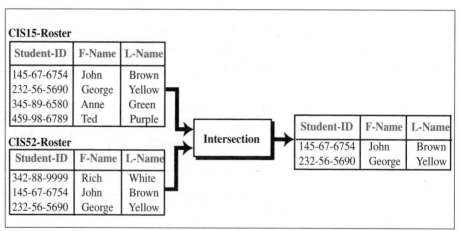

Figure 14.14 Intersection operation

DIFFERENCE

The **difference operation** is also a binary operation. It is applied to two relations with the same attributes. The tuples in the resulting relation are those that are in the first relation but not the second. For example, Figure 14.15 shows two input relations. The result of the difference operation is a relation with information about students taking CIS15 but not CIS52.

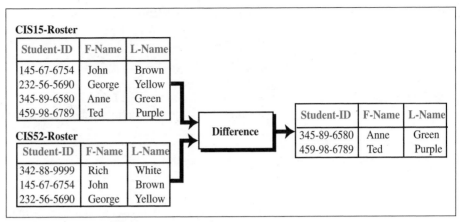

Figure 14.15 Difference operation

14.6 STRUCTURED QUERY LANGUAGE

The **Structured Query Language (SQL)** is the language standardized by the American National Standards Institute (ANSI) and the International Organization for Standardization (ISO) for use on relational databases. It is a declarative (not procedural) language, which means that the users declare what they want without having to write a step-by-step procedure. The SQL language was first implemented by the Oracle Corporation in 1979. New versions of SQL have been released since then.

In this section, we define common statements in the SQL language that are related to operations we defined in the previous section. It is by no means a tutorial for the SQL language. For more information, consult books on SQL.

STATEMENTS

The following statements are related to the operations we defined.

Insert

The insert operation uses the following format. The values clause defines all the attribute values for the corresponding tuple to be inserted.

```
insert into    RELATION-NAME
values    (. . ., . . ., . . .)
```

For example, the insertion operation in Figure 14.7 can be implemented in SQL using:

```
insert into    COURSES
values ("CIS52","TCP/IP Protocols", 6)
```

Note that string values are enclosed in quotation marks; numeric values are not.

Delete

The delete operation uses the following format. The criteria for deletion are defined in the where clause.

```
delete from RELATION-NAME
where criteria
```

For example, the deletion operation in Figure 14.8 can be implemented in SQL using:

```
delete from COURSES
where No ="CIS19"
```

Update

The update operation uses the following format. The attribute to be changed is defined in the set clause. The criteria for updating are defined in the where clause.

```
update    RELATION-NAME
set attribute1 = value1    attribute2 = value2, . . .
where    criteria
```

For example, the update operation in Figure 14.9 can be implemented in SQL using

```
update    COURSES
set    Unit = 6
where No ="CIS51"
```

Select

The select operation uses the following format. The asterisk signifies that all attributes are chosen.

```
select    *
from   RELATION-NAME
where    criteria
```

For example, the select operation in Figure 14.10 can be implemented in SQL using:

```
select *
from COURSES
where Unit = 5
```

Project

The project operation uses the following format. The names of the columns for the new relation are explicitly listed.

```
select    attribute-list
from RELATION-NAME
```

For example, the project operation in Figure 14.11 can be implemented in SQL using:

```
select No, Unit
from COURSES
```

Join

The join operation uses the following format. The attribute list is the combination of attributes from the two input relations; criteria explicitly define the attributes used as common attributes.

```
select    attribute-list
from RELATION1, RELATION2
where criteria
```

For example, the join operation in Figure 14.12 can be implemented in SQL using:

```
select No, Course-Name, Unit, Professor
from COURSES, TAUGHT-BY
where COURSES.No = TAUGHT-BY.No;
```

Union

The union operation uses the following format. Again, asterisks signify that all attributes are selected.

```
select  *
from RELATION1
union
select  *
from RELATION2
```

For example, the union operation in Figure 14.13 can be implemented in SQL using

```
select  *
from CIS15-Roster
union
select  *
from CIS52-Roster;
```

Intersection

The intersection operation uses the following format. Again, asterisks signify that all attributes are selected.

```
select  *
from RELATION1
intersection
select  *
from RELATION2
```

For example, the intersection operation in Figure 14.14 can be implemented in SQL using

```
select  *
from CIS15-Roster
intersection
select  *
from CIS52-Roster;
```

Difference

The difference operation uses the following format. Again, asterisks signify that all attributes are selected.

```
select  *
from RELATION1
minus
select  *
from RELATION2
```

For example, the difference operation in Figure 14.15 can be implemented in SQL using

```
select  *
from CIS15-Roster
minus
select  *
from CIS52-Roster;
```

Combination of Statements

The SQL language allows you to combine the foregoing statements to extract more complex information from a database.

14.7 OTHER DATABASE MODELS

The relational database is not the only common model today. The other two common models are distributed databases and object-oriented databases. We briefly discuss these two models here and leave further exploration to books about databases.

DISTRIBUTED DATABASES

The **distributed database** model is not actually a new model. It is based on the relational model. However, the data are stored on several computers that communicate through the Internet (or some private wide area network). Each computer (or site, as it is called) maintains part of the database or the whole database. In other words, data are either fragmented, with each fragment stored at one site, or data are replicated at each site.

Fragmented Distributed Databases

In a **fragmented distributed database,** data are localized. Locally used data are stored on the corresponding site. However, this does not mean that a site cannot access data stored at another site. Access is mostly local but occasionally global. Although each site has complete control over its local data, there is global control through the Internet. For example, a pharmaceutical company may have multiple sites in many countries. Each site has a database with information about its own employees, but a central personnel department has control of all the databases.

Replicated Distributed Databases

In a **replicated distributed database,** each site holds an exact replica of another site. Any modification in data stored in one site is exactly repeated at every site. The reason for having such a database is security. If the system at one site fails, the users at this site can access data at another site.

OBJECT-ORIENTED DATABASES

The relational database has a specific view of data that is based on the nature of the relational database (tuples and attributes). The smallest unit of data in a relational database is the intersection of a tuple and an attribute. However, today, some applications need to look at data in another form. Some applications like to see data as a structure (see Chapter 11) such as a record made of fields.

An **object-oriented database** tries to keep the advantages of the relational model and at the same time allows applications to access structured data. In an object-oriented database, objects and their relations are defined. In addition, each object can have attributes that can be expressed as fields.

For example, in an organization, one can define object types such as employee, department, and customer. The employee class can define the attributes of an employee object (first name, last name, social security number, salary, etc.) and how they can be accessed. The department object can define the attributes of the department and how they can be accessed. In addition, the database can create a relation between an employee object and a department object (an employee works in a department).

14.8 KEY TERMS

application program
cardinality
conceptual level
database
database management system
    (DBMS)
difference operation
distributed database
end user
external level
fragmented distributed database
hardware

hierarchical model
internal level
intersection operation
join operation
network model
object-oriented database
procedure
project operation
relation
relational database management
    system (RDBMS)
relational model

replicated distributed database
select operation
software
Standards Planning and Requirements
    Committee (SPARC)
Structured Query Language (SQL)
tuple
union operation
update operation
user

14.9 SUMMARY

■ A database is a collection of data that is logically, but not necessarily physically, coherent.

■ A database management system (DBMS) defines, creates, and maintains a database and allows controlled access to users.

■ A DBMS is composed of hardware, software, data, users, and procedures.

■ DBMS users can be humans or application programs.

■ A DBMS has three levels: internal, conceptual, and external.

■ The internal level of a DBMS interacts directly with the hardware and is concerned with low-level access methods and byte transfer to and from the storage device.

■ The conceptual level of a DBMS defines the logical view of the data as well as the data model and schema diagrams.

■ The external level of a DBMS interacts directly with the user.

■ The relational database management system (RDBMS) is the only database model in wide use today. The hierarchical and network models are obsolete.

■ A relation can be thought of as a two-dimensional table.

■ Each column in a relation is called an attribute. The number of attributes in a relation is its degree.

■ Each row in a relation is called a tuple. The number of rows in a relation is its cardinality.

■ Nine operations can be performed on relations.

■ An operation that operates on one relation is a unary operator. Unary operators include the insert, delete, update, select, and project operations.

■ An operation that operates on two relations is a binary operator. Binary operators include the join, union, intersection, and difference operations.

■ The Structured Query Language (SQL) is the language standardized by ANSI and ISO for use on relational databases.

14.10 PRACTICE SET

REVIEW QUESTIONS

1. What are the five necessary components of a DBMS?

2. Discuss the two types of users of a DBMS.

3. How do the three levels of a DBMS relate to each other?

4. What are the three database models? Which are popular today?

5. What is a relation in an RDBMS?

6. In a relation, what is an attribute? What is a tuple?

7. What is the difference between a unary operation and a binary operation?

8. Name the unary operations on relations in an RDBMS.

9. Name the binary operations on relations in an RDBMS.

10. What is the difference between the insert and the delete operations?

11. What is the difference between the update and the select operations?

12. What is the function of the project operation?

13. What does the output relation of the join operation have in common with the input relations?

14. What is the difference between the union operation and the intersection operation?

15. What is the function of the difference operation?

16. What is SQL?

17. In the SQL, how do you know on which relations the operators are operating?

MULTIPLE-CHOICE QUESTIONS

18. A DBMS _____ a database.
    a. defines
    b. creates
    c. maintains
    d. all of the above

19. The DBMS code that allows the user to access, maintain, and update is the _____.
    a. hardware
    b. data
    c. software
    d. user

20. The DBMS components such as the computer and hard disks that allow physical access to data are known as the _____.
    a. hardware
    b. software
    c. users
    d. application programs

21. The _____ of a DBMS can be a database administrator or a person who needs to access the database.
    a. end user
    b. application program
    c. programmer
    d. b and c

22. Both humans and _____ can be considered users of a database.
    a. data
    b. software
    c. application programs
    d. hardware

23. In a three-level DBMS architecture, the layer that interacts directly with the hardware is the _____ level.
    a. external
    b. conceptual
    c. internal
    d. physical

24. In a three-level DBMS architecture, the _____ level determines where data are actually stored on the storage device.
    a. external
    b. conceptual
    c. internal
    d. physical

25. The _____ level of a three-level DBMS architecture defines the logical view of the data.
    a. external
    b. conceptual
    c. internal
    d. physical

26. The data model and the schema of a DBMS are often defined in the _____ level.
    a. external
    b. conceptual
    c. internal
    d. physical

27. In a three-level DBMS architecture, the _____ level interacts directly with the users.
    a. external
    b. conceptual
    c. internal
    d. physical

28. Of the various database models, the _____ model is the most prevalent today.
    a. hierarchical
    b. network
    c. relational
    d. linked list

29. The _____ database model arranges its data in the form of an inverted tree.
    a. hierarchical
    b. network
    c. relational
    d. linked list

30. In the _____ database model, each entity can be accessed through multiple paths.
    a. hierarchical
    b. network
    c. relational
    d. linked list

31. The relation is a set of data organized logically as a(n) _____-dimensional table.
    a. one
    b. two
    c. three
    d. any

32. Each column in a relation is called _____.
    a. an attribute
    b. a tuple
    c. a union
    d. an attitude

33. The degree of a relation is the number of _____ in the relation.
    a. attributes
    b. tuples
    c. unions
    d. attitudes

34. Each row in a relation is called _____.
    a. an attribute
    b. a tuple
    c. a union
    d. an attitude

35. If a relation has five rows, then its _____ is five.
    a. difference
    b. cardinality
    c. duplicity
    d. relativity

36. A unary operator is applied to _____ relation(s) and creates an output of _____ relation(s).
    a. one; one
    b. one; two
    c. two; one
    d. two; two

37. A binary operator is applied to _____ relations(s) and creates an output of _____ relation(s).
    a. one; one
    b. one; two
    c. two; one
    d. two; two

38. The unary _____ operation always results in a relation that has exactly one more row than the original relation.
    a. insert
    b. delete
    c. update
    d. select

39. If you want to change the value of an attribute of a tuple, you use the _____ operation.
    a. project
    b. join
    c. update
    d. select

40. If you have tuples in a relation containing student information and want only the tuples of the female students, you can use the _____ operation.
    a. project
    b. join
    c. update
    d. select

41. The operation that takes two relations and combines them based on common attributes is the _____ operation.
    a. join
    b. project
    c. union
    d. intersection

42. If you need to delete an attribute in a relation, you can use the _____ operation.
    a. join
    b. project
    c. union
    d. intersection

43. You want to create a relation called New that contains tuples that belong to both relation A and relation B. For this, you can use the _____ operation.
    a. select
    b. union
    c. project
    d. intersection

44. Which of the following is a unary operator?
    a. intersection
    b. union
    c. join
    d. project

45. Which of the following is a binary operator?
    a. select
    b. update
    c. difference
    d. all of the above

46. _____ is a declarative language used on relational databases.
    a. PDQ
    b. SQL
    c. LES
    d. PBJ

EXERCISES

47. You have relations A, B, and C as shown in Figure 14.16. Show the resulting relation if you apply the following SQL statements:

        select *

        from A

        where A2 = 16

48. You have relations A, B, and C as shown in Figure 14.16. Show the resulting relation if you apply the following SQL statements:

        select A1 A2

        from A

        where A2 = 16

49. You have relations A, B, and C as shown in Figure 14.16. Show the resulting relation if you apply the following SQL statements:

        select A3

        from A

50. You have relations A, B, and C as shown in Figure 14.16. Show the resulting relation if you apply the following SQL statements:

        select B1

        from B

        where B2 = 216

51. You have relations A, B, and C as shown in Figure 14.16. Show the resulting relation if you apply the following SQL statements:

        update C

        set C1 = 37

        where C1 = 31

52. Using the design in Figure 14.5, show the SQL statement that creates a new relation containing only the course number and the number of units for each course.

53. Using the design in Figure 14.5, show the SQL statement that creates a new relation containing only the student ID and student name.

54. Using the design in Figure 14.5, show the SQL statement that creates a new relation containing only the professor name.

55. Using the design in Figure 14.5, show the SQL statement that creates a new relation containing only the department name.

56. Using the design in Figure 14.5, show the SQL statement that creates a new relation containing the courses taken by the student with ID 2010.

57. Using the design in Figure 14.5, show the SQL statement that creates a new relation containing the courses taught by Professor Blake.

58. Using the design in Figure 14.5, show the SQL statement that creates a new relation containing only the courses that are three units.

59. Using the design in Figure 14.5, show the SQL statement that creates a new relation containing only the name of students taking course CIS015.

60. Using the design in Figure 14.5, show the SQL statement that creates a new relation containing the department number of the Computer Science Department.

A		
A1	A2	A3
1	12	100
2	16	102
3	16	103
4	19	104

B	
B1	B2
22	214
24	216
27	284
29	216

C		
C1	C2	C3
31	401	1006
32	401	1025
33	405	1065

Figure 14.16   Exercise 47–53

61. Relational databases are based between entities in an organization. Find the entities in the design of Figure 14.5. For example, student and course are two of the entities in this design.

62. Relations between entities are said to be 1:1 (one to one), 1:M (one to many), and M:N (many to many). Using the design of Figure 14.5, find the relation type (1:1, 1:M, or M:N) between student and course.

63. Repeat Exercise 62 to find the relation type (1:1, 1:M, or M:N) between student and professor.

64. Repeat Exercise 62 to find the relation type (1:1, 1:M, or M:N) between department and professor.

65. Repeat Exercise 62 to find a one-to-one relationship between two entities.

66. Design a relational database for a library.

67. Design a relational database for a real estate company.

Advanced Topics

V

Data Compression 15

In recent days, technology has changed the way we transmit and store data. For example, fiber-optic cable allows us to transmit data much faster. And the DVD allows us to store huge amounts of data on a physically small medium. However, as in other aspects of life, the rate of demand from the public is ever increasing. Today, we want to download more and more data in a shorter and shorter amount of time. We also want to store more and more data in a smaller space.

Compressing data can reduce the amount of data sent or stored by partially eliminating inherent redundancy. Redundancy is created when we produce data. Through data compression, we make transmission and storage more efficient, and at the same time, we preserve the integrity of the data (to some extent).

Data compression means sending or storing a smaller number of bits. Although many methods are used for this purpose, in general these methods can be divided into two broad categories: lossless and lossy methods. Figure 15.1 shows the two categories and common methods used in each category.

We first discuss the simpler and easier to understand lossless compression methods. We then present the more complicated lossy compression methods.

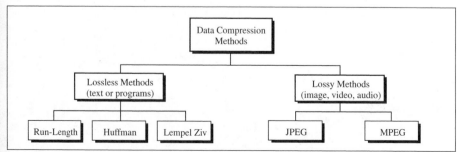

Figure 15.1　Data compression methods

15.1 LOSSLESS COMPRESSION

In **lossless data compression,** the integrity of the data is preserved. The original data and the data after **compression and decompression** are exactly the same because, in these methods, the compression and decompression algorithms are exactly the inverse of each other. No part of the data is lost in the process. Redundant data are removed in compression and are added during decompression.

These methods are normally used when you cannot afford to lose a single bit of data. For example, you do not want to lose data when you compress a text file or a program.

We discuss three lossless compression methods in this section: run-length encoding, Huffman coding, and the Lempel Ziv algorithm.

RUN-LENGTH ENCODING

Probably the simplest method of compression is **run-length encoding.** It can be used to compress data made of any combination of symbols. It does not need knowledge of the frequency of occurrence of symbols (as needed by the next method) and can be very efficient if data are represented as 0s and 1s.

The general idea behind this method is to replace consecutive repeating occurrences of a symbol by one occurrence of the symbol and the number of occurrences. For example, AAAAAAAA can be replaced by A08. Figure 15.2 shows an example of this simple compression method. Note that we use a fixed number of digits (two) to represent the count.

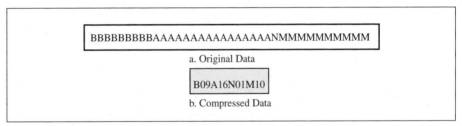

Figure 15.2 Run-length encoding example

The method can be even more efficient if the data use only two symbols (e.g., 0 and 1) in its bit pattern and one symbol is more frequent than the other. For example, let's say you have an image represented by mostly 0s and some 1s. In this case, you can reduce the number of bits by sending (or storing) the number of 0s occurring between two 1s (Figure 15.3).

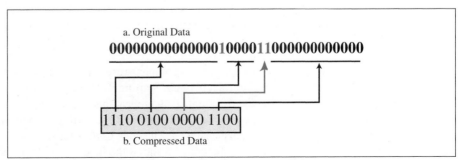

Figure 15.3 Run-length encoding for two symbols

We have represented the counts as a 4-bit binary number (unsigned integer). In an actual situation, you would find an optimal number of bits to avoid introducing extra redundancy. In Figure 15.3, there are fourteen 0s before the first 1. These fourteen 0s are compressed to the binary pattern 1110 (14 in binary). The next set of 0s is compressed to 0100 because there are four 0s. Next you have two 1s in the original data, which are represented by 0000 in the compressed data. Finally, the last twelve 0s in the data are compressed to 1100.

Note that, given a 4-bit binary compression, if there are more than fifteen 0s, they are broken into two or more groups. For example, a sequence of twenty-five 0s is encoded as 1111 1010. Now the question is how the receiver knows that this is twenty-five 0s and not fifteen 0s, then a 1, and then ten 0s. The answer is that if the first count is 1111, the receiver knows the next 4-bit pattern is a continuation of 0s. Now another question is raised: What if there are exactly fifteen 0s between two 1s? In this case, the pattern is 1111 followed by 0000.

HUFFMAN CODING

In **Huffman coding,** you assign shorter codes to symbols that occur more frequently and longer codes to those that occur less frequently. For example, imagine you have a text file that uses only five characters (A, B, C, D, E). We chose only five characters to make the discussion simpler, but the procedure is equally valid for a smaller or greater number of characters.

Before you can assign bit patterns to each character, you assign each character a weight based on its frequency of use. In this example, assume that the frequency of the characters is as shown in Table 15.1. Character A occurs 17 percent of the time, character B occurs 12 percent of the time, and so on.

Character	A	B	C	D	E
Frequency	17	12	12	27	32

Table 15.1 Frequency of characters

Once you have established the weight of each character, build a tree based on those values. The process for building this tree is shown in Figure 15.4. It follows three basic steps:

1. Put the entire character set in a row. Each character is now a **node** at the lowest level of a tree.

2. Find the two nodes with the smallest weights and join them to form a third node, resulting in a simple two-level tree. The weight of the new node is the combined weights of the original two nodes. This node, one level up from the leaves, is eligible to be combined with other nodes. Remember, the sum of the weights of the two nodes chosen must be smaller than the combination of any other possible choices.

3. Repeat step 2 until all of the nodes, on every level, are combined into a single tree.

Once the tree is complete, use it to assign codes to each character. First, assign a bit value to each **branch.** Starting from the root (top node), assign 0 to the left branch and 1 to the right branch and repeat this pattern at each node.

A character's code is found by starting at the root and following the branches that lead to that character. The code itself is the bit value of each branch on the path taken in sequence. Figure 15.5 shows the final tree with bits added to each branch. Note that we moved the leaf nodes to make the tree look like a **binary tree.**

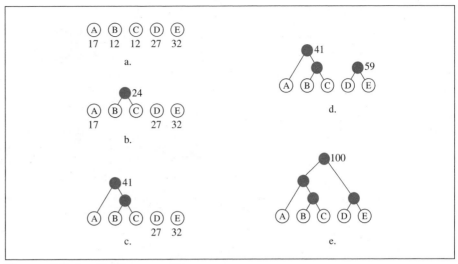

Figure 15.4   Huffman coding

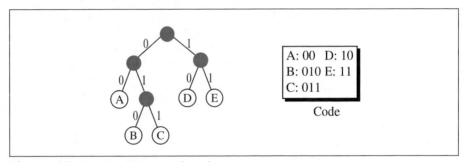

Figure 15.5   Final tree and code

Note these points about the codes. First, the characters with higher frequencies receive a shorter code (A, D, and E) than the characters with lower frequencies (B and C). Compare this with a code that assigns equal bit lengths to each character. Second, in this coding system, no code is a prefix of another code. The 2-bit codes, 00, 10, and 11, are not the prefix of any of the two other codes (010 and 011). In other words, you do not have a 3-bit code beginning with 00, 10, or 11. This property makes the Huffman code an instantaneous code. We will explain this property when we discuss encoding and **decoding** in Huffman coding.

Encoding

Let us see how to encode text using the code for our five characters. Figure 15.6 shows the original and the encoded text. Two points about this figure are worth mentioning. First, notice that there is a sense of compression even in this small and unrealistic code. If you want to send the text without using Huffman coding, you need to assign a 3-bit code to each character. You would have sent 30 bits, whereas with Huffman coding, you send only 22 bits.

Second, notice that we have not used any delimiters between the bits that encode each character. We write the codes one after another. The beauty of Huffman coding is that no code is the prefix of another code. There is no ambiguity in encoding; in addition, the receiver can decode the received data without ambiguity.

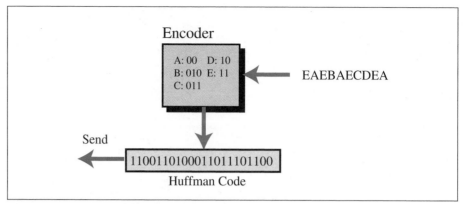

Figure 15.6   Huffman encoding

Decoding

The receiver has a very easy job in decoding the data that it receives. Figure 15.7 shows how decoding take place. When the receiver receives the first 2 bits, it does not have to wait for the next bit to make the decision. It knows that these 2 are decoded as E. The reason, as we mentioned earlier, is that these 2 bits are not the prefix of any 3-bit code (there is no 3-bit code that starts with 11). Likewise, when the receiver receives the next 2 bits (00), it also knows that the character must be A. The next 2 bits are interpreted the same way (11 must be E). However, when it receives bits 7 and 8, it knows that it must wait for the next bit because this code (01) is not in the list of codes. After receiving the next bit (0), it interprets the 3 bits together (010) as B. This is why Huffman code is called instantaneous code; the decoder can unambiguously decode the bits instantaneously (with the minimum number of bits).

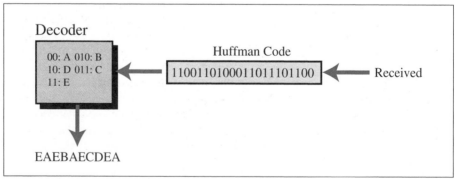

Figure 15.7   Huffman decoding

LEMPEL ZIV ENCODING

Lempel Ziv (LZ) encoding is an example of a category of algorithms called **dictionary-based encoding.** The idea is to create a dictionary (a table) of strings used during the communication session. If both the sender and the receiver have a copy of the dictionary, then already-encountered strings can be substituted by their index in the dictionary to reduce the amount of information transmitted.

Although the idea appears simple, several difficulties surface in the implementation. First, how can a dictionary be created for each session (it cannot be universal due to its length)? Second, how can the receiver acquire the dictionary made by the sender (if you send the dictionary, you are sending extra data, which defeats the whole purpose of compression)?

A practical algorithm that uses the idea of adaptive dictionary-based encoding is the Lempel Ziv (LZ) algorithm. The algorithm has gone through several versions (LZ77, LZ78, etc.). We introduce the basic idea of this algorithm with an example but do not delve into the details of different versions and implementations. In our example, assume that the following string is to be sent. We have chosen this specific string to simplify the discussion.

BAABABBBAABBBBAA

Using our simple version of the LZ algorithm, the process is divided into two phases: compressing the string and decompressing the string.

Compression

In this phase, there are two concurrent events: building an indexed dictionary and compressing a string of symbols. The algorithm extracts the smallest **substring** that cannot be found in the dictionary from the remaining noncompressed string. It then stores a copy of this substring in the dictionary (as a new entry) and assigns an index value. Compression occurs when the substring, except for the last character, is replaced with the index found in the dictionary. The process then inserts the index and the last character of the substring into the compressed string. For example, if the substring is ABBB, you search for ABB in the dictionary. You find that the index for ABB is 4; the compressed substring is therefore 4B. Figure 15.8 shows the process for our sample string.

Let us go through a few steps in this figure:

STEP 1   The process extracts the smallest substring from the original string that is not in the dictionary. Because the dictionary is empty, the smallest character is one character (the first character, B). The process stores a copy of it as the first entry in the dictionary. Its index is 1. No part of this substring can be replaced with an index from the dictionary (it is only one character). The process inserts B in the compressed string. So far, the compressed string has only one character: B. The remaining uncompressed string is the original string without the first character.

STEP 2   The process extracts the next smallest substring that is not in the dictionary from the remaining string. This substring is the character A, which is not in the dictionary. The process stores a copy of it as the second entry in the dictionary. No part of this substring can be replaced with an index from the dictionary (it is only one character). The process inserts A in the compressed string. So far, the compressed string has two characters: B and A (we have placed commas between the substrings in the compressed string to show the separation).

STEP 3   The process extracts the next smallest substring that is not in the dictionary from the remaining string. This situation differs from the two previous steps. The next character (A) is in the dictionary, so the process extracts two characters (AB), which are not in the dictionary. The process stores a copy of AB as the third entry in the dictionary. The process now finds the index of an entry in the dictionary that is the substring without the last character (AB without the last character is A). The index for A is 2, so the process replaces A with 2 and inserts 2B in the compressed string.

STEP 4   Next the process extracts the substring ABB (because A and AB are already in the dictionary). A copy of ABB is stored in the dictionary with an index of 4. The process finds the index of the substring without the last character (AB), which is 3. The combination 3B is inserted into the compressed string. You may have noticed that

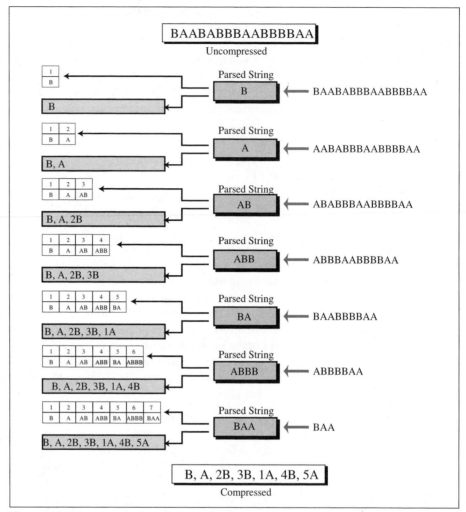

Figure 15.8   Example of Lempel Ziv encoding

in the three previous steps, we have not actually achieved any compression because we have replaced one character by one (A by A in the first step and B by B in the second step) and two characters by two (AB by 2B in the third step). But in this step, we have actually reduced the number of characters (ABB becomes 3B). If the original string has many repetitions (which is true in most cases), we can greatly reduce the number of characters.

The remaining steps are similar to one of the preceding four steps, and we let the reader follow through. Note that the dictionary was only used by the sender to find the indexes. It is not sent to the receiver, and the receiver must create the dictionary for itself as we will see in the next section.

Decompression

Decompression is the inverse of the compression process. The process extracts the substrings from the compressed string and tries to replace the indexes with the corresponding entry in the dictionary, which is empty at first and built up gradually. The whole idea is that when an index is received, there is already an entry in the dictionary corresponding to that index. Figure 15.9 shows the decompression process.

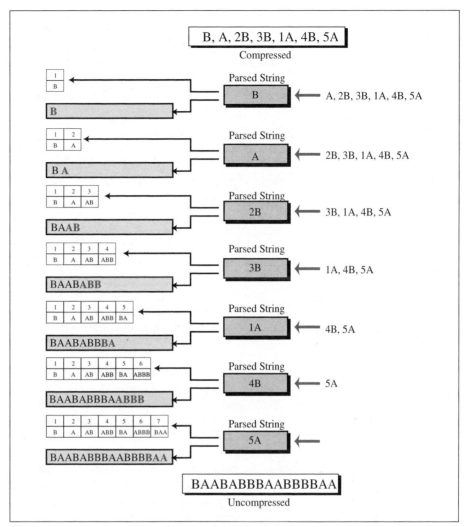

Figure 15.9   Example of Lempel Ziv decoding

Let us go through a few steps in the figure:

STEP 1   The first substring of the compressed string is examined. It is B without an index. Because the substring is not in the dictionary, it is added to the dictionary. The substring (B) is inserted into the decompressed string.

STEP 2   The second substring (A) is examined; the situation is similar to step 1. Now the decompressed string has two characters (BA), and the dictionary has two entries.

STEP 3   The third substring (2B) is examined. The process searches the dictionary and replaces the index 2 with the substring A. The new substring (AB) is added to the decompressed string, and AB is added to the dictionary.

STEP 4   The fourth substring (3B) is examined. The process searches the dictionary and replaces the index 3 with the substring AB. The substring ABB is now added to the decompressed string, and ABB is added to the dictionary.

We leave the exploration of the last three steps as an exercise. As you have noticed, we used a number such as 1 or 2 for the index. In reality, the index is a binary pattern (possibly variable in length) for better efficiency. Also note that LZ encoding leaves the last character uncompressed (which means less efficiency). A version of LZ encoding, called Lempel Ziv Welch (LZW) encoding, compresses even this single character. However, we leave the discussion of this algorithm to more specialized textbooks.

15.2 LOSSY COMPRESSION METHODS

Loss of information is not acceptable in a text file or a program file. It is, however, acceptable in a picture or video. The reason is that our eyes and ears cannot distinguish subtle changes. For these cases, you can use a **lossy data compression** method. These methods are cheaper and take less time and space when it comes to sending millions of bits per second for images and video.

Several methods have been developed using lossy compression techniques. **Joint photographic experts group (JPEG)** is used to compress pictures and graphics. **Motion picture experts group (MPEG)** is used to compress video.

IMAGE COMPRESSION: JPEG

As discussed in Chapter 2, an image can be represented by a two-dimensional array (table) of picture elements (pixels); for example, $640 \times 480 = 307,200$ pixels. If the picture is gray scale, each pixel can be represented by an 8-bit integer (256 levels). If the picture is color, each pixel can be represented by 24 bits (3×8 bits), with each 8 bits representing one of the colors in the RBG (or YIQ) color system. To simplify the discussion, we concentrate on a gray scale picture with 640×480 pixels.

You can see why you need compression. A gray scale picture of 307,200 pixels is represented by 2,457,600 bits, and a color picture is represented by 7,372,800 bits. In JPEG, a gray scale picture is divided into blocks of 8×8 pixel blocks (Figure 15.10).

The purpose of dividing the picture into blocks is to decrease the number of calculations because, as you will see shortly, the number of mathematical operations for each

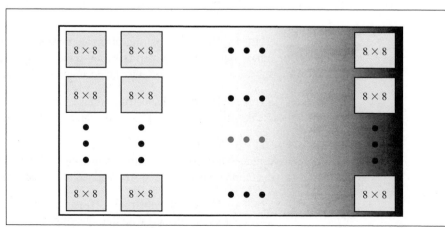

Figure 15.10 JPEG gray scale example, 640×480 pixels

picture is the square of the number of units. That is, for the entire image, you need $307,200^2$ operations (94,371,840,000 operations). If you use JPEG, you need 64^2 operations for each block; that's a total of $64^2 \times 80 \times 60$, or 19,660,800 operations. This decreases by 4800 times the number of operations.

The whole idea of JPEG is to change the picture into a linear (vector) set of numbers that reveals the redundancies. The redundancies (lack of changes) can then be removed using one of the lossless compression methods you studied previously. A simplified version of the process is shown in Figure 15.11.

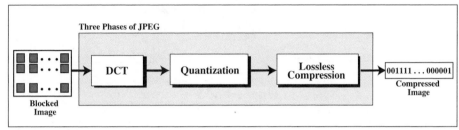

Figure 15.11 JPEG process

Discrete Cosine Transform (DCT)

In this step, each block of 64 pixels goes through a transformation called the **discrete cosine transform (DCT).** The transformation changes the 64 values so that the relative relationships between pixels are kept but the redundancies are revealed. The formula is given in Appendix F. $P(x, y)$ defines one value in the block; $T(x,y)$ defines the value in the transformed block. Appendix F shows the mathematical formula for a transformation.

To understand the nature of this transformation, let us show the result of the transformations for three cases.

Case 1 In this case, you have a block of uniform gray scale, and the value of each pixel is 20. When you do the transformations, you get a nonzero value for the first element (upper left corner). The rest of the pixels have a value of 0 because, according to the formula, the value of $T(0,0)$ is the average of the other values. This is called the **DC value** (direct current, borrowed from electrical engineering). The rest of the values, called **AC values,** in $T(x,y)$ represent changes in the pixel values. But because there are no changes, the rest of the values are 0s (Figure 15.12).

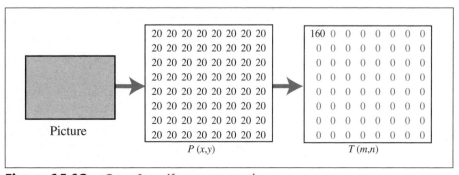

Figure 15.12 Case 1: uniform gray scale

Case 2   In the second case, you have a block with two different uniform gray scale sections. There is a sharp change in the values of the pixels (from 20 to 50). When you do the transformations, you get a DC value as well as nonzero AC values. However, there are only a few nonzero values clustered around the DC value. Most of the values are 0 (Figure 15.13).

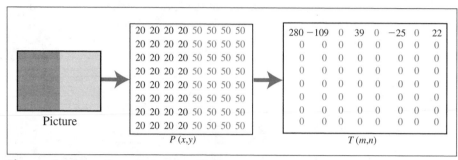

Figure 15.13   Case 2: two sections

Case 3   In the third case, you have a block that changes gradually. That is, there is no sharp change between the values of neighboring pixels. When you do the transformations, you get a DC value, with many nonzero AC values also (Figure 15.14).

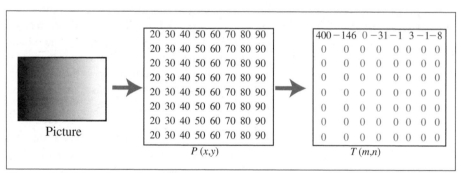

Figure 15.14   Case 3: gradient gray scale

From Figures 15.12, 15.13, and 15.14, we can state the following:

■ The transformation creates table T from table P.

■ The DC value gives the average value of the pixels.

■ The AC values gives the changes.

■ Lack of changes in neighboring pixels creates 0s.

Before we close the discussion of the DCT, note that the DCT transformation is reversible. Appendix F also shows the mathematical formula for a reverse transformation.

Quantization

After the T table is created, the values are quantized to reduce the number of bits needed for encoding. Previously in **quantization,** we dropped the fraction from each value and kept the integer part. Today, we divide the number by a constant and then drop the fraction. This reduces the required number of bits even more. In most implementations, a quantizing table (8 by 8) defines how to quantize each value. The divisor depends on the position of the value in the T table. This is done to optimize the number of bits and the number of 0s for each particular application.

Note that the only phase in the process that is not reversible is the quantizing phase. You lose some information here that is not recoverable. As a matter of fact, the only reason that JPEG is called lossy compression is because of the quantization phase.

Compression

After quantization, the values are read from the table, and redundant 0s are removed. However, to cluster the 0s together, the process reads the table diagonally in a zigzag fashion rather than row by row or column by column. The reason is that if the picture does not have fine changes, the bottom right corner of the T table is all 0s. Figure 15.15 shows the process. JPEG usually uses run-length encoding at the compression phase to compress the bit pattern resulting from the zigzag linearization.

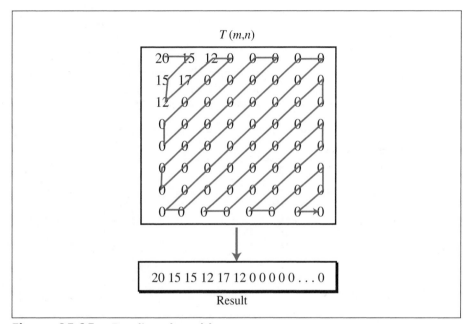

Figure 15.15 Reading the table

VIDEO COMPRESSION: MPEG

The Moving Picture Experts Group (MPEG) method is used to compress video. In principle, a motion picture is a rapid flow of a set of frames, where each frame is a picture. In other words, a frame is a spatial combination of pixels, and a video is a temporal combination of frames that are sent one after another. Compressing video, then, means spatially compressing each frame and temporally compressing a set of frames.

Spatial Compression   The **spatial compression** of each frame is done with JPEG (or a modification of it). Each frame is a picture that can be independently compressed.

Temporal Compression   In **temporal compression,** redundant frames are removed. When we watch television, we receive 30 frames per second. However, most of the consecutive frames are almost the same. For example, when someone is talking, most of the frame is the same as the previous one except for the segment of the frame around the lips, which changes from one frame to another.

A rough calculation points to the need for temporal compression for video. A 20:1 JPEG compression of one frame sends 368,640 bits per frame; at 30 frames per second, this is 11,059,200 bits per second. We need to reduce this number.

To temporally compress data, the MPEG method first divides frames into three categories: I-frames, P-frames, and B-frames.

- **I-frames.** An **intracoded frame (I-frame)** is an independent frame that is not related to any other frame (not to the frame sent before or to the frame sent after). They are present at regular intervals (e.g., every ninth frame is an I-frame). An I-frame must appear periodically due to some sudden change in the frame that the previous and following frames cannot show. Also, when a video is broadcast, a viewer may tune in his or her receiver at any time. If there is only one I-frame at the beginning of the broadcast, the viewer who tunes in late will not receive a complete picture. I-frames are independent of other frames and cannot be constructed from other frames.

- **P-frames.** A **predicted frame (P-frame)** is related to the preceding I-frame or P-frame. In other words, each P-frame contains only the changes from the preceding frame. The changes, however, cannot cover a big segment. For example, for a fast-moving object, the new changes may not be recorded in a P-frame. P-frames can be constructed only from previous I- or P-frames. P-frames carry much less information than other frame types and carry even fewer bits after compression.

- **B-frames.** A **bidirectional frame (B-frame)** is relative to the preceding and following I-frame or P-frame. In other words, each B-frame is relative to the past and the future. Note that a B-frame is never related to another B-frame.

Figure 15.16 shows a sample sequence of frames.

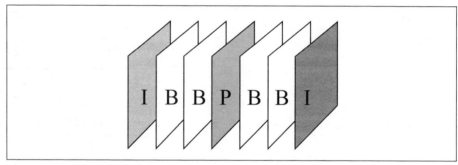

Figure 15.16   MPEG frames

Figure 15.17 shows how the I-, P-, and B-frames are constructed from a series of seven frames.

MPEG has gone through many versions. MPEG 1 was designed for a CD-ROM with a data rate of 1.5 Mbps. MPEG 2 was designed for high-quality DVD with a data rate of 3–6 Mbps. MPEG 3 (or MP3) is a standard for audio compression.

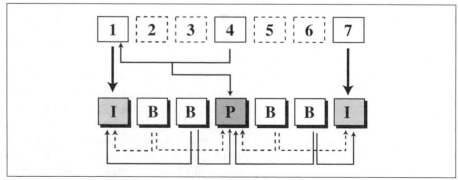

Figure 15.17   MPEG frame construction

15.3 KEY TERMS

AC value
bidirectional frame (B-frame)
binary tree
branch
compression
data compression
DC value
decoding
decompression

dictionary-based encoding
discrete cosine transform (DCT)
Huffman coding
intracoded frame (I-frame)
Joint Photographic Experts Group
 (JPEG)
Lempel Ziv (LZ) encoding
lossless data compression
lossy data compression

Moving Picture Experts Group
 (MPEG)
node
predicted frame (P-frame)
quantization
run-length encoding
spatial compression
substring
temporal compression

15.4 SUMMARY

- Data compression methods are either lossless (all information is recoverable) or lossy (some information is lost).

- Data compression takes the original message and reduces the number of bits that are to be transmitted.

- In lossless compression methods, the received data are the exact replica of the sent data.

- Three lossless compression methods are run-length encoding, Huffman coding, and Lempel Ziv (LZ) encoding.

- In run-length encoding, repeated occurrences of a symbol are replaced by a symbol and the number of occurrences of the symbol.

- In Huffman coding, the code length is a function of symbol frequency; more frequent symbols have shorter codes than less frequent symbols.

- In LZ encoding, repeated strings or words are stored in variables. An index to the variable replaces the string or word.

- LZ encoding requires a dictionary and an algorithm at both sender and receiver.

- In lossy compression methods, the received data need not be an exact replica of the sent data.

- Joint Photographic Experts Group (JPEG) is a method to compress pictures and graphics.

- The JPEG process involves blocking, the discrete cosine transform, quantization, and lossless compression.

- Motion Pictures Experts Group (MPEG) is a method to compress video.

- MPEG involves both spatial compression and temporal compression. The former is similar to JPEG, and the latter removes redundant frames.

15.5 PRACTICE SET

REVIEW QUESTIONS

1. What are the two categories of data compression methods?

2. What is the difference between lossless compression and lossy compression?

3. What is run-length encoding?

4. How does Lempel Ziv encoding reduce the amount of bits transmitted?

5. What is Huffman coding?

6. What is the role of the dictionary in LZ encoding?

7. What is the advantage of LZ encoding over Huffman coding?

8. What are two lossy compression methods?

9. When would you use JPEG? When would you use MPEG?

10. How is MPEG related to JPEG?

11. In JPEG, what is the function of blocking?

12. Why is the DCT needed in JPEG?

13. How does quantization contribute to compression?

14. What is a frame in MPEG compression?

15. What is spatial compression compared to temporal compression?

16. Discuss the three types of frames used in MPEG.

MULTIPLE-CHOICE QUESTIONS

17. Data are compressed using a dictionary with indexes to strings. This is _____.
    a. differential encoding
    b. Lempel Ziv encoding
    c. Morse coding
    d. lossy coding

18. A string of one hundred 0s is replaced by two markers, a 0, and the number 100. This is _____.
    a. run-length encoding
    b. Morse coding
    c. differential encoding
    d. Lempel Ziv encoding

19. An example of lossy compression is _____.
    a. differential encoding
    b. Lempel Ziv encoding
    c. run-length encoding
    d. JPEG

20. In a _____ data compression method, the received data are an exact copy of the original message.
    a. lossless
    b. lossy
    c. lessloss
    d. glossy

21. In a _____ data compression method, the received data need not be an exact copy of the original message.
    a. lossless
    b. lossy
    c. lessloss
    d. glossy

22. _____ encoding is a lossless data compression method.
    a. Huffman
    b. Run-length
    c. LZ
    d. all of the above

23. In _____ encoding, the more frequently occurring characters have shorter codes than the less frequently occurring characters.
    a. Huffman
    b. run-length
    c. LZ
    d. all of the above

24. In _____ encoding, PPPPPPPPPPPPPPP can be replaced by P15.
    a. Huffman
    b. run-length
    c. LZ
    d. all of the above

25. In _____ encoding, a string is replaced by a pointer to the stored string.
    a. Huffman
    b. run-length
    c. LZ
    d. all of the above

26. LZ encoding requires _____.
    a. a dictionary
    b. a buffer
    c. an algorithm
    d. all of the above

27. JPEG encoding involves _____, a process that reveals the redundancies in a block.
    a. blocking
    b. the DCT
    c. quantization
    d. vectorization

28. In JPEG encoding, the _____ process breaks the original picture into smaller blocks and assigns a value to each pixel in a block.
    a. blocking
    b. DCT
    c. quantization
    d. vectorization

29. The last step in JPEG, _____, removes redundancies.
    a. blocking
    b. quantization
    c. compression
    d. vectorization

30. _____ is a lossy compression method for pictures and graphics; whereas _____ is a lossy compression method for video.
    a. DCT; MPEG
    b. MPEG; JPEG
    c. JPEG; MPEG
    d. JPEG; DCT

EXERCISES

31. Encode the following bit pattern using run-length encoding with 5-bit codes:

eighteen zeros, 11, fifty-six zeros, 1, fifteen zeros, 11

32. Encode the following bit pattern using run-length encoding with 5-bit codes:

1, eight zeros, 1, forty-five zeros, 11

33. Encode the following characters using Huffman coding with the given frequencies:

A (12), B (8), C (9), D (20), E (31), F (14), G (8)

34. Encode the following characters using Huffman coding. Each character has the same frequency (1):

A, B, C, D, E, F, G, H, I, J

35. Can the following be a Huffman coding? Explain.

A: 0   B: 10   C:11

36. Can the following be a Huffman code? Explain.

A: 0   B:1   C: 00   D: 01   E: 10   F: 11

37. Encode the message BAABBBBAACAA using the following Huffman code:

A: 0   B: 10   C: 11

38. Decode the message 0101000011110 using the following Huffman code:

A: 0   B: 10   C: 11

39. Use a transformation to transform a 4 by 4 table. The rules are as follows:

$$T(0,0) = (1/16) [P(0,0) + P(0,1) + P(0,2) + \ldots]$$

$$T(0,1) = (1/16) [0.95P(0,0) + 0.9P(0,1) + 0.85P(0,2) + \ldots]$$

$$T(0,2) = (1/16) [0.90P(0,0) + 0.85P(0,1) + 0.80P(0,2) + \ldots]$$

. . .

Compare and contrast this method with the DCT. Is the DCT actually a weighted average calculation like the preceding transformation? If so, what is the weight?

16 Security

Security plays a very important role in computer science today. With the growth of the Internet, more and more data are being exchanged, and those data need to be secure. For example, when you shop on the Internet, you expect that information you send to the vendor is kept secret and used only by the vendor. Also, when you receive a message, you sometimes need to authenticate the sender. In this chapter, we touch on the subject of **security.** The subject is so vast that entire books are devoted to it. The concepts and ideas presented here are motivators for further study.

We can say that there are four aspects of security: privacy (confidentiality), message authentication, message integrity, and nonrepudiation (Figure 16.1).

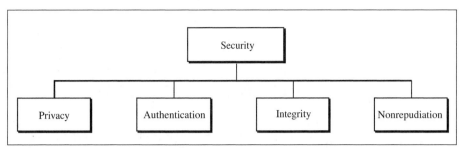

Figure 16.1 Aspects of security

PRIVACY

In a secure communication, the sender and the receiver expect privacy, or confidentiality. In other words, only the sender and the receiver of the message are able to understand the contents of the message.

AUTHENTICATION

Confidentiality of the message is not enough in a secure communication; **authentication** is also needed. The receiver needs to be sure of the sender's identity.

INTEGRITY

Secrecy and authentication are only two elements of a secure communication. The integrity of the message also needs to be preserved. Neither the sender nor the receiver is happy if the contents of the message are changed during transmission. For example, in a banking transaction, neither the customer nor the bank is satisfied if the customer's transfer of $1000 is changed to $10,000 during the transmission. The change could happen either maliciously, be caused by an intruder who benefits from the change, or happen accidentally as the result of a hardware or software malfunction.

NONREPUDIATION

Although it is not very obvious, one of the elements of a secure communication is **nonrepudiation**—that is, prevention of repudiation (denial) from the sender. In other words, a secure system needs to prove that the sender actually sent the message. For example, when a customer sends a message to transfer money from one account to another, the bank must have proof that the customer actually requested this transaction.

16.1   PRIVACY

Privacy requires that the message be somehow encrypted at the sender site and decrypted at the receiver site so that a potential intruder (eavesdropper) cannot understand its contents.

ENCRYPTION/ DECRYPTION

Today, privacy can be achieved using encryption/decryption methods. The data are encrypted at the sender and decrypted at the receiver. Two categories of encryption/decryption methods in use today are secret key and public key.

Privacy with Secret Key Encryption

The simplest way to encrypt data is to use a **secret key.** The sender uses this key and an **encryption** algorithm to encrypt data; the receiver uses the same key and the corresponding **decryption** algorithm to decrypt the data (Figure 16.2).

The data, when they are not encrypted, are called **plaintext;** when data are encrypted, they are called **ciphertext.** Note that both user A and B use the secret key, which is exactly the same. However, the encryption and decryption algorithms are the

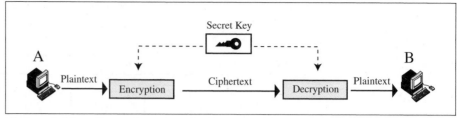

Figure 16.2   Secret key encryption

inverse of each other in the sense that, for example, if the encryption algorithm adds something to the data, the decryption algorithm subtracts the same thing from the data.

> In secret key encryption, the same key is used in encryption and decryption. However, the encryption and decryption algorithms are the inverse of each other.

Note that the secret key encryption algorithms are often referred to as symmetric encryption algorithms because the same secret key can be used in bidirectional communication.

Data Encryption Standard (DES)   Secret key encryption has been used for more than two millennia. At first, the algorithms were very simple, and the keys were very easy to guess. Today, we use very sophisticated algorithms; the most common is called the **data encryption standard (DES).**

DES encrypts and decrypts at the bit level. The data are first transformed into a string of bits. They are broken into segments of 64 bits (extra 0s are added to the last section if it is not 64 bits). Each section is then encrypted using a 56-bit key (actually, the key is 64 bits long, but 8 bits are for error control). Figure 16.3 shows the general layout of this method.

The whole idea is to scramble the data and the key in such a way that every bit of ciphertext depends on every bit of plaintext and the key. This makes it very difficult for an intruder to guess the bits of plaintext from the bits of ciphertext.

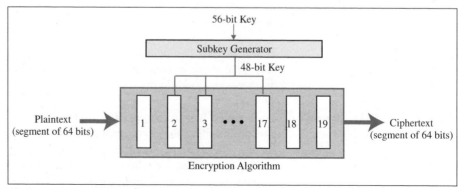

Figure 16.3   DES

Stages 1, 18, and 19 of the algorithm are just **permutation** operations (not using the key). Stages 2 to 17 are identical stages. The right 32 bits of a stage become the left 32 bits of the next stage. The left 32 bits of a stage are scrambled with the key and become the right 32 bits of the next stage. The scrambling is complex and beyond the scope of this book.

Advantage and Disadvantages   The secret key algorithms have one big advantage: efficiency. They take less time to encrypt or decrypt compared with the public key algorithms we will discuss shortly. They are very good candidates for long messages. However, secret key algorithms have two big disadvantages. Each pair of users must have a secret key. This means that if N people in the world want to use this method, there need to be $N(N-1)/2$ secret keys. For example, for 1 million people to communicate, a half-trillion secret keys are needed. In addition, the distribution of the keys between two parties can be difficult. You will see shortly how to solve this problem.

Privacy with Public Key Encryption

The second type of encryption/decryption is **public key encryption.** In this method, there are two keys: a private key and a public key. The **private key** is kept by the receiver. The **public key** is announced to the public (maybe via the Internet).

When user A wants to send a message to user B, A uses the public key to encrypt the message. When the message is received by B, she uses her private key to decrypt the message (Figure 16.4).

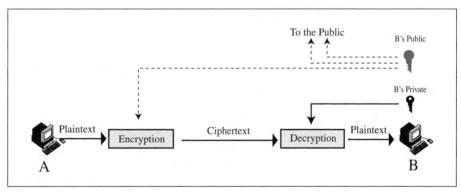

Figure 16.4   Public-key encryption

The whole idea of this method is that the encryption and decryption algorithms are not the inverse of each other. Although an intruder has the public key and encryption and decryption algorithms, he cannot decrypt the message without the private key.

RSA   The most common public-key algorithm is named after its inventors, **Rivest-Shamir-Adleman (RSA) encryption.** The private key is a pair of numbers (N, d); the public key is also a pair of numbers (N, e). Note that N is common to the private and public keys.

The sender uses the following algorithm to encrypt the message:

$$C = P^e \bmod N$$

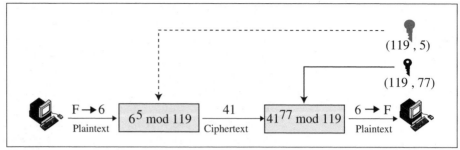

Figure 16.5 RSA

In this algorithm, P is the plaintext, which is represented as a number. C is the number that represents the ciphertext. The two numbers e and N are components of the public key. P is raised to the power e and divided by N. The mod term indicates that the remainder is sent as the ciphertext.

The receiver uses the following algorithm to decrypt the message:

$$P = C^d \bmod N$$

In this algorithm, P and C are the same as before. The two numbers d and N are components of the private key.

Here is an example. Imagine the private key is the pair (119, 77) and the public key is the pair (119, 5). The sender needs to send the character F. This character can be represented as number 6 (F is the sixth character in the alphabet). The encryption algorithm calculates $C = 6^5 \bmod 119 = 41$. This number is sent to the receiver as the ciphertext. The receiver uses the decryption algorithm to calculate $P = 41^{77} \bmod 119 = 6$ (the original number). The number 6 is then interpreted as F. Figure 16.5 shows the process.

The reader may question the effectiveness of this algorithm. If an intruder knows the decryption algorithm and $N = 119$, the only thing missing is $d = 77$. Why couldn't the intruder use trial and error to find d? The answer is that in this trivial example, an intruder could easily guess the value of d. But a major concept of the RSA algorithm is the use of very large numbers for d and e. In practice, the numbers are so large (on the scale of tens of digits) that the trial-and-error approach to breaking the code takes a long time (months, if not years) even with the fastest computers available today.

Choosing Public and Private Keys   One question that comes to mind is how to choose the three numbers N, d, and e for encryption and decryption to work. The inventors of the RSA algorithm mathematically proved that using the following procedure guarantees that the algorithms will work. Although the proof is beyond the scope of this book, we outline the procedure:

- Choose two large prime numbers, p and q.
- Compute $N = p \times q$.
- Choose e (less than N) such that e and $(p-1)(q-1)$ are relatively prime (having no common factor other than 1).
- Choose d such that $(e \times d) \bmod [(p-1)(q-1)]$ is equal to 1.

Advantage and Disadvantage   The advantage of the public key algorithm is the number of keys. Each entity can use the foregoing procedure to create a pair of keys, keep the private one (*N, d*), and distribute publicly the other one (*N, e*). Individuals can even post their public key on their Web site. In addition, note that in this system, for 1 million users to communicate, there is a need for only 2 million keys, not a half-trillion as was the case in the secret key algorithm. However, the big disadvantage of the public key method is the complexity of the algorithm. If you want the method to be effective, you need large numbers. Calculating the ciphertext from plaintext using the long keys takes a lot of time. This is the main reason that public key encryption is not recommended for large amounts of text.

PRIVACY USING THE COMBINATION

You can combine the advantage of the secret key algorithm (efficiency) and the advantage of the public key algorithm (easy distribution of keys). The public key is used to encrypt the secret key; the secret key is used to encrypt the message. The procedure is as follows:

1. The sender chooses a secret key. This secret key is called the one-session key; it is used only once.
2. The sender uses the public key of the receiver to encrypt the secret key (as text) and sends the encrypted secret key to the receiver. Note that we said the public key method is good for a short message. A secret key is a short text message.
3. The receiver uses the private key to decrypt the secret key.
4. The sender uses the secret key to encrypt the actual message.

Figure 16.6 shows the idea of combination.

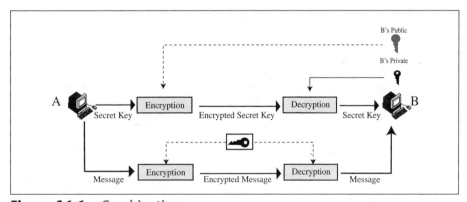

Figure 16.6   Combination

16.2   DIGITAL SIGNATURE

Surprisingly, the other three aspects of security (integrity, authentication, and nonrepudiation) can be achieved using a single concept. The concept comes from the signing (authenticating) of a document by its author or originator. When an author signs a document, it cannot be changed. As an analogy, if you cross out something on a document such as a check, you must put your signature or initials by the change. In this way, you cannot deny it later (nonrepudiation). When you send a document electronically, you can also sign it. This is called **digital signature.**

Digital signature can be done in two ways. You can sign the whole document or you can sign a digest of the document.

SIGNING THE WHOLE DOCUMENT

You can use public key encryption to sign the whole document. However, the use of the public key here is different from that for privacy. Here, the sender uses his or her private key (not the private key of the receiver) to encrypt the message. The receiver, on the other hand, uses the public key of the sender (not his or her private key) to decrypt the message. In other words, the private key is used for encryption and the public key for decryption. This is possible because the encryption and decryption algorithms used today, such as RSA, are mathematical formulas and their structures are the same. Figure 16.7 shows how this is done.

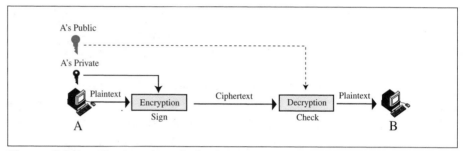

Figure 16.7   Signing the whole document

Let us see how this type of encryption can provide integrity, authentication, and non-repudiation. We claim that the integrity of the message is preserved because, if an intruder intercepts the message and partially or totally changes the message, the decrypted message would be (with a high probability) unreadable and not even look like a message. The message can also be authenticated because if an intruder sends a message (pretending that it is coming from the true author), she uses her own private key. The message is then not decrypted correctly by the public key of the true author (it is unreadable). The method also provides nonrepudiation. Although the sender can deny sending the message, she must reveal (in court) her private key that must correspond with the public key. If you encrypt and decrypt the received message, you get the sent message.

Note two important points. First, you cannot provide these aspects of security using the secret key (we leave the reasoning behind it for an exercise). Second, the method does not provide secrecy; anybody can use the public key of the sender to read the message. To add secrecy to this technique, you need another level of encryption (either with secret key or with public key encryption).

SIGNING THE DIGEST

We said earlier that one of the disadvantages of public key encryption is that it is very inefficient. This is true when you use public key encryption to sign the whole document (the whole document must be encrypted and decrypted).

To make the process more efficient, you can let the sender sign a digest of the document instead of the whole document. In other words, the sender makes a miniature of the document and signs it (encrypts it with his or her private key); the receiver then checks the signature on the miniature (decrypts it with the sender's public key).

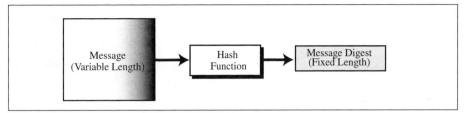

Figure 16.8   Signing the digest

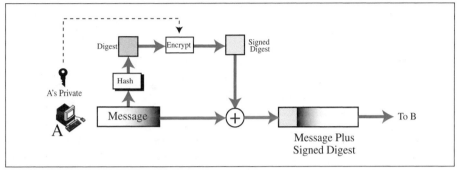

Figure 16.9   Sender site

The method uses a technique called a hash function to create a digest of the message. No matter what the length of the message, the digest is of fixed size (usually 128 bits) as shown in Figure 16.8.

The two most common hash functions are called Message Digest 5 (MD5) and Secure Hash Algorithm 1 (SHA-1). The first produces a 128-bit digest. The second produces a 160-bit digest.

Note that the hash function has two properties to guarantee its success. First, hashing should be one-way; the digest can only be created from the message, but not vice versa. Second, hashing should be one-to-one; it should be very difficult to find two messages that create the same digest. You will see the reason for this condition shortly.

After the digest has been created, it is encrypted (signed) using the sender's private key. The encrypted digest is attached to the original message and sent to the receiver. Figure 16.9 shows the sender site.

The receiver receives the original message and the encrypted digest. She separates the two. She applies the same hash function to the message to create a second digest. She also decrypts the received digest using the public key of the sender. If the two digests are the same, it is obvious that all three aspects of security are preserved. Figure 16.10 shows the receiver site.

We know that these three properties are preserved for the copy of the digest received by the receiver. Now let us see why these properties are preserved for the message.

1. The digest has not been changed, and the message creates a replica of the digest. So the message has not been changed (remember, no two messages can create the same digest).

2. The digest comes from the true sender, so the message also comes from the true sender. If an intruder had initiated the message, the message would not have created the same digest.

3. The sender cannot deny the message because she cannot deny the digest; the only message that can create that digest is the received message.

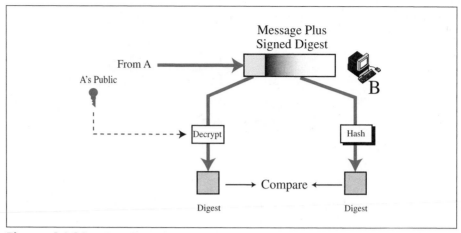

Figure 16.10   Receiver site

Again note that this method of digital signature does not provide privacy; if privacy is needed, it should be added using another level of encryption with either secret key encryption or public key encryption, or both.

16.3   KEY TERMS

authentication	nonrepudiation	Rivest-Shamir-Adleman (RSA)
ciphertext	permutation	encryption
data encryption standard (DES)	plaintext	secret key
decryption	private key	security
digital signature	public key	
encryption	public key encryption	

16.4   SUMMARY

- Security involves the issues of privacy, authentication, integrity, and nonrepudiation.

- Privacy is achieved through encryption. Encryption renders a message (plaintext) unintelligible to unauthorized personnel.

- An encryption/decryption method can be classified as either a secret key method or a public key method.

- In secret key encryption, only the sender and the receiver know the key.

- DES is a popular secret key encryption method.

- In public key encryption, the public key is known to everyone, but the private key is known only to the receiver.

- One commonly used public key encryption method is based on the RSA algorithm.

- Authentication, integrity, and nonrepudiation are achieved through a method called digital signature.

- You can use digital signature on the whole document or on a digest of the document.

16.5 PRACTICE SET

REVIEW QUESTIONS

1. What are the four conditions necessary for the security of transmitted data?

2. How can you assure the privacy of a message?

3. How can you authenticate the sender of a message?

4. How can you preserve the integrity of a message?

5. Give an example of nonrepudiation.

6. What are the two main categories of encryption methods?

7. How is plaintext related to ciphertext?

8. What is DES?

9. Discuss the secret key, the public key, and the private key. Who has possession of each key? What type of encryption uses each key?

10. Why is the RSA algorithm so powerful?

11. What are the disadvantages of secret key encryption?

12. What is the disadvantage of public key encryption?

13. What is the difference between signing the whole document and signing the digest?

14. How does the digital signature relate to privacy concerns?

MULTIPLE-CHOICE QUESTIONS

15. In encryption/decryption, the _____ key is known by everyone.
    a. secret
    b. private
    c. public
    d. skeleton

16. _____ is achieved through encryption/decryption.
    a. Authentication
    b. Integrity
    c. Privacy
    d. Nonrepudiation

17. In the secret key method of encryption and decryption, _____ possession of the secret key.
    a. only the sender has
    b. only the receiver has
    c. both the sender and the receiver have
    d. the general public has

18. One of the advantages of public key encryption is _____.
    a. the short amount of time required for encryption/decryption
    b. a smaller number of keys is needed
    c. integrity is preserved
    d. everyone knows all the keys

19. The RSA algorithm is the basis of a _____ encryption method.
    a. public key
    b. secret key
    c. private key
    d. all of the above

20. To create a digest of a document, you can use _____.
    a. a digital signature
    b. a prime number
    c. DES
    d. a hash function

21. In the digital signature method, the sender uses his or her _____ key to encrypt the message.
    a. public
    b. private
    c. secret
    d. skeleton

22. In the digital signature method, the receiver uses the _____ key to decrypt the message.
    a. public
    b. private
    c. secret
    d. skeleton

23. What is 10 mod 3?
    a. 1
    b. 3
    c. 3.33
    d. 10

24. In a digital signature involving a digest, the hash function is needed _____.
    a. only at the receiver
    b. only at the sender
    c. at both the sender and receiver
    d. by the general public

25. The digital signature method does not provide
_____.
    a. privacy
    b. authentication
    c. integrity
    d. nonrepudiation

EXERCISES

26. One of the early secret key methods was called mono-alphabetic substitution (or the Caesar Cipher, attributed to Julius Caesar). In this method, each character in the plaintext is shifted forward n characters. Characters are wrapped around if necessary. For example, if n is 5, character A is replaced by F, character B by G, and so on. What is the key here? What is the encryption algorithm? What is the decryption algorithm?

27. Using the Caesar Cipher, and 6 as the key, encrypt the message Hello.

28. Discuss the effectiveness of the Caesar Cipher. Can an intruder guess the key by looking only at the ciphertext? If so, how?

29. One of the operations used in a secret key algorithm is the permutation of bits. An 8-bit plaintext is permuted (scrambled). Bit 1 becomes bit 3, bit 2 becomes bit 7, and so on. Draw a diagram to show the encryption and decryption. Choose your own scrambling. What is the key here? What is the encryption algorithm? What is the decryption algorithm?

30. One operation in a secret key algorithm is the XOR operation (see Chapter 4). A fixed-size bit pattern (plaintext) is XORed with the same size bit pattern (key) to create a fixed-sized ciphertext. What is the encryption algorithm here? What is the decryption algorithm? Use the fact that an XOR algorithm is a reversible algorithm.

31. Use the public key (15, 3) to encrypt the number 7. Use the private key (15, 11) to decrypt the result of the previous encryption. Draw a diagram to show the flow of information between the sender and receiver.

32. Prove that the role of the public key and private key can be changed by repeating the previous exercise, but encrypt the number 7 with the private key (15, 11) and decrypt it with the public key (15, 3). Draw a diagram to show the flow of information between the sender and receiver.

33. Discuss why secret key encryption/decryption cannot be used for nonrepudiation.

34. Discuss why secret key encryption/decryption cannot be used for authentication.

35. Add a layer of secret key encryption/decryption to Figure 16.7 to provide privacy.

36. Add a layer of public key encryption/decryption to Figure 16.7 to provide privacy.

Theory of Computation 17

Several questions puzzled computer scientists at the beginning of the computer era:

- Which problems can be solved by a computer? Which cannot?
- How long does it take to solve a problem using a particular language?
- Is one language superior to another? That is, can a computer program written in one language solve a problem that another cannot?
- What is the minimum number of statements needed for a language to solve a problem?
- Before running a program, can it be determined if the program will halt (terminate) or run forever?

To answer these questions, we turn to a discipline called the *theory of computation*. First, we introduce a language, called the Simple Language, to show that the minimum number of statements needed to solve any problem that is solvable by a computer is three. In other words, we prove that all languages that have these three basic statements are equal. Second, we introduce another tool, a computer model called the Turing machine. We show that a problem that can be solved by our Simple Language, can also be solved by the Turing machine. Third, we prove that no program can tell if another program halts or not. This proof is itself an indication that there are problems that cannot be solved by a computer. Finally, we briefly discuss the complexity of algorithms.

17.1 SIMPLE LANGUAGE

We can define a language with only three statements: the *increment, decrement,* and *while* loop (Figure 17.1). In this language, you use only the integer data type. There is no need for any other data type because you can simulate other data types with the integer type. The language uses only a few symbols such as { and }.

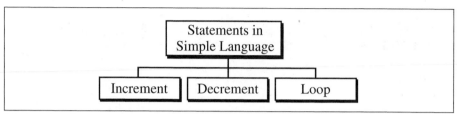

Figure 17.1 Statements in simple language

INCREMENT STATEMENT

The **increment statement** adds 1 to the variable (e.g., X). The format is

```
incr  X
```

DECREMENT STATEMENT

The **decrement statement** subtracts 1 from the variable (e.g., X). The format is

```
decr  X
```

LOOP STATEMENT

The **loop statement** repeats an action (or a series of actions) while the value of the variable (e.g., X) is not 0. The format is

```
while X
{
    Action(s)
}
```

POWER OF THE SIMPLE LANGUAGE

Inductively, we can prove that this simple programming language with only three statements is as powerful (though not necessarily as efficient) as any sophisticated language in use today, such as C. To do so, we show how we can simulate several statements found in some popular languages.

Macros in the Simple Language

We call each simulation a **macro** and use it in other simulations without the need to repeat code.

First Macro: X ⟵ 0   The following code shows how to use the statements in this language to assign 0 to a variable X. The macro notation for this is X ⟵ 0. It is sometimes called clearing a variable.

```
while X
{
   decr X
}
```

Second Macro: X ⟵ n   The following code shows how to use the statements in this language to assign a positive integer to a variable X. The macro notation for this is X ⟵ n. First clear the variable X; then increment X *n* times.

```
X    ⟵   0
incr X
incr X
  .  .  .

  .  .  .

  .  .  .
incr X
```

Third Macro: Y ⟵ X   Every programming language has a statement that copies the value of one variable to another without losing the value of the original variable. This macro can be simulated in the Simple Language using the following series of statements. Note that the second loop uses a temporary variable (TEMP) to restore the value of X.

```
Y       ⟵   0
TEMP    ⟵   0
while X
{
    incr Y
    decr X
    incr TEMP
}
while TEMP
{
    decr TEMP
    incr X
}
```

Fourth Macro: Z ⟵ X + Y   This macro adds the values of X and Y and stores the result in Z. You do this in two steps. First store the value of X in Z (third macro) and then increment Z Y times.

```
Z       ⟵   X
TEMP    ⟵   Y
while TEMP
{
    incr Z
    decr TEMP
}
```

Fifth Macro: Z ⟵ X * Y   This macro multiplies the values of X and Y and stores the result in Z. You use the fourth macro because multiplication is repeated addition.

```
Z       ⟵   0
TEMP    ⟵   Y
while TEMP
{
    Z   ⟵   Z  + X
    decr TEMP
}
```

Sixth Macro: Z ← X ** Y This macro raises X to the power Y and stores the result in Z. You do this using multiplication because exponentiation is repeated multiplication.

```
Z     ←  1
TEMP  ←  Y
while TEMP
{
    Z  ←  Z  *  X
    decr TEMP
}
```

Seventh Macro: comp (X) This macro complements the value of X. If the value of X is 0 (false), change it to 1 (true). If it is not 0 (true), change it to 0 (false). The first loop changes the value of X to 0 if it is not 0 (positive). If you enter this loop (X is not 0), then the value of TEMP is set to 0, which means you never enter the second loop. If you never enter the first loop (X is 0), then you definitely enter the second loop and change the value of X to 1 (the loop is iterated only once because the value of TEMP is 1).

```
TEMP  ←  1
while  X
{
    X     ←  0
    TEMP  ←  0
}
while  TEMP
{
    incr (X)
    decr TEMP
}
```

Eighth Macro: if X then A1 else A2 This macro simulates the decision-making (if-then-else) statement of modern languages. If the value of X is not 0, A1 (an action or a series of actions) is executed in the first loop. However, the loop is executed only once because, after the first iteration, the value of TEMP becomes 0 and you come out of the loop. If the value of X is 0, the first loop is skipped. The value of TEMP, which is the same as the value of X, is complemented (becomes not 0), and the second loop is executed just once.

```
TEMP  ←  X
while TEMP
{
    A1
    TEMP  ←  0
}
    TEMP  ←  X
    comp (TEMP)
    while  TEMP
{
    A2
    TEMP  ←  0
}
```

Other Macros You may have guessed that you need more macros to make the Simple Language compatible with the contemporary languages. Creating other macros is possible, though not trivial. We have left some challenging macros as exercises.

Input and Output

You may have wondered about input/output statements. For example, how can you read data into a variable and how can you print the result of a program? For a language such as this, there is no need for input or output. You can simulate the input, such as `read X`, by an assignment statement ($X \longleftarrow n$). You can also simulate the output by assuming the last variable used in a program holds what should be printed. Remember that this is not a practical language; it is designed to prove some theorems in computer science.

CONCLUSION

The Simple Language is as powerful as any other language discussed in Chapter 9. This means that if you cannot solve a problem in this language, you cannot solve it in any other language. Later, we show that the *halting problem* is not solvable in any language because it is not solvable by the Simple Language.

17.2 TURING MACHINE

The **Turing machine** was introduced in 1936 by Alan M. Turing to solve computable problems. It is the foundation of modern computers. In this section, we introduce a very simplified version of this machine to show how it works. We then show how it implements the statements in the Simple Language.

TURING MACHINE COMPONENTS

A Turing machine is made of three components: a tape, a controller, and a read/write head (Figure 17.2).

Tape

Although modern computers use a random access storage device with finite capacity, the Turing machine's memory is infinite. The **tape,** at any one time, holds a sequence of characters from the set of characters acceptable by the machine. For our purpose, we assume that the machine can accept only a few symbols: the pound sign (#), ampersand (&), the digit 1, and the blank. Figure 17.3 shows an example of data on a tape in this machine. The # defines beginning of the number, the number stored on the tape is represented by 11111, and the & defines the end of the number. The rest of the tape contains blank characters.

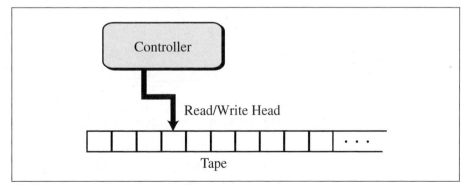

Figure 17.2 Turing machine

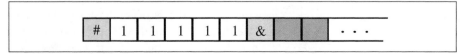

Figure 17.3 Tape

We also assume that the tape processes only positive integer data represented in unary arithmetic. In this arithmetic, a positive integer is made only of 1s. For example, the integer 4 is represented as 1111 and the integer 7 is represented as 1111111. The absence of 1s represents 0.

Read/Write Head

The read/write head at any moment points to one symbol on the tape. We call this symbol the current symbol. The read/write head reads and writes one symbol at a time from the tape. After reading and writing, it moves to the left, to the right, or stays in place. Reading, writing, and moving are all done under instructions from the controller.

Controller

The **controller** is the theoretical counterpart of the central processing unit (CPU) in modern computers. It is a finite state automaton, a machine that has a predetermined finite number of states and moves from one state to another based on the input. At any moment, it can be in one of these states.

Figure 17.4 shows the transition diagram for a controller as a finite state automaton. In this figure, the automaton has four states (A, B, C, D). The diagram shows the change of state as a function of the character read. The following describes the figure:

■ If the controller is in state A and it reads 1 or a blank, it goes to state B. If it reads # or &, it goes to state C.

■ If the controller is in state B and it reads 1, it goes to state C. If it reads any other character, it goes to state A.

■ If the controller is in state C and it reads 1, it goes to state B. If it reads any other character, it goes to state D.

■ If the controller is in state D and it reads any character except a blank, it goes to state B. But if it reads a blank, it stays at state D.

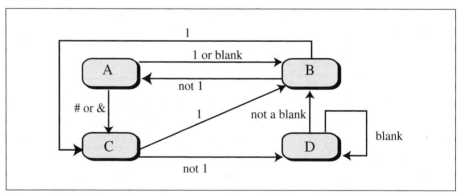

Figure 17.4 Transition state

For each reading of a symbol, the controller writes a character, defines the next position of the read/write head, and changes the state. In the transition diagram, we showed only one of these three; a transition table can show all three. The transition table, as shown in Table 17.1, has five columns: the current state, the character read, the character written, the next position of the read/write head, and the new state.

For each problem, we should define the corresponding table. This is similar to a program written in a computer language. A program is a modern implementation of the transition table.

Current State	Read	Write	Move	New State
A	1 or blank	#	$\longrightarrow$	B
A	# or &	&	$\longleftarrow$	C
B	1	1	$\longleftarrow$	C
B	not 1	same as read		A
C	1	blank	$\longrightarrow$	B
C	not 1	1	$\longrightarrow$	D
D	not a blank	same as read	$\longrightarrow$	B
D	blank	1	$\longleftarrow$	D

Table 17.1 Transition table

SIMULATION OF SIMPLE LANGUAGE

Let us see if we can write programs (create transition tables) that implement the statements of the Simple Language.

Increment Statement

Let us implement the statement (incr X) using the Turing machine. Figure 17.5 shows the transition diagram for this statement. We interpret X as the data already on the tape delimited by the # sign (at the beginning) and the & sign (at the end). For simplicity, we have omitted some states (e.g., the error state) from Figure 17.5.

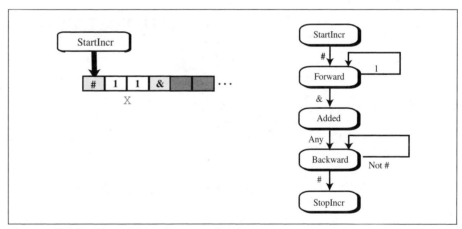

Figure 17.5 Transition diagram for incr X

Table 17.2 shows the transition table for this statement.

Current State	Read	Write	Move	New State
StartIncr	#	#	$\longrightarrow$	Forward
Forward	1	1	$\longrightarrow$	Forward
Forward	&	1	$\longrightarrow$	Added
Added	any	&	$\longleftarrow$	Backward
Backward	not #	same as read	$\longleftarrow$	Backward
Backward	#	#	none	**StopIncr**

Table 17.2 Transition table for incr X statement

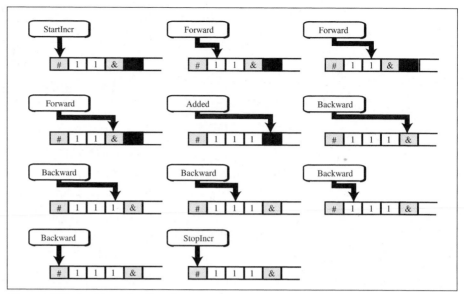

Figure 17.6   Steps in the `incr X` statement

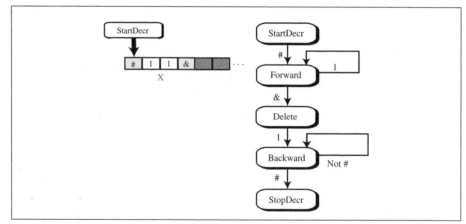

Figure 17.7   Transition diagram for `decr X`

Figure 17.6 shows how the state of the controller will change and how the read/write head moves.

Decrement Statement

The decrement statement (`decr X`) is similar to the increment statement. Figure 17.7 shows the transition diagram.

Table 17.3 shows the transition table for this statement.

Current State	Read	Write	Move	New State
StartDecr	#	#	$\longrightarrow$	Forward
Forward	1	1	$\longrightarrow$	Forward
Forward	&	blank	$\longleftarrow$	Delete
Delete	1	&	$\longleftarrow$	Backward
Backward	not #	same as read	$\longleftarrow$	Backward
Backward	#	#	none	**StopDecr**

Table 17.3   Transition table for `decr X` statement

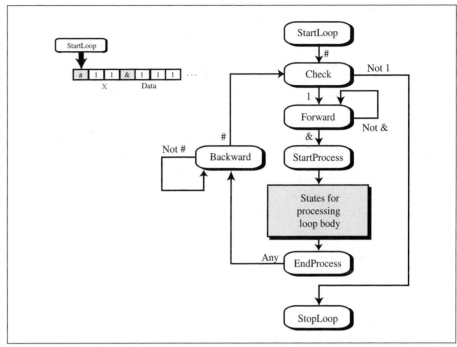

Figure 17.8 Transition diagram for the loop statement

Loop Statement

To simulate the loop, assume that X is stored after the # symbol. The & marks the end of X and the beginning of data that are processed in the body of the loop (it can be more than one data item). Figure 17.8 shows the transition diagram.

Table 17.4 shows the transition table.

Current State	Read	Write	Move	New State
StartLoop	#	#	$\longrightarrow$	Check
Check	Not 1	Same as read	$\longleftarrow$	**StopLoop**
Check	1	1	$\longrightarrow$	Forward
Forward	Not &	Same as read	$\longrightarrow$	Forward
Forward	&	&	None	StartProcess
. . .	. . .	. . .	. . .	. . .
. . .	. . .	. . .	. . .	. . .
EndProcess	Any	Same as read	$\longleftarrow$	Backward
Backward	Not #	Same as read	$\longleftarrow$	Backward
Backward	#	#	None	Check

Table 17.4 Transition table for the loop statement

CONCLUSION

The Turing machine is as powerful as our Simple Language. Any problem that can be solved by the Simple Language can also be solved by the Turing machine. But what about the other side of the coin? Is there a problem solvable by the Turing machine that is not solvable by the Simple Language? Although we cannot prove it, during the latter decades, computer scientists are convinced that this cannot happen. It is referred to as the Church thesis (after Alonzo Church), which states that simple languages like the Simple Language and the Turing machine are equivalent. Every problem that can be solved by the Simple Language can also be solved by the Turing machine, and vice versa.

17.3 GÖDEL NUMBERS

In theoretical computer science, an unsigned number is assigned to every program that can be written in a specific language. This is usually referred to as the **Gödel number** (after Kurt Gödel).

This assignment has many advantages. First, programs can be used as a single data item as input to another program. Second, programs can be referred to by just their integer representations. Third, the numbering can be used to prove that some problems cannot be solved by a computer by showing that the total number of problems in the world is much larger than the total number of programs that can ever be written.

Different methods have been devised for numbering programs. We use a very simple transformation to number programs written in our Simple Language. The Simple Language uses only 15 symbols (Table 17.5). Note that in this language you use only X, X1, X2, . . . , X9 as variables. To encode these variables, you handle Xn as two symbols X and n (X3 is X and 3). If you have a macro with other variables, they need to be changed to Xn.

Symbol	Hex code	Symbol	Hex code
1	1	9	9
2	2	**incr**	A
3	3	decr	B
4	4	while	C
5	5	{	D
6	6	}	E
7	7	X	F
8	8		

Table 17.5   Code for symbols used in the Simple Language

REPRESENTING A PROGRAM

Using the table, you can represent any program written in our Simple Language by a unique positive integer. Follow these steps:

1. Replace each symbol with the corresponding hexadecimal code from the table.

2. Interpret the resulting hexadecimal number as an unsigned integer.

EXAMPLE 1

What is the Gödel number for the program `incr X`?

SOLUTION

Replace each symbol by its hexadecimal code:

```
incr    X
A       F
175 (in decimal)
```

So this program can be represented by the number 175.   ■

INTERPRETING A NUMBER

To show that the numbering system is unique, use the following steps to interpret a Gödel number:

1. Convert the number to hexadecimal.
2. Interpret each **hexadecimal digit** as a symbol using Table 17.5 (ignore a 0).

Note that while any program written in the Simple Language can be represented by a number, not every number can be interpreted as a valid program. After conversion, if the symbols do not follow the syntax of the language, the number is not a valid program.

EXAMPLE 2

Interpret 3058 as a program.

SOLUTION

Change the number to hexadecimal and replace each digit with the corresponding symbol:

```
3058
B   F 2
decr X 2
```

Note that in our Simple Language, each program includes input and output. This means that the combination of a program and its inputs defines the Gödel number. ∎

17.4 HALTING PROBLEM

Almost every program written in a programming language involves repetition (loops or recursive functions). A repetition construct may never terminate (halt); that is, a program can run forever if it has an infinite loop. For example, the following program in the Simple Language never terminates.

```
X ⟵ 1
while X
{
}
```

A classical programming question is

> Can you write a program that tests whether or not any program, represented by its Gödel number, will terminate?

The existence of this program would save programmers a lot of time. Running a program without knowing if it halts or not is a tedious job. Unfortunately, it has now been proven that this program cannot exist (a big disappointment for programmers).

HALTING PROBLEM IS NOT SOLVABLE

Instead of saying that the testing program does not exist and can never exist, the computer scientist says: "The halting problem is not solvable".

Proof

Let us give an informal proof about the nonexistence of this testing program. Our method is often used in mathematics: Assume that it does exist and then show that its existence creates a contradiction. Therefore, it cannot exist. We use three steps to show the proof in this approach.

STEP 1   In this step, we assume that a program, called Test, exists. It can accept any program such as P, represented by its Gödel number, as input, and outputs either 1 or 0. If P terminates, the output of Test is 1; if P does not terminate, the output of Test is 0 (Figure 17.9).

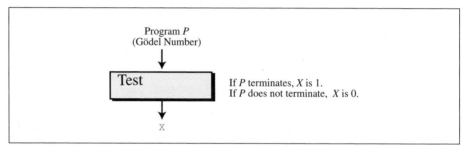

Figure 17.9   Step 1 in proof

STEP 2   In this step, we create another program called Strange that is made of two parts: a copy of Test at the beginning and an empty loop (loop with an empty body) at the end. The loop uses X as the testing variable, which is actually the output of the Test program. This program also uses P as the input. We call this program Strange for the following reason. If P terminates, the first part of Strange, which is a copy of Test, outputs 1. This 1 is input to the loop. The loop does not terminate (infinite loop), and consequently, Strange does not terminate. If P does not terminate, the first part of Strange, which is a copy of Test, outputs 0. This 0 is input to the loop; the loop does terminate (finite loop), and consequently, Strange does terminate.

In other words, we have these strange situations:

> If P terminates, Strange does not terminate.
>
> If P does not terminate, Strange terminates.

Figure 17.11 shows step two in the proof.

STEP 3   Now having made the program Strange, we test this program with itself (its Gödel number) as input. This is legitimate because we did not put any restrictions on P. Figure 17.10 shows the situation.

Contradiction   Do you see the contradiction?

> If we assume that Test exists, we have the following contradictions:
>
> Strange does not terminate if Strange terminates.
>
> Strange terminates if Strange does not terminate.

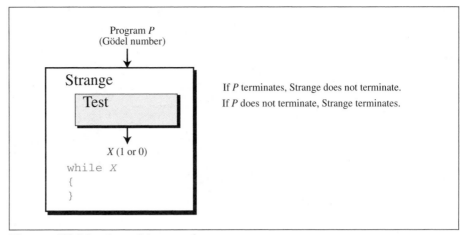

Figure 17.10 Step 2 in proof

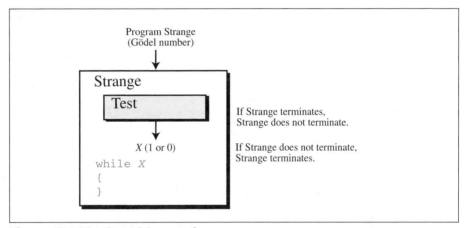

Figure 17.11 Step 3 in proof

This proves that the Test program cannot exist and that we should stop looking for it. The halting problem is unsolvable.

17.5 SOLVABLE AND UNSOLVABLE PROBLEMS

Now that we have shown that at least one problem is unsolvable by a computer, let us touch on this important issue a bit more. In computer science, we can say that, in general, problems can be divided into two categories: **solvable problems** and **unsolvable problems.** The solvable problems can themselves be divided into two categories: polynomial and nonpolynomial problems (Figure 17.12).

UNSOLVABLE PROBLEMS

There are an infinite number of problems that cannot be solved by a computer; one is the halting problem. One method to prove that a problem is not solvable is to show that if that problem is solvable, the halting problem is solvable too. In other words, prove that the solvability of a problem results in the solvability of the halting problem.

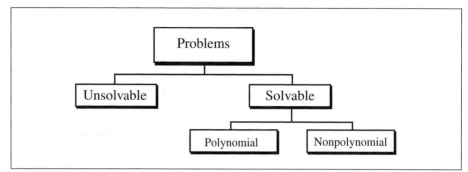

Figure 17.12   Taxonomy of problems

SOLVABLE PROBLEMS

There are many problems that can be solved by a computer. Often, we want to know how long it takes for the computer to solve that problem. In other words, how complex is the program?

The complexity of the program can be measured in several different ways, such as the run time, the memory needed, and so on. One approach is the run time: How long does it take to run a program?

Complexity of Solvable Problems

One way to measure the complexity of a solvable problem is to find the number of operations executed by the computer when it runs the program. In this way, the complexity is independent of the speed of the computer that runs the program. This measure of complexity can depend on the number of inputs. For example, if a program is processing a list (sorting a list), the complexity depends on the number of elements in the list.

Big-O Notation   With the speed of computers today, we are not as concerned with exact numbers as with general orders of magnitude. For example, if the analysis of two programs shows that one executes 15 operations (or a set of operations) while the other executes 25, they are both so fast that you can't see the difference. On the other hand, if the numbers are 15 versus 1500, you should be concerned.

This simplification of efficiency is known as **big-O notation.** We give the idea of this notation without delving into its formal definition and calculation. In this notation, the number of operations (or a set of related operations) is given as a function of the number of inputs. The notation O (n) means a program does n operations for n inputs; the notation O (n^2) means a program does n^2 operations for n inputs.

EXAMPLE 3

Imagine you have written three different programs to solve the same problem. The first one has a complexity of O $(\log_{10} n)$, the second O (n), and the third O (n^2). Assuming an input of 1 million, how long does it take to execute each of these programs on a computer that executes one instruction in 1 microsecond (1 million per second)?

SOLUTION

The following shows the analysis:

```
1st Program: n=1,000,000  O(log₁₀ n) → 6      Time → 6 μs
2nd Program: n=1,000,000  O(n) → 1,000,000    Time → 1 sec
3rd Program: n=1,000,000  O(n²) → 10¹²         Time → 277 hrs
```

Polynomial Problems   If a program has a complexity of $O(\log n)$, $O(n)$, $O(n^2)$, $O(n^3)$, $O(n^4)$, or $O(n^k)$ (with k a constant), it is called *polynomial*. With the speed of computers today, you can get solutions to **polynomial problems** with a reasonable number of inputs (e.g., 1000 to 1 million).

Non-polynomial Problems   If a program has a complexity that is greater than a polynomial—for example, $O(10^n)$ or $O(n!)$—it can be solved if the number of inputs is very small (fewer than 100). If the number of inputs is large, one could sit in front of the computer for months to see the result of a **nonpolynomial problem.** But who knows? At the rate the speed of computers is increasing, you may be able to get a result for this type of problem in less time.

17.6 KEY TERMS

controller	loop statement	tape
decrement statement	macro	Turing machine
Gödel number	nonpolynomial problem	unsolvable problem
hexadecimal digit	polynomial problem	
increment statement	solvable problem	

17.7 SUMMARY

- The theory of computation can help computer scientists answer intrinsic questions.

- Three statements (increment, decrement, and loop) are all that are needed to simulate all other types of statements in a computer language. For example, you can clear a variable, assign a value to a variable, copy the value of one variable to another, and add the values of two variables using the three basic statements.

- The Turing machine can implement statements in our Simple Language.

- A Turing machine has a tape, a controller, and a read/write head.

- The tape in a Turing machine holds a sequence of characters from an acceptable character set.

- The read/write head at any moment in a Turing machine points to a character. After reading and writing, the head can move left, right, or remain stationary

- The controller in a Turing machine controls the read/write head. It is the theoretical counterpart of the CPU in today's computers..

- A transition diagram is a pictorial representation of the states of the controller.

- A transition table is a matrix representation of information about the controller states.

- You can assign a Gödel number to every program in a specific computer language.

- There is no program that can predict whether or not another program will terminate.

- You use big-O notation to denote the efficiency of a program.

- Problems are either solvable or unsolvable. Solvable problems can be categorized as either polynomial or nonpolynomial.

- Nonpolynomial problems usually take longer to solve than polynomial problems if the number of inputs is very large.

17.8 PRACTICE SET

REVIEW QUESTIONS

1. Why do you need the theory of computation?

2. Name and give the functions of the three basic statements that are the foundation of other statements in a computer language.

3. Show how assigning the value of one variable to another (with the original variable retaining its value) uses the three basic statements.

4. What is the relationship between the Turing machine and our Simple Language?

5. What are the components of the Turing machine and what is the function of each component?

6. What is one way to delimit the data on a Turing machine tape?

7. When a read/write head finishes reading and writing a symbol, what are its next options?

8. How is a transition diagram related to a Turing machine controller?

9. How is a transition diagram related to a transition table? Do they have the same information? Which has more information?

10. What is a Gödel number?

11. How do you use a Gödel number to prove that the halting problem is not solvable?

12. How can you indicate the efficiency of a program?

13. Compare and contrast the complexity of a polynomial solvable problem and a nonpolynomial solvable problem.

MULTIPLE-CHOICE QUESTIONS

14. A simple computer language can be designed with only _____ statements.
    a. one
    b. two
    c. three
    d. four

15. The _____ statement adds 1 to the variable.
    a. increment
    b. decrement
    c. loop
    d. complement

16. The _____ statement repeats one or more actions.
    a. increment
    b. decrement
    c. loop
    d. complement

17. The _____ statement subtracts 1 from the variable.
    a. increment
    b. decrement
    c. loop
    d. complement

18. To clear a variable, use the _____ statement(s).
    a. increment
    b. decrement
    c. loop
    d. b and c

19. To assign a number to a variable, use the _____ statement(s).
    a. increment
    b. decrement
    c. loop
    d. all of the above

20. To copy the value of one variable to another variable with the first variable retaining its value, use the _____ statement(s).
    a. increment
    b. decrement
    c. loop
    d. all of the above

21. You call the macro that changes 0 to 1 and a positive integer to 0 the _____ macro.
    a. decr X
    b. Y X
    c. comp (X)
    d. switch (X)

22. A Turing machine has these components: _____.
    a. tape, memory, and read/write head
    b. disk, controller, and read/write head
    c. tape, controller, and read/write head
    d. disk, memory, and controller

23. In a Turing machine, the _____ holds a sequence of characters.
    a. disk
    b. tape
    c. controller
    d. read/write head

24. After reading a symbol, the read/write head _____.
    a. moves to the left
    b. moves to the right
    c. stays in place
    d. any of the above

25. The _____ is the theoretical counterpart of the CPU.
    a. disk
    b. tape
    c. controller
    d. read/write head

26. The controller has _____ states.
    a. three
    b. four
    c. a finite number of
    d. an infinite number of

27. A _____ is a pictorial representation of the states and their relationships to each other.
    a. transition diagram
    b. flowchart
    c. transition table
    d. Turing machine

28. A _____ shows, among other things, the movement of the read/write head, the character read, and the character written.
    a. diagram
    b. flowchart
    c. transition table
    d. Turing machine

29. The Gödel number is _____ number assigned to a program in a specific language.
    a. a binary
    b. an integer
    c. a signed
    d. an unsigned

30. The Gödel number for `decr  X` in decimal is _____.
    a. 367
    b. 175
    c. 174
    d. 191

31. The Gödel number for `decr  X` in hexadecimal is _____.
    a. B C
    b. C B
    c. B F
    d. A F

32. You use _____ to denote a program's complexity.
    a. the Turing number
    b. big-O notation
    c. factorials
    d. the Simple Language

33. If the complexity of $O(n^3)$ is 8, then the number of inputs is _____.
    a. one
    b. two
    c. three
    d. four

34. If the complexity of $O(n!)$ is 24, then the number of inputs is _____.
    a. one
    b. two
    c. three
    d. four

35. The complexity is $O(log*10 n)$ and the computer executes 1 million instructions per second. How long does it take to run the program if the number of inputs is 10,000?
    a. 1 microsecond
    b. 2 microseconds
    c. 3 microseconds
    d. 4 microseconds

EXERCISES

36. Simulate the following macro using the previously defined statements or macros in the Simple Language:
    ```
    Z ← X - Y
    ```

37. Simulate the following macro using the previously defined statements or macros in the Simple Language:
    ```
    if X < Y then A1 else A2
    ```

38. Simulate the following macro using the previously defined statements or macros in the Simple Language:
    ```
    if X > Y then A1 else A2
    ```

39. Simulate the following macro using the previously defined statements or macros in the Simple Language:
    ```
    while X > Y
    {
      actions
    }
    ```

40. Simulate the following macro using the previously defined statements or macros in the Simple Language:
    ```
    while X < Y
    {
      actions
    }
    ```

41. Simulate the following macro using the previously defined statements or macros in the Simple Language:

```
while X == Y
{
  actions
}
```

42. Show the transition diagram for the Turing machine that simulates $X \longleftarrow 0$.

43. Show the transition diagram for the Turing machine that simulates $X \longleftarrow n$.

44. Show the transition diagram for the Turing machine that simulates $Y \longleftarrow X$.

45. Show the transition diagram for the Turing machine that simulates the macro $Z \longleftarrow X + Y$.

46. Show the transition diagram for the Turing machine that simulates the macro $Z \longleftarrow X * Y$.

47. Show the transition diagram for the Turing machine that simulates the macro comp (X).

48. Show the transition diagram for the Turing machine that simulates the macro if X then A1 else A2.

49. What is the Gödel number for the macro $X1 \longleftarrow 0$?

50. What is the Gödel number for the macro $X2 \longleftarrow n$?

51. What is the Gödel number for the macro $X3 \longleftarrow X1 + X2$?

ASCII Code

The American Standard Code for Information Interchange (ASCII) is a seven-bit code that represents 128 characters as shown in Table A.1.

Decimal	Hexadecimal	Binary	Character	Description
0	00	0000000	NUL	Null
1	01	0000001	SOH	Start of header
2	02	0000010	STX	Start of text
3	03	0000011	ETX	End of text
4	04	0000100	EOT	End of transmission
5	05	0000101	ENQ	Enquiry
6	06	0000110	ACK	Acknowledgment
7	07	0000111	BEL	Bell
8	08	0001000	BS	Backspace
9	09	0001001	HT	Horizontal tab
10	0A	0001010	LF	Linefeed
11	0B	0001011	VT	Vertical tab
12	0C	0001100	FF	Formfeed
13	0D	0001101	CR	Carriage return
14	0E	0001110	SO	Shift out
15	0F	0001111	SI	Shift in
16	10	0010000	DLE	Data link escape
17	11	0010001	DC1	Device control 1
18	12	0010010	DC2	Device control 2
19	13	0010011	DC3	Device control 3
20	14	0010100	DC4	Device control 4
21	15	0010101	NAK	Negative acknowledgment
22	16	0010110	SYN	Synchronous idle
23	17	0010111	ETB	End of transmission block
24	18	0011000	CAN	Cancel
25	19	0011001	EM	End of medium
26	1A	0011010	SUB	Substitute
27	1B	0011011	ESC	Escape
28	1C	0011100	FS	File separator
29	1D	0011101	GS	Group separator
30	1E	0011110	RS	Record separator
31	1F	0011111	US	Unit separator
32	20	0100000	SP	Space
33	21	0100001	!	Exclamation point
34	22	0100010	"	Double quote
35	23	0100011	#	Pound sign
36	24	0100100	$	Dollar sign
37	25	0100101	%	Percent sign
38	26	0100110	&	Ampersand
39	27	0100111	'	Apostrophe
40	28	0101000	(	Open parenthesis
41	29	0101001	)	Close parenthesis
42	2A	0101010	*	Asterisk
43	2B	0101011	+	Plus sign
44	2C	0101100	,	Comma
45	2D	0101101	-	Hyphen
46	2E	0101110	.	Period
47	2F	0101111	/	Slash

Table A.1   ASCII table

Decimal	Hexadecimal	Binary	Character	Description
48	30	0110000	0	
49	31	0110001	1	
50	32	0110010	2	
51	33	0110011	3	
52	34	0110100	4	
53	35	0110101	5	
54	36	0110110	6	
55	37	0110111	7	
56	38	0111000	8	
57	39	0111001	9	
58	3A	0111010	:	Colon
59	3B	0111011	;	Semicolon
60	3C	0111100	<	Less than sign
61	3D	0111101	=	Equal sign
62	3E	0111110	>	Greater than sign
63	3F	0111111	?	Question mark
64	40	1000000	@	At sign
65	41	1000001	A	
66	42	1000010	B	
67	43	1000011	C	
68	44	1000100	D	
69	45	1000101	E	
70	46	1000110	F	
71	47	1000111	G	
72	48	1001000	H	
73	49	1001001	I	
74	4A	1001010	J	
75	4B	1001011	K	
76	4C	1001100	L	
77	4D	1001101	M	
78	4E	1001110	N	
79	4F	1001111	O	
80	50	1010000	P	
81	51	1010001	Q	
82	52	1010010	R	
83	53	1010011	S	
84	54	1010100	T	
85	55	1010101	U	
86	56	1010110	V	
87	57	1010111	W	
88	58	1011000	X	
89	59	1011001	Y	
90	5A	1011010	Z	
91	5B	1011011	[	Open bracket
92	5C	1011100	\	Backslash
93	5D	1011101	]	Close bracket
94	5E	1011110	^	Caret
95	5F	1011111	_	Underscore

Table A.1 ASCII table (Continued)

Decimal	Hexadecimal	Binary	Character	Description
96	60	1100000	`	Grave accent
97	61	1100001	a	
98	62	1100010	b	
99	63	1100011	c	
100	64	1100100	d	
101	65	1100101	e	
102	66	1100110	f	
103	67	1100111	g	
104	68	1101000	h	
105	69	1101001	i	
106	6A	1101010	j	
107	6B	1101011	k	
108	6C	1101100	l	
109	6D	1101101	m	
110	6E	1101110	n	
111	6F	1101111	o	
112	70	1110000	p	
113	71	1110001	q	
114	72	1110010	r	
115	73	1110011	s	
116	74	1110100	t	
117	75	1110101	u	
118	76	1110110	v	
119	77	1110111	w	
120	78	1111000	x	
121	79	1111001	y	
122	7A	1111010	z	
123	7B	1111011	{	Open brace
124	7C	1111100	|	Bar
125	7D	1111101	}	Close brace
126	7E	1111110	~	Tilde
127	7F	1111111	DEL	Delete

Table A.1 ASCII table (Continued)

Unicode B

Unicode is a 16-bit code that can represent up to 65,536 symbols. Using hexadecimal notation, the code can range from 0000 to FFFF. Note that it takes tens, if not hundreds, of pages to show all the individual symbols (characters). We show only some ranges here.

ALPHABETS

Codes 0000 to 1FFF define different alphabets. Some are shown in Table B.1 Note the following about this table:

1. Codes 0000 to 007F (Basic Latin) are exactly the same as defined in ASCII code.
2. Codes 0080 to 00FF (Latin-1 supplement) are the same as the Latin-1 characters defined by ISO. The Windows operating system uses a variation of these symbols. The Basic Latin characters are supplemented with accent characters, umlauts, the upside-down question mark, and so on.

Range	Description
0000–007F	Basic Latin
0080–00FF	Latin-1 supplement
0100–017F	Latin extended-A
0180–024F	Latin extended-B
0250–02AF	International Phonetic Alphabet (IPA) extension
02B0–02FF	Spacing modifier letters
0300–036F	Combining diacritical marks
0370–03FF	Greek
0400–04FF	Cyrillic
0530–058F	Armenian
0590–05FF	Hebrew
0600–06FF	Arabic
0700–074F	Syriac
0780–07BF	Thaana
0900–097F	Devinagari
0980–09FF	Bengali
0A00–0A7F	Gumurkhi
0A80–0AFF	Gujarati
0B00–0B7F	Oriya
0B80–0BFF	Tamil
0C00–0C7F	Teluga
0C80–0CFF	Kannada
0D00–0D7F	Malayalam
0D80–0DFF	Sinhala
0E00-0E7F	Thai
0E80-0EFF	Lao
0F00–0FFF	Tibetan
1000–109F	Myanmar
10A0–10FF	Georgian
1100–11FF	Hangul Jamo
1200–137F	Ethiopic
13A0–13FF	Cherokee
1400–167F	Unified Canadian Aboriginal Syllabic
1680–169F	Ogham
16A0-16FF	Runic
1780–17FF	Khmer
1800-18AF	Mongolian
1E00–1EFF	Latin extended additional
1F00–1FFF	Greek extended

Table B.1 Alphabets (0000-1FFF)

SYMBOLS AND PUNCTUATION MARKS

Codes 2000 to 2FFF define symbols and punctuation marks. Some are shown in Table B.2.

Range	Description
2000–2067	General punctuation
2070–209F	Subscripts and superscripts
20A0–20CF	Currency symbols
20D0–20FF	Combining marks for symbols
2100–214F	Letterlike symbols
2150–218F	Number forms
2190–21FF	Arrows
2200–22FF	Mathematical operations
2300–23FF	Miscellaneous technical
2400–243F	Control pictures
2440–245F	Optical character recognition
2460–24FF	Enclosed alphanumeric
2500–257F	Box drawing
2580–259F	Block drawing
25A0–25FF	Geometric shapes
2600–26FF	Miscellaneous symbols
2700–27BF	Dingbats
2800–28FF	Braille patterns
2E80–2EFF	CJK radical supplement
2F00–2FDF	Kangxi radical
2FF0–2FFF	Ideographic description characters

Table B.2 Symbols and punctuation (2000 to 2FFF)

CJK AUXILIARIES

Codes 3000 to 33FF define the Chinese, Japanese, and Korean (CJK) auxiliaries. Some are shown in Table B.3.

Range	Description
3000–303F	CJK symbols and punctuation
3040–309F	Hiragana
30A0-30FF	Katakana
3100–312F	Bopomofo
3130-318F	Hangul compatibility Jamo
3190-319F	Kanbun
31A0–31BF	Bopomofo extended
3200–32FF	Enclosed CJK letters and months
3300–33FF	CJK compatibility

Table B.3 CJK auxiliaries (3000 to 33FF)

CJK UNIFIED IDEOGRAPHS

Codes 4000 to 9FFF define CJK unified ideographs.

SURROGATES   Codes D800 to DFFF define surrogates.

PRIVATE USE   Codes E000 to F8FF are for private use.

MISCELLANEOUS   Codes F900 to FFFF define miscellaneous characters and symbols.
CHARACTERS
AND SYMBOLS

Flowcharts

A very effective tool to show the logic flow of a program is the flowchart. In a programming environment, it can be used to design a complete program or just part of a program.

The primary purpose of a flowchart is to show the design of an algorithm. At the same time, it frees programmers from the syntax and details of a programming language while allowing them to concentrate on the details of the problem to be solved.

A flowchart gives a pictorial representation of an algorithm. This is in contrast to another programming design tool, pseudocode (see Appendix D), that provides a textual design solution. Both tools have their advantages, but a flowchart has the pictorial power that other tools lack.

C.1   AUXILIARY SYMBOLS

A flowchart is a combination of symbols. Some symbols are used to enhance the readability or functionality of the flowchart. They are not used directly to show instructions or commands. They show the start and stop points, the order and sequence of actions, and how one part of a flowchart is connected to another. These auxiliary symbols are shown in Figure C.1.

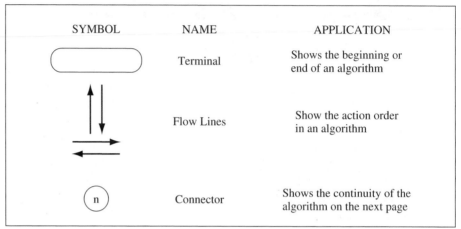

SYMBOL	NAME	APPLICATION
	Terminal	Shows the beginning or end of an algorithm
	Flow Lines	Show the action order in an algorithm
n	Connector	Shows the continuity of the algorithm on the next page

Figure C.1   Auxiliary symbols in flowcharting

START AND STOP

An oval is used to show the beginning or end of an algorithm. When it is used to show the beginning of an algorithm, write the word START in the oval. When it is used to show the end of an algorithm, write STOP in the oval.

One of the first rules of structured programming is that each algorithm should have only one entry point and one exit. This means that a well-structured flowchart should have one and only one START and one and only one STOP. Ovals should be aligned to show clearly the flow of the action in an algorithm. For example, a flowchart for a program that does nothing is shown in Figure C.2. This program starts and stops without doing anything.

An oval can also be used to show the beginning and the end of a module. When used at the beginning, write the name of the module inside (instead of the word START); when used at the end, write the word RETURN (instead of STOP).

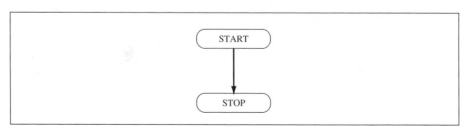

Figure C.2   Start and stop symbols

FLOW LINES

Flow lines are used to show the order or sequence of actions in a program. They connect symbols. Usually, a symbol has some entering and some exiting lines. The START oval has only one exiting line. The STOP oval has only one entering line. We have already shown the use of flow lines in Figure C.2. We will show other flows in the examples that follow.

CONNECTORS

You use only one symbol, a circle with a number in it, to show connectivity. It is used when you reach the end of the page, with your flowchart still unfinished. At the bottom of the page, use a connector to show that the logic flow is continued at the top of the next page. The number in the connector can be a simple serial number or it can be a combination of a page and symbol in the form *page.number*. Figure C.3 shows an off-page connector.

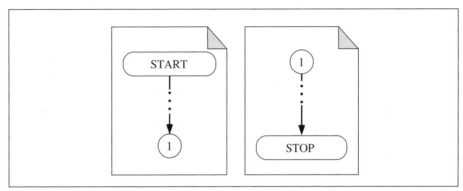

Figure C.3 Connectors

C.2 MAIN SYMBOLS

Main symbols are used to show the instructions or actions needed to solve the problem presented in the algorithm. With these symbols, it is possible to represent all five structured programming constructs: sequence, decision, `while` loop, `for` loop, and `do-while` loop.

SEQUENCE STATEMENTS

Sequence statements simply represent a series of actions that must continue in a linear order. Although the actions represented in the sequence symbol may be very complex, such as an input or output operation, the logic flow must enter the symbol at the top and flow out at the bottom. Sequence symbols do not allow any decisions or flow changes within the symbol.

There are five sequence symbols: null, assignment, input/output, module call, and compound statement. The latter four are shown in Figure C.4.

Null Statement

It is worth noting that *do nothing* is a valid statement. It is commonly referred to as a null statement. The null statement is considered a sequence statement because it cannot change the flow direction of a program. There is no symbol for a null statement. It is simply a flow line. Figure C.2 is an example of a null statement.

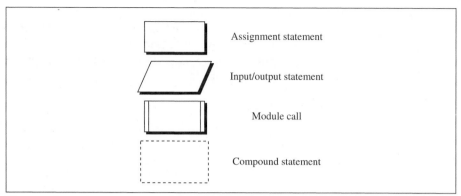

Figure C.4   Sequence symbols

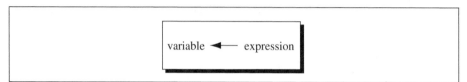

Figure C.5   Assignment statement

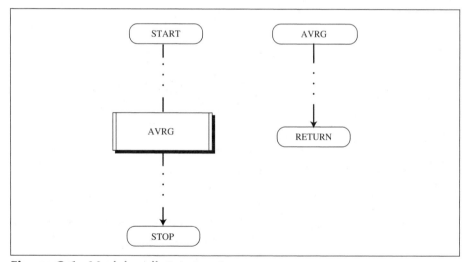

Figure C.6   Module-call statement

Assignment Statement

The assignment statement is shown using a rectangle. Within the rectangle, the assignment operator is shown as a left-pointing arrow. At the right side of the arrow is an expression whose value must be stored in the variable at the left side. Figure C.5 shows an assignment statement.

Input/Output Statement

A parallelogram is used to show any input or output, such as reading from a keyboard or writing to the system console.

Module-Call Statement

The symbol for calling a module is a rectangle with two vertical bars inside. The flowchart for the called module must be somewhere else. In other words, each time you see a module-call statement, look for another flowchart with the module name (Figure C.6).

Compound Statement

Although there is no actual symbol to show a compound statement, we encapsulate all statements that make a compound statement in a broken-line rectangle.

SELECTION STATEMENTS

Unlike the sequence statement, selection statements can cause the flow of the program to change. They allow the execution of selected statements and the skipping of other statements. There are two selection statements in structured programming: two-way and multiway selection.

Two-Way Selection

The two-way symbol is the diamond. When it is used to represent an `if-else` statement, the true condition logic is shown on the right leg of the logic flow and the false condition, if present, is shown on the left leg of the logic flow. With the `if-else`, there must always be two logic flows, although often one of them is null. (Remember that the null statement is represented by a flow line; there is no symbol for null.) Finally, the statement ends with a connector where the true and false flows join. In this case, the connector has nothing in it.

Although you will often see decisions drawn with the flow from the bottom of the diamond, this is not good style. Even when one of the flows is null, it still must flow from the left or right side of the diamond.

Figure C.7 shows the use of the decision symbol in the `if-else` statement. As we pointed out, there are always two branches. On each branch, you are allowed to have one and only one statement. Of course, the statement in each branch can be a null or a compound statement. But only one statement is allowed in each branch; not less, not more. Also remember that the whole figure is only one statement, not two or three; it is one `if-else` statement.

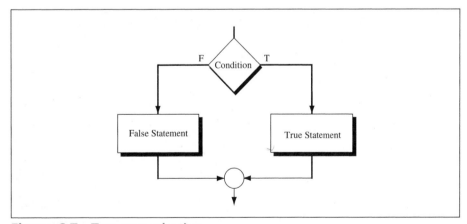

Figure C.7   Two-way selection

Multiway Selection

The second application of the selection symbol used in structured programming is multiway selection (Figure C.8). As you can see, you can have as many branches as you need. On each branch, you are allowed to have one, and only one, statement. Of course, the statement in each branch can be a null or a compound statement. But remember that only one statement in each branch is allowed; not less, not more. Also remember that the whole figure is only one statement, not two or three.

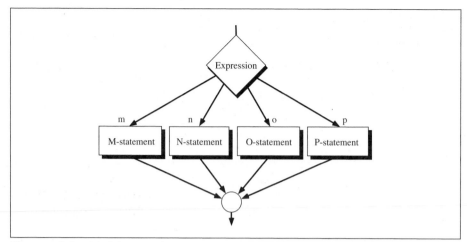

Figure C.8   Multiway selection

LOOPING STATEMENTS

There are three looping statements: `for`, `while`, and `do-while`.

for Statement

The `for` statement is a counter-controlled loop. It is actually a complex statement that has three parts, any of which can be null: (1) the loop initialization, which normally sets the loop counter; (2) the limit test; and (3) the end-of-loop action statements, which usually increment a counter. Since the `for` statement is a pretest loop, it is possible that the loop may not be executed. If the terminating condition is true at the start, the body of the `for` statement is skipped.

As is the case in all structured programming constructs, the body of the loop can contain one and only one statement. As is the case with the other constructs, this one statement can be null or a compound statement. Figure C.9 shows the `for` loop.

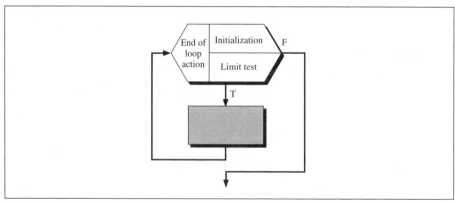

Figure C.9   `for` loop

while Statement

The second looping construct is the `while` statement. The major difference between the `for` and `while` loops is that the `while` loop is not a counting loop. Both are pretest loops; this means that, like the `for`, the body of the `while` loop may never be executed.

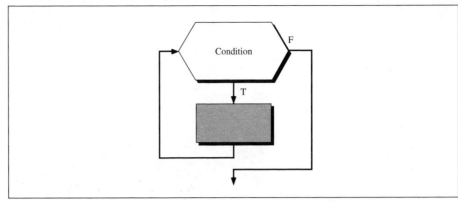

Figure C.10 `while` loop

You use the same basic symbol for the `while` loop, but because there is only a limit test, the internal divisions are not necessary. Figure C.10 shows the basic format of the `while` statement.

do-while Statement

The third application of the loop symbol is the `do-while` statement (Figure C.11). Because of the inherent differences between the `for` and `while` loops and the `do-while` loop, it is presented differently in a flowchart. There are two major differences between the `while` and the `do-while`:

1. A `while` loop is a pretest loop. The `do-while` loop is a posttest loop.
2. The body of a `while` loop may never be executed. The body of a `do-while` loop is executed at least once.

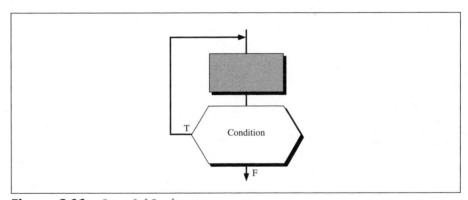

Figure C.11 `do-while` loop

Pseudocode

One of the most common tools to define algorithms is pseudocode. Pseudocode is an Englishlike representation of the code required for an algorithm. It is part English and part structured code. The English part provides a relaxed syntax that is easy to read. The code part consists of an extended version of the basic algorithmic constructs: sequence, selection, and iteration. Algorithm D.1 shows an example of pseudocode.

Algorithm D.1

Algorithm: Finding Smallest
Purpose: This algorithm finds the smallest number among a list of numbers.
Pre: List of numbers
Post: None
Return: The smallest

1. Set smallest to the first number
2. **loop** (not end of list)
   2.1 **if** (next number < smallest)
       2.1.1 set smallest to next number
   2.2 **end** if
3. **end** loop
4. **return** smallest
End Finding Smallest

D.1   COMPONENTS

An algorithm written in pseudocode can be decomposed into several elements and constructs.

ALGORITHM HEADER

Each algorithm begins with a header that names it. For example, in Algorithm D.1, the header starts with the word *Algorithm,* which names the algorithm as "Finding Smallest".

PURPOSE, CONDITIONS, AND RETURN

After the header, you normally mention the purpose, the pre- and postconditions, and the data returned from the algorithm.

Purpose

The purpose is a short statement about what the algorithm does. It needs to describe only the general algorithm processing. It should not attempt to describe all of the processing. In Algorithm D.1, the purpose starts with the word *Purpose* and continues with the goal of the algorithm.

Precondition

The precondition lists any precursor requirements. For example, in Algorithm D.1, we require that the list be available to the algorithm.

Postcondition

The postcondition identifies any effect created by the algorithm. For example, perhaps the algorithm specifies the printing of data.

Return

We believe that every algorithm should show what is returned from the algorithm. If there is nothing to be returned, we advise that null be specified. In Algorithm D.1, the smallest value found is returned.

STATEMENT NUMBERS

Statements are numbered as shown in Algorithm D.1 (1, 2, 3, . . .). The dependent statements are numbered in a way that shows their dependencies (1.1, 2.4, . . .).

STATEMENT CONSTRUCTS

When Niklaus Wirth first proposed the structured programming model, he stated that any algorithm could be written with only three programming constructs: sequence, selection, and loop. Our pseudocode contains only these three basic constructs. The implementation of these constructs relies on the richness of the implementation language. For example, the loop can be implemented as a `while`, `do-while`, or `for` statement in the C language.

SEQUENCE

A sequence is a series of statements that do not alter the execution path within an algorithm. Although it is obvious that statements such as assign and add are sequence statements, it is not so obvious that a call to other algorithms is also considered a sequence statement. The reason lies in the structured programming concept that each algorithm has only one entry and one exit. Furthermore, when an algorithm completes, it returns to the statement immediately after the call that invoked it. Therefore, you can properly consider the algorithm call a sequence statement. Algorithm D.2 shows a sequence.

Algorithm D.2

```
. . .
7.  set x to first number
8.  set y to second number
9.  multiply x by y and store the result in z
. . .
```

SELECTION

Selection statements evaluate one or more alternatives. If true, one path is taken. If false, a different path is taken. The typical selection statement is the two-way selection (`if-else`). Whereas most languages provide for multiway selections, we provide none in pseudocode. The alternatives of the selection are identified by indentation, as shown in Algorithm D.3.

Algorithm D.3

```
. . .
5.  if (x < y)
        5.1 increment x
        5.2 print x
6.  else
        6.1 decrement y
        6.2 print y
7.  end if
. . .
```

LOOP

A loop iterates a block of code. The loop in our pseudocode most closely resembles the `while` loop. It is a pretest loop; that is, the condition is evaluated before the body of the loop is executed. If the condition is true, the body is executed. If the condition is false, the loop terminates. Algorithm D.4 shows an example of a loop.

Algorithm D.4

```
. . .
3.  loop (not end of file File 1)
        3.1   read the next line
        3.2   delete the leading spaces
        3.3   copy the line to file File 2
4.  end loop
. . .
```

Structure Charts

The structure chart is the primary design tool for a program. As a design tool, it is created before you start writing your program.

E.1   STRUCTURE CHART SYMBOLS

Figure E.1 shows the various symbols used in a structure chart.

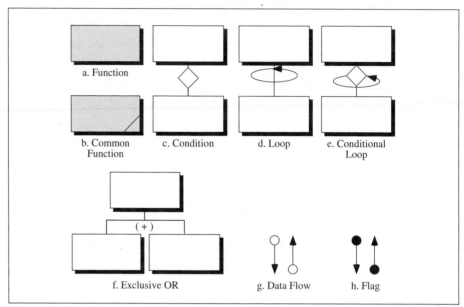

Figure E.1   Structure chart symbols

FUNCTION SYMBOL   Each rectangle in a structure chart represents a function *that you write*. The name in the rectangle is the name you give to the function (Figure E.2).

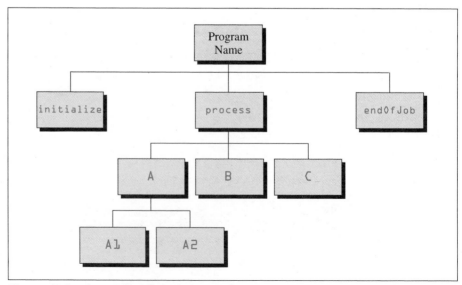

Figure E.2   Example of a structure chart

**SELECTION
IN STRUCTURE
CHARTS**

Figure E.3 shows two symbols for a function that is called by a selection statement: the condition and the exclusive OR.

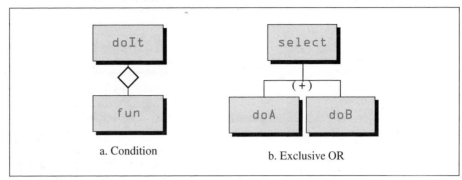

a. Condition   b. Exclusive OR

Figure E.3   Selection in a structure chart

In Figure E.3a., the function `doIt` contains a conditional call to a subfunction, `fun`. If the condition is true, you call `fun`. If it is not true, you skip `fun`. This situation is represented in a structure chart as a diamond on the vertical line between the two function blocks.

Figure E.3b. represents the selection between two different functions. In this example, the function `select` chooses between `doA` and `doB`. One and only one of them will be called each time the selection statement is executed. This is known as an exclusive OR; one of the two alternatives is executed to the exclusion of the other. The exclusive OR is represented by a plus sign between the processes.

Now consider the design found for a series of functions that can be called exclusively. This occurs when a multiway selection contains calls to several different functions. Figure E.4 contains an example of a selection statement that calls different functions based on color.

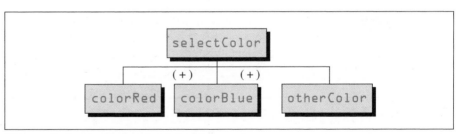

Figure E.4   Example of a selection

**LOOPS
IN STRUCTURE
CHARTS**

Let's look at how loops are shown in a structure chart. The symbols are very simple. Loops go in circles, so the symbol used is a circle. Programmers use two basic looping symbols. The first is a simple loop, shown in Figure E.5a. The other is the conditional loop, shown in Figure E.5b.

When the function is called unconditionally, as in a `while` loop, the circle flows around the line above the called function. On the other hand, if the call is conditional, as in a function called in an `if-else` statement inside a loop, then the circle includes a decision diamond on the line.

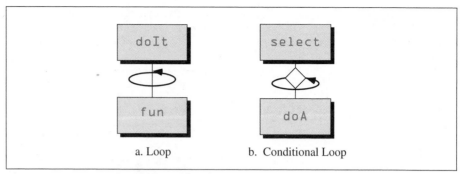

Figure E.5   Loops in a structure chart

Figure E.6 shows the basic structure for a function called `process`. The circle is *below* the function that controls the loop. In this example, the looping statement is contained in `process`, and it calls three functions, `A`, `B`, and `C`. The exact nature of the loop cannot be determined from the structure chart. It could be any of the three basic looping constructs.

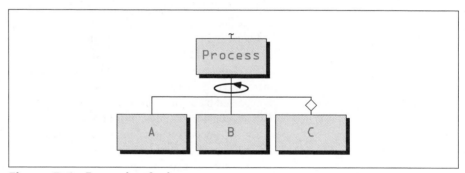

Figure E.6   Example of a loop

DATA FLOWS

It is not necessary to show data flows and flags, although it may be helpful in certain circumstances. If they are shown, inputs are to the left of the vertical line and outputs are to the right. When they are included, the name of the data or flag should also be indicated.

E.2   READING STRUCTURE CHARTS

Structure charts are read *top-down* and *left-right*. Referring to Figure E.2, this rule says that Program Name (`main`) consists of three subfunctions: `initialize`, `process`, and `endOfJob`. According to the left-right rule, the first call in the program is to `initialize`. After `initialize` is complete, the program calls `process`. When `process` is complete, the program calls `endOfJob`. In other words, the functions on the same level of a structure chart are called in order from left to right.

The concept of top-down is demonstrated by `process`. When `process` is called, it calls `A`, `B`, and `C` in turn. Function `B` does not start running, however, until `A` is finished. While `A` is running, it calls `A1` and `A2` in turn. In other words, all functions in a line from `process` to `A2` must be called before function `B` can start.

Often, a program will contain several calls to a common function. These calls are usually scattered throughout the program. The structure chart will show the call wherever it logically occurs in the program. To identify common structures, the lower right corner of the rectangle will contain crosshatching or will be shaded. If the common function is complex and contains subfunctions, these subfunctions need to be shown only once. An indication that the incomplete references contain additional structure should be shown. This is usually done with a line below the function rectangle and a cut (~) symbol. This concept is seen in Figure E.7, which uses a common function, `average`, in two different places in the program. Note, however, that you never graphically show a function connected to two calling functions.

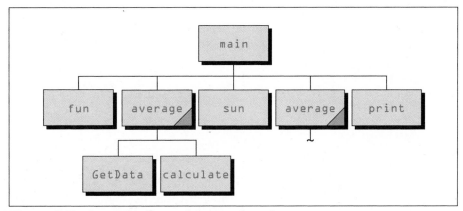

Figure E.7   Several calls to the same function

E.3   RULES OF STRUCTURE CHARTS

We summarize the rules discussed in this section:

- Each rectangle in a structure chart represents a function written by the programmer.
- The name in the rectangle is the name that will be used in the coding of the function.
- The structure chart contains only function flow. No code is indicated.
- Common functions are indicated by crosshatching or shading in the lower right corner of the function rectangle.
- Data flows and flags are optional. When used, they should be named.
- Input flows and flags are shown to the left of the vertical line; output flows and flags are shown to the right.

Discrete Cosine Transform

In this appendix, we give the mathematical background for the discrete cosine and inverse discrete cosine transforms.

F.1   DISCRETE COSINE TRANSFORM

In this transformation, each block of 64 pixels goes through a transformation called the discrete cosine transform (DCT). The transformation changes the 64 values so that the relative relationship between pixels is kept but redundancies are revealed. The formula follows. $P(x,y)$ defines one particular value in the picture block; $T(m,n)$ defines one value in the transformed block.

$$T(m,n) = 0.25c(m)c(n) \sum_{x=0}^{7} \sum_{y=0}^{7} P(x,y) \cos\left(\frac{(2x+1)m\pi}{16}\right)\cos\left(\frac{(2y+1)n\pi}{16}\right)$$

where

$$c(i) = \begin{cases} \dfrac{1}{\sqrt{2}} & \text{if } i = 0 \\ 1 & \text{otherwise} \end{cases}$$

F.2   INVERSE TRANSFORM

The inverse transform is used to create the $P(x,y)$ table from the $T(m,n)$ table.

$$P(x,y) = 0.25c(x)c(y) \sum_{m=0}^{7} \sum_{n=0}^{7} T(m,n) \cos\left(\frac{(2m+1)x\pi}{16}\right) \cos\left(\frac{(2n+1)y\pi}{16}\right)$$

where

$$c(i) = \begin{cases} \dfrac{1}{\sqrt{2}} & \text{if } i = 0 \\ 1 & \text{otherwise} \end{cases}$$

Acronyms

ADT: abstract data type
ALU: arithmetic/logic unit
ANSI: American National Standards Institute
ASCII: American Standard Code for Information Interchange
bit: binary digit
CD-ROM: compact disc, read-only memory
CD-R: compact disc, recordable
CD-RW: compact disc, rewritable
CISC: complex instruction set computer
COBOL: COmmon Business-Oriented Language
CPU: central processing unit
DBMS: database management system
DES: data encryption standard
DMA: direct memory access
DRAM: dynamic RAM
DVD: digital video disk
EBCDIC: Extended Binary-Coded Decimal Interchange Code
EEPROM: electronically erasable PROM
EPROM: erasable PROM
FIFO: first-in first-out
FORTRAN: FORmula TRANslation
FTP: File Transfer Protocol
HTML: HyperText Markup Language
HTTP: HyperText Transfer Protocol
IP: Internetworking Protocol
ISO: International Organization for Standardization
JPEG: Joint Photographic Experts Group
LIFO: last-in, first-out

LISP: List processing
LAN: local area network
LZ: Lempel-Ziv
LZW: Lempel-Ziv-Welch
MAN: metropolitan area network
MPEG: Motion Picture Experts Group
OSI: Open Systems Interconnection
PERL: Practical Extraction and Report Language
PC: personal computer
pixel: picture element
PROM: programmable ROM
RAM: random access memory
RDBMS: relational database management system
RISC: reduced instruction set computer
ROM: read-only memory
RSA: Rivest, Shamir, and Adelman
SCSI: small computer system interface
SMTP: Simple Mail Transfer Protocol
SQL: Structured Query Language
SRAM: static RAM
TCP: Transmission Control Protocol
TCP/IP: Transmission Control Protocol/Internetworking Protocol
TELNET: Terminal Network
UDP: User Datagram Protocol
URL: Uniform Resource Locator
USB: Universal Serial Bus
WAN: wide area network
WORM: write once, read many
WWW: World Wide Web

Glossary

abstract data type (ADT): a data declaration packaged together with operations that are meaningful on the data type.

abstraction: the generalization of an algorithm's operations without a specified implementation.

AC value: the value that changes with time.

access method: a technique for reading data from a secondary (auxiliary) storage device.

accuracy: the quality factor that addresses the correctness of a system.

active document: in the World Wide Web, a document executed at the local site using Java.

active hub: a hub that regenerates received signals (a repeater).

actual parameters: the parameters in the function calling statement that contain the values to be passed to the function. Contrast with *formal parameters.*

Ada: a high-level concurrent programming language developed by the U.S. Department of Defense.

address bus: the part of the system bus used for address transfer.

address space: a range of addresses.

adjacency list: a method of representing a graph that uses a linked list to store the vertices and a two-dimensional linked list array to store the lines.

adjacency matrix: a method of representing a graph that uses an array for the vertices and a matrix (square two-dimensional array) to store the lines.

adjacent vertices: two vertices in a graph that are connected by a line.

ADT: See *abstract data type.*

algorithm: the logical steps necessary to solve a problem with a computer; a function or a part of a function.

American National Standards Institute (ANSI): an organization that creates standards in programming languages, electrical specifications, communication protocols, and so on.

American Standard Code for Information Interchange (ASCII): an encoding scheme that defines control and printable characters for 128 values.

analog: a continuously varying entity.

analysis phase: a phase in the software system life cycle that defines requirements that specify what the proposed system is to accomplish.

Analytical Engine: the computer invented by Charles Babbage.

ancestor: any node in the path from the current node to the root of a tree.

AND operation: one of the bit-level operations; the result of the operation is 1 only if both bits are 1s; otherwise it is 0.

AND operator: the operator used in the AND operation.

application layer: the seventh layer in the OSI model; provides access to network services.

arc: a directed line in a graph. Contrast with *edge.*

arithmetic logic unit (ALU): the part of a computer system that performs arithmetic and logic operations on data.

arithmetic operation: an operation that takes two numbers and creates another number.

arithmetic operator: the operator used in an arithmetic operation.

array: a fixed-sized, sequenced collection of elements of the same data type.

ASCII: See *American Standard Code for Information Interchange.*

assembler: system software that converts a source program into executable object code; traditionally associated with an assembly language program. See also *compiler.*

assembly language: a programming language in which there is a one-to-one correspondence between the computer's machine language and the symbolic instruction set of the language.

assignment operator: in C and C++, the operator that assigns a value to a variable.

authentication: verification of the sender of the message.

auxiliary storage device: any storage device outside main memory; permanent data storage; external storage; secondary storage.

B

backbone: the media and devices that create connectivity to small networks.

backtracking: an algorithmic process, usually implemented with a stack or through recursion, that remembers the path through a data structure and can retrace the path in reverse order.

balance: a tree node attribute representing the difference in height between the node's subtrees.

balance factor: in a tree, the difference between the height of the right subtree and left subtree.

bar chart: a graph with values represented by bars.

batch operating system: the operating system used in early computers, in which jobs were grouped before being served.

bidirectional frame (B-frame): in MPEG, a frame that is related to both the preceding and following frames.

big-O notation: a measure of the efficiency of an algorithm with only the dominant factor considered.

binary digit (bit): the smallest unit of information (0 or 1).

binary file: a collection of data stored in the internal format of the computer. Contrast with *text file*.

binary operation: an operation that needs two input operands.

binary operator: any operator that is used in a binary operation.

binary search: a search algorithm in which the search value is located by repeatedly dividing the list in half.

binary system: a numbering system that uses two symbols (0 and 1).

binary to decimal conversion: the changing of a binary number to a decimal number.

binary tree: a tree in which no node can have more than two children; a tree with a maximum outdegree of 2.

binary tree traversal: the process of visiting each node in a binary tree.

bit: acronym for *bi*nary digi*t*. In a computer, the basic storage unit with a value of either 0 or 1.

bit pattern: a sequence of bits (0s and 1s).

bit-level encryption: an encryption method in which the data are first divided into blocks of bits before being encrypted.

bitmap graphic: a graphic representation in which a combination of pixels defines the image.

black box: a device with internal mechanisms unknown to the operator.

black box testing: testing based on the system requirements rather than a knowledge of the program.

block: a group of statements treated as a whole.

body: the part of a function that contains the definitions and statements; all of a function except the header declaration. Contrast with *function header*.

branch: a line in a tree that connects two adjacent nodes.

breadth-first traversal: a graph traversal method in which nodes adjacent to the current node are processed before their descendants.

bridge: a connecting device operating at the first two layers of the OSI model with filtering and forwarding capabilities.

browser: an application program that displays a WWW document.

bubble sort: a sort algorithm in which each pass through the data moves (bubbles) the lowest element to the beginning of the unsorted portion of the list.

bucket: in a hashing algorithm, a location that can accommodate multiple data units.

bucket hashing: a hashing method that uses buckets to reduce collision.

bus: the physical channel that links hardware components in a computer; the shared physical medium used in a bus-topology network.

bus topology: a network topology in which all computers are attached to a shared medium.

byte: a unit of storage, usually 8 bits.

C

C language: a procedural language developed by Dennis Ritchie.

C++ language: an object-oriented language developed by Bjarne Stroustrup.

cache memory: a small, fast memory used to hold data items that are being processed.

carry: in addition, the value that must be added to the next column.

central processing unit (CPU): the part of a computer that contains the control components to interpret instructions. In a personal computer, a microchip containing a control unit and an arithmetic logic unit.

changeability: the quality factor that addresses the ease with which changes can be accurately made to a program.

`char`**:** the C language type for character.

character-level encryption: an encryption method in which the character is the unit of encryption.

child: a node in a tree or graph that has a predecessor.

ciphertext: the encrypted data.

class: the combination of data and functions joined together to form a type.

class diagram: a diagram in object-oriented programming that shows the relationship between objects.

clear: in masking, a technique to make a bit 0; also known as force to 0.

client: in a client-server program, the application that requests services from a server.

client-server model: the model of interaction between two application programs in which a program at one end (client) requests a service from a program at the other end (server).

COBOL: a business programming language (*CO*mmon *B*usiness-*O*riented *L*anguage) developed by Grace Hopper.

code: a set of bit patterns designed to represent text symbols.

cohesion: the attribute of a module that describes how closely the processes written in a module are related to one another.

coincidental cohesion: the combination of procedures that are not related.

collision: in hashing, an event that occurs when a hashing algorithm produces an address for an insertion, and that address is already occupied.

collision resolution: an algorithmic process that determines an alternative address after a collision.

command-line argument: in a C program, a parameter specified on the run-time execute statement and passed to the program for its use.

comment: in a C program, a note to the program reader that is ignored by the compiler.

communicational cohesion: a design attribute in which module processes are related because they share the same data.

compact disc: a direct access optical storage medium with a capacity of 650 megabytes.

compact disc read-only memory (CD-ROM): a compact disc in which the data are written to the disc by the manufacturer and can only be read by the user.

compact disc recordable (CD-R): a compact disc that a user can write to only once and read from many times.

compact disc rewritable (CD-RW): a compact disc that can be written to many times and read from many times.

compiler: system software that converts a source program into executable object code; traditionally associated with high-level languages. See also *assembler.*

complete tree: a tree with a restricted outdegree that has the maximum number of nodes for its height.

complex instruction set computer (CISC): a computer that defines an extensive set of instructions, even those that are used less frequently.

compound statement: in some programming languages, a collection of statements (instructions) treated as one by the language.

compression: the reduction of a message without significant loss of information.

computer language: any of the syntactical languages used to write programs for computers, such as machine language, assembly language, C, COBOL, and FORTRAN.

computer network: See *network.*

computer science: the study of issues related to a computer.

conceptual level: relating to the logical structure of a database. It deals with the meaning of the database, not its physical implementation.

connecting devices: devices such as routers, bridges, and repeaters that connect LANs or WANs.

constant: a data value that cannot change during the execution of the program. Contrast with *variable.*

control bus: the bus that carries information between computer components.

content coupling: the direct reference to the data in one module by statements in another module; the lowest form of coupling and one to be avoided.

control coupling: communication between functions in which flags are set by one module to control the actions of another.

control unit: the component of a CPU that interprets the instructions and controls the flow of data.

controller: a component of a Turing machine that is equivalent to a computer's CPU.

correctability: the quality factor that addresses the ease with which errors in a module can be fixed.

counter-controlled loop: a looping technique in which the number of iterations is controlled by a counter.

coupling: a measure of the interdependence between two separate functions. See also *content coupling, control coupling, data coupling, global coupling,* and *stamp coupling.*

CPU: See *central processing unit.*

cycle: a graph path with a length greater than 1 that starts and ends at the same vertex.

D

data bus: the bus inside a computer used to carry data between components.

data compression: the reduction of the amount of data without significant loss.

data coupling: communication between modules in which only the required data are passed; considered the best form of coupling.

data encryption standard (DES): the U.S. government encryption method for nonmilitary and nonclassified use.

data file: a file that contains only data, not programs.

data-link layer: the second layer in the OSI model; responsible for node-to-node delivery of data.

data processor: an entity that inputs data, processes them, and outputs the result.

data register: an area that holds data to be processed inside the CPU.

data structure: the syntactical representation of data organized to show the relationship among the individual elements.

data transfer: moving data from one computer to another.

data type: a named set of values and operations defined to manipulate them, such as character and integer.

database: a collection of organized information.

database management system (DBMS): a program or a set of programs that manipulates a database.

datagram: the packet sent by the IP protocol.

DC value: the value that does not change with time.

deadlock: a situation in which the resources needed by one job to finish its task are held by other jobs.

decimal system: a method of representing numbers using 10 symbols (0 to 9).

decimal to binary conversion: the changing of a decimal number to a binary number.

declaration: in C, the association of a name with an object, such as a type, variable, structure, or function. See also *definition*.

declarative language: a computer language that uses the principle of logical reasoning to answer queries.

decoding: the process of restoring an encoded message to its preencoded form.

decompression: the action performed on compressed data to obtain the original data.

decrement statement: the statement that subtracts 1 from the value of a variable.

decryption: the recovery of the original message from the encrypted data. See *encryption*.

definition: in C, the process that reserves memory for a named object, such as a variable or constant. See also *declaration*.

degree: the number of lines incident to a node in a graph.

delete operator: in a relational database, the operator that deletes a tuple from the relation.

demand paging: a memory allocation method in which a page of a program is loaded into memory only when it is needed.

demand paging and segmentation: a memory allocation method in which a page or a segment of a program is loaded into memory only when it is needed.

demand segmentation: a memory allocation method in which a segment of a program is loaded into memory only when it is needed.

depth-first traversal: a traversal method in which all of a node's descendants are processed before any adjacent nodes (siblings).

dequeue: delete an element from a queue.

derived type: a composite data type constructed from other types (array, structure, union, pointer, and enumerated type).

descendant: any node in the path from the current node to a leaf.

design phase: a phase in the software system life cycle that defines how the system will accomplish what was defined in the analysis phase.

device manager: a component of an operating system that controls access to the input/output devices.

dictionary-based encoding: a compression method in which a dictionary is created during the session.

difference operation: an operation in two sets. The result is the first set minus the common elements in the two sets.

difference operator: an operator in a relational database that is applied to two relations with the same attributes. The tuples in the resulting relation are those that are in the first relation but not the second.

digital: a discrete (noncontinuous) entity.

digit extraction: selecting digits from a key for use as an address.

digit extraction hashing: a hashing method that uses digit extraction.

digital signature: a method used to authenticate the sender of the message and to preserve the integrity of the data.

digital versatile disk (DVD): a direct access optical storage medium that can store up to 17 gigabytes (a 2-hour movie).

digraph: a directed graph.

direct hashing: a hashing method in which the key is obtained without algorithmic modification.

direct memory access (DMA): a form of I/O in which a special device controls the exchange of data between memory and I/O devices.

directed graph: a graph in which the direction is indicated on the lines (arcs).

discrete cosine transformation (DCT): a mathematical transformation used in JPEG.

disjoint graph: a graph that is not connected.

disk: an auxiliary storage medium for computer data and programs.

distributed database: a database in which data are stored on several computers.

distributed system: an operating system that controls the resources located in computers at different sites.

division remainder hashing: a type of hashing in which the key is divided by a number and the remainder is used as the address.

dotted-decimal notation: the notation devised to make the IP addresses easier to read; each byte is converted to a decimal number; numbers are separated by a dot.

double hashing: a hashing collision resolution method in which the collision address is hashed to determine the next address.

double-precision format: a standard for storing floating-point numbers in memory with more exactness than single-precision format.

doubly linked list: an ordered collection of data in which each element contains two pointers, one pointing to the previous element and one pointing to the next element.

do-while loop: in the C and C++ languages, an event-controlled posttest loop.

dynamic document: a Web document created by running a program at the server site.

dynamic RAM (DRAM): RAM in which the cells use capacitors. DRAM must be refreshed periodically to retain its data.

E

EBCDIC: See *Extended Binary Coded Decimal Interchange Code.*

edge: a graph line that has no direction.

efficiency: the quality factor that addresses the optimum use of computer hardware or responsiveness to a user.

electronic mail (email): a method of sending messages electronically based on a mailbox address rather than host-to-host exchange.

electronically erasable programmable read-only memory (EEPROM): programmable read-only memory that can be programmed and erased using electronic impulses without being removed from the computer.

encapsulation: the software engineering design concept in which data and their operations are bundled together and maintained separately from the application using them.

encryption: converting a message into an unintelligible form that is unreadable unless decrypted.

end user: the entity that uses the final product.

enqueue: insert an element into a queue.

erasable programmable read-only memory (EPROM): programmable read-only memory that can be programmed; erasing EPROM requires removing it from the computer.

error report file: in a file update process, a report of errors detected during the update.

event-controlled loop: a loop whose termination is predicated upon the occurrence of a specified event. Contrast with *counter-controlled loop.*

Excess system: a number representation method used to store the exponential value of a fraction.

executable file: a file that can be executed (run); a program.

execute: run a program.

exclusive OR (XOR): a binary logical operation in which the result is true only if one of the operands is true and the other is false.

expression: a sequence of operators and operands that reduces to a single value.

expression statement: in C, an expression terminated by a semicolon.

expression tree: a tree in which the leaves are data items and the internal node and the root are operators.

extended ASCII: a character set that extends basic ASCII. The extra characters represent characters from foreign languages as well as other symbols.

Extended Binary Coded Decimal Interchange Code (EBCDIC): the character set designed by IBM for its large computer systems.

external level: the part of the database that interacts with the laser.

F

fetch: the part of the instruction cycle in which the instruction to be executed is brought in from memory.

field: the smallest named unit of data that has meaning in describing information. A field may be either a variable or a constant.

FIFO: See *first in, first out.*

file: a named collection of data stored on an auxiliary storage device. Contrast with *list.*

file manager: the component of the operating system that controls access to the files.

File Transfer Protocol (FTP): an application-layer service in TCP/IP for transferring files from and to a remote site.

FireWire: an I/O device controller with a high-speed serial interface that transfers data in packets.

first in, first out (FIFO): an algorithm in which the first data item that is added to a list is removed from the list first.

flag: an indicator used in a program to designate the presence or absence of a condition; switch.

flexibility: the quality factor that addresses the ease with which a program can be changed to meet user requirements.

flip: changing a bit from 0 to 1 or from 1 to 0.

float: a floating-point type.

floating-point number: a number that contains both an integer and a fraction.

flowchart: a program design tool in which standard graphical symbols are used to represent the logical flow of data through a function.

for loop: a counter-controlled loop in C and C++.

force to change: the bit manipulation concept used to change selected bits from 0 to 1 or from 1 to 0.

force to 1: the bit manipulation concept used to change selected bits to 1.

force to 0: the bit manipulation concept used to change selected bits to 0.

formal parameters: the parameter declaration in a function to describe the type of data to be passed to the function.

FORTRAN: a high-level procedural language used for scientific and engineering applications.

fraction: a part of a whole number.

fragmented distributed database: a distributed database in which data are localized.

frame: a data unit at the data-link layer.

frequency array: an array that contains the number of occurrences of a value or of a range of values. See also *histogram*.

function: a named block of code that performs a process within a program; an executable unit of code, consisting of a header, function name, and a body, that is designed to perform a task within the program.

function body: the code within a function that is contained in the function's definition and statement sections.

function call: a statement that invokes another function.

function declaration: in C, a prototype statement that describes a function's return type, name, and formal parameters.

function definition: in C, the implementation of a function declaration.

function header: in a function definition, that part of the function that supplies the return type, function identifier, and formal parameters. Contrast with *body*.

functional cohesion: a design attribute in which all of the processing is related to a single task. The highest level of cohesion.

functional language: a programming language in which a program is considered to be a mathematical function.

G

gateway: a device that connects two separate networks that use different communication protocols.

general list: a list in which data can be inserted or deleted anywhere in the list.

global coupling: a communication technique in which data are accessible to all modules of a program; considered to be a very poor method for intraprogram communication.

Gödel number: a number assigned to every program that can be written in a specific language.

graph: a collection of nodes, called vertices, and line segments, called edges or arcs, connecting pairs of nodes.

H

hardware: any of the physical components of a computer system, such as a keyboard or a printer.

hashed file: a file that is searched using one of the hashing methods.

header: the information added to the beginning of a packet for routing and other purposes.

height: a tree attribute indicating the length of the path from the root to the last level; the level of the leaf in the longest path from the root plus 1.

hexadecimal digit: a symbol in the hexadecimal system.

hexadecimal notation: a numbering system with base 16. Its digits are 0, 1, 2, 3, 4, 5, 6, 7, 8, 9, A, B, C, D, E, and F.

hierarchical model: a database model that organizes data in a treelike structure that can be searched from top to bottom.

high-level language: a (portable) programming language designed to allow the programmer to concentrate on the application rather than the structure of a particular computer or operating system.

histogram: a graphical representation of a frequency distribution. See also *frequency array*.

hold state: the state of a job that is waiting to be loaded into memory.

home address: in a hashed list, the first address produced by the hashing algorithm.

home page: the main page of a hypertext document available on the Web.

HTML: See *Hypertext Markup Language*.

hub: a device that connects other devices in a network.

Huffman coding: a statistical compression method using variable-length code.

hybrid topology: a topology made of more than one basic topology.

hypertext: a document with reference to other documents.

Hypertext Markup Language (HTML): the computer language for specifying the contents and format of a Web document; allows text to include fonts, layouts, embedded graphics, and links to other documents.

Hypertext Transfer Protocol (HTTP): the protocol that is used to retrieve Web pages on the Internet.

I

identifier: the name given to an object in a programming language.

if-else statement: a construct that implements a two-way selection.

image: data in the form of graphics or pictures.

imperative language: another name for a procedural language.

implementation phase: a phase in the software system life cycle in which the actual programs are created.

increment statement: in C or C++, the statement that adds 1 to an integer value.

incremental model: a model in software engineering in which the entire package is constructed with each module consisting of just a shell; the modules gain complexity with each iteration of the package.

indegree: the number of lines entering a node in a tree or graph.

index: the address of an element in an array.

indexed file: the file that uses an index for random access.

infix: an arithmetic notation in which the operator is placed between two operands.

inheritance: the ability to extend a class to create a new class while retaining the data objects and methods of the base class and adding new data objects and methods.

initializer: a statement that initializes the value of a variable.

inorder traversal: a binary tree traversal method in which the root is traversed after the left subtree and before the right subtree.

input data: user information that is submitted to a computer to run a program.

input/output (I/O) controller: a device that controls the access to input/output devices.

input/output subsystem: the part of the computer organization that receives data from the outside and sends data to the outside.

insert operator: an operator in a relational database that inserts a tuple in a relation.

insertion sort: a sort algorithm in which the first element from the unsorted portion of the list is inserted into its proper position in the sorted portion of the list.

instruction: a command that tells a computer what to do.

instruction register: a register in the CPU that holds the instruction before being interpreted by the control unit.

integer: an integral number; a number without a fractional part.

integrated circuit: transistors, wiring, and other components on one single chip.

internal level: the part of the database that defines where data are actually stored.

internal node: any tree node except the root and the leaves; a node in the middle of a tree.

internal sort: a sort in which all of the data are held in primary storage during the sorting process.

International Organization For Standardization (ISO): a worldwide organization that defines and develops standards for a variety of topics.

internet: abbreviation for internetwork.

Internet: the global internet that uses the TCP/IP protocol suite.

Internet address: a 32-bit address used to uniquely define a computer on the Internet.

Internet Protocol (IP): the network-layer protocol in the TCP/IP protocol responsible for transmitting packets from one computer to another across the Internet.

internetwork: a network of networks.

internetworking device: devices such as routers or gateways that connect networks to form an internetwork.

interoperability: the quality factor that addresses the ability of one system to exchange data with another.

interrupt driven I/O: a form of I/O in which the CPU, after issuing an I/O command, continues serving other processes until it receives an interrupt signal that the I/O operation is completed.

intersection operation: an operation on two sets in which the result is a set with the common elements between the two sets.

intersection operator: an operator in relational algebra that finds tuples that are common between two relations.

intersector gap: the gap between sectors on a disk.

intertrack gap: the gap between tracks on a tape.

intracoded frame (I-frame): in MPEG, an independent frame.

inverted file: a file sorted according to a second key.

IP address: See *Internet address.*

IP datagram: the data unit in the network layer.

isolated I/O: a method of addressing an I/O module in which the instructions used to read/write memory are totally different from the instructions used to read/write to input/output devices.

iteration: a single execution of the statements in a loop.

J

Java: an object-oriented programming language for creating stand-alone programs or dynamic documents on the Internet.

job scheduler: a scheduler that selects a job for processing from a queue of jobs waiting to be moved to memory.

join operator: an operator in a relational database that takes two relations and combines them based on common attributes.

Joint Photographic Experts Group (JPEG): a standard for compressing images.

K

key: one or more fields used to identify a record (structure).

keyboard: an input device consisting of alphanumeric keys and function keys used for text or control data.

keywords: See *reserved words.*

L

land: on an optical disc, an area not hit by the laser in the translation of a bit pattern; usually represents a bit.

last in, first out (LIFO): an algorithm in which the last data item that is added to a list is removed from the list first.

leaf: a graph or tree node with an outdegree of 0.

Lempel Ziv (LZ) encoding: a compression algorithm that uses a dictionary.

Lempel Ziv Welch (LZW) encoding: an enhanced version of LZ encoding.

level: an attribute of a node indicating its distance from the root.

LIFO: See *last in, first out.*

line: a graph element that connects two vertices in the graph. See also *arc* and *edge.*

linear list: a list structure in which each element, except the last, has a unique successor.

link: in a list structure, the field that identifies the next element in the list.

linked list: a linear list structure in which the ordering of the elements is determined by link fields.

linked list resolution: a collision resolution method in hashing that uses a separate area for synonyms, which are maintained in a linked list.

linked list traversal: a traversal method in which every element of a linked list is processed in order.

linker: the function in the program creation process in which an object module is joined with precompiled functions to form an executable program.

Linux: an operating system developed by Linus Torvalds to make UNIX more efficient when run on an Intel microprocessor.

LISP: a list processing programming language in which everything is considered a list.

list: an ordered set of data contained in main memory. Contrast with *file.*

literal constant: an unnamed constant coded in an expression.

loader: the operating system function that fetches an executable program into memory for running.

local area network (LAN): a network connecting devices inside a limited area.

local login: a login to a computer attached directly to the terminal.

logical address: an address defined at the network layer.

logical cohesion: a design attribute that describes a module in which the processing within the module is related only by the general type of processing being done. Considered as unacceptable in structured programming.

logical data: data with a value of either true or false.

logical operation: an operation in which the result is a logical value (true or false).

logical operator: an operator that performs a logical operation.

loop: in a program, a structured programming construct that causes one or more statements to be repeated; in a graph, a line that starts and ends with the same vertex.

loop statement: a statement that causes the program to iterate a set of other statements.

loose coupling: a type of coupling between modules that makes them more independent.

lossless data compression: data compression in which no data are lost; used for compressing text or programs.

lossy data compression: data compression in which some data are allowed to be lost; used for image, audio, or video compression.

M

machine cycle: the repetitive sequence of events in the execution of program instructions (fetch, decode, and execute).

machine language: the instructions native to the central processor of a computer that are executable without assembly or compilation.

macro: a custom-designed procedure that can be used over and over again.

magnetic disk: a storage medium with random access capability.

magnetic tape: a storage medium with sequential capability.

main memory: See *primary memory.*

mantissa: the part of a floating-point number that shows the precision.

mask: a variable or constant that contains a bit configuration used to control the setting of bits in a bitwise operation.

master disk: the disk holding the master file in file updating.

master file: a permanent file that contains the most current data regarding an application.

memory: the main memory of a computer consisting of random access memory (RAM) and read-only memory (ROM); used to store data and program instructions.

memory manager: the component of the operating system that controls the use of main memory.

memory-mapped I/O: a method of addressing an I/O module in a single address space; used for both memory and I/O devices.

mesh topology: a topology in which each device is connected to every other device.

metropolitan area network (MAN): a network that can span a city or a town.

microcomputer: a computer small enough to fit on a desktop.

minimum spanning tree: a tree extracted from a connected network such that the sum of the weights is the minimum of all possible trees contained in the graph.

model: the specification set by a standards organization as a guideline for designing networks.

module: See *subalgorithm*.

modulo division: dividing two numbers and keeping the remainder.

monitor: the visual display unit of a computer system; usually a video display device.

monoprogramming: the technique that allows only one program to be in memory at a time.

Moving Pictures Experts Group (MPEG): a lossy compression method for compressing video (and audio).

multidimensional array: an array with elements having more than one level of indexing.

multiprogramming: a technique that allows more than one program to reside in memory while being processed.

multiway selection: a selection statement that is capable of evaluating more than two alternatives. In C, the `switch` statement. Contrast with *two-way selection*.

N

named constant: a constant that is given a name by the programmer.

natural language: any spoken language.

nearly complete tree: a tree with a limited outdegree that has the minimum height for its nodes and in which the leaf level is being filled from the left.

negative integer: an integer ranging from negative infinity to 0.

network: a system of connected nodes that can share resources.

network layer: the third layer in the OSI model; responsible for delivery of packets from the original host to the final destination.

network model: a database model in which a record can have more than one parent record.

new master file: the master file that is created from an old master file when the file is updated.

node: in a data structure, an element that contains both data and structural elements used to process the data structure.

node-to-node delivery: the delivery of data from one node to the next.

nonpolynomial problem: a problem that cannot be solved with polynomial complexity.

nonrepudiation: a quality of a received message that does not allow the sender to deny sending it.

nonstorage device: an I/O device that can communicate with the CPU/ memory, but cannot store information.

normalization: in a relational database, the process of removing redundancies.

NOT operation: the operation that changes a 0 bit to 1 or a 1 bit to 0.

NOT operator: the operator used in a NOT operation.

null pointer: the pointer that points to nothing.

null tree: a tree with no nodes.

O

object module: the output of a compilation consisting of machine language instructions.

object-oriented database: a database in which data are treated as structures (objects).

object-oriented language: a programming language in which the objects and the operations to be applied to them are tied together.

octal notation: a numbering system with a base of 8; the octal digits are 0 to 7.

old master file: the master file that is processed in conjunction with the transaction file to create the new master file.

one-dimensional array: an array with only one level of indexing.

one's complement: the bitwise operation that reverses the value of the bits in a variable.

one's complement representation: a method of integer representation in which a negative number is represented by complementing the positive number.

online update: an update process in which transactions are entered and processed by a user who has direct access to the system.

open addressing resolution: a collision resolution method in which the new address is in the home area.

Open Systems Interconnection (OSI): a seven-layer model designed by ISO as a guide to data communication.

operability: the quality factor that addresses the ease with which a system can be used.

operand: an object in a statement on which an operation is performed. Contrast with *operator*.

operating system: the software that controls the computing environment and provides an interface to the user.

operator: the syntactical token representing an action on data (the operand). Contrast with *operand*.

optical storage device: an I/O device that uses light (laser) to store and retrieve data.

OR operation: a binary operation resulting in an output of 0 only if the two inputs are 0s; otherwise it is 1.

OR operator: the operator used in an OR operation.

ordered list: a list in which the elements are arranged so that the key values are placed in ascending or descending sequence.

outdegree: the number of lines leaving a node in a tree or graph.

output data: the results of running a computer program.

output device: a device that can be written to but not read from.

overflow: the condition that results when there are insufficient bits to represent a number in binary.

P

page: one of a number of equally sized sections of a program.

paging: a multiprogramming technique in which memory is divided into equally sized sections called frames.

parallel system: an operating system with multiple CPUs on the same machine.

parameter: a value passed to a function.

parameter list: a list of values passed to a function.

parent: a tree or graph node with an outdegree greater than 0; that is, with successors.

parsing: a process that breaks data into pieces or tokens.

partitioning: a technique used in multiprogramming that divides the memory into variable-length sections.

Pascal: a programming language designed with a specific goal in mind: to teach programming to novices by emphasizing the structured programming approach.

pass by reference: a parameter passing technique in which the called function refers to a passed parameter using an alias name.

pass by value: a parameter passing technique in which the value of a variable is passed to a function.

passive hub: a type of connecting device that does not regenerate data.

path: a sequence of nodes in which each vertex is adjacent to the next one.

PERL: a high-level language (with a syntax similar to C) using regular expressions that allow the parsing of a string of characters into components.

permutation: scrambling.

personal computer (PC): a computer designed for individual use.

physical address: the address of a device at the data-link layer.

physical layer: the first layer in the OSI model; responsible for signaling and transmitting bits across the network.

picture element (pixel): the smallest unit of an image.

pit: on an optical disc, an area hit by the laser in the translation of a bit pattern; usually represents a 0 bit.

pixel: See *picture element.*

plaintext: the text before being encrypted.

pointer: a constant or variable that contains an address that can be used to access data stored elsewhere.

polycarbonate resin: in CD-ROM production, a material injected into a mold.

polymorphism: in C++, defining several operations with the same name that can do different things in related classes.

polynomial problem: a problem that can be solved with polynomial complexity.

pop: the stack delete operation.

port address: the address used in TCP and UDP to distinguish one process from another.

portability: the quality factor relating to the ease with which a system can be moved to other hardware environments.

postfix: an arithmetic notation in which the operator is placed after its operands.

positive integer: an integer ranging from 0 to positive infinity.

postorder traversal: a binary tree traversal method in which the left subtree is processed first, then the right subtree, and then the root.

postponement: changing the accessing order of data.

posttest loop: a loop in which the terminating condition is tested only after the execution of the loop statements. Contrast with *pretest loop.*

predicted frame (P-frame): in MPEG, a frame that is related to the preceding I-frame or B-frame.

prefix: an arithmetic notation in which the operator is placed before the operands.

prefix increment: in C, the operator (e.g., ++a) that adds 1 to a variable before its value is used in an expression; also known as *unary increment.*

preorder traversal: a binary tree traversal in which the left subtree is traversed first, the root is traversed next, and the right subtree is traversed last.

preprocessor: the first phase of a C compilation in which the source statements are prepared for compilation and any necessary libraries are loaded.

preprocessor directives: commands to the C precompiler.

presentation layer: the sixth layer in the OSI model; responsible for formatting data, encryption/decryption, and compression.

pretest loop: a loop in which the terminating condition is tested before the execution of the loop statements. Contrast with *posttest loop*.

primary expression: an expression consisting of only a single operator; the highest priority expression.

primary memory: the high speed memory of a computer, where programs and data are stored when the program is being executed. The primary memory is volatile, which means that the content is erased when the computer is turned off; main memory.

prime area: in a hashed list, the memory that contains the home address.

private key: one of the two keys used in public key encryption.

probe: in a hashing algorithm, the calculation of an address and test for success; in a search algorithm, one iteration of the loop that includes the test for the search argument.

procedural cohesion: a design attribute in which the processing within the module is related by control flows. Considered acceptable design only at the higher levels of a program.

procedural language: a computer language in which a set of instructions is usually executed one by one from beginning to end.

procedure: another term for a subalgorithm.

process: a program in execution.

process manager: an operating system component that controls the processes.

process scheduler: an operating system mechanism that dispatches the processes waiting to get access to the CPU.

process synchronization: an operating system mechanism that controls the access of a resource by more than one process.

program: a set of instructions.

program counter: a register in the CPU that holds the address of the next instruction in memory to be executed.

programmable data processor: a machine that takes input data and a program to produce output data.

programmable read-only memory (PROM): memory with contents electrically set by the manufacturer; may be reset by the user.

programmed I/O: a form of I/O in which the CPU must wait for the I/O operation to be completed.

programming language: a language with limited words and limited rules designed to solve problems on a computer.

project operation: an operation in a relational database in which a set of columns is selected based on a criterion.

project operator: a relational algebra operator (used in relational database) in which a column or columns of data are extracted based on given criteria.

Prolog: a high-level programming language based on formal logic.

protocol: a set of rules for data exchange between computers.

pseudocode: Englishlike statements that follow a loosely defined syntax and are used to convey the design of an algorithm or function.

public key: one of the keys in a public key encryption; it is revealed to the public.

public key encryption: an encryption method using two keys: private and public. The private key is kept secret; the public key is revealed to the public.

push: the stack insert operation.

Q

quality circle: a diagram in circular form of the steps to quality software.

quality software: software that satisfies the user's explicit and implicit requirements, is well documented, meets the operating standards of the organization, and runs efficiently on the hardware for which it was developed.

quantization: assigning a value from a finite set of values.

queue: a linear list in which data can only be inserted at one end, called the rear, and deleted from the other end, called the front.

queue simulation: a modeling activity used to generate statistics about the performance of a queue.

R

random access: a storage method that allows data to be retrieved in an arbitrary order.

random access memory (RAM): the main memory of the computer that stores data and programs.

random list: a list with no ordering of the data.

read-only memory (ROM): permanent memory with contents that cannot be changed.

ready state: in process management, the state of processing in which the process is waiting to get the attention of the CPU.

record: the information related to one entity.

recursion: a function design in which the function calls itself.

reduced instruction set computer (RISC): a computer that uses only frequently used instructions.

register: a fast stand-alone storage location that holds data temporarily.

relation: a table in a relational database.

relational database: a database model in which data are organized in related tables called relations.

relational database management system (RDBMS): a set of programs that handles relations in a relational database model.

relational model: See *relational database.*

relational operator: an operator that compares two values.

reliability: the quality factor that addresses the confidence or trust in a system's total operation.

remote login: logging on to a computer connected to the local computer.

repeater: a connecting device that regenerates the signal.

replicated distributed database: a database in which each site holds a replica of another site.

reserved words: the set of words in a language that has a predetermined interpretation and cannot be user-defined.

restricted list: a list in which data can only be added or deleted at the ends of the list and processing is restricted to operations on the data at the ends.

retrieval: the location and return of an element in a list.

reusability: the quality factor that addresses the ease with which software can be used in other programs.

ring topology: a topology in which the devices are connected in a ring; each device receives a data unit from one neighbor and sends it to the other neighbor.

Rivest-Shamir-Adleman (RSA) encryption: a popular public key encryption method.

root: the first node of a tree.

rotational speed: the spin rate of a magnetic disk.

router: a device operating at the first three OSI layers that connects independent networks. A router routes a packet based on its destination address.

routing: the process performed by a router.

routing table: the table used by a router to route a packet.

row-major storage: a method of storing array elements in memory in which the elements are stored row by row.

run-length encoding: a lossless compression method in which a run of symbols is replaced by the symbol and the number of repeated symbols.

running state: in process management, a state in which a process is using the CPU.

S

sampling: taking measurements at equal intervals.

scheduling: allocating the resources of an operating system to different programs and deciding which program should use which resource when.

scheme: the de facto standard of the LISP language.

search a list: See *searching.*

searching: the process that examines a list to locate one or more elements containing a designated value known as the search argument.

secondary storage device: See *auxiliary storage device.*

secret key: a key that is shared by two participants in secret key encryption.

sector: a part of a track on a disk.

security: the quality factor that addresses the ease or difficulty with which an unauthorized user can access data.

seek time: in disk access, the time required to move the read/write head over the track where data are.

select operation: an operation in a relational database that selects a set of tuples.

select operator: a relational algebra operator that extracts tuples based on the supplied criteria.

selection statement: a statement that chooses between two or more alternatives. In C, the `if-else` or `switch` statements.

self-referential record: a record in which part of the record is used to point to another record of the same type.

self-referential structure: a structure that contains a pointer to itself.

sequential access: an access method in which the records in a file are accessed serially beginning with the first element.

sequential cohesion: a design attribute in which the processing within the module is such that the data from one process are used in the next process.

sequential file: a file structure in which data must be processed serially from the first element in the file.

sequential search: a search technique used with a linear list in which the searching begins at the first element and continues until the value of an element equal to the value being sought is located or until the end of the list is reached.

server: in a client-server system, the centralized computer that provides auxiliary services (server programs).

session layer: the fifth layer in the OSI model; responsible for establishing and terminating sessions and controlling dialogs.

set: in masking, a technique to make a bit 1.

siblings: nodes in a tree with the same parent.

side effect: a change in a variable that results from the evaluation of an expression; any input/output performed by a called function.

sign-and-magnitude representation: a method of integer representation in which 1 bit represents the sign of the number and the remaining bits represent the magnitude.

Simple Mail Transfer Protocol (SMTP): the TCP/IP protocol for email service.

single-user operating system: an operating system in which only one program can be in memory at a time.

singly linked list: an ordered collection of data in which each element contains only the location of the next element. Contrast with *doubly linked list.*

small computer system interface (SCSI): an I/O device controller with a parallel interface.

software: the application and system programs necessary for computer hardware to accomplish a task.

software engineering: the design and writing of structured programs.

software life cycle: the life of a software package.

solvable problem: a problem that can be solved by a computer.

sort pass: one loop during which all elements are tested by a sorting program.

sorting: the process that orders a list or file.

source file: the file that contains program statements written by a programmer before they are converted into machine language; the input file to an assembler or compiler.

source-to-destination delivery: the delivery of a data packet from the source to the destination.

spanning tree: a tree extracted from a connected graph that contains all of the vertices in the graph.

spatial compression: compression done by JPEG on a frame.

SQL: See *Structured Query Language.*

stack: a restricted data structure in which data can be inserted and deleted only at one end, called the top.

stamp coupling: the communication technique between modules in which data are passed as a structure; often results in unrequired data being passed.

star topology: a topology in which all computers are connected to a common hub.

starvation: a problem in the operation of an operating system in which processes cannot get access to the resources they need.

state diagram: a diagram that shows the different states of a process.

statement: a syntactical construct in C that represents one operation in a function.

static document: a Web page that is created at the remote site and is retrieved by the local site. Contrast with *dynamic document.*

static RAM (SRAM): a technology that uses the traditional flip-flop gates (a gate with two states: 0 and 1) to hold data.

statistical compression: a compression method in which encoding is based on the frequency of symbols.

storage device: an I/O device that can store large amounts of information for retrieval at a later time.

strongly connected graph: a graph in which there is a path from every node to every other node. Contrast with *weakly connected graph.*

structure chart: a design and documentation tool that represents a program as a hierarchical flow of functions.

Structured Query Language (SQL): a database language that includes statements for database definition, manipulation, and control.

subalgorithm: a part of an algorithm that is independently written. It is executed when called inside the algorithm.

subprogram: See *subalgorithm.*

subroutine: See *subalgorithm.*

subscript: an ordinal number that indicates the position of an element within an array. See also *index.*

substring: a part of a string.

subtree: any connected structure below the root of a tree.

summation: addition of a series of numbers.

switch: See *flag.*

switch statement: the C implementation of the multiway selection.

symbolic constant: a constant that is represented by an identifier.

symbolic language: a computer language, one level removed from machine language, that has a mnemonic identifier for each machine instruction and has the capability of symbolic data names.

synchronization point: a point introduced into the data by the session layer for the purpose of flow and error control.

synonym: in a hashed list, two or more keys that hash to the same home address.

syntax: the "grammatical" rules of a language. In C, the set of keywords and formatting rules that must be followed when writing a program.

system development life cycle: a sequence of steps required to develop software; begins with the need for the software and concludes with its implementation.

system documentation: a formal structured record of a software package.

T

TELNET (Terminal Network): a general-purpose client-server program that allows remote login.

temporal cohesion: a module design in which processes are combined because they all need to be processed in the same time sequence.

temporal compression: compression done by MPEG on frames.

terminated state: in process management, a state in which a process has finished executing.

testability: an attribute of software that measures the ease with which the software can be tested as an operational system.

testing phase: a phase in the software life cycle in which experiments are carried out to prove that a software package works.

text: data stored as characters.

text editor: software that creates and maintains text files, such as a word processor or a source program editor.

text file: a file in which all data are stored as characters. Contrast with *binary file*.

timeliness: an attribute of software that measures the responsiveness of a system to a user's time requirements.

time sharing: an operating system concept in which more than one user has access to a computer at the same time.

token: a syntactical construct that represents an operation, a flag, or a piece of data.

top-down design: a program design concept in which a design progresses through a decomposition of the functions beginning with the top of the structure chart and working toward the lowest modules.

topology: the structure of a network, including the physical arrangement of devices.

track: a part of a disk.

trailer: control information appended to a data unit.

transaction file: a file containing relatively transient data that are used to change the contents of a master file.

transfer time: the time to move data from the disk to the CPU/memory.

translation unit: in C, a temporary compilation file used to store modified source code.

translator: a generic term for any of the language conversion programs. See also *assembler* and *compiler*.

Transmission Control Protocol (TCP): one of the transport-layer protocols in the TCP/IP protocol suite.

Transmission Control Protocol/Internet Protocol (TCP/IP): the official protocol of the Internet, made of five layers.

transmission rate: the number of bits sent per second.

transport layer: the fourth layer in the OSI model; responsible for end-to-end delivery of the whole message.

traversal: an algorithmic process in which each element in a structure is processed once and only once.

tree: a set of connected nodes structured so that each node has only one predecessor.

truth table: a table listing all the possible logical input combinations with the corresponding logical output.

tuple: in a relational database, a record (a line) in a relation.

Turing machine: a computer model with three components (tape, controller, and read/write head) that can implement statements in a computer language.

two-dimensional array: an array with elements having two levels of indexing. See also *multidimensional array*.

two's complement: a representation of binary numbers in which the complement of a number is found by complementing all bits and adding a 1 after that.

two's complement representation: a method of integer representation in which a negative number is represented by leaving all the rightmost 0s and the first 1 unchanged and complementing the remaining bits.

two-way selection: a selection statement that is capable of evaluating only two alternatives. In C, the `if-else` statement. Contrast with *multiway selection*.

type: a set of values and a set of operations that can be applied on these values.

U

UML (Unified Modeling Language): a tool used for design in computer science and business.

unary operation: an operation that needs only one input operand.

unary operator: an operator that performs a unary operation.

underflow: an event that occurs when an attempt is made to delete data from an empty data structure.

undirected graph: a graph consisting only of edges; that is, a graph in which there is no indication of direction on the lines.

Unicode: a 65,536-character code that includes the symbols and alphabets from most languages in the world.

Uniform Resource Locator (URL): a string of characters that defines a page on the Internet.

union operation: an operation on two sets in which the result contains all the elements from both sets without duplicates.

union operator: in relational algebra, an operator that combines rows from two relations.

universal serial bus (USB): a serial I/O device controller that connects slower devices such as the keyboard and mouse to a computer.

UNIX: a popular operating system among computer programmers and computer scientists.

unset: See *force to 0*.

unsigned integer: an integer without a sign; its value ranges between 0 and positive infinity.

unsolvable problem: a problem that cannot be solved by a computer.

update operation: an operation in a relational database in which the operation about one tuple is changed.

update operator: in a relational database, an operator that changes some values in a tuple.

user datagram: the name of the data unit used by the UDP protocol.

User Datagram Protocol (UDP): one of the transport-layer protocols in the TCP/IP protocol suite.

user interface: a program that accepts requests from users (processes) and interprets them for the rest of the operating system.

V

variable: a memory storage object whose value can be changed during the execution of a program. Contrast with *constant*.

vector graphic: the type of graphics in which lines and curves are defined using mathematical formulas.

vertex: a node in a graph.

video: a representation of images (called frames) in time.

virtual memory: the memory resulting from swapping programs in and out of memory during execution to give the impression of a larger main memory than really exists.

von Neumann model: a computer model (consisting of memory, arithmetic logic unit, control unit, and input/output subsystems) upon which the modern computer is based.

W

waiting state: a state in which a process is waiting to receive the attention of the CPU.

waterfall model: a software development model in which each module is completely finished before the next module is started.

WAN: See *wide area network*.

weakly connected graph: a graph in which there is at least one node with no path to at least one other node. Contrast with *strongly connected graph*.

Web: see *World Wide Web*.

Web page: a unit of hypertext or hypermedia available on the Web.

weighted graph: a graph with weighted lines. Each line has an integer that defines the weight.

while loop: an event-controlled loop in C and C++.

white box testing: program testing in which the internal design of the program is considered; also known as *clear box testing*. Contrast with *black box testing*.

whitespace: in C, the space, vertical and horizontal tabs, newline, and formfeed characters.

whole number: See *integer*.

wide area network (WAN): a network that spans a large geographical distance.

World Wide Web (WWW): a multimedia Internet service that allows users to traverse the Internet by moving from one document to another via links.

write once, read many (WORM): another name for a CD-R.

X

XOR operation: a bitwise operation in which the result of the operation is 1 only if one of the operands is 1.

XOR operator: the operator used in an XOR operation.

Index